Discourse in English Language Education

'*Discourse in English Language Education* provides a solid introduction to the major concepts and issues in discourse analysis and its applications in language teaching and learning. Examples of real-world discourse in diverse international settings help to make the concepts and theories accessible. This text will be an important resource for advanced undergraduates and postgraduates in applied linguistics, language education, and TESOL.'

Jane Jackson, *The Chinese University of Hong Kong*

Discourse in English Language Education introduces students to the major concepts and questions in Discourse Studies and their applications to language education. Each chapter draws on key research to examine critically a particular approach in the field, providing a review of important literature, examples to illustrate the principal issues concerned and an outline of the implications for their application to pedagogy.

Features include:

- coverage of a broad range of approaches in the field, including Systematic Functional Linguistics and Register, Speech Acts, the Cooperative Principle and Politeness, Conversation Analysis, Genre Analysis, Critical Discourse Analysis and Corpus Linguistics;
- analysis of a wide range of discourse examples that include casual conversation, newspapers, fiction, radio, classrooms, blogs and real-life learner texts;
- a selection of illustrations and tables carefully chosen to enhance students' understanding of different concepts and approaches;
- stimulating discussion questions at the end of each chapter, specially designed to foster critical thinking, reflection and engagement with the topics covered.

Engaging, accessible and comprehensive, *Discourse in English Language Education* richly demonstrates how Discourse Studies can inform the teaching of English and other languages, both as a foreign language and in the mother tongue.

It will be essential reading for upper undergraduates and postgraduates with interests in Applied Linguistics, TESOL and Language Education.

John Flowerdew is Professor in the English Department, City University of Hong Kong.

Discourse in English Language Education

JOHN FLOWERDEW

Routledge
Taylor & Francis Group

LONDON AND NEW YORK

First published 2013
by Routledge
2 Park Square, Milton Park, Abingdon, Oxon OX14 4RN

Simultaneously published in the USA and Canada
by Routledge
711 Third Avenue, New York, NY 10017

Routledge is an imprint of the Taylor & Francis Group, an informa business

British Library Cataloguing in Publication Data
A catalogue record for this book is available from the British Library

Library of Congress Cataloging in Publication Data
Flowerdew, John, 1951–
Discourse in English language education / John Flowerdew.
p. cm.
1. English language–Discourse analysis.
2. English language–Study and teaching.
3. Functionalism (Linguistics) 4. Systemic grammar.
5. Action research in education. I. Title.
PE1422.F56 2012
420.1'41–dc23
2012019912

ISBN: 978–0–415–49964–4 (hbk)
ISBN: 978–0–415–49965–1 (pbk)
ISBN: 978–0–203–08087–0 (ebk)

Typeset in Akzidenz-Grotesk
by Swales & Willis Ltd, Exeter, Devon

MIX
Paper from
responsible sources
FSC® C004839
www.fsc.org

Printed and bound in Great Britain by
TJ International Ltd, Padstow, Cornwall

Contents

List of figures and tables

FIGURES

TABLES

Acknowledgements

I would like to acknowledge very useful feedback given to me on various chapters of this book from a number of people, as follows: Joseph Alvaro, Anne Barron, Tom Cobb, Peter Grundy, Chris Jenks, Rodney Jones, Michelle Lazar, Graham Lock, Numa Markee, Jim Martin, Brian Paltridge, Christine Tardy, Geoff Thompson, Hansun Zhang Waring, Martin Weisser, Jean Wong and Lawrence Wong.

Further feedback was given to me by my MA English Studies, Discourse Analysis students in the Department of English at City University of Hong Kong and this is gratefully acknowledged.

I would like to thank very much Nadia Seemungal, commissioning editor at Routledge, for originally commissioning this book and for her patience during the rather long time that it took to complete it. I would also like to thank very much Isabelle Cheng, editorial assistant at Routledge, for regularly checking on the progress of the book, extremely diligent work in securing copyright permissions and various other advice and assistance.

Finally, I would like to acknowledge the editorial help of two of my students, Antonio Domingo and Meilin Chen.

The authors and publishers would like to thank the following copyright holders for permission to reproduce the following material:

Excerpt from *The Waves* by Virginia Woolf, copyright 1931 by Harcourt Inc. and renewed 1959 by Leonard Woolf, reprinted by permission of Houghton Miffin Harcourt Publishing Company. All rights reserved. (Chapter 1)

Figure 1.2 'Schematic representation of communicative competence' (Celce-Murcia) from E. Alcon Soler and Safont Jorda (Eds): *Intercultural Language Use and Language Learning*, 2007, p. 45, in chapter 'Rethinking the Role of Communicative Competence in Language Teaching' by M. Celce-Murcia. Reproduced with kind permission from Springer Science + Business Media B.V.

Extract from *The Bangkok Secret* by Anthony Grey reprinted by permission of Peters Fraser & Dunlop (www.petersfraserdunlop.com) on behalf of Anthony Grey. (Chapter 3)

Table 3.1 'Examples of exophoric reference as specific to the community' reprinted from Martin, J. R. *English Text: System and structure* (1992) Reproduced with kind permission of John Benjamins Publishing Co.

Extract from *Pagan Passions* by Randal Garrett and Larry M. Harris (1959). Reproduced with kind permission of JABberwocky Literary Agency and the Laurence Janifer estate (Chapter 3).

Verlag Walter de Gruyter GmbH & Co. for permission to reprint Figure Chain interaction in text, from Hoey, M. (1991) 'Another perspective on coherence and cohestive harmony', in E. Ventola

(Ed.) *Functional and Systematic Linguistics: Approaches and uses* (pp. 385–414), Berlin: Mouton de Gruyter. Reproduced by kind permission. (Figure 3.2)

Figure 'Lexical links in a non-narrative text'. Reproduced by permission of Oxford University Press. From *Oxford Applied Linguistics: Patterns of Lexis in Text* by M. Hoey © Oxford University Press 1991. (Figure 3.3)

Extract from *Desert Island Discs* (Sunday 12 June 1988 broadcast). Reproduced with kind permission of BBC Commercial Agency. (Chapter 3)

Slightly adapted excerpt from Pacific Coffee's website at www.pacificcoffee.com/eng/ index.php. Reproduced with kind permission. (Chapter 4)

From the *Financial Times*, 22 August 2010: 'View from the lanes of Pompeii', Tim Bradshaw. The Financial Times Limited 2010 ©. All Rights Reserved. (Chapter 4)

'A postal carrier…' joke from www.pricelessparrots.com. Reproduced with kind permission. (Chapter 4)

Extract from 'How To Make an Omelette English style' at www.accessentertainment.co.uk/Eatingin/ Recipes/Omelettes.htm. Reproduced with kind permission of Ian Jenkins. (Chapter 4)

E-mail chain excerpt from www.mail-archive.com/correct-my-english@googlegroups.com/ msg00515.html. Reproduced with kind permission of Asim Khan. (Chapter 4)

Excerpt from *Goon Show Classics*. Vol. 3 [sound recording] / script, Spike Milligan and Larry Stephens, BBC Enterprises, 1989. © Spike Milligan Productions Ltd. Reproduced with kind permission of Spike Milligan Productions Ltd. (Chapter 6)

The excerpt from the Limerick Corpus of Irish English (LCIE) reproduced in Chapter 6 is produced with the permission of the copyright holders at the University of Limerick and Mary Immaculate College, Ireland. LCIE is a one-million-word spoken corpus of mostly casual conversations, created under the direction of Dr Fiona Farr, University of Limerick and Dr Anne O'Keeffe, Mary Immaculate College, Limerick, Ireland.

Excerpt from Schegloff, E.A. (2007) *Sequence Organisation in Interaction: A primer in conversation analysis* (vol. 1), 2007, Cambridge University Press. Copyright © Cambridge University Press, reproduced with permission. (Chapter 7)

'Instructions text' reproduced with kind permission of Alishan International Guest House. (Chapter 8)

Table 'Schematic structures of key elemental genres as developed by the Sydney school' with kind permission of *Hong Kong Journal of Applied Linguistics*. (Table 8.3)

Figure 4: 'Map of genres in school' from J R Martin and D Rose (2012) *Learning to Write, Reading to Learn: Genre, knowledge and pedagogy in the Sydney school* (p. 110), London: Equinox. © Equinox Publishing Ltd 2012. (Figure 8.3)

Table from C. Tribble (2002), Corpus and corpus analysis: New windows on academic writing. In J. Flowerdew eds. *Academic Discourse* (pp. 131–149), Longman, Pearson Educated Limited, 2012. © Pearson Education Limited. Reproduced by kind permission. (Table 9.2)

While the publishers have made every effort to contact copyright holders of material used in this volume, they would be grateful to hear from any they were unaable to contact.

CHAPTER 1

Introduction

This chapter focuses on the various meanings of the terms 'discourse' and 'Discourse Analysis/Studies', highlights a number of features of discourse and Discourse Analysis/Studies, considers the notion of communicative competence and its relation to discourse and explains how it is an appropriate goal for Language Education. The chapter concludes with a brief overview of the rest of the book.

1.1 DEFINING DISCOURSE

There are various usages of the term *discourse*, but we will begin here by defining it broadly as language in its contexts of use. In considering language in its contexts of use, the concern is also with language above the level of the sentence. The emphasis on contexts of use and the suprasentential level is important, because for much of the history of modern linguistics, under the influence of the generative linguist Chomsky, language has been analysed as separate from context, as *decontextualised* sentences. The rationale for a contextualised and suprasentential consideration of language is based upon the belief that knowing a language is concerned with more than just grammar and vocabulary: it also includes how to participate in a conversation or how to structure a written text. To be able to do this, it is necessary to take into account the context, or situation, in which a particular use of language occurs and how the units of language combine together and structure the overall discourse.

More restricted in sense, the term 'discourse' can also be used to refer to a particular set of ideas and how they are articulated, such as the discourse of environmentalism, the discourse of neoliberalism or the discourse of feminism. In this case, the term refers to a type of specialised knowledge and language used by a particular social group. This meaning is associated with French post-structuralist thinkers such as Michel Foucault. It will be particularly important in Chapter 10.

The discourse analyst Gee (2011a) memorably refers to the first of the two meanings of discourse considered thus far – discourse as language in the contexts of its use and above the level of the sentence – as little 'd' discourse and the second meaning – discourse as ideas and how they are articulated – as big 'D' discourses (note the first is always singular, while the second can be pluralised).

1.2 DEFINING DISCOURSE STUDIES AND DISCOURSE ANALYSIS

Following our definition of discourse in the previous section, *Discourse Analysis*, or, to use a more recent term, *Discourse Studies* can be defined as the study of language in its contexts of use and above the level of the sentence. The more recent term *Discourse Studies* is perhaps more appropriate than the older term, *Discourse Analysis*, because it gets away from the misconception that the field is only concerned with analysis (that it is just a method), while it is also concerned with theory and application (and it comprises a host of methods) (van Dijk, 2001b). Both terms will be used in this book: *Discourse Analysis* to refer to the actual analysis, and *Discourse Studies* to refer to the field, or discipline, in general.

Discourse Studies, as a discipline, is arguably most closely associated with linguistics, but is essentially an interdisciplinary activity, employed in such diverse fields as anthropology, business studies, communication studies, cultural studies, educational studies, environmental studies, law, literary studies, media studies, philosophy, politics, psychology, sociology, and many others, in addition to linguistics.

1.3 DISCOURSE ANALYSIS MAY EMPHASISE DISCOURSE STRUCTURE OR DISCOURSE FUNCTION OR BOTH

As in physics, chemistry or biology, Discourse Analysis may involve structural analysis. Here a text or group of texts would be broken down into their component parts. These parts (which are, in fact, usually determined in terms of their functions, or meanings) might be based on the topics or turns at speaking, in spoken discourse, or the paragraphs and sentences, or propositions, in written discourse (more technical units will be presented later). A structural approach to Discourse Analysis might also look at how elements of language are held together in coherent units.

Instead of, or in addition to, a structural analysis, Discourse Analysis might take a functional approach. Here the discourse analyst considers the particular meanings and communicative forces associated with what is said or written. This approach to discourse considers language as a type of *communicative action*. It considers questions such as the following: How is language used persuasively – e.g. to request, accept, refuse, complain? What sort of language is polite language? How do people use language to convey meanings indirectly? What constitutes racist or sexist language? How do people exercise power through their use of language? What might be the hidden motivations behind certain uses of language?

Alternatively, in a functional approach, the discourse analyst might look at particular discourse *genres* (Chapter 8). Here the discourse analyst asks: How is language used in academic essays, in research articles, in conference presentations, in letters, in reports and in meetings? Here the concern is again with communicative purposes or communicative action, but the focus is on particular contexts of use.

Then again, in a functional approach to discourse, the analyst might consider how language is used by particular social groups (known as register analysis: see Chapter 2). How do teachers or politicians or business executives use language? How do men and women vary in their use of language? What is particular about the language used by such people that it identifies them as belonging to particular social groups?

Functional analysis suggests a qualitative rather than a quantitative methodology and, indeed, most Discourse Analysis is qualitative in nature. The concern is not with measuring and counting, but with describing. However, with the use of computers, quantitative analysis has received more attention and discourse analysts may also use computers to derive quantitative findings; for example, on the relative frequency of particular language patterns by different individuals or social groups in particular texts or groups of texts. This approach to Discourse Analysis is known as Corpus Linguistics and will be dealt with in Chapter 9.

1.4 DISCOURSE ANALYSIS MAY FOCUS ON ANY SORT OF TEXTS

Discourse Analysis may focus on any sort of text, written or spoken. The term 'text', in Discourse Analysis, refers to any stretch of spoken or written language. In written text, Discourse Analysis may consider texts as diverse as news reports, textbooks, company reports, personal letters, business letters, e-mails and faxes. In spoken discourse, it may focus on casual conversations, business and other professional meetings, service encounters (buying and selling goods and services) and classroom lessons, among many others.

While Discourse Analysis has traditionally focused on written and spoken text, in recent years it has started to extend its field of activity to consider *multimodal* discourse, where written and/or spoken text is combined with visual or aural dimensions, such as television programmes, movies, websites, museum exhibits and advertisements of various kinds. These texts, which form the data of Discourse Analysis, may be contemporary or historical. Indeed, Discourse Analysis has much to offer historical studies (Flowerdew, 2012a).

1.5 THERE ARE VARIOUS APPROACHES TO DISCOURSE STUDIES

Discourse Studies may adopt various approaches to analysis. Some of the main approaches will be used as the organising principle of this book: they include *register analysis* (Chapter 2), which studies the typical features of particular fields of activity or professions; *cohesion, coherence* and *thematic development* (Chapters 3–4), which investigate how text is held together, in terms of both structure and function; *Pragmatics* (Chapters 5–6), which studies language in terms of the actions it performs; *Conversation Analysis* (Chapter 7), which takes a microanalytic approach to spoken interaction; *Genre Analysis* (Chapter 8), which studies language in terms of the different recurrent stages it goes through in specific contexts; *Corpus-based Discourse Analysis* (Chapter 10), which uses computers in the analysis of very large bodies of text (known as *corpora* – singular *corpus*) in order to identify particular *phraseologies* (wordings) and rhetorical patterning; and *Critical Discourse Analysis* (Chapter 10), which interprets texts from a social perspective, analysing power relations and cases of manipulation and discrimination in discourse. These are just some of the approaches. There are numerous others and many discourse analysts adopt an eclectic or hybrid approach.[1]

1.6 DISCOURSE ANALYSIS IS CONDUCTED IN MANY FIELDS OF ACTIVITY

Discourse Analysis is conducted in many fields, both informal and institutional. In informal fields, Discourse Analysis has been used to analyse how people interact in conversation and in service encounters, as already mentioned, and to analyse how they tell stories, how they gossip and how they chat. In formal fields, Discourse Analysis has been fruitfully employed in the political arena, in analysing the media, in the law, in healthcare, and in business and other forms of bureaucracy.

1.7 DISCOURSE STUDIES FOCUS ON LANGUAGE IN ITS CONTEXTS OF USE

The definition given above for Discourse Studies refers to the study of language in its contexts of use. But what is meant exactly by this term *context*? Another word for context is situation. In order to understand the meaning of an *utterance*[2], one needs to know the particular features of the situation in which it was uttered. In a very well-known study, Hymes (1972a) identified 16 features of situation, or context, some of which are listed as follows:

- the physical and temporal setting;
- the participants (speaker or writer, listener or reader);
- the purposes of the participants;

- the channel of communication (e.g. face to face, electronic, televised, written);
- the attitude of the participants;
- the genre, or type of speech event: poem, lecture, editorial, sermon;
- background knowledge pertaining to the participants.

How do features of context such as these affect meaning and the analyst's interpretation of meaning? We can understand the role of context if we consider in what situations certain utterances might or might not be appropriate. To take some examples, first, for the contextual feature *participants*, an expression such as 'Sit down!' is likely to be interpreted as appropriate when spoken by a parent to a child. When addressed to a superior, however, it would likely be interpreted as rude. The important variable, therefore, in this example, is the participants, whether one of them is a child or a superior. To take another example, this time for *channel of communication*, the following might be perfectly acceptable as a text message sent via the channel of a mobile phone: 'CUL8ER' (that is to say, 'see you later'), but sent by means of another channel, such as a business letter, it would more likely be perceived as uneducated or rude. To take a third example, here for *background knowledge*, suppose two people are playing a game and one says to the other 'Make sure you follow all the rules.' This person is relying on the other person knowing what these rules are. It would be redundant to have to specify all of the rules. In this way, background knowledge makes communication more efficient.

Another element of context that needs to be considered is the text surrounding an utterance, what has come before and what comes later. Consider the following exchange:

A.   These bananas cost 3 dollars.
B.   I'll take them.

In this exchange, *them* in B's statement can only be interpreted in the light of part of what has been mentioned previously by A, that is to say, *bananas*. Consider now the following two statements, which are linked together:

I have a problem. I haven't got any money.

Problem, here, can be explicated by what follows it, that is to say, the *problem* is that I do not have enough money. This type of context is commonly referred to as *co-text* or *linguistic context* (in contrast to *extralinguistic context*).

van Dijk (2008: x) stresses how contexts are 'not some kind of objective condition or direct cause', but are, rather, subjective constructs that develop over the course of an interaction. Individuals each develop and define their own contexts according to their '(on-going) subjective interpretations of communicative situations' (van Dijk, 2008: x). Context, for van Dijk, is thus not just a social phenomenon, but a sociocognitive one.

In Chapter 2, we will consider another model of context, that of Systemic Functional Linguistics, which consists of three broad parameters: field (the subject matter of the text), tenor (the relations between the participants and their attitudes) and mode (how the language is organised and functions in the text).

In Discourse Analysis, as Blommaert (2001: 15) has warned, the analyst's selection of what is relevant in the context in order to interpret a text is crucial. An emphasis on a particular element of the context is likely to affect the analyst's interpretation of the text.

1.8 DISCOURSE IS INTERTEXTUAL

The simplest form of Discourse Analysis is of a single text. Increasingly, though, discourse analysts have come to accept the importance of considering other texts in the analysis of a given text. One text cannot be understood except in relation to other texts which have gone before (and, indeed, which are likely to follow). Other texts, of course, are one facet of context. For instance, in the reference to the rules of the game in section 1.7 above, presumably, in assuming common knowledge of the rules, the participants in the interaction would have come across these rules on previous occasions in (spoken or written) texts. The *intertextuality* (Bhaktin, 1981) in this example – how one text relates back to another text or texts – is made explicit. Another example of intertextuality, which is even more explicit, would be direct quotation of one text in another, indicated through the use of inverted commas.

Very often, however, intertextual links are implicit. Implicit intertextuality is extremely common in newspaper headlines and various types of advertisement. The following is an example of language promoting the AXN television channel: 'There's a time to ask not what you can do for your country, but what you can watch on AXN.' The intertextuality here is based on a famous statement made by the US President, John F. Kennedy: 'Ask not what your country can do for you, but what you can do for your country.' The intertextuality with the AXN promotion is created through the use of parallel syntactic, semantic and prosodic structures.

Here are some other examples of intertextuality from newspaper headlines:

Merkel is no Bond Girl
(German leader Angela Merkel says that she will not support the issuance of Eurobonds; intertext: James Bond movies, each of which features a 'Bond girl'

American Airlines is Terminal
(The airline is on the verge of bankruptcy; intertext: aircraft operate out of terminals)

It's Acropolis Now, Greece!
(Greece is on the verge of bankruptcy; intertext: the Vietnam War film *Apocalypse Now!* directed by Francis Ford Coppola)

Implicit intertextuality is intrinsic to poetry. Many, if not most, poems can be related to other poems or works of art. Much English poetry, for example, employs imagery which has its roots in the St James's Bible. In her poetic novel, *The Waves,* the English writer, Virginia Woolf, uses intertextuality to recast the opening of the first line of the Gospel of St John in the Bible. St John's Gospel begins with 'In the beginning there was the word', while Woolf begins *The Waves* with 'In the beginning, there was a nursery, with windows opening on to a garden, and beyond that the sea.'

Intertextuality is a major obstacle to effective communication in a foreign or second language, because it depends very much on background knowledge, which is often very culturally specific.

1.9 DISCOURSE AND COMMUNICATION

It should already be clear from the above discussion that Discourse Studies have a lot to offer to those concerned with Language Education, whether in the mother tongue or as a second or foreign language. In this section and in those that follow, we will consider the relationship between discourse and Language Education more explicitly. In the foregoing, we have used the terms *communicative* and *communication* a number of times. That is because discourse is the vehicle by means of which communication takes place. A traditional, although now largely discredited (by linguists, at any rate), model of communication is the so-called *code model*, or *conduit metaphor model*, as shown in Figure 1.1 (Reddy, 1979; Sperber & Wilson, 1995).

According to this model of communication, which has existed in various forms for hundreds,

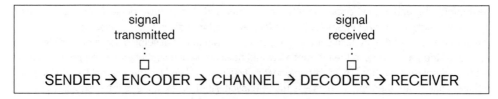

Figure 1.1   The code, or conduit, metaphor model of communication.

if not thousands, of years, the sender encodes a message which passes along the communication channel in the form of a signal, which is then decoded by the receiver. Provided that there is no deficiency in the channel and that both sender and receiver are using the same code, success-ful communication is guaranteed. According to this model, communication can take place without any reference to the speaker, hearer or wider context. However, this is to leave out the important dimension of context, as discussed in section 1.7. Our interpretation of a message is affected by the context in which it is sent.

According to more recent models of communication, referred to as inferential models, speakers take into account the context and what they understand to be the background and world knowl-edge of their addressees. Speakers are then able to calibrate what they say to match up with this assumed hearer knowledge. They do not need to say everything, but can rely on their addressees to fill in any details that are not explicitly communicated.

To give an example, at the time of writing, the British television personality, Jeremy Clarkson, who is best known for his BBC programme, *Top Gear* (which is about cars), was interviewed on a television chat show. He was asked about an industrial strike that was disrupting the country and replied: 'I would have them [the strikers] all shot. I would take them outside and execute them in front of their families'. If this statement was interpreted according to the code model, it would be taken literally, that this is really what Clarkson wanted to happen. As Clarkson commented in a public apol-ogy later, however, it was said for 'comic effect'. Clarkson intended his audience to go further in their interpretation than the literal meaning of his statement and to assume that he did not mean what he said to be taken literally. Unfortunately for Clarkson, however, some members of the British public took his remarks at face value and accused him of offensive behaviour, thereby illustrating how ver-bal communication is not always successful, as suggested by the code model, and can sometimes lead to misunderstanding.

1.10 DISCOURSE AND COMMUNICATIVE COMPETENCE

Language educators are concerned with encouraging learners to communicate in the most effec-tive ways possible. It is self-evident, therefore, that an understanding of discourse and its role in communication will be of value to such students or professionals.

In the 1960s, the leading theory of language was that of Chomsky (1965), who made a famous distinction between *competence* and *performance*: competence, referring to the underlying gram-matical system that he claimed to be intuitively known by all native speakers of a language and performance, referring to actual language use in real situations. Chomsky was only interested in competence, viewing performance – which incorporated memory limitations, distractions and slips of the tongue – as a distortion of the ideal model that is competence.

In reaction to Chomsky, Hymes (1972b) argued that there was more to language than ide-alised grammar, invoking the term *communicative competence* to refer to the competence that is required in real communication. Language use was also worthy of study and had its own (situationally defined) conventions and patterns, according to Hymes. His famous dictum was 'there are rules of use without which the rules of grammar would be useless' (1972b: 278). To investigate these situationally defined conventions and patterns, Hymes developed his model of contextual variables, referred to above in section 1.7.

Hymes's ideas on communicative competence were taken up by applied linguists, who *recontextualised* (appropriated from one field to another) his theory (Leung, 2005) as a goal for teaching and learning, in what became known as the *communicative approach* to language teaching (CLT). As Dubin (cited in Leung, 2005: 124) has noted, these applied linguists shifted Hymes's agenda away from researching what was happening in language communities to a set of standards for an ideal teaching and learning curriculum. Nevertheless, in spite of this shift in orientation, with the notion of communicative competence acting as what Leung has referred to as its 'intellectual anchor', CLT rapidly became the predominant paradigm for language development internationally and has remained so up to the present.

The most commonly cited model of communicative competence in language teaching is that of Canale and Swain (1980)[3], who broke communicative competence down into three subcomponents:

1. *Grammatical competence*: knowledge and skill with regard to lexical items and rules of morphology, syntax, sentence grammar semantics and phonology.
2. *Sociolinguistic competence*: Hymes's rules of use; knowledge and skill regarding formality, politeness and appropriateness of meaning to situation.
3. *Strategic competence*: strategies to compensate for breakdowns in communication and to enhance language learning.

Later, Canale (1983) added a fourth component, discourse competence, which referred to the knowledge of and skill in combining linguistic elements to achieve a unified textual whole. A problem with adding this extra component, however, is that it seems to be at a different level; it would seem that grammatical competence, sociolinguistic competence and strategic competence are all component parts of overall discourse competence. Realising this, Celce-Murcia (2007),[4] has put forward a more complex, but better integrated, model of communicative competence, which highlights this central role for discourse competence. Celce-Murcia's revised model is shown in Figure 1.2.

In the model, *sociocultural competence* refers to the speaker's pragmatic knowledge, that is to say, Hymes's rules of speaking; it includes *social contextual factors*, such as the participants' age, gender and status; *stylistic appropriateness*, such as politeness strategies; and *cultural factors*, including background knowledge about the target language group.

Linguistic competence is equivalent to Canale and Swain's grammatical competence.

Formulaic competence is the counterpart to linguistic competence; it refers to the fixed, prefabricated chunks of language which do not behave in the generative way that grammatical items do. This will be dealt with in Chapter 9, when we discuss corpus approaches to discourse.

Interactional competence includes *actional* competence (the ability to perform *speech acts*: see Chapter 5) and *conversational competence* (the ability to operate the turn-taking system of conversation: see Chapter 7).

Strategic competence consists of strategies for language learning or maintaining the flow of interaction; it is similar to Canale and Swain's original *strategic competence* component. This component is represented in Figure 1.2 as going around and linking up the other components, because it allows for the resolution of ambiguities and deficiencies in these other parts of the model.

Discourse competence, in Celce-Murcia's model, plays a central, controlling role; it 'refers to the selection, sequencing and arrangement of words, structures, and utterances to achieve a unified spoken message' (Celce-Murcia, 2007: 46). This is where the other elements in the model come together; where the lexical and linguistic levels, the formulaic patterns and the sociocultural and

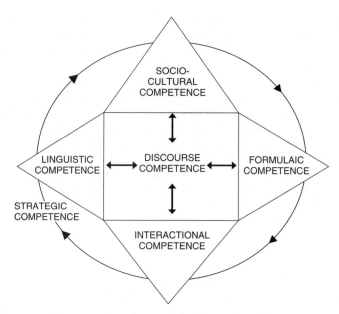

Figure 1.2   Schematic representation of communicative competence (Celce-Murcia, 2007: 45).

interactional knowledge are united in the creation of coherent text. Discourse competence is thus a level above the other subcompetencies in Celce-Murcia's model, a level which both incorporates and controls all of the other elements.

With Celce-Murcia, we should stress that the model should be viewed not as a static product, as might be suggested by Figure 1.2, but as a dynamic process, with a constant interaction of the component parts.

1.11 ORGANISATION OF THE BOOK

One of the challenges for anyone entering the field of Discourse Studies is the plethora of different features of discourse to focus upon, on the one hand, and the abundance of theoretical and methodological approaches, on the other. The solution offered to this problem in this book is to organise the chapters according to specific approaches or areas within Discourse Studies which are judged to be of particular relevance to Language Education and to allow the reader to decide which might be of most value. At the same time, it is worth noting that Discourse Analysis is becoming more and more eclectic and approaches and methods are increasingly being combined. The book does not argue for any one particular view, although astute readers may be able to note some of the author's preferences in the way that the chapters have been selected and written.

The topics of the individual chapters are as follows: Chapter 2 deals with the *Systemic Functional Linguistics* approach to discourse and the theory of *register*, how language varies systematically according to situation. Chapter 3 focuses on *cohesion*, the linguistic features which hold texts together. Chapter 4 is also concerned with how a text coheres, but here, not in terms of formal links, but rather of the *thematic development* of a text, how the organisation of the information in the clauses that make up a text functions to make the text hold together. In Chapters 5–6 the focus changes to consider features of discourse dealt with in the field know as *Pragmatics*, namely *speech act theory* (Chapter 5), how language is used to perform communicative actions, and the *Cooperative Principle* and *Politeness* (Chapter 6), two pragmatic phenomena which guide cooperative communicative behaviour. In Chapter 7, we overview the approach to discourse known as *Conversation Analysis*, which looks at the structures which create order in conversation and other forms of spoken interaction. Chapter 8 introduces the concept of *genre*, the staged, goal-oriented activities shared by particular communities. Chapter 9 deals with computer-assisted approaches to the analysis of discourse, as embodied in the field known as *Corpus Linguistics*. Chapter 10 centres on a particular approach to Discourse Analysis, *Critical Discourse Analysis*, which views language as a form of social practice and looks for structures of power, manipulation and control in discourse.

Each chapter follows a fairly systematic organisation, beginning with the introduction of key concepts and questions in the field and discussion of their relevance to Language Education, reviewing the key literature to exemplify the concepts and questions (sometimes from my own work), sometimes introducing original textual analysis to illustrate key issues, and concluding with sections devoted to critiques of the approaches described, and implications for application to pedagogy. In selecting the literature to review, attention has been paid to ensuring that the seminal publications are included, as well as more recent work.

1.12 QUESTIONS FOR DISCUSSION

1. What are some of the 'big D' discourses you come into contact with on a daily basis? What are their distinctive features? What are the ideas and attitudes they express? Can you think of any particular linguistic features of these discourses?
2. Think of someone you know. How do they identify themselves through their use of language, perhaps because of their age, their job, or some other contextual factors?
3. Can you think of (or make up) any examples of intertextuality, maybe in newspaper headlines or advertisements you have come across?
4. Can you think of any examples of intertextuality that would be difficult for a foreigner entering your country or an English-speaking country you are familiar with?
5. Why do you think the conduit model has remained so popular over the centuries?
6. Do you think non-native speakers can acquire the same level of linguistic competence as posited by Chomsky for native speakers?
7. Do you think non-native speakers can acquire the same level of communicative competence as posited by Hymes for native speakers?
8. Which do you think is more important in learning a language: linguistic (grammatical) competence or communicative competence?
9. Can you think of any 'rules of use', as referred to by Hymes? Think of a particular context, such as the classroom, the library, a particular type of shop or a bank.
10. Are you familiar with any strategies that you (or others) use as part of your strategic competence when you speak a second/foreign language?
11. What do you think about Celce-Murcia's model of communicative competence? What are its strengths and weaknesses?

1.13 FURTHER READING

Bhatia *et al.*, 2008; Celce-Murcia, 2007; Hymes, 1972b; Johnson, 2008; Jones, 2012; Paltridge, 2005/2006; Renkema, 2004; Van Dijk, 2011.

CHAPTER 2

Systemic Functional Linguistics and Register

2.1 INTRODUCTION

Systemic Functional Linguistics (SFL) is a theory of language and discourse developed by M.A.K. Halliday and his followers. *Systemic* in SFL refers to a conception of language as a network of systems, or choices, for expressing meaning. *Functional* refers to a concern for what language does and how it does it, in contrast to more structural approaches.

Halliday began to develop his theory in the 1960s. He was influenced by the British linguist Firth, his teacher, from whom he inherited the notions of language as a set of systems and the importance of context in the interpretation of meaning. Malinowski, a social anthropologist of Polish origin, but working at London University, also had an important impact on Halliday, with his emphasis on the relation between language and context, that is, his idea that you need to be in the particular context to understand the meaning of an utterance, and his notion of multiplicities of languages according to situations. Another influence on Halliday was the American linguist, Whorf, who also insisted on how language was influenced by environment. Another body of work drawn upon by Halliday was that of the Danish linguist, Hjelmslev, and his notion of language as the level of expression of a higher-level semiotic system. A final influence on Halliday was the functional approach of the Prague school of linguistics, especially with regard to the textual metafunction (see below).

Although first and foremost a linguist, Halliday is very much concerned with the role of language in society, particularly education. One of his earliest publications (Halliday *et al.*, 1964) was entitled *The Linguistic Sciences and Language Teaching*. Many of Halliday's ideas are already present in this early publication and we will draw on it for the account of Halliday's approach in this chapter. Other key texts to be drawn on here are the book Halliday wrote with his wife (Halliday & Hasan, 1985/1989), *Language, Context, and Text: Aspects of language in a social-semiotic perspective*, which gives a good account of Halliday's theory of register; *Spoken and Written Language* (Halliday, 1989), which compares the salient features of these two linguistic channels; and the latest version of his book setting out his model of grammar, *An Introduction to Functional Grammar* (revised by Matthiessen [Halliday & Matthiessen, 2004]). We will begin, however, with Halliday's model of first language acquisition, as set out in a book entitled *Learning How to Mean* (Halliday, 1975).

2.2 A FUNCTIONAL PERSPECTIVE ON CHILD LANGUAGE ACQUISITION

Through a diary study of his child, Nigel, Halliday (1975) developed a theory of language development. The theory is a functional one, as might be expected with a title such as *Learning How to Mean*, with development seen as taking place in a social context, through interaction, rather than as some innate biological process. The first stage of Nigel's language learning is described by Halliday as a *protolanguage*; this is when Nigel developed a small set of words which he developed to express certain functions. The *proto-words* that made up this set were not learned from the social environment but came from Nigel himself, words such as *da, na, a* and *yi*. Nevertheless these words were discovered to perform particular functions, of which Halliday identified six, as follows:

1. *Instrumental*: to obtain goods or services – the 'I want' function.
2. *Regulatory*: to control the behaviour of others – the 'do as I tell you' function.
3. *Interactional*: to interact with others – the 'me and you' function.
4. *Personal*: to express the personality of the child – the 'here I come' function.
5. *Heuristic*: to explore and learn about the environment – the 'tell me why' function.
6. *Imaginary*: to create the child's own environment – the 'let's pretend' function.

Later, a seventh function is added to the child's repertoire, the *informative* function – the 'I've got something to tell you' function.

Halliday explains the development of the protolanguage as follows:

> A child begins by creating a proto-language of his own, a meaning potential in respect of each of the social functions that constitute his developmental semiotic.
>
> (Halliday, 1978: 124)

As the various functions of the protolanguage develop, so does the need for a language code through which they can be expressed:

> The text-in-situation by which [the child] is surrounded is filtered through his own functional-semantic grid, so that he processes just as much of it as can be interpreted in terms of his own meaning potential at the time.
>
> (Halliday, 1978: 124)

In this way, with gradually increasing degrees of sophistication, language forms come to be attached to the meaning that the child wishes to express. As the child begins to be involved in more and more complex social relations, so do the demands grow greater and so does the language system increase to cope with them. By the time of secondary schooling, for example, the young adult is introduced to the concept of *grammatical metaphor*, how one type of process is represented in the grammar of another, to use a noun to refer to a process. For example, *The student's refusal to participate ...* as opposed to *The student refused to participate ...* (see below for more on this).

Since Halliday's original study, four other longitudinal case studies have been reported (Painter, 2009), each confirming Halliday's basic position that: 'the nature of development cannot be viewed as some kind of flowering that occurs independently with the child, or through the child's autonomous explorations of the environment, but must be seen from its inception as a profoundly social process' and that 'the SFL account of language development is one that has always stressed the dialogic, interpersonal nature of the process from birth onwards ...' (Painter, 2009: 95).

2.3 SYSTEMIC FUNCTIONAL LINGUISTICS

We already mentioned that the term *systemic* in SFL refers to how language is viewed as a network of interrelated systems or set of choices for making meanings. Figure 2.1 is a systems network for *mood*, the system of verb forms used to indicate the speaker's attitude toward a statement, in the English clause.

We also mentioned how the term *functional* is in opposition to *formal*, that is, language is construed as a practical means of expressing meanings rather than as an abstract set of relations,

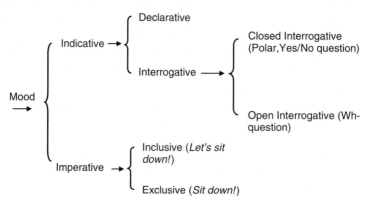

Figure 2.1   Mood system of the English clause.

which is the approach of many other schools of linguistics, in particular Chomskyan generative grammar. SFL views grammar and lexis (vocabulary) as working together in making meanings: this combination is referred to as *lexicogrammar*.

According to SFL, meanings are expressed according to three broad *metafunctions*: *ideational*, *interpersonal* and *textual*. The ideational metafunction is concerned with things (real or imagined) in the world. It is to do with actions, events and states (referred to as *processes*), for example, *run*, *occur*, *be*; *participants* in those processes, for example, *he*, *she*, *man*, *car*, *weather*, and the *circumstances* in which those processes occur, that is, how, when, and where. It is divided into two components: the *experiential* component (to do with experience and understanding of the world) and the *logical* component (to do with logical relations). The interpersonal function has to do with relationships between participants, not only in spoken texts, but also in written texts (with regard to how the writer interacts with the reader). The textual metafunction relates to the construction of text, how it is held together and what gives it *texture*. The textual function is an enabling function, because the two other functions 'depend on being able to build up sequences of discourse, organizing the discursive flow, creating cohesion and continuity as it moves along' (Halliday & Matthiessen, 2004: 30).

It is important to note that the three metafunctions are not independent of each other and that any stretch of language expresses, or *realises*, the three functions simultaneously. Hasan (1995: 231) refers to this relationship as like a chemical solution, where each factor affects each of the others. Having said that, while the three metafunctions freely combine together, they do not constrain each other (Halliday & Matthiessen, 2004: 30). Thus, certain linguistic features are more typically expressive of one of the functions than the others. Lexis is typically associated with ideational meanings, for example, while modal verbs are associated with the interpersonal function. Conjunctions, on the other hand, are closely associated with the textual metafunction. Nevertheless, there is overlap. Thus, for example, although lexis, is, as we have said, primarily associated with the ideational metafunction, it may also have an interpersonal dimension to its meaning; for example, words like *disgusting*, *revolting* and *sordid* are typically used to expressed an individual's negative attitude towards something or somebody; similarly, pronouns may play both an interpersonal and textual role, interpersonal to show relationships between interlocutors and textual to link up one stretch of text with another.

The metafunctions are related to, or realise, features of what in SFL is called the *context of situation*. These features are referred to as *contextual parameters*. Thus, ideational meanings realise what is called the *field* of discourse (the purpose of the communication and what it is about), interpersonal meanings realise what is called the *tenor* (the relations between the participants in the text) and textual meanings realise what is referred to as the *mode* (how the language is organised and functions in the interaction, for example, whether it is written or spoken or some combination of the two

Table 2.1   Different levels of analysis in Systemic Functional Linguistics

Contextual parameters	Field	Tenor	Mode
Metafunctions	Ideational	Interpersonal	Textual
Lexicogrammar	Lexis Transitivity	Mood Modality Person	Cohesion Theme–rheme

(as in various electronic modalities), whether it is expository, or didactic or persuasive, and so forth. Hudson (1980: 49) offers an *aide-mémoire* to help understand these contextual features: field refers to 'why' and 'about what' a communication takes place; tenor is about 'to whom' the communication is directed, that is, how the speaker or writer sees the person with whom s/he is communicating; and mode is about 'how' the communication takes place. The relations between the different levels of contextual parameters, metafunctions and lexicogrammar can be represented as in Table 2.1.

It is important to note that context is not a fixed, deterministic phenomenon, but is dynamic and evolving. Context and language are mutually constitutive. Context constrains choices in language while at the same time choices in language shapes context.

2.4 REGISTER[1]

In any given context of situation, a certain set of contextual parameters comes together in what is called a *register*. Halliday and Hasan (1985/1989: 38–39), accordingly, define register as 'a configuration of meanings that are typically associated with a particular situational configuration of field, mode, and tenor'. To put it more simply, register is a set of linguistic choices associated with a particular situation. These situations are usually related to professional activity (the language of teachers, doctors, students, and so forth) or interests (bridge-playing, bird-watching, music-making, and so forth). Examples of registers would be church services, school lessons or sports commentaries (Halliday *et al.*, 1964). As Halliday *et al.* (1964: 87) point out, a single sentence from any of these registers might enable us to identify it correctly. We can guess that 'let us pray' probably comes from a church service, that 'open your books at page 1' probably comes from a school lesson and that 'three players are on yellow cards' probably comes from a soccer commentary. Nevertheless, it should be noted that the boundaries between registers are difficult, if not impossible, to specify. Thus, register is an idealised concept which allows us to make predictions about what lexicogrammatical features are likely to occur in any given situation. One thing that can be said from the point of view of learners, whether they be first- or second-language (L1 or L2) learners, is that the mixing of items from different registers is a frequent problem. The PhD applicant who wrote to me for the first time using the term of address *Hi Sir* is just one example.

Taking the contextual parameters one by one, under the heading of field – what is going on in the text and the area of language activity (Halliday *et al.*, 1964: 90) – registers may be identified according to the event of which the language activity forms a part. In some situations, language accounts for the great part of the activity, for example, an essay or academic discussion. Here, the register can be defined in terms of the subject matter, for example, politics, history or biology. In other situations, language plays only a minimal role and here the register refers to the whole event, for example, domestic chores, playing games, performing medical operations.

With regard to registers identified according to tenor – the relations between the participants – level of formality is a primary distinction, colloquial and formal registers being differentiated, although they are related on a cline, rather than as distinct categories. Tenor relations may be more or less permanent. The relationship between a husband and wife is a fairly permanent one (at least traditionally). Casual encounters are likely to vary with the situation. An encounter at a party is likely to be informal, whilst one in an office is likely to be more formal. Some relationships are socially defined, such as that between teacher and pupil and that between doctor and patient. Some relationships are directly encoded in the language. The *tu/vous* distinction of many languages is determined according to the formality of the relationship. Some languages, such as Japanese, reserve certain grammatical forms for men and others for women.

As for mode, the primary distinction here is between spoken and written, but, within this primary classification there can be subdivisions into, for example, literature, newspaper and advertising for written registers and casual conversation and formal interview and sports commentary for spoken registers. There may also be registers which blur the spoken/written distinction, for example, plays, which are written to be spoken, or political speeches, which are written to be read aloud. Registers labelled at a higher level of classification can be further subclassified. Thus, literature can be broken down into prose and verse; the news register can be broken down into reportage, editorial writing and features writing.

The three dimensions taken together can be used to determine a register. Halliday *et al.* (1964: 93) give the example of a lecture on biology at a technical college. They describe this as being in the scientific field, the polite tenor and the lecturing mode. As another example, they point out that the same lecturer, 5 minutes later, in the staff common room, may switch to the field of cinema, tenor of man among colleagues and mode of conversation, with corresponding changes in linguistic choices.

If we take a concrete example of a text in a certain register, say a biology lecture, to use the example of Halliday*et al.*, we can create a description of its contextual parameters and associated likely lexicogrammar, as in Table 2.2.

2.5 LEXICOGRAMMAR

In order to come up with lexicogrammatical specifications of registers, it is necessary to be familiar with the descriptive apparatus of SFL. With reference to a very short text, this next section will map out what might be considered to be the most important features of this apparatus, from a discourse analytic point of view. Given the limited space, a lot more will be left out than can be included, but a flavour of the approach can still be given. At this point, a warning is perhaps warranted that there is rather a lot of terminology to grasp in SFL description. This is off-putting, it must be admitted, for some people, especially as traditional grammatical categories are often replaced by new ones. The rationale for this, however, is to emphasise the functional, semantic (meaning-focused) approach to description. The labels refer to semantic phenomena, whereas the labelling of traditional grammar is more focused on form.

In order to exemplify the various lexicogrammatical features of English as they relate to the

Table 2.2   Contextual parameters and associated lexicogrammar for the biology lecture register

Contextual parameter	Lexicogrammar
Field An area of information about the given biological topic	Biological lexis Relational process clauses (verbs of being and existing) and material process clauses (verbs of doing and happening)
Tenor Participants: lecturer as expert giver of knowledge and students as novice recipients of knowledge	Mostly declarative clauses Occasional use of imperatives, for example, *look at this slide*; *write this down* Occasional use of interrogatives if interacting with the audience
Mode Informal spoken monologue with occasional breaks for questions Supported by visual elements Expository	Discourse markers to signal structuring of the lecture such as *well, OK, so, right, now*

My favourite pet

My favourite pet is my parrot. He is an African Grey. We got him about 5 years ago. He has a grey body and a red tail. His beak is very sharp and he can bite you. He can say lots of words, like 'Hello', 'How are you today?' and 'Who's a pretty boy then?' He hasn't got a name. We just call him 'parrot'.

Figure 2.2   Short children's text about a pet parrot.

contextual parameters of field tenor and mode and to the ideational, interpersonal and textual metafunctions, we will use a very short text which was written by my son when he was in primary school (Figure 2.2).

2.5.1 Features related to field and the ideational function

2.5.1.1 Lexis

The first thing to note with respect to field is how the lexis relates semantically to the topic of the text, *my parrot*, that is to say, *my favourite pet – my parrot – an African Grey – a grey body – a red tail – his beak – very sharp – can bite*. Lexis is the most obvious way to recognise the field of any text.

2.5.1.2 Rank hierarchy

SFL works with a hierarchy of units, or *ranks,* as follows:

    clause complex
    clause
    group
    word

Each of these units consists of one or more of the units below it. Thus a group consists of one or more words, a clause consists of one or more groups, and a clause complex consists of one or more clauses. SFL does not use the term *sentence* in this hierarchy, considering *sentence* to be part of the system of orthography (writing) rather than grammar.

Let us take an example clause complex from our sample text: *His beak is very sharp and he can bite you*. This is a clause complex consisting of two clauses (connected by *and*), as follows:

    Clause 1: *his beak is very sharp*
    Clause 2: *he can bite you*

If we consider the composition of these clauses, we see that the first one, *his beak is very sharp*, consists of three groups:

    a nominal group: *his beak*
    a verbal group: *is*
    an adjectival group: *very sharp*

We see that the first of these groups consists of two words, the second of just one word and the third of two words. In the second clause, *he can bite you,* we have the following breakdown:

a nominal group: *he*
a verbal group: *can bite*
a second nominal group: *you*

Here, there are two nominal groups, each consisting of just one word, but the verbal group is made up of two words (a main verb *bite* and a modal verb *can*).

Because this text was written by a child, the groups are short. Some nominal groups, particularly in technical and bureaucratic registers, can be rather long. Here is quite an extreme example consisting of 44 words from a book on linguistics (Thibault 2004: 16) (complex nominal group underlined):

I conclude that language and other semiotic modalities emerge from <u>the primordial many degrees of freedom of the prior, sensor-motor based modalities of semiosis which constitute our earlier, always embodied, always semiotically mediated, transactions with the topological richness and variety of the physical-material processes and flows of the world in which we are immersed.</u>

2.5.1.3 Clauses

The clause is the basic unit of analysis in SFL. A clause is made up of *processes* (expressed as verbal groups), *participants* (expressed as nominal groups) and *circumstances* (expressed as adverbial groups or prepositional phases). These are functional labels, indicating the role of each element in the clause, that is to say, *processes* involve *participants* in certain *circumstances*.

The following is our sample text broken down into clauses.

1. My favourite pet is my parrot.
2. He is an African Grey.
3. We got him about 5 years ago.
4. He has a grey body and a red tail.
5. His beak is very sharp
6. [and] he can bite you.
7. He can say lots of words, like 'Hello', 'How are you today?' and 'Who's a pretty boy then?'
8. He hasn't got a name.
9. We just call him 'parrot'.

Most of the clauses in this simple text consist of two participants and a process. For example, the first two clauses can be labelled as follows.

My favourite pet	is	my parrot
He	is	an African Grey
Participant	**Process**	**Participant**

There is always a process in any clause and usually one or more participants. The final clause in our sample text has three participants.

We	call	him	parrot
Participant	**Process**	**Participant**	**Participant**

The fifth clause is the only clause in our sample text to contain a circumstance. Circumstances are optional elements in the clause.

We	got	him	about 5 years ago
Participant	Process	Participant	Circumstance

The process element of a clause may be finite, that is to say, it is marked for tense and takes a *subject,* or non-finite, that is, it is not marked for tense and does not take a subject. All of the clauses in our sample text are finite. Non-finites are associated more with more complex and more adult registers.

2.5.1.4 Process types: transitivity

Transitivity, in traditional grammar, refers to whether a verb is transitive or intransitive, the former taking a direct object and the latter not. Transitivity in SFL, however, is much broader than this. It is concerned with the whole clause, not just the verb. It includes the different types of processes involved, their relations to the roles of the participants and how the processes, roles and circumstances relate one to another. When we analyse the roles of the participants, the processes and the circumstances in a text, we can see the relationships between the people and the things involved, the processes they engage in and the sort of circumstances in which they occur.

There are six process types: *relational, material, verbal, mental, existential* and *behavioural,* only the first three of which occur in our sample text.

2.5.1.5 Relational process clauses

Relational process clauses are to do with being and existing. The most common relational process verb by far is the verb *be,* although other verbs may also express states of being and existing, such as *seem, look, become* and *have.* In our sample text there are many relational process clauses, three with *be* and two with *have.* This is because it is a descriptive text expressing relations of being and existing.

The participants in relational process clauses depend on whether the relational process clause is *identifying* or *attributive.* In identifying relational process clauses, the participants are *identifier,* which usually precedes the verb, and *identified,* which usually follows the verb. The obligatory participant in attributive relational process clauses is the *carrier,* which comes before the verb. The verb is followed by an *attribute,* which may be an adjectival or nominal group.

We have examples of each type in our sample text, as follows.

Identifying clauses

My favourite pet	is	my parrot
Identifier	Relational process	Identified

Attributive clauses

He	has	a grey body and a red tail
His beak	is	very sharp
He	hasn't got	a name
Carrier	Relational process	Attribute

A way to differentiate attributive and identifying clauses is that with the latter it is possible to reverse the participants; for example, *My favourite pet is my parrot* and *My parrot is my favourite pet* are both possible; with the attributive type this is not the case.

2.5.1.6 Material process clauses

Material process clauses contain verbs of doing. They are about actions performed. Typical material process verbs are *run*, *jump*, *arrive*, *leave, eat* and *drink*. Material process clauses have an *actor* as participant and may have a *goal* as a second participant. There are two material process verbs in our sample text, *got* and *bite*.

We	got	him	about 5 years ago
He	[can] bite	you	˙
Actor	**Material process**	**Goal**	**Circumstance**

2.5.1.7 Verbal process clauses

Verbal process clauses refer to processes of saying. The participants are: *sayer*, *receiver* and *verbiage*. We have two examples of a verbal process clause in the parrot text, *He can say lots of words* and *We just call him 'parrot'*.

He	[can] say		lots of words, like 'Hello', 'How are you today?' and 'Who's a pretty boy then?'
We	call	him	parrot
Sayer	**Verbal process**	**Receiver**	**Verbiage**

2.5.1.8 Mental process clauses

Mental processes are to do with thinking and feeling, with things that go on in the mind. Typical mental process verbs are *think, feel, see, believe, want* and *like*. In addition to the verb, mental process clauses may contain two participants: a *senser* and a *phenomenon*. There are no clauses of this type in our sample text, so here are some made-up examples. Note how the ordering of senser and phenomenon is variable, either one coming before or after the verb.

I	[can't] see	my keys
Senser	**Mental process**	**Phenomenon**

His outstanding personality	impresses	me
Phenomenon	**Mental process**	**Senser**

2.5.1.9 Existential process clauses

Existential process clauses are clauses referring to existence which are introduced by the 'empty' category there, usually with the verb *be*. Existential process clauses contain only one participant, the existent. There are no existential process clauses in our example text, so here is a made-up one.

There	is	a desk	in the corner
Existential process		**Existent**	**Circumstance**

2.5.1.10 Behavioural process clauses

The behavioural process category is intermediate between material and mental, such processes incorporating elements of both types of meaning. Examples include *watch, listen, laugh* and *cry*. Note how these verbs involve both material action and a mental state. There is usually only one participant in behavioural process clauses, the *behaver*, although there may also be a *behaviour*. There are no existential process clauses in our example text, so here are some made-up examples.

He	stared		out of the window
She	breathed	a sigh of relief	
Behaver	**Behavioural process**	**Behaver**	**Circumstance**

2.5.2 Features related to tenor and the interpersonal function: person, modality and mood

So far, we have been talking about field, as realised through the ideational metafunction, and how it relates to our sample text. Let us now turn to the tenor, as expressed through the interpersonal metafunction, that is, the personal relationships involved in a text between writer/speaker and reader/listener, and in our sample text in particular. The relationship in our sample text here is one of school pupil to teacher; the school pupil is telling the teacher about his parrot. We can note that, although this is a description, it is quite personalised, with the use of first-person pronouns: *my* favourite pet, *we* got him, *we* just call him (also one second-person pronoun: he can bite *you*). Descriptive text is not usually personalised like this, certainly not in academic contexts.

One feature of more sophisticated descriptive registers (for example, science textbooks) that this primary school text does have, however, is the near absence of modal verbs. Modal verbs such as *might, must, may, can* and *should* are used to express our attitude to what we are saying, to indicate how confident or not we are about the truth of what we are saying. In our text, there are two modal verbs, in he **can** bite you and in he **can** say lots of words. However, this is more expressive of the parrot's ability, not the writer's attitude towards what he is saying. The paucity of modal verbs in our text indicates that the school pupil is confident about what he is telling his teacher and at the same time makes the text less personalised.

This impersonality is further reinforced by the *mood* of the text, by the fact that it only has declarative clauses; there are no interrogatives (except for the reported interrogatives of the parrot) or imperatives.

2.5.3 Features related to mode and the textual metafunction: cohesion, theme and thematic development

When we consider the mode and textual metafunction of a text, in terms of lexicogrammar, we are concerned with the linguistic features which hold the text together and give it its characteristic texture (see Chapters 3 and 4 for more on this).

First, we can consider the *cohesion*, the links between the clauses[2]. In our sample text we find that cohesion is created primarily through the use of personal pronouns and the possessive pronouns *he* and *his* to refer to the parrot. In fact, we can note a chain of such items relating back to *my parrot* in the first clause, as follows: *my parrot – he – him – he – his – he – he – he – him.*

After cohesion, we can consider *theme* and *thematic development*.[3] Theme is the point of departure of a clause, what the clause is about, while thematic development refers to the pattern of themes across a stretch of text. We see that the parrot or a body part of the parrot (referred to respectively as *he* or *his* in our text) is made the theme of most of the sentences, in order to maintain attention on what is being described.

2.6 SUMMARY OF ANALYSIS OF THE *PARROT* TEXT

This brings us to the end of this brief analysis, which we can now summarise in Table 2.3.

2.7 A TEXT IN A SIMILAR, YET DIFFERENT, REGISTER

In order to see how SFL analysis can identify distinctions in registers, let us now look at another text (Figure 2.3) from a similar, yet different, register. This text is taken from some notes for students of elementary biology, not at primary school level, as in the parrot text, but at secondary level. If we conduct a similar analysis on this text as we did for the *parrot* text, we can highlight the similarities and differences of this more advanced register.

Table 2.3   Contextual parameters and lexicogrammar of the *parrot* text

Contextual parameter	Lexicogrammar
Field	
A boy's parrot; its attributes	Field-related lexis
	Relational process clauses (verbs of being and existing) (the majority); material process clauses (verbs of doing and happening); one verbal process clause; no mental, existential or behavioural process clauses
Tenor	
Social roles – school pupil to teacher	Use of first-person pronouns
Social distance – familiar	Very few markers of modality
	All clauses declarative
Mode	
Written to be read	Cohesion by means of personal pronouns and possessive adjectives
Descriptive	Theme–theme–theme pattern

The iris

(1.) The iris is a circular, coloured structure located in the front of the eye. (2.) In the centre of the iris is a small hole called the pupil. (3.) The iris is made up of radial muscles that contract to dilate the pupil and relax to make the pupil smaller. (4.) The function of the iris is to regulate the amount of light that enters the eye by contracting or dilating the pupil.

Figure 2.3   Short biology text about the iris (clause numbers added).

2.7.1 Field and the ideational metafunction

An important thing to note with respect to field in this *iris* text is the technical nature of the field-related lexis, for example, *the iris, the pupil, radial muscles, contract, dilate, relax, regulate*. While the *parrot* text had terms all relating to parrots, they were everyday terms, already a part of the child's vocabulary. The lexis of the iris text would likely not be understood by a primary school pupil (at least in the early years), so part of the educational process is to acquire technical vocabularies of the various registers of the school curriculum.

Another important difference between our two texts is the greater complexity of the one about the iris. We can see this, first, in the longer nominal groups. In the first clause of the iris text, we have a nominal group consisting of 11 words: *a circular, coloured structure located in the front of the eye*. The *head noun* of this group is *structure*. This head noun is modified by the indefinite article and the two adjectives preceding it, the *pre-modifier* – *circular* and *coloured*. However, most of its length is made up of what follows the head noun, the *post-modifier* – *located in the front of the eye*. The phenomenon which allows for this additional lengthy material as post-modifier in the nominal group is referred to as *embedding*. Embedding is a process which allows for the addition of an element to a group which is from a higher (or sometimes lower) level unit or rank (sometimes also called *downranking* or *rank-shifting*). Similar types of embedding occur in clauses 3 and 4, although we do not have space to analyse them here.

This type of embedding is indicative of the great flexibility of nominals in English to be expanded (it is not so easily done with verbs, which do not allow such embedding). It is a typical feature of the scientific textbook register. (See Halliday, 1989, Chapter 5, for a more detailed account of the role of embedding in written scientific language along similar lines to the one presented here.)

Alongside embedding, a related phenomenon which also creates greater textual complexity is *grammatical metaphor*, which was briefly introduced above. Grammatical metaphor refers to the use of a particular grammatical form to express a phenomenon that would be expressed more *congruently* by another grammatical form. Things are most congruently expressed by nouns, while processes are most congruently expressed by verbs. So a process expressed by a noun (also referred to as *nominalisation*) is a case of grammatical metaphor (and is, indeed, the most common pattern for the phenomenon). To exemplify this, Halliday (2004: 56) gives the following (made-up) example, where expression (a) is the congruent form and expression (b) is its rewording with grammatical metaphor:

(a)   The driver drove the bus too rapidly down the hill, so the brakes failed.
(b)   The driver's overrapid downhill driving of the bus resulted in brake failure.

This example does not sound very scientific in either of the two forms, but (b), because of the grammatical metaphor/nominalisation, perhaps sounds more 'scientific' than (a). Halliday also provides some authentic examples (p. 59), some of which are presented as follows (grammatical metaphor/nominalisation in bold [added]):

- Rapid **changes** in the **rate** of **evolution** are caused by external **events**.
- The thermal **losses** typical of an **insulating** system are measured in **terms** of a **quantity** called the thermal **loss** coefficient.
- This **breeding effort** was anchored in the American species' **resistance** to phylloxera.
- The **growth** of **attachment** between infant and mother signals the first **step** in the child's **capacity** to discriminate among people.

In the iris text, we only have one clause incorporating grammatical metaphor, the fourth clause: *The function of the iris is to regulate the amount of light that enters the eye by contracting or dilating the pupil*. In fact, there are two examples of grammatical metaphor in this clause, both *function* and *amount* having more congruent wordings.[4] A more congruent wording of the clause might thus be something like *the iris **does something** to regulate **how much** light ....*

What both embedding and grammatical metaphor highlight is the greater complexity of technical/academic writing as compared to 'everyday' language. This complexity can be opaque to the uninitiated and getting to grips with it is an essential part of the educational process, in both first- and second-language contexts. A practical learning activity to deal with this issue is to practise 'unpacking' and 'repacking' clauses which contain embedding and grammatical metaphor.

Returning to the *iris* text, we can note that, in spite of the greater complexity of the clauses, the process types employed are similar to those of the *parrot* text. As in the *parrot* text, the majority of the processes in the iris text are relational: *is, is, is [made up of], is*. The second most frequent type, as in the parrot text again, is material processes: *contract, dilate, relax, regulate, enters*. This similarity is a register feature of field to do with the fact that both texts are talking about structure (relational processes) and function (material processes), albeit at different levels of technicality. It is also interesting to note that both texts contain verbal processes: *call* and *say* in the *parrot* text and *called* in the *iris* text. Both texts involve the *naming* of structures and their parts.

2.7.2 Tenor and the interpersonal function and mode and the textual function

We can also note some register-specific features of the *iris* text as compared to the *parrot* text in the tenor and mode contextual parameters and their interpersonal and textual counterparts.

Considering, first, the tenor/interpersonal dimension, we noted that the *parrot* text was for the most part impersonal, but with some use of first-person pronouns. The *iris* text, on the other hand, is completely impersonal. There are no first- or second-person pronouns, only third-person ones. This subtle difference in tenor/interpersonal function between the two texts is indicative of the different relationship between writer and reader; in the expertise of the textbook writer, compared to the novice-like writing of the school pupil.

Turning now to mode/textual function, whereas in the *parrot* text, cohesion was created by the use of personal pronouns and adjectives, in the *iris* text, it is created primarily by lexical repetition. The nominal groups *the pupil* and *the iris* are each mentioned four times in the *iris* text. Lexical repetition like this is a common feature of scientific writing. Whereas in other types of writing we may be encouraged to avoid repetition and to strive for what is sometimes referred to as *elegant variation* (Fowler & Fowler, 1973), in scientific writing, clarity is considered more important than style. The school pupil/writer of the *parrot* text has clearly not learned this convention of scientific writing yet.

Another feature of mode/textual function in the *iris* text which is not present in the *parrot* text is the use of *marked theme*. In the *iris* text, *iris* is made the theme of each of the sentences to maintain attention on what is being discussed, just as *parrot* or a part of the parrot is the theme of clauses of the *parrot* text. However, in the second clause of the *iris* text, a *marked* pattern is employed, with the circumstance – *in the centre of the iris* – being placed in initial position. Such use of marked themes is a typical feature of the scientific textbook register, especially in descriptions of structure, where attention is drawn to particular structural parts.

2.7.3 Summary of analysis of the *iris* text

Table 2.4 is a summary of the analysis of the *iris* text, for the purposes of comparison with Table 2.3, the summary of the *parrot* text.

Table 2.4   Contextual parameters and lexicogrammar of the *iris* text

Contextual parameter	*Lexicogrammar*
Field	
Biology	Field-related (biological) lexis
	Relational process clauses (verbs of being and existing) and material process clauses (verbs of doing and happening)
Tenor	
Teacher to student; impersonal	Third person
	No modal forms
	All clauses declarative
Mode	
Written to be read	Lexical repetition
Descriptive and didactic	Theme–theme–theme pattern
	One example of marked theme
	Complex nominal groups
	One case of nominalisation
	Embedded clauses

2.8 CONVERSATION AS REGISTER

To complement the focus on written text thus far, this section will consider Halliday's approach to the analysis of the conversational register. We will draw for our account primarily on Eggins and Slade (2005), Halliday and Matthiessen (2004), Martin (1992) and Thornbury and Slade (2006). (In Chapter 7, we will consider a different, but complementary, approach to analysing conversation, that of *Conversation Analysis*.)

Halliday's model of speech exchange is based on two pairs of variables. According to Halliday, there are two basic functions in conversational interaction: giving and demanding. The speaker either gives something to the listener, or demands something. The two imply each other: giving implies receiving and demanding implies giving. Another pair of variables concerns what is given or demanded: this may be either goods and services or information. If I say something with the aim of getting you to give me something or to do something, this is an exchange of goods and services. If I say something with the aim of getting you to tell me something, this is an exchange of information. The two pairs of variables – giving and demanding, on the one hand, and goods or services and information, on the other hand – give four primary speech functions: offering, commanding, stating and questioning, as shown in Table 2.5.

Each of the speech functions carries with it a desired response: offering implies accepting, commanding implies complying, stating implies acknowledging and questioning implies answering. At the same time, the listener has the option of rebuffing a speech function once it is initiated: an offer may be rejected, a command may be refused, a statement may be contradicted and a question may be disclaimed. These options are shown in Table 2.6.

Table 2.5   Giving or demanding goods and services or information (Halliday and Matthiessen, 2004: 107, adapted)

	Commodity exchanged	
Role in exchange	*Goods and services*	*Information*
1. Giving	Offer: *Would you like this pen?*	Statement: *He's giving her the pen.*
2. Demanding	Command: *Give me that pen!*	Question: *What is he giving her?*

Table 2.6   Speech functions and responses (Halliday & Matthiessen, 2004: 108, adapted)

Initiating speech function	Responding speech functions	
	Supporting	Confronting
Offer	**Acceptance**	**Rejection**
Shall I get you a coffee?	*Yes, please do*	*No, don't bother*
Command	**Compliance**	**Refusal**
Get me a coffee, please	*All right*	*No, I can't*
Statement	**Acknowledgement**	**Contradiction**
He's getting her a coffee	*Oh, is he?*	*No, he isn't*
Question	**Answer**	**Disclaimer**
Are you having a coffee?	*Yes, I am*	*I don't know*

Although there is no one-to-one relation, with the exception of offering, the examples in Table 2.6 suggest typical grammatical realisations of the different functions. This is done through the mood system. Thus, interrogative clauses are typically used to ask questions, imperatives are typically used to realise commands and declaratives are typically used to express statements.

Halliday refers to typical grammatical realisations of speech function as *congruent*, while alternative realisations are referred to as *incongruent*. Thus, where *Get me a coffee, please*, with its imperative mood for a command, is a congruent pattern, an incongruent alternative might be *I'd like a coffee* (declarative) or *Could you get me a coffee?* (interrogative).

It is also worth noting how the responding speech functions may echo the initiation with a part of the verbal group called an operator (for example, *do/don't, does/doesn't, will/won't, can/can't, has/hasn't*), as in *Are you having a coffee? Yes, I am.* This seems to be a particular feature of the English language and has traditionally been an important focus in English language teaching.

Halliday's model of speech function has been applied and developed by Eggins and Slade (2005). Eggins and Slade use the term *move* to refer to speech functional units. A move is typically realised as a speaker turn at talk, but often a single turn may consist of more than one move in a *move complex*. We can see this in the analysis presented in Table 2.7, which is a conversational transcript from an advising session conducted by two students (with one acting as consultant). The conversation is broken down into speaker turns and moves.

Table 2.7   Extract from student advising session (Michigan Corpus of Academic Spoken English: MICASE) (http://quod.lib.umich.edu/cgi/c/corpus/corpus?c=micase;page=simple)

Speaker/turn	Move/move complex	
S1	Statement	so. i see that you're from Hartland Michigan
S2	Acknowledgement	Yes
S1	Statement	this is, right up the road
S2	Acknowledgement	mhm,
S1	Statement	like forty minutes from here
S2	Acknowledgment	Yeah
S1	Statement	and uh, you say that you're interested in prebusiness and economics
S2	Acknowledgement	Mhm, i wro- i w- i'm interested in the um, international aspect
	Acknowledgement	more, of a um, of a, program or whatnot
	Acknowledgement	so, like the international, business i was gonna do,
	Acknowledgement	it's a really, you know open field,
	Acknowledgement	you know like all that stuff
	Acknowledgement	but i don't, think that that's what i wanna do anymore, so
S1	Question	Okay, so what, what changed your mind and what has it been changed to?
S2	Answer	um, i, don't know if i wanna sp- like i wanna experience like you know, cultures and and the world

We can see in this table that there is one rather lengthy turn which is broken down into separate moves which together make up an acknowledgment move. It must be said, however, that the boundaries of such moves are often difficult to identify. For example, the final exchange has been coded as a question and answer, but it might be argued that the question is not one move but two, given that there are two separate questions here: *Okay, so what, what changed your mind?* and *What has it been changed to?*

One feature which can help in recognising discourse boundaries is rhythm and intonation. Speakers are able to speed up and slow down in order to control the turns in an interaction. Thus, a decision as to whether the two questions mentioned above make up one move or two might be decided by whether the speaker runs on from one to the other or creates a pause. Although we do not have detailed prosodic information for our transcript from the MICASE corpus, the corpus transcript does indicate where longer pauses occur. Given that no pause is indicated here, the decision can be made to count it as one move.

What this sort of analysis can do is to demonstrate how an interaction progresses. It can show who does the initiating and who responds (S1, the adviser, does all of the initiating here); what form the initiations take: offers, commands, statements or questions (statements and one question here, but mostly statements, which lead up to the question); what form the responses take: supporting or confronting? (supporting here; S2 is in a less powerful position than S1). And, in terms of the grammatical realisations, it can show whether they are congruent or incongruent (all congruent here). In short, it is a powerful tool in the analysis of interaction. It also offers potential for organising (part of) a language syllabus.

2.9 SINCLAIR AND COULTHARD'S MODEL OF CLASSROOM INTERACTION

In the 1970s, two linguists in Birmingham in the UK, Sinclair and Coulthard, directed a research project analysing classroom interaction in English primary schools. Sinclair and Coulthard were interested in seeing if Halliday's rank hierarchy for grammatical analysis could be extended to classroom discourse. The findings of this project were published in a book entitled *Towards an Analysis of Discourse: The English used by teachers and pupils* (Sinclair & Coulthard, 1975).

In Halliday's model of speech functions, as we have seen, exchanges consist of two units:

Initiation: Would you like a chocolate?
Response: Yes, please.

Sinclair and Coulthard noticed, however, that in their classroom data, exchanges are made up of three units, which, anticipating Eggins and Slade (2005), they referred to as *moves*: an *initiation*, a *response* and a *follow-up*, as in:

Initiation: What's the capital of France?
Response: Paris
Follow-up: Right

The pattern is predominant in classrooms, because the interaction is concerned with the *display* of information: teachers ask questions to which they already know the answer; pupils respond with the required information; and teachers follow up with confirmation to pupils as to whether they are right or not. The following example of a three-part exchange is from Sinclair and Coulthard's data:

Initiation: What makes a road slippery?
Response: You might have rain or snow on it.
Follow-up: Yes, snow, ice.

(Sinclair and Coulthard, 1975: 68).

Another phenomenon noted by Sinclair and Coulthard, again anticipating Eggins and Slade (2005), was that moves do not necessarily correspond to turns at talk. A given turn may consist of one or more moves. In the following extract, for example, the teacher's second turn consists of two moves: follow-up (*Yes. To keep you strong*) and initiation (*Why do you want to be strong?*):

Teacher: Can you tell me why you eat all that food?
            Yes?
Pupil: To keep you strong.
Teacher: Yes. To keep you strong.
            Why do you want to be strong?

Sinclair and Coulthard were not only concerned with moves and exchanges, however. As already mentioned, their research was an attempt to apply Halliday's rank scale for grammar to classroom discourse. Based on the data they collected from primary schools, Sinclair and Coulthard proposed the following ranks:

Lesson
Transaction
Exchange
Move
Act

The highest level, the lesson, is divided up into transactions, whose boundaries are marked by discourse markers such as *now, then, right*. Transactions consist of series of exchanges which are characterised by the initiation–response–follow-up (IRF) pattern. Exchanges are made up of moves, which are the single actions of initiation–response–follow-up. Acts, of which there are over 20 types, are the specific actions assigned to moves, such as eliciting an answer, bidding for a turn, providing information, and so forth. Thus, in the previous extract of data quoted, the teacher's initiation consists of two acts: an *elicit* (*Can you tell me why you eat all that food?*) and a *cue* (*Yes?*).

As with Halliday's rank scale model, each level consists of one or more units of the level below. Sinclair and Coulthard were partially successful in their application of Halliday's approach, although they were only able to specify the boundaries of transactions and not their internal structure.

A lot has been written about IRF and its effectiveness (or not) as a teaching tool. Some writers have noted how the pattern does not allow the student any initiative; the teacher does all of the initiating and follow-up work and thus is in overall control of the discourse. If we consider this in the light of language classes, it is clear that the students are not only getting no opportunity to initiate or follow up, but are overall getting very little opportunity to produce English (this apart from any ideological issues concerning the unequal distribution of power in the classroom). This insight lends support to a move away from teacher-fronted classrooms towards pair and group work, where learners are given the opportunity to participate more fully in the interaction.

Another insight from the model is that display questions are very specific to certain discourse situations, such as classrooms, and quizzes; such discourse is inauthentic in so far as it does not correspond to how people normally interact outside these institutional contexts.

On the other hand, if we look at Sinclair and Coulthard's data, we can see that IRF is interspersed with *informing* moves, moves where the teacher introduces new knowledge. In the following extract, for example, the student does not get the correct answer, thus allowing the teacher to introduce new information into the discourse, with an informing move.

Initiation:	And these symbols have a special name. Does anybody know that special name?
Response:	Is it Arabic?
Follow-up:	No, it isn't Arabic.
Inform:	Well, they're called hieroglyphics. It's hieroglyphic writing. And these, each one of these is an hieroglyph.

(Sinclair and Coulthard, 1975: 68).

In addition, the pattern allows the opportunity for *scaffolding* – support for learners on the part of the teacher when they are struggling for words – as shown in the following dialogue from Walsh (cited in McCarthy & Slade, 2007: 863):

[the class are discussing parking fines]

Pupil:	… or if my car
Teacher:	**is parked**
Pupil:	is parked illegally, the policeman take my car and … er … go to the police station, not police station, it's a big place where they have some cars, they
Teacher:	**Yes, where they collect the cars=**
Pupil:	= collect the cars and if I have a lot of … erm
Teacher:	**stickers … or fines**
Pupil:	stickers … or fines
Teacher:	**yeah**
Pupil:	Erm I I don't know … because no erm, if I have for example 100 fines [Teacher: **fines**] and I have money in the bank the government take the money from the bank [Teacher: **good**], no consult

2.10 SPEECH AND WRITING

A fundamental distinction can be made with regard to the contextual parameter of mode between spoken and written language. Halliday's main contribution to the literature on speech and writing is his book *Spoken and Written Language* (Halliday, 1989). Here we will consider this work, but also contributions from other linguists. A comparison of any transcribed spoken text and a written text is likely to reveal a number of significant differences, (consider, for example, the texts in Figures 2.2 and 2.3, above). According to Chafe and Danielewicz (1987), spoken text is fragmented (loosely structured) and involved (interactive with the listener). Written text is integrated (densely structured) and detached (lacking in interaction with the listener).

Some linguistic features of spoken text are as follows:

* phonological contractions and assimilations;
* hesitations, false starts and filled pauses;
* repetition;
* sentence fragments rather than complete sentences;
* structured according to prosodic features rather than clauses;
* high incidence of discourse markers at the beginning or end of tone groups;

- relatively frequent use of questions and imperatives;
- first- and second-person pronouns;
- deixis (reference outside the text – *this, that, here, there*).

Linguistic features of written text, on the other hand, are:

- longer information units (complete clauses and sentences);
- complex relations of coordination and subordination;
- high incidence of attributive adjectives;
- wider range and more precise choice of vocabulary than in speech;
- high degree of nominalisations;
- longer average word length;
- greater use of passive voice.

In spite of these differences, however, spoken and written text are not two totally distinct categories. Halliday (1989: 46) argues that there is a cluster of registers that share the written medium, on the one hand, and a cluster of registers that share the spoken medium, on the other, but that there are nevertheless certain features which are characteristic of either mode. With the advent of electronic media, the distinction between certain registers is becoming blurred, many 'virtual' texts exhibiting features typical of both speech and writing.

Different spoken and written registers can be situated along a continuum marking different degrees of 'spokenness' and 'writtenness' and exhibiting to a greater or lesser extent the linguistic features listed above. Casual conversation would be at one extreme of spokenness, while academic writing might be at the other extreme of writtenness. Other registers, such as radio news, academic lectures, formal ceremonies (for example, marriages and coronations), and so forth, for spoken language, and business letters, fiction, personal letters, e-mails and text messages, and so forth, for written language, would be situated at different points along the continuum. If we compare the *parrot* text and the *iris* text used as examples in this chapter, we can see the *parrot* text as closer to the 'spoken' end of the continuum and the *iris* text closer to the 'written' end.

Ochs (1979) suggests that the positioning of the different registers along the spoken/written continuum depends at least in part to what degree the language of a given register is *planned* or *unplanned*. Clearly, casual conversation is unplanned, while academic writing is carefully planned. Academic lectures, on the other hand, are less spontaneous than casual conversation, but more spontaneous than academic writing.

McCarthy and Slade (2007) add a further dimension, that of explicitness, with written text being more explicit and spoken language more implicit and dependent on context. McCarthy and Slade (2007: 860) present a diagram to show the differences on the various scales we have mentioned, as shown in Figure 2.4.

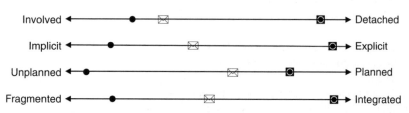

Figure 2.4   Comparison of some spoken and written text types (adapted from McCarthy & Slade, 2007: 860).

2.11 LEXICAL DENSITY

In spite of the arguments for no absolute distinctions between speech and writing, it is nevertheless possible to talk of general tendencies. One way of contrasting the relative complexity of speech and writing is in terms of *lexical density* (Halliday, 1989; Ure, 1971). Lexical density is a statistical measure of the relative frequency of lexical words and grammatical words in a stretch of text. The category of lexical words (also referred to as *content words*) includes nouns, verbs, adjectives and adverbs. Grammatical words (also referred to as *function words*) include determiners, pronouns, prepositions, conjunctions, numerals and auxiliary verbs. Given that a text consists of only these two types of words, we can express lexical density as the ratio of lexical words to the total number of words.[5]

To take an example, if a stretch of text has, say, 60 lexical items and 40 grammatical items, the ratio of lexical items to the total (100 words) is 60 per cent or 0.6, which is the lexical density, depending upon how you want to express it.

The formula can be stated as in Figure 2.5.

Typically, written text will have a higher lexical density than spoken text. Halliday is keen to stress, however, that this does not mean that written text is more complex than spoken. Both types of text have their individual type of complexity. Halliday describes writing as the world of 'things' rather than 'happenings', of 'product' rather than 'process', and of 'being' rather than 'becoming'. Spoken text, on the other hand, is the world of happening, of processes and of becoming, Writing reflects upon the world, while speech represents the world as action or process. In terms of the grammar, written text is characterised by lexical intricacy, while spoken text is characterised by complex chains of clauses. '[T]he complexity of written language is lexical, while that of spoken language is grammatical' (Halliday, 1989: 63).

To illustrate this, Halliday (1989: 81) provides two sets of wordings that are paraphrases of each other, one typical of writing and the other of speech, as shown in Table 2.8.

The written versions of these paraphrases are characterised by nominals: *visit, sense, futility, action, violence, improvements, costs, installation, opinion, change, enthusiasm*; the spoken versions are characterised by verbs: *had visited, had ended up feeling, tried to do, had been, has improved, install, doesn't cost, rejoiced, change*. Both sets of paraphrases represent different types of complexity.

2.12 APPRAISAL

Developed by Martin and White (Martin, 2000; Martin & White, 2005), *appraisal*, or *appraisal theory*, is an attempt to develop the minutiae of the interpersonal function.[6] Appraisal is concerned with the ways we express our views and react to the views of others. It can be identified at the level of the word or group. There are three systems in appraisal – graduation, attitude and engagement. We will deal with them very briefly in turn, drawing extensively on two very useful websites: http://www.grammatics.com/appraisal/ and http://www.alvinleong.info/sfg/sfgappraisal.html (see Martin & White, 2005).

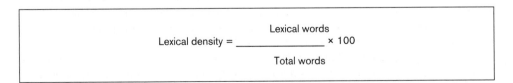

$$\text{Lexical density} = \frac{\text{Lexical words}}{\text{Total words}} \times 100$$

Figure 2.5   Formula for lexical density.

Table 2.8   Written and spoken paraphrases (Halliday, 1989: 81, adapted)

1.
Written Every previous visit had left me with a sense of the futility of further action on my part.
Spoken   Whenever I'd visited there before, I'd ended up feeling that it would be futile if I tried to
do anything more.
2.
Written Violence changed the face of once peaceful Swiss cities.
Spoken   The cities in Switzerland had once been peaceful, but they changed when people became violent.
3.
Written Improvements in technology have reduced the risks and high costs associated with
simultaneous installation.
Spoken   Because the technology has improved it's less risky than it used to be when you install
them at the same time, and it doesn't cost as much either.
4.
Written Opinion in the colony greeted the promised change with enthusiasm.
Spoken   The people in the colony rejoiced when it was promised that things would change in this way.

2.12.1 Graduation

Graduation is concerned with grading and scaling of the interpersonal force attaching to utterances. There are two subsystems: *force*, which is to do with intensity of interpersonal force (*slightly, somewhat, very, completely*); and *focus*, which concerns the precision of our interpersonal focus (*I kind of like this, this is the genuine article*).

2.12.2 Attitude

Attitude is to do with how speakers and writers express their attitude towards people and phenomena. It has three subsystems: *affect*, which refers to emotional attitude (*I love/hate you*); *judgement*, which refers to evaluation of behaviour (*She played very well/badly*); and *appreciation*, which relates to the evaluation of objects and products in terms of their aesthetic or other value (*He played a beautiful shot*; *That's a really dangerous place*).

2.12.3 Engagement

Engagement is how we express our commitment to what is stated in what we say or write. It has four subsystems: *disclaiming*, in which we distance ourselves from what has been said or written (*It is said that*; *I deny that*); *proclamation*, where we assert that something is true (*It is true that*; *I must say that*); *acknowledgement*, where we acknowledge a range of possibilities (*It is possible that*; *It seems that*); and *attribution*, through which we report something that has been said or written (*Scientists have discovered that*; *According to Smith (2010)*).

2.13 CRITIQUE

Hallidayan theory and SFL in general have been critiqued on a number of counts. Most of these are rather technical and we will not go into them here. We will merely point out some of the more salient ones (see Butler, 2003, for some of the more technical ones). First, from the point of view of the student and from the point of view of the applied practitioner, many find the terminology off-putting, as already mentioned, and not always intuitive. The counterargument, as already mentioned again, is that the labels are semantic ones which point to the functional value of the categories. In addition, using only traditional terms restricts us to talking about only certain areas of grammar. A huge number of grammatical features (that often cause severe problems for learners) are simply ignored in traditional grammar because there is no metalanguage for talking about them – especially, for example, in the area of transitivity.

Some have critiqued SFL for dealing in binary oppositions, thereby not allowing for scalar gradations of meaning, as is possible, for example, in more pragmatic accounts of language (see Chapters 5 and 6). Everything has to be either/or and never somewhere in between. The counterargument here is that it is possible to go to ever more delicate distinctions. Thus, where there is a choice, say, of mood between indicative and imperative, indicative can be further differentiated between interrogative and declarative, interrogative can be divided according to closed/polar (yes/no) and open ('Wh'-), and so forth.

Another criticism is the lack of an empirical basis for the claim for three contextual parameters and three corresponding metafunctions. Other linguists have come up with other functions. Jakobson (1960), for example, has six contextual parameters and corresponding functions. Related to this is the more general critique that SFL does not devote enough attention to analysing context (contrast this with more ethnographic or sociocognitive approaches), preferring to focus more on the lexicogrammar (van Dijk, 2008). On the other hand, proponents of SFL would argue that it is the only school with a robust model to link the text and context systematically. It is no good talking about context if you cannot show how it is systematically construed or expressed by the lexicogrammar.

Finally, even if the tripartite divisions are accepted, it may be difficult to decide which features of the lexicogrammar correspond to which metafunction and contextual parameter.

In spite of these possible criticisms, as will be emphasised in the next section, Halliday's framework offers great potential for application to pedagogy.

2.14 APPLICATION TO PEDAGOGY

We mentioned in the introduction to this chapter that Halliday has always been concerned with 'applied' issues. He refers to his model as *appliable* linguistics and the research centre set up in his name in 2005 at City University of Hong Kong is called the Halliday Centre for Intelligent Applications of Language Studies. As well as coauthoring *The Linguistic Sciences and Language Teaching*, Halliday was director of two influential curriculum development projects in the UK in the 1960s and early 1970s. Both of these projects (*Breakthrough to Literacy* at primary level and *Language in Use For Secondary Schools*) were very influential in reforming the teaching of English in the British school system. Fundamental to these projects was the concept of register, as set out in *The Linguistic Sciences and Language Teaching,* and the need for the child 'to be taught the varieties of the language appropriate to different situations: the range and use of its registers and restricted languages' (Halliday *et al.*, 1964: 241). Halliday's social commitment comes through in these projects, as it does in the following quotation from *The Linguistic Sciences and Language Teaching*:

> We cannot afford in any way to neglect the language requirements of those who are going to become nurses, engineers, technicians, draughtsmen, transport workers, private secretaries, shorthand typists or members of any other of the thousand and one occupations that by some miracle feed, clothe and house us … Each of us has to learn to manipulate English in a range of varieties, some of which are developing very rapidly. … What can we tell the compiler of a computer programming manual about the use of English in that restricted language?
>
> (Halliday *et al.*, 1964: 243).

Halliday's theory was very influential in the Council of Europe's Common European Framework project for language teaching and his model of acquisition underpins the basic theory of communicative language teaching. After Halliday moved to Australia in the 1970s, Halliday and Hallidayan theory were again influential in the development of programmes for both first-language teaching and the teaching of immigrants in that country.

Halliday's theory of register can be seen to underpin the development of the English for Specific Purposes (ESP) movement, the concept of register as situated variety of language being fundamental to that movement. Needs analysis – the specification of the language that learners are likely to need in a given target situation – and essential to ESP, indeed, can be seen as a form of register analysis.

> Let us take as examples the questions 'what kind of English?' and 'for what purposes?' The items to be taught are absolutely determined by the answers to these questions, and obviously the reply 'we should teach the whole of English' – which would imply English as spoken and written at all times, in all places, about all subjects – is an unreal one and therefore useless.
>
> (Halliday *et al.*, 1964: 202).

As we have seen in this chapter, Halliday sees language as a resource for making meanings. Through interaction, we shape our world and our individual identity. As Halliday's study of his child, Nigel, showed, the acquisition of language is an interactive process through which the learner develops control of the functions of language and the grammatical resources required for their realisation. This model can be seen to be operating in the communicative approach to language teaching, with its emphasis on the importance of interaction as both the means and goal of language teaching.

2.15 QUESTIONS FOR DISCUSSION

1. Do you agree with Halliday's model of language development as based on interaction? What are the strengths and weaknesses of this theory, as compared to the competing theory that says that humans have an innate ability for language acquisition and are preprogrammed to learn their first language? What about second-language learning?
2. Think of a register and then write down some typical phrases that might help you to identify it if you heard or read them. Show these typical phrases to your classmates. Can they recognise the register?
3. Compare a register you are familiar with in your first language with the same register in your second language, if you know one. What differences are there in field, tenor or mode when they are compared, if any?
4. Make lists of at least five material process verbs, five relational process verbs and five verbal process verbs.
5. If you have ever learned an additional language, what approach did your teachers use: Sinclair and Coulthard's model of exchange structure or pair and group work? Did all of your teachers use the same approach?
6. Sinclair and Coulthard's model of exchange structure has been claimed by some to apply also in everyday language. Write down at least two three-part exchanges that might occur in everyday interaction.
7. Draw a vertical line and write down casual conversation at the top and research articles at the bottom. Write in other spoken and written registers you are familiar with along this line according to how 'spoken' or 'written' you judge them to be.
8. Take a short text and see if you can identify any of the features of appraisal in it, as listed in this chapter.
9. In a group or with a partner, discuss the potential advantages and disadvantages of SFL and register theory as they relate to language teaching.

2.16 FURTHER READING

Halliday, 1975, 1987; Halliday and Matthiessen, 2004; Halliday *et al.*, 1964; Thompson, 2004.

CHAPTER 3

Cohesion

3.1 INTRODUCTION

With *cohesion*, we are concerned with the formal (but at the same time semantic) links between clauses, how an item – a pronoun, a noun or a conjunction – in one clause may refer backwards or forwards to another clause. Cohesion needs to be distinguished from *coherence*, which is concerned with the overall interpretation of a text as a unified piece of discourse, not just the formal links. As many linguists have argued (for example, Brown and Yule, 1983; Carrell, 1982; de Beaugrande and Dressler, 1981; Enkvist, 1978; Widdowson, 1978), it is possible (although unusual) to have coherence without cohesion. Widdowson (1978: 29) gives the often-quoted example of an exchange between two people:

A: That's the telephone.
B: I'm in the bath.
A: OK.

This piece of discourse has no formal links between the three clauses that make it up, but at the same time it can be understood as a coherent piece of discourse; one person is summoning someone to answer the telephone and the other is saying that s/he is not able to answer it because s/he is having a bath. Short, made-up examples which display no cohesion such as these are interesting, but most coherent texts will at the same time display a range of cohesive devices. We can say that cohesion contributes to coherence, although it is not a sufficient condition. We will return to this issue later in this chapter.

Halliday and Hasan (1976: 4) describe cohesion as follows:

Cohesion occurs where the INTERPRETATION of some element in the discourse is dependent on that of another. The one PRESUPPOSES the other, in the sense that it cannot be effectively decoded except by recourse to it. When this happens, a relation of cohesion is set up, and the two elements, the presupposing and the presupposed, are thereby at least potentially integrated into the text.

Halliday and Hasan (1976: 2) give the following example:

Wash and core **six cooking apples**. Put **them** into a fireproof dish.

In this example, *them* in the second sentence refers back to the *six cooking apples* of the first sentence. The cohesive relation is created both by the referring item, *them*, and the item it refers back to, the *six cooking apples*. It is the resolution of what is presupposed by *them* (*six cooking apples*) which creates the cohesive relation between the two sentences. Another way of putting this is to say that, in a cohesive relation such as this, one of the two elements is interpreted by reference to another (Halliday & Hasan, 1976: 11). We can only interpret what is meant by *them* by referring back to the *six cooking apples*.

The relation between the two elements in a cohesive relationship such as the one in the above example is referred to as a *tie*. Because there is a meaning relation such as this in cohesive ties, Halliday and Hasan describe cohesion as a *semantic* phenomenon.

Cohesion can occur both within the clause and across clauses and sentences, although most linguists focus their attention on the *interclausal* or *intersentential*, as opposed to the *intraclausal*, variety (Christiansen, 2011: 25). A sentence is understood here in the way that Halliday and Matthiessen (2004) define it, in the sense of one or more clauses. Thus, in the following example (a), which is a single clause and at the same time a sentence, the tie is intrasentential, *her* referring back to *Mary* in this same clause/sentence.

    a)   **Mary** put the money in **her** purse.

In the next example (b), which is a sentence consisting of two clauses, *it* and *her* refer back to *the money* and *Mary* respectively. The links are interclausal, but not intersentential.

    b)   **Mary** took **the money** and put **it** in **her** purse.

In a third example (c), where we have two simple sentences, each consisting of one clause, we have two intersentential links, between *she* and *her*, on the one hand, and *Mary* and *the money*, on the other.

    c)   **Mary** took **the money**. Then **she** put it in **her** purse.

Halliday and Hasan classify cohesive devices into five categories: reference, substitution, ellipsis, conjunction and lexical cohesion, categories which have been taken up by most other linguists. We will deal with them below.

3.2 REFERENCE

3.2.1 Definition, forms and functions

The examples we have been discussing so far are cases of reference. A reference item is a word or phrase, the identity of which can be determined by referring to other parts of the text or the situation.

Reference items in English include personal pronouns, such as *I, you, he, she, it*; possessive adjectives, such as *my, your, his, her*; possessive pronouns, such as *mine, yours, his, hers*; demonstratives, such as *this, that, these, those*; and the definite article, *the*.

As well as within the text – called endophoric reference – as in our examples so far, reference may also be outside the text – called exophoric reference. An example of exophoric reference would be when someone refers to something which is part of the context of situation, but does not appear in the text, as in **That** *picture is beautiful*, referring to a picture which is hanging on the wall, or *Look at **them***, referring to a group of people standing nearby.

Because it does not bind two elements together in a text, exophoric reference is not included as part of cohesion (Halliday & Hasan, 1976: 18). Nevertheless, exophoric reference interacts with the cohesion system and, like cohesion, is an important property of texts, contributing to their overall coherence.

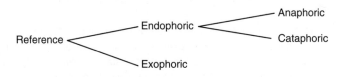

Figure 3.1 The English reference system.

Within endophoric reference, there are two categories: anaphoric (referring back) and cataphoric (referring forward). The reference system can thus be represented as shown in Figure 3.1.

We have already noted examples of anaphoric reference (a–c above). In those examples, it is easy to see the link to be made between the reference item and its *antecedent* and how the reference item presupposes that its antecedent has already been mentioned. Here are a few more examples:

a) **Jocelyine Hampson** read again the six words that had been typed with a faint ribbon: '*The Bangkok Secret* by Adam Hapson'. **She** breathed in slowly, flicked over the page and read the first paragraph again.

b) **Prapoth** struggled frantically to tear himself from my grip. **His** mouth was agape with fear and **his** eyes were rolling.

c) And **the allegations concerning a member of the royal family**. What about **those**?

(examples from The Bangkok Secret, Anthony Grey)

With regard to the cataphoric type, it must be said that this pattern is much less frequent than either the anaphoric or exophoric types. An example of cataphoric reference would be the following: *Remember* **this**. *Never trust a stranger*. In this example, we can see how a reference item can refer to a whole sentence (or, in many cases, more), not just a single noun or noun phrase. *This*, in this example, refers forward to the whole following sentence, *Never trust a stranger*. In written text, cataphoric reference often occurs after a colon, semicolon or dash following the reference item, as in this next example: ***The following*** *are the winners: Susan, Christopher and Ali*. Strictly speaking, cases such as these are not interclausal at all, but they are often treated as such. In fact, a case can be made for such examples to be considered as interclausal, if what comes after the colon is taken as *ellipitical* (that is to say, reduced – see below on ellipsis). Thus in our example, *Susan, Christopher and Ali* could be expanded to [*they are*] *Susan, Christopher and Ali*.

3.2.2 Definite reference

We listed the definite article, *the*, as an item that can be used as a referring item. This is a less transparent type of reference, as many learners of English, even very advanced ones, have learned to their peril. Here is an example:

d) In the centre of the dimly lit execution yard **a cross of wood** had been erected. Close to **the cross** stood a rectangular frame over which a blue curtain was drawn.

(The Bangkok Secret, Anthony Grey)

Referential *the* has no content of its own. It obtains its meaning by attaching itself to another item and in doing so makes that item specific and identifiable, that is to say, that it can be recovered somewhere in the context, either textual or situational. Thus, if I say '*the tree*' or '*the enemy*', or '*the cross*' (as in example d, above), I am presupposing that there is some tree or some enemy or some cross in the context in which I am using these expressions and that this tree or this enemy or this cross can be identified.

Probably the most frequent use of definite reference is exophoric. Halliday and Hasan identify two ways in which exophoric definite reference refers. First, it may refer to something which is specific to the given situation. If I say, *The water's too cold* when standing with my interlocutor by a swimming pool, I am clearly referring to the water in the pool. When London underground operators say *Mind the gap!* they are referring to the gap between the train and the platform, with which alighting passengers are familiar. Second, exophoric definite reference may refer to something which is specific to a community (referred to by Martin [1992] as *context of culture*), for example, *the president, the baby, the piano*. This type of reference is also sometimes called *unique reference* or *homophora*. Martin (1992: 122) provides a set of examples of this type of definite exophoric reference related to the community, or context of culture, as shown in Table 3.1.

Exophoric definite reference may also refer to a whole class of items: *the newspapers, the possibilities, the differences*; or an individual considered as a representative of a whole class (referred to also as *generic reference*): *the lion, the alligator*, as in **The lion** (Panthera leo) *is one of the four big cats in the genus* Panthera, or **The alligator** *is notorious for its bone-crushing bites* (both examples from Wikipedia).

Halliday and Hasan refer to two uses of the definite article which are endophoric, as opposed to the exophoric examples mentioned so far. The first is cataphoric, where the reference item refers forward to the modifier in a noun phrase, for example, *The title of the book, The capital of France, The boy sitting in the corner, The man who fixed our drains for us*. In examples such as these, the definite article signals forward that the modifier is to be taken as the defining feature of the item in question. It answers the question *Which book? Which capital? Which boy? Which man?* These uses are not cohesive, given that they only refer within the nominal group.

The second type of endophoric reference is anaphoric. This is the only type of those discussed which is truly cohesive. With this category, *the* may attach itself to a repeated noun, a synonym or a semantically related noun. The following are examples.

a) Last year I bought a new house. *The* house is very well built.
b) Last year I bought a new house. *The* place is very well built.
c) I went into the house. *The* rooms were very dark.

Given the complexity of the system of reference, it is not surprising that learners – even advanced learners – have difficulty mastering it. As Lock (1996: 36) points out, and as we have seen here, the relationships between referring items and reference categories are not one-to-one. Choice of referring item requires a high degree of sensitivity to context. As Lock (1996: 36) points out again, generalisations or rules regarding each form illustrated with decontextualised examples are not likely to be successful. Learners need to understand and practise the various types of reference in extended contexts.

Table 3.1   Examples of exophoric reference as specific to the community (context of culture): (Martin, 1992: 122)

Community (context of culture)	Homophoric nominal group
English speakers	The sun, the moon
Nations	The president, the governor
States	The premier, the Department of Education
Businesses	The managing director, the shareholders
Offices	The secretary, the photocopier
Families	The car, the baby, the cat

3.3 SUBSTITUTION AND ELLIPSIS

Substitution and ellipsis are closely related to each other, as they both involve the replacement (substitution) or removal (ellipsis) of material which would otherwise be anticipated in the text. Compared to reference, both categories are relatively local phenomena in so far as they are limited to linking two adjoining clauses, whereas reference links can stretch across long stretches of text in cohesive chains (see below).

3.3.1 Substitution

With substitution, a substitute word of phrase is replaced by another, for example, *Which book do you want? I'll take the red* **one**. In this example the word *book* is substituted by *one*. Substitution may be nominal, as in the example just given; it may be verbal, for example, *I have coffee every morning and he* **does** *too*, where *have coffee every morning* is substituted by *does;* or it can be at the level of the whole clause, for example, A: *I am so ugly*, B: *Okay, if you say* **so**, where the whole clause, *I am so ugly*, is replaced by *so*.

3.3.2 Ellipsis

Halliday and Hasan refer to ellipsis as a variation on substitution. It is described by them as 'substitution by zero' (p. 142), that is to say, something is omitted. Where ellipsis occurs, something is left unsaid, it is true, but, at the same time, it is nevertheless understood. As with substitution, ellipsis may be at the level of the noun group, verbal group or complete clause. The following are examples of each:

a) He potted the pink ball and then the black. (nominal)
b) John played tennis and Peter football. (verbal)
c) A: Do you play tennis?
    B: No. (clausal)

In (a), *ball* is ellipsed at the end of the second of the two clauses; in (b), the verb *played* is ellipsed in the second clause; and in (c), the whole clause, *I don't play tennis* is ellipsed.

The intricacies of ellipsis and substitution are quite complex, with many categories and subcategories, and they are beyond the scope of this chapter. However, see Halliday and Hasan (1976) for a full treatment.

Some of the more common patterns of substitution and ellipsis are typically treated in language courses as part of the grammar. Question and answer routines involving substitution and ellipsis are typically practised in drills such as the following:

A. Do, you like tennis?
B. Yes, I do./No, I don't.

A. Does she like tennis?
B. Yes, she does./No, she doesn't.

A. Do they like tennis?
B. Yes, they do./No, they don't.

It is certainly true that patterns such as these cause problems for learners who do not have such patterning in their first language.

3.4 CONJUNCTION

Christiansen (2011: 161) describes conjunction as 'perhaps the most explicit and obvious cohesive devices in a text', because, with this type of cohesion, the meaning relation is contained in the cohesive item itself. Halliday and Matthiessen (2004: 536) describe conjunction as a system for marking what they refer to as *logicosemantic relations*. Halliday and Hasan (1976) distinguish four major types of conjunction in English for marking these relations:

ADDITIVE (for example, *and, in addition, besides, furthermore*)
ADVERSATIVE (for example, *but, yet, though, however*)
CAUSAL (for example, *so, then, therefore*)
TEMPORAL (for example, *then, next, after that, finally*)

Halliday and Hasan (1976: 174) make the point that there is 'no single uniquely correct inventory' of conjunctive types and indeed Halliday and Mathiessen (2004: 541) provide a rather different classification to that of Halliday and Hasan (1976), although the one presented here has the advantage of being simple and relatively transparent.
Some conjunctions may occur at various places in the clause:

a)   Mark is an excellent teacher. **However**, David is even better.
b)   Mark is an excellent teacher. David, **however**, is even better.
c)   Mark is an excellent teacher. David is, **however**, even better.
d)   Mark is an excellent teacher. David is even better, **however**.

In contrast, others can only occur at the beginning of the second clause or sentence:

a)   Mark is an excellent teacher **and** Alice is too.
b)   Mark is an excellent teacher **but** Alice is better.
c)   Mark is an excellent teacher, **so** we are lucky to have him.

Halliday and Matthiessen (2004: 536) explain how conjuncts can link text spans of varying extent, ranging from pairs of clauses (as in the examples so far) to longer spans of text. In the following example, we can see how the contrastive conjunct, *however*, links up with a series of clauses, not just a single clause, about Bill Dobrow's drumming career:

These days *Bill Dobrow* is a successful drummer, having recorded and toured with a whole host of successful acts that include *The Black Crowes*, *Sean Lennon*, and *Martha Wainwright*; **however** a career in music wasn't always his dream …
(http://www.lettersofnote.com/2011/01/however-since-you-are-twelve.html)

Halliday and Hasan (1976) list over 40 different conjunctions. However, spoken discourse, although making very frequent use of conjunctions, typically uses a much narrower range of items (most typically *oh, well, and, so, then, but, because, now* and *then*), as compared to written text. Schiffrin (1987) refers to such conjuncts as *discourse markers*. The following is an extract from Schiffrin's data (p. 39), showing the pervasiveness of the discourse marker *and* in informal spoken discourse:

I believe in that. Whatever's gonna happen is gonna happen.

I believe … that … **y'know** it's fate.

It really is.

Because eh my husband has a brother, that was killed in an automobile accident.

and at the same time there was another fellow, in there, that walked away with not even a scratch on him.

And I really fee−

I don't feel y'can push fate.

and I think a lot of people do.

But I feel that you were put here for so many, years or whatever the case is,

and that's how it was meant to be.

Because like when we got married.

we were supposed t'get married uh: like about five months later.

My husband got a notice t'go into the service

and we moved it up.

And my father died the week … after we got married.

While we were on our honeymoon.

And I just felt, that move was meant to be,

because if not, he wouldn't have been there.

So eh **y'know** it just s−seems that that's how things work.

The logicosemantic relations in spoken text such as the above example seem to be a lot less specific than those found in formal written text. Coming as they do at the beginning of clauses, they also seem to have a more topic-organising function, breaking the discourse into chunks and indicating when the speaker is continuing with a topic or shifting to a new one. Georgakopoulou and Goutsos (2004: 93) argue that the strongest meaning of discourse markers is not ideational, but interpersonal. It is true that in our example, *y'know* at the beginning of the extract does seem to indicate the speaker's attitude to what she is saying.

One consideration in the teaching of conjunction concerns the danger of overuse. Consider the following learner text concerning the possible development of a village in Hong Kong (Shalo):

As golf playing is a popular sport in the world, **however**, we have only a few courses in the area, **therefore** in order to promote tourism and recreation, it is the time for us to construct a private golf course.

   The present situation of Shalo is a small village and it is only connected by a footpath. **Moreover**, most of the areas surrounding it are abandoned fields, grassland and woodland. **In view of the above**, we find that the inconvenience caused to the surrounding area is minimal. **Besides**, the resource of land will be better utilized as most of the area is abandoned land. **Moreover**, after initial contact with the villagers of Shalo, all of them accepted the proposed compensation.

(author's data)

This text was produced by a Hong Kong learner. In public examinations at the time of its writing, a certain number of marks were assigned for the use of conjuncts. It is quite possible, therefore, that the learner inserted so many conjuncts in the expectation of being given credit for them.

3.5 LEXICAL COHESION

Halliday and Hasan (1976) divide cohesion into two distinct categories: grammatical and lexical. So far, we have summarised the different grammatical categories. In spite of lexical cohesion being one of the two sides of this binary classification, however, it takes up only a few pages of Halliday and Hasan's lengthy treatment of the general topic of cohesion. This is especially surprising when, as Tanskanen (2006: 31) points out, in the example text analysis which Halliday and Hasan provide at the back of their book, lexical cohesion makes up almost half of the cohesive ties they analyse. In spite of this, or perhaps because of it, lexical cohesion is in many ways the most interesting (and problematic) part. We will begin in this section with Halliday and Hasan's (1976) original treatment of the topic, briefly discuss their later revisions to their model, and then, in subsequent sections, consider a number of alternative models.

Halliday and Hasan (1976) have two subcategories of lexical cohesion: reiteration and collocation.

Reiteration of a lexical item in a text may be by repetition of a word, use of a synonym, a near synonym, a superordinate or a general class word. The following are examples of each:

a) I would like to introduce **Dr Johnson**. **Dr Johnson** is our head of department. (repetition)
b) He has worked in a **coal mine** all his life. He first went down **the pit** when he was a boy. (synonym)
c) Our **computer system** is one of the most sophisticated in the country. The **network** has been running for several years now. (near synonym)
d) As part of our **America** week, RTHK revels in some of the most expressive music of **that continent**. (superordinate)

Broadly defined, collocation is the way in which words are used regularly together (Halliday and Hasan, 1976: 284). The term 'collocation' is also used in lexicography and Corpus Linguistics (see Chapter 9), where it tends to mean relations between adjacent items. However, Halliday and Hasan apply it to interclausal relationships. Words may be related with each other semantically without being coreferential (referring to the same thing) (which, as we have just seen, is the case with reiterations). Thus 'there is cohesion between any pair of lexical items that stand to each other in *some* recognizable lexicosemantic (word meaning) relation' (p. 285, emphasis added).

Two systems operate within collocation: *hyponomy* and *antonymy*. *Hyponomy* concerns the relations between groups of words all falling under one *superordinate*. Thus *apple*, *orange*, *banana* and *lemon* are all hyponyms of the superordinate *fruit*. *Chair*, *desk*, *sofa* and *table* are hyponyms of the superordinate *furniture*. Antonymy is concerned with opposites; thus *large* and *small* and *happy* and *sad* are pairs of antonyms.

In addition, there may be other semantic relations, such as ordered sets, as in the days of the week, part–whole relationships (for example, *mouth*, *eyes*, *nose* – *face*), and even relations which are difficult to describe systematically (for example, *laugh–joke, blade–sharp, garden–dig, ill–doctor*). Halliday and Hasan (1976: 286) write that these relationships depend more on their tendency to occur in adjacent contexts than on any systematic semantic relationship. Halliday and Hasan also point out that these relationships build up into chains across whole stretches of text, not just in adjacent clauses. We can see this already in the following short extract:

The muzzle of the US Army Colt .45 pistol wavered slightly, then steadied. It was fully loaded and its safety catch was in the 'off' position. From a distance of only a few inches, it was pointing directly at the head of King Rama VIII of Siam.

(*The Bangkok Secret*, Anthony Grey)

Lexical chains

a) *muzzle of the US Army Colt .45 pistol, loaded, safety catch, 'off' position*
b) *wavered, steadied, pointing*

In a revised version of this model of lexical cohesion, Hasan (in Halliday & Hasan, 1985/1989) reorganised the system into two major categories: *general* and *instantial*. The general category includes all of those systems which can be described semantically, including repetition, synonymy, hyponymy, meronymy (part–whole relations) and antonymy. The instantial category deals with those relations which cannot be described semantically. Thus, it includes the sort of relations that in the earlier model were dealt with under the heading of collocation and which Hasan (in Halliday & Hasan, 1985/1989: 81) argues are specific to individual texts. Thus, in one of the children's narratives studied by Hasan, the words *sailor* and *daddy* are related to each other by a relation of equivalence, even though these two words are not systematically related to each other outside this text.

Separately, Halliday, too, has reorganised the earlier system. In the latest version (Halliday & Matthiessen, 2004), Halliday now has three major categories: *elaborating relations* (which include repetition, synonymy and hyponymy), *extending relations* (meronymy) and *collocation*. Of this last category, he emphasises its probabilistic nature, how a collocation sets up expectations of what is likely to come next in a text, and how this probability can vary according to how frequently any two words typically occur together in a given corpus. It is notable that Halliday's revised model is closer to the original one than is Hasan's.

3.6 GENERAL NOUNS AND SIGNALLING NOUNS

There is one type of lexical cohesion discussed in Halliday and Hasan (1976) which they describe (p. 275) as being on the border of grammatical and lexical cohesion, and which, they argue, has been neglected by linguists. Halliday and Hasan (1976) refer to this type of cohesion as *general nouns*, which they describe as 'a small set of nouns having generalized reference within the major noun classes, those such as "human noun", "place noun", "fact noun" and the like.' (p. 274). Halliday and Hasan (1976: 274) provide the following examples and classes:

a)   people, person, man, woman, child, boy, girl – human;
b)   creature – non-human animate;
c)   thing, object – inanimate concrete count;
d)   stuff – inanimate concrete mass;
e)   business, affair, matter – inanimate abstract;
f)   move – action;
g)   place – place;
h)   question, idea – fact.

The following are some examples found on the internet:

a)   Israel wanted **Blair** to head up the Quartet, as did the U.S. for the simple reason that it would be yet another biased group purporting to be honest brokers in the conflict. Naturally, the Palestinians can't stand **the man**.

(http://deskofbrian.com/2011/01/palestinian-officials-complain-
tony-blair-is-pro-israel/)

b)   **The phone hacking scandal** has become so complicated we wanted to create the ultimate wallchart showing what happened when in **the affair**.

(http://www.guardian.co.uk/media/phone-hacking)

c)   He had one arm around Gerda's waist and he was grinning up at her, and, sideways, at Forrester with a look that made them co-conspirators in **what was certainly planned to be Gerda's seduction**. Forrester didn't like **the idea**.

(http://www.freefictionbooks.org/books/p/11144-pagan-passions-by-
garrett-and-janifer?start=53)

d) **Dreams come true**. Without **that possibility**, nature would not incite us to have them.

(http://quotationsbook.com/quote/11545/)

These nouns are described as being on the border of grammatical and lexical cohesion, because, as lexical items, they are members of an open set, while, as grammatical items, they can at the same time be considered to be part of a closed set. Like other lexical items, general nouns are superordinates which refer back to members of their class which have been referred to earlier in the text. In common with other grammatical items, however, accompanied as they usually are by the definite article or demonstrative adjective, they are very similar to reference items; indeed, as Halliday and Hasan (1976: 275) point out, there is very little difference in meaning between an utterance such as *it seems to have made very little impression on **the man*** and *it seems to have made very little impression on **him***; in both cases, in order to understand the utterance, it must be referred back to something that has preceded it.

While the human and concrete members of the general noun category are in other ways fairly unremarkable, since Halliday and Hasan (1976), quite a lot of attention has been given to the abstract ones (including animate and concrete nouns such as *thing* and *stuff* used metaphorically in abstract senses) and it is possible to view these items as a separate class. Various linguists have used different terms to describe this type, including *type 3 vocabulary* (Winter, 1977), *anaphoric nouns* (Francis, 1986), *advance labels* (Tadros, 1985), *carrier nouns* (Ivanic, 1991), *metalanguage nouns* (Winter, 1992), *shell nouns* (Schmid, 2000) and *signalling nouns* (Flowerdew, 2003a, b, c, 2006, 2010). The proliferation in terms is due to distinctive approaches to the nouns in question being adopted, both in terms of their discursive functions and in terms of what constitutes a member or not of the given class.

Table 3.2 lists some of the most frequent signalling nouns from my corpus of academic language, which consists of lectures, textbook chapters and research articles.

A lot can be said about these nouns (which will be referred to using my preferred term, signalling nouns [SNs]), far more than comes within the scope of this book. However, a number of features can be highlighted.

1. SNs can be both anaphoric and cataphoric, as indicated by the following two examples (examples from here on in this section are from my academic corpus):

Table 3.2   Frequent signalling nouns in an academic corpus (author's data)

1. example	21. condition	41. assumption	61. hypothesis
2. case	22. right	42. step	62. implication
3. result	23. solution	43. period	63. advantage
4. way	24. function	44. stage	64. definition
5. problem	25. change	45. purpose	65. observation
6. theory	26. value	46. discussion	66. notion
7. idea	27. argument	47. failure	67. characteristic
8. point	28. possibility	48. attempt	68. phenomenon
9. thing	29. ability	49. feature	69. target
10. question	30. difference	50. potential	70. difficulty
11. reason	31. concept	51. technique	71. indication
12. effect	32. analysis	52. topic	72. suggestion
13. method	33. conclusion	53. instance	73. opinion
14. process	34. situation	54. evidence	74. belief
15. factor	35. policy	55. role	75. effort
16. fact	36. view	56. objective	76. need
17. principle	37. response	57. decision	77. chance
18. issue	38. relationship	58. behaviour	78. response
19. approach	39. strategy	59. intention	79. emphasis
20. procedure	40. consequence	60. prediction	80. innovation

... after the earth was formed, it was subjected to a period of heavy bombardment with large (100 km diameter) comets and meteorites. During this **time** ... (anaphoric)

Resources are not unlimited. Shortages, temporary or permanent, can result from several **causes**. Brisk demand may bring in orders that exceed manufacturing capacity or outpace the response time required to gear up a production line ... (cataphoric)

SN is a functional category, rather than a formal one. This means that a given abstract noun may potentially function as an SN, but that in a given context such a noun may or not function as such. Indeed, many uses of abstract nouns are exophoric and do not refer back or forward in the text, depending on the interlocutor's background knowledge for explication.

2. As well as across clauses, as in the previous examples, SNs may be realised within the clause:

The **aim** of this paper is to elucidate the interaction of metabolic effects of the foraminifer and the chemical environment.

The major **premise** of the theory is that an action is strengthened or weakened by its own consequence.

3. Where they are realised across clauses, SNs may relate anaphorically or cataphorically to large stretches of text, not just single clauses. In the following example, which discusses how one researcher has approached the issue of women and work, several sentences of exposition are labelled anaphorically as a *perspective*:

Catherine Hakim's work draws on evidence to show that: Women are on average less committed to paid work and careers than are men. There is a clear division between women who want to develop a career and those who see marriage and child-rearing as their priority. Lack of affordable and good-quality childcare does not explain women's lower rates of labour force participation because most part-time women workers have no childcare commitments. Women have higher rates of job turnover and higher rates of absenteeism than men. This **perspective** on women and work suggests that it is not true that women are forced, through lack of choice, to take time out to raise children or to accept part-time work while their children are growing up.

And in the next example, which is a cataphoric one, in a discussion of Marxist theory, the SN *assumptions* introduces a whole list of such assumptions which are assumed by Marxists:

Several very crucial **assumptions** about the nature of politics are contained in this theory:

1. Politics is less important than economics.
2. All societies are divided into classes, with the RULING class always dominant.
3. The state or political system exists merely to help the dominant class retain its control (to Marx, it was self-evident that in a capitalist society, the state would represent the interests of capitalists).
4. Ideologies, religions, culture, and all other value systems exist to rationalize the power of the ruling class. (This is why Marx labelled ideologies 'false consciousness' and religion 'the opiate of the people.')

3.7 COHESIVE CHAINS

So far in our discussion of cohesion we have focused on individual ties. It is important to bear in mind, however, that (as briefly illustrated earlier) cohesive ties do not operate in isolation, but combine together in *cohesive chains*. Here is an extract from *Women in Love* by D.H. Lawrence:

One day at this time Birkin was called to London. He was not very fixed in his abode. He had rooms in Nottingham, because his work lay chiefly in that town. But often he was in London, or in Oxford. He moved about a great deal, his life seemed uncertain, without any definite rhythm, any organic meaning.

(Project Gutenburg: http://www.gutenberg.org/files/4240/4240-h/
4240-h.htm#chap05)

In this extract we can see two major chains in operation, as follows:

a)   Birkin – he – his – he – his – he – he – his
b)   London – Nottingham – that town – London – Oxford

Following Hasan (in Halliday & Hasan, 1985/1989), we can make a number of points about cohesive chains. First of all, the links in a chain can be either grammatical or lexical. In our example above, all of the links in chain (a) are grammatical, while those in chain (b) are all lexical. Chains may also be made up of combinations of lexical and grammatical links. Hasan (in Halliday & Hasan, 1985/1989: 83) states that '[i]n a typical text, grammatical and lexical cohesion move hand in hand, the one supporting the other.'

Second, in any text, it is likely that different chains are operating simultaneously. This is the case, of course, in our example above, with the two chains overlapping with each other.

Third, with Hasan again (in Halliday & Hasan, 1985/1989), we can distinguish two types of chain: *identity chains* and *similarity chains*. Chain (a) in our example is an identity chain. In identity chains, all of the links in the chain refer to the same entity, they are *co-referential*. Chain (a) is in many ways a paradigm example for identity chains, in so far as it clearly identifies the participant at the outset (Birkin) and then continuously refers back to this person (as *he/his*) throughout the text. This is a typical feature of third-person narratives.

With similarity chains, the links in the chain are not related by identity of reference, but by similarity; they all belong to the same class of entities. Similarity relations may be cases of *co-classification* (belonging to the same class) or *co-extension* (belonging to the same general field of meaning). In our example text extract, chain (b) is a good example of a similarity chain. Each of the items refers to a city/town (co-classification).

3.8 COHESIVE HARMONY

Starting with the notion of cohesive tie and then moving on to cohesive chains, Hasan (1985, in Halliday & Hasan, 1985/1989) goes a stage further in the analysis of cohesion in texts, arguing that for there to be what she refers to as *cohesive harmony* – what it is that makes a text coherent, according to Hasan – there must be interaction between chains; the presence of multiple chains does not mean on its own that a text will be coherent. Hasan refers to this as *chain interaction*. She argues that, for chains to interact, there must be at least two members of a given chain which are in the same relation to two members of another chain. This can be represented as in Figure 3.2, which is a simplified version of the original one in Halliday and Hasan (1985/1989), as created by Hoey (1991a) (the chains here read from top to bottom and the interactions are horizontal):

Hasan divides the tokens in a text into two types: *relevant tokens* and *peripheral tokens*. Relevant tokens are those that are part of chains. Peripheral tokens are those which do not belong to chains. Relevant tokens are sub-divided into *central tokens*, which are those that interact with tokens in other chains, and *non-central tokens*, which are those which do not interact. A hierarchy of tokens is thereby established, in terms of their contribution to cohesive harmony. Using these categories, Hasan is able to define cohesive harmony as: (1) a low relation of peripheral tokens to relevant ones; (2) a high relation of central tokens to non-central ones; and (3) few ruptures in the chains.

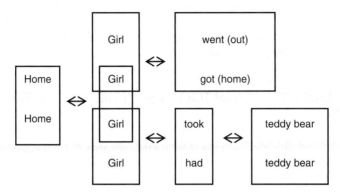

Figure 3.2   Chain interaction in text (adapted and simplified by Hoey (1991a) from Halliday & Hasan, 1985/1989)

3.9 COHESION, COHERENCE AND TEXTURE

Hasan grounds her discussion of cohesive harmony in the context of what she refers to as *texture* (see also Halliday & Hasan, 1976), which she equates with *textual unity* (Hasan, 1985: 70). Texture and textual unity are in turn identified with *coherence* (Hasan, 1985: 72). From this, it seems, therefore, that, for Hasan, the greater the cohesive harmony of a text, the greater will be its coherence. Indeed, she explicitly states that 'variation in coherence is the function of variation in the cohesive harmony of a text' (Hasan, 1985: 94).

At the same time, however, in an earlier publication (Hasan, 1984a), she stressed that coherence is 'a relative, not an absolute property' (1984a: 184). And in Halliday and Hasan (1976: 296) she also emphasised the relative nature of texture, writing with Halliday that:

> Textuality is not a matter of all or nothing, of dense clusters of cohesive ties or else none at all. Characteristically we find variation in texture which serves to signal that the meanings of the parts are strongly interdependent and that the whole forms a single unity. In other instances, however, the texture will be much looser.

So there is some confusion here. It may be that, for the children's story narratives which were the focus of Hasan's research, greater cohesive harmony did correlate with coherence. However, for other text types, this seems to be counterintuitive. Surely, one might argue, some spoken texts, while quite coherent, are less cohesive, making use of other semiotic resources than cohesion, such as exophoric reference, intonation and body language. Other written texts may display a greater degree of cohesive harmony than Hasan's children's stories, but does that make them any less coherent than cohesively harmonious children's stories? Surely, each is coherent in its own right.

Indeed, other studies have demonstrated it to be the case that there is a gradation in the degree to which cohesion and cohesive harmony contribute towards coherence. Hoey (1991b), for example, whose model we will deal with in the next section, has demonstrated how expository text exhibits a much higher level of cohesive harmony than do Hasan's children's narratives. Hoey states that 'in non-narratives the number of chains proliferate vigorously' (p. 386). He also found in his own study that the cohesive links in his data did not follow a linear chain pattern, one clause linking up with the preceding one, but formed a pattern more like a web, with overlapping and nesting of related sets. On the other hand, Taboada (2004) has shown how, in conversation, there is very low interaction in cohesive chains and that major chains in such texts do not interact with each other. Taboada states that '[t]he dialogues [in the texts in her study], although perfectly functional, seem to contain very low cohesive harmony' and suggests that 'different measures of cohesive harmony are necessary for different genres'. Similarly, Thompson (1994), in her investigation of university lecture monologue, found that, in addition to lexicogrammatical cohesive devices, intonation and clause relations (which may or may not be signalled linguistically) contributed to the coherence of her data.

3.10 PATTERNS OF LEXIS IN TEXT: HOEY'S MODEL OF (LEXICAL) COHESION

Hoey's (1991b) study, *Patterns of Lexis in Text*, is concerned with non-narrative text. In non-narrative text, Hoey (1991b: 10) claims, it is the lexical cohesive links which dominate the cohesion. For Hoey, lexical cohesion is:

> the dominant mode of creating texture. In other words, the study of the greater part of cohesion is the study of lexis, and the study of cohesion in text is to a considerable degree the study of patterns of lexis in text.

In addition to being more pervasive than grammatical links in non-narrative texts, Hoey argues, lexical links differ from grammatical links because they do not depend on each other for their meaning; a grammatical link, such as a pronoun, depends on its referent for its meaning, but a lexical link is a meaningful semantic unit in its own right. For this reason, Hoey assigns greater salience to lexical cohesion as compared to grammatical cohesion, even though he does include grammatical links in his model.

For Hoey, lexical cohesion involves multiple relationships; a given lexical item has the potential to link with more than one other item. As he states, '[l]exical cohesion is the only type of cohesion that regularly forms multiple relationships.' Non-narrative text, unlike narrative text, which is built up from a a series of links from one clause to the next, is built on repeated links. An example of such links is shown in Figure 3.3, which is taken from Hoey (1991b: 37).

Drawing on Winter (1974, 1979), Hoey argues that the basic cohesive relationship is one of repetition. 'It is the common repeating function of much cohesion that is important, not the classificatory differences between types of cohesion', he states (Hoey, 1991a: 20). It is for this reason that

1   A **drug** known to **produce** violent reactions in **humans** has been **used** for **sedating grizzly bears** *Ursus arctos* in Montana, USA, according to a report in the *New York Times*.
2   After one **bear**, known to be a peaceable animal, killed and ate a camper in an unprovoked attack, scientists discovered it had been **tranquillized** 11 times which phencyclidine, or 'angel dust', which **causes** hallucinations and sometimes gives the **user** an irrational feeling of destructive power.
3   Many wild **bears** have become 'garbage junkies', feeding from dumps around **human** developments.
4   To avoid potentially dangerous clashes between **them** and **humans**, scientists are trying to rehabilitate the **animals** by **drugging** them and releasing them in uninhabited areas.
5   Although some biologists deny that the mind–altering **drug was responsible for** uncharacteristic behaviour of this particular bear, no research has been done into the effects of giving **grizzly bears** or other mammals repeated doses of phencyclidine.

Figure 3.3   Lexical links in a non-narrative text (Hoey, 1991b: 37).

he includes some grammatical items in his model; they have the capacity to repeat, just as do lexical items, although, for Hoey, as already stated, these links are weaker.

Hoey's (1991b) model of cohesion has the following categories.

a) simple lexical repetition (*a bear – bears*);
b) complex lexical repetition (*a drug – drugging*);
c) simple paraphrase (*to sedate – to drug*);
d) complex paraphrase (*heat – cold*);
e) substitution (*a drug – it*);
f) co-reference (*Mrs Thatcher – the Prime Minster*);
g) ellipsis (*a work of art – the work*);
h) deixis (*Plato and Artistotle – these writers*).

Hoey is primarily interested in those items in a text which have above-average numbers of links, these items establishing what he refers to as *bonds*. As already stated, the weight of links varies, with a higher weighting given to lexical over grammatical links. In fact, the order of strength follows the ordering of the list of categories given above. In this way, Hoey is able to differentiate between central and marginal sentences, based upon the number and strength of the bonds.

Following on from this, lexical cohesive bonds combine together and relate to other items in networks (referred to as *nets*). These nets, in bringing together central sentences and omitting marginal sentences, have the capacity to produce a meaningful paraphrase of the whole text.

3.11 TANSKANEN'S APPROACH TO LEXICAL COHESION

A further development of the original Halliday and Hasan model is that of Tanskanen (2006). Tanskanen views cohesion as a resource which communicators use to contribute towards coherence, hence the title of her monograph, *Collaborating towards Coherence*. Tanskanen's work is particularly interesting from a discourse point of view, because her model is developed in order to analyse cohesion in different text types. This comparative empirical purpose leads to a number of innovations into her model. The elements of the model are as follows (p. 49):

Reiteration
1. simple repetition
2. complex repetition
3. substitution
4. equivalence
5. generalisation
6. specification
7. co-specification
8. contrast

Collocation
1. ordered set
2. activity-related collocation
3. elaborative collocation

Some of these categories look familiar and are based on those used by others, as described thus far in this review of lexical cohesion. Some of their particular features are singled out below.

First, simple and complex repetition: simple repetition applies to items of an identical form or with a difference in grammatical form; complex repetition concerns items which are identical but serve different grammatical functions or are not identical but share a lexical morpheme. Importantly, pronouns are also included, as Tanskanen notes that, following Hoey (1991b), although pronouns are normally treated as part of grammatical cohesion, their function is very similar to full repetitions.

The third category, substitution, like repetition, also includes pronouns, for the same reason given above. Tanskanen cites Halliday and Hasan in support of this decision. Halliday and Hasan (1976: 212) argue that it is possible to shift the perspective on reference 'from the grammatical to the lexical and look at reference from the lexical angle, interpreting it as a means of avoiding the repetition of lexical items'. Tanskanen also cites Hasan (1984b) in support of this decision. Hasan argues that leaving out grammatical cohesion in analysis of cohesive chains in her study was at the expense of a consideration of the text's fundamental semantic unity.

The fourth category, equivalence, basically corresponds to synonymy. The use of the different term is to acknowledge the textual basis for the classification of items, as opposed to applying a ready-made system. A particular text may treat items as synonymous, but they may not correspond to an abstract systematic class. This is Hasan's distinction between *general* and *instantial* relations.

Generalisation, the fifth category, corresponds to what other linguists refer to as superordinates, while specification, the sixth category is the counterpart of generalisation, usually referred to as meronymy, the parts of a whole.

Co-specification refers to what are elsewhere referred to as co-meronyms or co-hyponyms.

Finally, contrast corresponds to what in other systems is referred to as antonymy.

Turning now to collocation, like Halliday and Hasan (1976), Tanskanen defines this in terms of relationships established through habitual co-occurrence. In spite of this, she nevertheless has three different classes. Ordered sets, as in Halliday and Hasan, refer to sets such as months of the year, days of the week and colours. Activity-related collocations are items which relate to each other in terms of an activity: *meals – eat, ciphers – decode* and *car – drive* are examples of these. Finally, elaborative collocation is a catch-all category for those items which are part of neither ordered sets nor activity relations. Tanskanen tries to capture relationships under this category in terms of frame theory (see, for example, Fillmore, 1985). Frames are knowledge structures which are evoked by lexical items. Tanskanen gives the example in her data of *Cambridge* and *Mill Lane lecture theatre.* *Cambridge* invokes a university frame, which thereby sets up the link with *Mill Lane lecture theatre.*

One interesting point about Tanskanen's contribution is that, because she is developing an empirical study, as opposed to developing a theory *per se*, she adopts the *lexical unit* rather than the individual word as the unit of analysis. What this means in practice is that some of the items she identifies as *cohesive units* may be multiword as well as single-word. These multiword units include items like phrasal verbs and idioms, but also lexical items such as *cultural determinism, social services, Standard English, the working people* and *out of fashion.* The justification for including multiword units such as these is that items are defined by the words with which they co-occur, not in the abstract. Thus, a phrase like *cultural determinism* achieves its meaning in relation to other social theories with which it is related in the text. To take *cultural* or *determinism* as separate units would allow for much larger numbers of possible relations than taking the two words together as one item. Once one begins to deal with actual text, it soon becomes clear that this is the right way to go.

Turning now to the results of Tanskanen's study, interesting qualitative conclusions were that, in all texts, reiteration and collocation take part in the formation of cohesive chains and that all texts show both longer and shorter chains. Furthermore, cohesive chains are capable of marking topical segments. The beginning or end of a cohesive change corresponds with the beginning or end of a topic. Again, all texts exhibited this phenomenon.

I noted that Tanskanen compared different text types. Here the quantitative findings of her study are interesting. One finding was in the density of cohesive ties in each text type used in the study. The frequency of ties (per thousand words) in each of the text types was as follows:

Two-party conversations	160
Prepared speeches	153
Mailing list 1	151
Mailing list 2	134
Three-party conversations	120
Academic writing	105

Particularly striking in these findings is the positioning of two-party conversation as the highest density and academic writing as the lowest. Based on our knowledge of lexical density, which tells us that, of the common text types, academic writing is the most dense lexically, while conversation is the least dense (see Chapter 1), one might have anticipated exactly the opposite. Further studies are needed, of course, to corroborate this finding.

Another interesting quantitative finding in Tanskanen's study was the relatively low frequency of collocation, as compared to reiteration. Frequency of ties per thousand words for the different text types ranged from 10 to 16.5 for collocation, while for reiteration the numbers ranged from 90 to 146. One conclusion from the study, therefore, is that collocation is relatively rare as a cohesive feature.

3.12 PROPOSITIONAL RELATIONS

In their discussion of conjunction, Halliday and Hasan (1976: 229) make the point that it is often the case that a conjunctive relation may often be identified without it being overtly expressed by means of a conjunction at all. They provide the following set of examples to illustrate this point (p. 228):

a)   A snowstorm followed the battle.
b)   After the battle, there was a snowstorm.
c)   After they had fought a battle, it snowed.
d)   They fought a battle. Afterwards, it snowed.

In each of these examples, two events, or *propositions*, are referred to in a sequential relationship, but only in (d) is there a conjunction overtly relating the two. In another set of examples, Halliday and Hasan illustrate some of the different ways that an adversative propositional relationship may be established:

a)   He fell asleep, in spite of his great discomfort.
b)   Although he was very uncomfortable, he fell asleep.
c)   He was very uncomfortable. Nevertheless he fell asleep.

Propositional relations such as these, whether overtly signalled or not, have been the focus of the work of a considerable number of linguists. Here is another example, this time from Crombie (1985: 6), where a propositional relation, that of *reason–result*, in this case, is established, without the use of an overt signal:

I missed the train. I'm going to be late for work.

A variety of approaches has been adopted to researching propositional relations, with a range of different terms being used. Thus, Winter (1974, 1977) and Hoey (1983, 1991b) use the term *clause relations*, Beekman and Callow (1974) discuss *relations between propositions*, Grimes (1975) discusses *rhetorical predicates*, Longacre (1976) discusses *combinations of predications*, Hobbs (1978, 1979) has *coherence relations*, van Dijk (1977a, 1980) has *semantic relations between propositions*, Martin (1984) has *conjunctive relations*, Crombie (1985) has *binary discourse values*, Mann and Thompson (1988) have *rhetorical structures* and Renkema (2009) has *discourse relations*.

Here, we will focus on Crombie's approach, because her work was developed with the aim of direct application to language syllabus design. *Binary discourse values*, Crombie's preferred term, are defined by Crombie (1985: 2) as 'the significance that attaches to utterances by virtue of the specific type of relationship which they bear to one another.' Binary discourse values are divided into two groups: functional components of conversation (which will not concern us here, although see Chapter 7 on Conversation Analysis) and *general semantic relations*, which are concerned with relations between the propositional content of utterances.

Crombie (1985) develops a taxonomy of nine general semantic relations, as follows:

1. temporal;
2. matching;
3. cause–effect;
4. truth and validity;
5. alternation;
6. bonding;
7. paraphrase;
8. amplification;
9. setting/conduct.

These nine basic categories are further subclassified into between one and four subcategories. Thus category 1, temporal relations, is divided into *chronological sequence* and *temporal overlap*; category 4, truth and validity, is broken down into *statement–affirmation, statement–denial, denial–correction* and *concession–contra-expectation*; while category 7, paraphrase, on the other hand, is not subdivided.

The following are some examples of possible realisation forms for the subcategories for temporal relations and truth and validity:

1. Paris seized Helen and left Greece.
   (temporal relations – chronological sequence)
2. As he left, Paris looked over his shoulder.
   (temporal relations – temporal overlap)
3. A: Achilles should resume the fight.
   B: Absolutely/I agree.
   (truth and validity – statement–affirmation)
4. A: Achilles was right.
   B: No, he wasn't / I deny that.
   (truth and validity – statement–denial)
5. He wasn't a soldier, he was a priest.
   (truth and validity – denial–correction)
6. Although the seeds were sown and nurtured, the plants failed to appear.
   (truth and validity – concession–contra-expectation)

Types of relation can be identified by the application of a simple question test. The following are some example questions:

a.   For simple contrast:

   • Is A said to differ from B in a particular respect?

b.   For simple comparison:

  •   Is A said to be similar to B in a particular respect?

c.   For paraphrase (where P and Q are statements):

  •   Does Q have the same conceptual context as P?

d.   For denial–correction:

  •   Does Q provide a corrective substitute for a negated term in P?

This is a very neat means of identification, requiring, as it does, only one question for each category.

The linguistic realisation of discourse values, or propositional relations, as already suggested, can be either explicit or implicit. Where they are explicit, some signalling items are more explicit than others. Thus subordinators, such as *if, because* and *although*, and connectives, such as *similarly, however* and *nevertheless*, are more explicit than coordinators such as *and* and *but*. Propositional relations are not only signalled by conjuncts such as these, however. The presence of certain lexical items such as *different, difference* and *result* can also indicate particular relations. Where propositional relations are implicit, a number of factors may contribute to their interpretation. These include juxtaposition, sequencing, lexical selection and general background, or situational, knowledge. In addition, interpretation may be by guided by Gricean cooperative maxims (see Chapter 6) and, in spoken discourse, by intonation.

An aspect of Crombie's approach of particular significance for the language syllabus is the fairly detailed specification she is able to provide of linguistic forms capable of realising the various relations. Thus, for the chronological sequence relations, for example, she is able to specify the following signalling devices:

1.   subordinators (*once, until, when*, etc.);
2.   prepositions (*after, before, since*, etc.);
3.   conjuncts (*first, second, finally*, etc.);
4.   time adjuncts (*today, last night*, etc.);
5.   syntactic constructions (which Crombie lists).

In developing a pedagogical approach to propositional relations, there are, in theory, two possible approaches. The first is to start with the linguistic items and then work out their possible semantic functions; the second is to start with a set of semantic categories and work from there to their possible linguistic realisations, or signals. In actual practice, as is the case with Crombie, most researchers adopt a combination of the two approaches.

Among those emphasising the more formal approach is Hoey (1983: 20), who states that 'discussion of types of relation cannot be sensibly carried on apart from the means whereby those relations are identified'. Another is Martin (1983), who bases his relational classification on 'conjunctive relations', the syntactic devices used to connect clauses. A third is Winter (1977: 2), who states that the finite number of 'clause relations' that he specifies can be 'named' by a special vocabulary of words such as *affirm, cause, compare, deny, different, effect, example, follow* and *mean*, referred to by him as vocabulary 3. A danger of this formal approach is that, as Crombie points out in discussion of Winter, it confuses what she refers to as *relations* with *relational encoding*, or, put another way, cohesion is confused with underlying coherence. It may be that the linguistic system does not have overt signals for realising all and every relation; it may be that in English, or in other languages, there may exist relations which are not identifiable by specific lexical means.

It is on this point that the other approach to propositional relations comes in, the semantics-first one. The best-known model using this approach is that of Mann and Thompson (Taboada & Mann,

2006a, b). The original set of propositional relations put forward by Mann and Thompson consisted of 24 types and the current version of the model is working with 30 (Taboada & Mann, 2006a). These categories are put forward using the semantics-first approach and hence are not dependent on any linguistic realisation for their identification. Indeed, this approach insists that certain relations are 'rarely or never signalled' (Taboada & Mann, 2006a: 436). A problem with this approach, however, is that any textual analysis is likely to be rather subjective, because the categories cannot be formally recognised in text.

3.13 PARALLELISM

A cohesive feature not included by Halliday and Hasan (1976), but which can, for the sake of completeness, be dealt with briefly here is *parallelism*. Parallelism is where elements – be they syntactic, lexical or phonological – of one clause are repeated, often for stylistic effect, in a following clause or clauses. Halliday and Hasan (1976: 10) exclude this category, which they refer to as 'syntactic parallelism', from their study of cohesion on the grounds that it is a purely formal device, not a meaningful relation. Nevertheless parallelism is cohesive in so far as it is a means of relating one clause to another.

Many examples of parallelism can be found in oratory, as the following examples show:

a. One small step for man.
    One giant step for mankind.

(statement made by the first man on the moon)

b. And so my fellow Americans: Ask not what your country can do for you. Ask what you can do for your country.
    My fellow citizens of the world: Ask not what America will do for you, but what together we can do for the freedom of man.

(from US President J.F. Kennedy's inaugural speech)

However, parallelism operates in many types of text, both written and spoken (advertisements are another type of text where it is pervasive).

Parallelism can operate at the level of syntax, lexis and phonology. In the following extract from a cookery book, syntactic parallelism is particularly noticeable, with the repeated use of imperative verb forms at the beginning of each clause.

Cheese and Onion Dip
Put the yoghurt and soup mix into the bowl and **process** until well blended. **Allow** to stand for 30 minutes. **Add** the cheese and seasoning and **process** until smoothly blended. **Transfer** to a serving bowl and chill. **Serve** garnished with chopped chives.

(Paige, 1984)

In the following extract, we can observe the three types of parallelism together, this time in casual conversation:

Marge: Can I have one of these Tabs?
         Do you want to split it?
         Do you want to split a Tab
Kate: Do you want to split MY Tab [laughter]
Vivian: No.
Marge: Kate, do you want to split my Tab!?
Kate: No, I don't want to split your Tab.

(Tannen, 1989: 57)

In this extract, on the syntactic level, parallelism is found in the repeated use of the interrogative form. Lexical parallelism is established by repetition of the phrase 'Do you want (or 'I don't want') to split my (or 'a' or 'your') tab?' and of the lexical item 'Tab' (occurring in every clause except one). Phonological parallelism is created by the parallel rhythm and sounds of each of the clauses (except for Vivian's 'No', which creates a contrastive effect).

3.14 CRITIQUE

In evaluating various approaches to cohesion, especially that of Halliday and Hasan (1976), some have critiqued the place assigned to it within overall coherence. It is true that, as already suggested earlier in this chapter, at times, Halliday and Hasan (1976, 1985/1989) seem to be inconsistent in writing about the relationship between cohesion, texture and coherence. In places, they identify cohesion with texture and texture with coherence. In other places, they claim that texture is more than just cohesion, involving also features such as register, propositional relations and thematic development.

At the beginning of Halliday and Hasan (1976: 2), for example, they state:

The concept of TEXTURE is entirely appropriate to express the property of 'being a text.' A text has texture, and that is what distinguishes it from being something that is not a text. It derives the texture from the fact that it functions as a unity with respect to its environment.

Then a little later (p. 9.), they state that 'cohesive ties between sentences stand out more clearly because they are the ONLY source of texture (original emphasis).' But then, on page 23, they claim that texture is more than just cohesion, also including register, and that neither is sufficient without the other. Again, in the concluding sections of the book, they claim that, in addition to cohesion, texture involves both how the sentences of a text are structured in such a way as to relate to the context (thematic development: see Chapter 4) and 'macrostructure', what establishes a text as one of a particular kind, such as conversation or narrative. The following is the quotation:

Texture involves much more than merely cohesion. In the construction of text the establishment of cohesive relations is a necessary component; but it is not the whole story.

In the most general terms there are two other components of texture. One is the textual structure that is internal to the sentence: the organization of the sentence and its parts in a way which relates it to its environment. The other is the 'macrostructure' of the text, that establishes it as a text of a particular kind – conversation, narrative, lyric, commercial correspondence and so on (Halliday and Hasan, 1976: 324).

Those linguists who have strongly critiqued Halliday and Hasan (for example, Brown & Yule, 1983; Carrell, 1982) may thus have overlooked the ambiguity we have just noted in their target, preferring to find in Halliday and Hasan a stronger claim for cohesion than was perhaps intended. Nevertheless, there is certainly ambiguity.

3.15 APPLICATION TO PEDAGOGY

3.15.1 The case for cohesion

Cohesion is fundamental to text construction, but is neglected in many learning materials, preference being given to grammar and lexis (although not lexical cohesion).

So what is the case for a focus on cohesion? Most obviously, there are formal differences between how cohesion is signalled, or realised, in different languages. Reference, substitution, ellipsis, conjunction and lexical cohesion differ in this respect and therefore, obviously, need to be the focus of teaching and learning.

On another level, though, the functional one, there is another reason for there to be a need for cohesion to be in the language syllabus. If we take as an example a language which is typologically distant from English, say Chinese, we can see how this operates in terms of function.

Chinese is often referred to as a 'high-context' language. That is, it relies greatly on context in the interpretation of meaning. English, on the other hand, can be described as a relatively 'low-context' language. It tends to signal meaning explicitly though the linguistic system rather than relying so much on the context (although context is still vital). What this means with regard to cohesion is that certain cohesive features which are signalled in the linguistic system in English are left to be determined by the context in Chinese.

In English, for example, after a participant has been introduced into the discourse, it will be typically reiterated in subsequent clauses by means of cohesive devices such as pronouns. In Chinese, however, in contrast to English, after the introduction of a participant into the discourse, this participant is generally understood from the context and does not need to be reiterated by means of cohesive devices. Similar differences in cohesion between English and Chinese are to be found in other areas of discourse.

Although, because of its typological distance from English, Chinese is a good example to talk about functional differences in cohesion, differences in cohesive functions also occur in languages which are typologically closer. If we take Spanish, which is much closer to English, as another example, that language, in common with Chinese, also does not need to reiterate participants in a text in the way that English does. However, there is less reliance on context in Spanish than in Chinese, because the verb itself will be marked to indicate who or what is being referred to, that is to say, cohesion will be signalled through the form of the verb. But nevertheless, in Spanish, as in Chinese, there is no need to use pronouns to signal continuity in the text.

3.15.2 Ties, chains and bonds

Some aspects of cohesion have traditionally been featured in language teaching, for example, substitution and ellipsis, even if they have not been dealt with under that rubric, but treated as aspects of grammar. A lot of those teaching and learning materials which do deal with cohesion focus on connecting pairs of sentences, using a slot and filler or 'fill in the blanks' approach. Reference items can be practised in this way and this can be a useful exercise in raising learners' awareness of the forms and functions of reference in English (which will both likely differ from their L1).

However, although the cohesive tie linking two clauses is the fundamental unit in cohesion, attention needs also to be focused on the role of chains and bonds. Cohesion varies from register to register (Hoey, 1991b; Tanskanen, 2006). An understanding of such variation is not likely to be developed through practice in linking pairs of clauses.

Hatch (1983: 115) uses the following text to highlight the subtleties needed to deal with what might seem even quite simple identity chains (although Hatch does not use this term):

> Our speaker today is Dr. Sheryl M. Strick. _____ is a professor in the Department of Vegetarian Diet at the College of Agriculture and Environment at UCLA. _____ graduated from Florida State University, and after a summer as an assistant seed breeder for the Burpee Company in Texts, _____ went on to do graduate work in plant genetics at UC San Diego. After receiving _____'s Ph.D., _____ jointed the Pennsylvania State University faculty where _____ remained except for trips to the Himalayas and Outer Mongolia to collect potato varieties and do research on potatoes. _____ wrote that _____ was bitten by the potato bug in _____'s grade school

days and never completely recovered. _____ remembers all the excitement _____ felt when _____ placed _____'s first mail order for seed and how _____ did everything wrong in sowing the seeds. Later, while still at home, _____ spent every available hour working on the farm that _____'s mother managed. It was clear even then in _____'s life _____ would deal with plants. It is a pleasure to introduce to you _____ who will speak to us on 'The Potato.' _____. Sherry.

Is it the case that each of the blanks in this text should be replaced by a simple *she* or *her*? At some points, it would seem appropriate to reintroduce either the full or partial name. Such reintroductions might be because the name has not been mentioned for a while and the listener needs to be reminded of it; or because other characters have been mentioned since the name was last used and there may hence be possible confusion? Is there a need to put the emphasis on the person being introduced rather than her accomplishments? Hatch raises all of these possibilities and they all might feed into a consciousness-raising discussion of the structure and functions of reference chains in discourse. Similar intricacies are likely to be at stake with similarity chains.

To exemplify this issue with regard to second-language usage, the following text was written by a Hong Kong secondary school student.[1]

1. Playing computer games has become such a popular hobby that many teenagers spend a lot of time and effort in the virtual world. Some people think that playing computer games is a harmful hobby which wastes time and money, while others believe that it can be a serious activity that requires practice and may turn into a career. So I strongly believe that playing computer games is a harmful hobby.
2. It is easy to get addicted to computer games. As we know that, computer games are attractive and it takes quite a long period of time to win the games. After you have won the first round, you may want to continue playing because you are attracted by the game. As the result, it is easy to get addicted.
3. **It** (1) may lead to eye strain and other health problems. We all know that playing computer games for too many hours will make our eyes feel tired or dry and **it** (2) would lead to eye strain. **It** (3) also will cause mental problems as it may affect their feeling or attitudes. **It** (4) may make them feel angry or sad or carry away and may occur accidents. **It** (5) is quite dangerous for the people who cannot control him or her emotion because you don't know when she or he loss the game, what will happen next.

If we look at the third paragraph of this text, we see that there is an identity chain involving five uses of *it* (bolded and numbered). With the first example of *it* at the beginning of the first sentence in paragraph 3, the referent of *it* is already unclear, although, with careful analysis of the text, this referent may be traced back to the previous sentence 'it is easy to get addicted' (which itself is a repetition of the first sentence of the paragraph). *Getting addicted* (worded as *to get addicted*) is, therefore, the beginning of this chain. The student might have done better by writing 'Such addiction' rather than just *it*, to establish clearly this first link in the chain. As the identity chain develops, however, by repetitions of *it* and with no use or repetition of the full nominal (*addiction*), the meaning becomes increasingly difficult to unravel. There is a place, here, therefore, for pedagogic intervention, in terms of cohesion.

3.15.3 Lexis

This brings us to the role of lexis. Students need be made aware of lexical fields and lexical sets to build up the various semantic relations involved in lexical cohesion. As Hoey (1991b) argues, students need to learn how to repeat, but not just by repeating with the same word or phrase (although in some registers, such as scientific ones, this may be more preferred), but to master the full range of words from the relevant semantic field. As McCarthy (1991: 71) argues with regard to conversation:

> The way in which we can observe speakers moving from superordinates to hyponyms and from synonyms to antonyms and back again is a common feature of conversation and learners can be equipped to use this skill by regular practice.

McCarthy is concerned with conversation, but the same applies whatever the register.

3.15.4 Propositional relations

Crombie (1985) proposes using propositional relations as an organising principle for syllabus design. She argues that propositional relations are a universal phenomenon, common to all languages (p. 33, p. 83) (see also Hatim & Mason, 1990 on this). She argues that propositional relations can provide a framework for introducing the signalling items of the target language and also how the relations may be expressed by other means (referred to as 'unsignalled value assignments'):

> For the language teacher and syllabus designer, the introduction into teaching programmes of the value signalling systems of the target language provides a framework for the introduction of the learner to language as a communicative dynamic and for a movement towards unsignalled value assignments. The ultimate aim is that the learner should reach a degree of competence at which he can not only recognize and use value signals, but also recognize where and when they need not be introduced and where and when they must not be (p. 36).

The following exercise from McCarthy *et al.* (1997: 8), where students are asked to match what are referred to as text organisers with chunks of text, illustrates how students might work with the way relations are signalled.

Text organisers	
Background	Railways declining because of growth in car ownership. Government investment in railways now very low
Problem	
Issue	Should we go on building more roads or revive our railways?
Question	
Move	The government has set up a committee to decide on transport policy
Decision	
Features	Cost per mile. Staffing costs. Pollution. Social service. Freedom of choice
Aspects	
View	Whatever committee decides, railways declining so fast that it's too late to stop decline
Conclusion	

3.16 CONCLUSION

In this chapter, we have seen the vital role that cohesion plays in the creation of text. Cohesion thus demands our attention in second-language course design. Thornbury (2005a: 34) summarises some of the general teaching implications arising from a consideration of cohesion:

1. Expose learners to texts rather than to isolated sentences only.
2. Draw attention to, and categorise, the features that bind text together.
3. Encourage learners to reproduce these features, where appropriate, in their own texts.
4. Provide feedback not only on sentence-level features of learners' texts, but on the overall cohesiveness as well.

Although cohesion is a vital property of texts, we need to bear in mind that cohesion does not correspond to coherence. As Halliday and Hasan put it (1976: 298–299):

Cohesion is a necessary, though not a sufficient condition for the creation of text. What creates text is the TEXTUAL, or text-forming component of the linguistic system, of which cohesion is one part.

In subsequent chapters, we will consider some of the other phenomena contributing towards coherence, beginning with the next chapter, which will deal with thematic development.

3.17 QUESTIONS FOR DISCUSSION

1. Identify the reference ties in the following examples by saying what relates to what and whether the ties are anaphoric, cataphoric or exophoric.

    1. The skeleton of a young child has been found on the roof of a building in Mong Kok. It was found inside a water tank by a man.
    2. Two years ago, this property cost 1 million pounds. Today, it costs 5 million.
    3. He bought some red wine and some white wine. The white wine he put in the fridge. (two links)
    4. Do you prefer these or those?
    5. The sun rises in the east.

2. Examine the following pieces of discourse and say what is wrong with the cohesion in each case:

    a) From an interview with the British Foreign Secretary, Douglas Hurd, on the radio programme *Desert Island Discs*:
        Douglas Hurd: My father said: 'Don't go straight into politics from Cambridge, you won't have anything to say.
        Programme Hostess: And indeed you didn't.
    b) From a staff association notice board:
        For those who have children and don't know it, we have a nursery.
    c) From a leaflet about migraine:
        Migraines strike twice as many women as do men.

3. Examine the following text extract from *A Study in Scarlet* by Arthur Conan Doyle about his famous fictional detective, Sherlock Holmes. Indicate the similarity chain in this text, starting with the first word of the paragraph, *Holmes*.

Holmes was certainly not a difficult man to live with. He was quiet in his ways, and his habits were regular. It was rare for him to be up after ten at night, and he had invariably breakfasted and gone out before I rose in the morning. Sometimes he spent his day at the chemical laboratory, sometimes in the dissecting-rooms, and occasionally in long walks, which appeared to take him into the lowest portions of the City. Nothing could exceed his energy when the working fit was upon him; but now and again a reaction would seize him, and for days on end he would lie upon the sofa in the sitting-room, hardly uttering a word or moving a muscle from morning to night. On these occasions I have noticed such a dreamy, vacant expression in his eyes, that I might have suspected him of being addicted to the use of some narcotic, had not the temperance and cleanliness of his whole life forbidden such a notion.

(Project Gutenberg: http://www.gutenberg.org/files/244/244-h/ 244-h.htm#2HCH0001)

4. Now indicate the similarity chain following the word *rooms* in the first sentence and the word *things* in the fourth sentence of the following paragraph (which is from the same Sherlock Holmes story as the one in the previous question).

We met next day as he had arranged, and inspected the **rooms** at No. 221B, Baker Street, of which he had spoken at our meeting. They consisted of a couple of comfortable bed-rooms and a single large airy sitting-room, cheerfully furnished, and illuminated by two broad windows. So desirable in every way were the apartments, and so moderate did the terms seem when divided between us, that the bargain was concluded upon the spot, and we at once entered into possession. That very evening I moved my **things** round from the hotel, and on the following morning Sherlock Holmes followed me with several boxes and portmanteaus. For a day or two we were busily employed in unpacking and laying out our property to the best advantage. That done, we gradually began to settle down and to accommodate ourselves to our new surroundings.

(Project Gutenberg: http://www.gutenberg.org/files/244/244-h/ 244-h.htm#2HCH0001)

5. Take any text that comes to hand and analyse it for: (a) its reference; (b) its conjunction; and (c) its lexical cohesion. Is the lexical cohesion better described with a 'chain' or a 'net' metaphor?
6. Rank the following types of cohesion according to the difficulty they are likely to cause learners: reference, substitution/ellipsis, conjunction, lexical cohesion, structural parallelism. Give reasons why each type is more or less problematic.
7. To what extent do you think (a) a consciousness raising approach and (b) an overt treatment of conjunction can be useful to first- or second-language learners in the teaching of writing?

3.18 FURTHER READING

Halliday and Hasan, 1976, 1985/1989; Hoey, 1991b; Tanskanen, 2006.

CHAPTER 4

Thematic development

4.1 DEFINITION OF THEME

Halliday and Matthiessen (2004) define theme as 'the point of departure for the message'. Theme in English is realised by initial position in the clause. McCarthy (1991) provides the following fuller definition:

> In English, what we decide to bring to the *front* of the clause (by whatever means) is a signal of what is to be understood as the *framework* within which what we say can be understood. The rest of the clause can be seen as transmitting 'what we want to say within this framework'. Items brought to front-place we shall call the theme of their clauses.

The remainder of the clause, what is not part of the theme, is referred to as the *rheme*. Brown and Yule (1983: 126) bring the terms *theme* and *rheme* together:

> We shall use the term theme to refer to a formal category, the left-most constituent of the sentence. Each simple sentence has a theme 'the starting point of the utterance' and a rheme, everything else in the sentence which consists of what the speaker states about, or in regard to, the starting point of the utterance.

4.2 THEME IN GRAMMAR AND DISCOURSE

Theme is an area where grammar and discourse seem very close to each other. The importance of theme in discourse, as opposed to grammar, centres on:

* the effect theme choice may have on the overall focus of a text;
* the degree of shared knowledge presupposed between writer/reader, speaker/listener.

The relevance of a discourse-based approach to theme for language teaching is:

* more control of theme development and overall text focus;
* an awareness of varying the manner of presenting and developing theme in text, leading to more complex and effective student speech and writing;
* the possible highlighting of differences in thematisation strategies between L1 and English;
* informed choice from a variety of theme configurations will also help the student in the manipulation of 'style' and lead to more 'effective' and 'authentic' writing in a variety of genres.

In order to understand the discourse functions of theme, we first of all need to know something about the grammar associated with it, because the grammar is organised in such a way as to allow theme to realise its various functions in discourse.

4.3 THEME IN DECLARATIVE CLAUSES

Here is a simple example of a declarative clause with its theme in italics:

1. *The American president* visited China.

You will notice that in this example the theme is also the subject; this is usually the case, although not always. Here are some other examples of theme as subject:

1. *I* like chocolate a lot.
2. *Foxes* can be found living in many cities nowadays.
3. *These students* all passed the exam.
4. *Hungarian* is a very difficult language to learn.

As subject, these themes are in the form of nominal groups. It is worth noting that, sometimes, where a nominal group is acting as theme of a clause, it can be very extensive. Such themes are very common in technical and bureaucratic language:

1. *The diffusion-reaction model for the carbonate system in a spherical geometry* has been discussed in detail by X.
2. *General guidelines to obtain estimates of the risk to soil-dwelling organisms* are provided by, for example, the International Organisation for Biological Control.
3. *Plans to make sure London keeps moving during the 2012 Games and that athletes, officials, media and the Olympic family can get to venues on time* have been published today.

When analysing texts with complex nominal groups as theme such as these, McCarthy's (1991) definition of theme as 'a signal of what is to be understood as the *framework* within which what we say of theme' is a useful point of reference.

In some cases, more than one nominal group may occur as theme:

Susan, Peter and Henry passed the exam.
Both the Democrats and the Republicans supported the new legislation.

Where the first element in a clause is not the subject/nominal group, it often occurs as an adjunct.[1]

Yesterday, I went to the cinema.
Usually, I play tennis on Sundays.
Next to the common room, you will find the library.
In common with many other people, I object to sports which are cruel to animals.
Out of all of the flats that we looked at to rent, the first one was actually the nicest.

We can refer to this type of pattern where adjuncts take on the role of theme as *marked themes*. We call them marked because they are not the typical form. They are often used to indicate a shift in topic, place or time.

We can also have marked theme in declarative clauses with certain other elements (usually object/complement) besides the subject or an adjunct. This is unusual and, when it does occur, may be used in order to mark a strong emphasis or a contrast with what has come before:

> I have a number of new books. *This one I* found in a shop on the high street.
> I've managed to buy a lot of different French cheeses, but *some I* just can't get hold of.
> He bought some red wine and some white wine. *The white wine he* put in the fridge.

Where we have a marked theme, the elements following the marked theme, up to, but not including, the verb will also be considered to be theme (that is why the elements following the marked theme in the above examples are also in italics). Indeed, this will be our overall definition of theme, that is, theme is that part of the sentence which includes everything up to, but not including, the verb. In this we are departing somewhat from other writers on theme such as Halliday and Matthiessen (2004) and Thompson (2004), who only include that part of the sentence up to the first experiential element.[2] By experiential, they mean an element which refers to a process, a participant or a circumstance (see Chapter 2). We are departing from these other linguists because our approach is more insightful when we look at how theme develops in discourse; the other linguists are focused more on grammar.

4.4 THEME AND RHEME

So far, we have not said much about rheme. We have been content to define it negatively, as what is not the theme. When we look at connected discourse, we see better the role played by rheme, in its interaction with theme. As already stated, the rheme follows the theme. Everything in the clause which is not theme is the rheme. In connected texts, theme–rheme patterns are found between:

- rheme and theme, where the rheme of clause (a) becomes the theme of clause (b);

Clause a		Clause b	
Theme a	*Rheme a*	*Theme b*	*Rheme b*
He	picked up the gun.	The gun	was loaded.

Following McCarthy (1991: 55), this can be represented graphically by the following diagram:

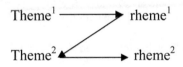

- theme and theme, where the theme of clause (a) becomes the theme of clause (b).

Clause a		Clause b	
Theme a	*Rheme a*	*Theme b*	*Rheme b*
I	am a teacher.	I	live in London.

Following McCarthy (1991: 55) again, this can be represented graphically, as follows:

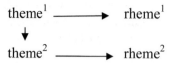

When we say that a theme or rheme 'becomes' another theme or rheme, this is not to imply that there must be an exact repetition; the reiteration may be a pronoun, a *synonym* (a word with a similar meaning, for example, book is a synonym of volume), *hyponym* (a word denoting a member of a class, for example, banana is a hyponym of fruit), a *meronym* (a word that is part of a larger whole, for example, *bumper* is a meronym of *car*) or a *superordinate* (a general word that includes members of its class).

Here are some examples of rheme and theme where there are respectively a synonym (war/ conflagration) and a meronym (family/brothers).

	Clause a		Clause b	
Marked theme	Theme a	Rheme a	Theme b	Rheme b
	I	have a large family.	My three brothers	are all older than me.
Between 1914 and 1918	there was	a terrible war in Europe.	The conflagration	led to the loss of millions of lives.

And here are some examples of theme and theme with a meronym (fruits/bananas) and a superordinate (Manchester United/team) respectively:

Clause a		Clause b	
Theme a	Rheme a	Theme b	Rheme b
Fruits	are plentiful in the market at the moment.	Bananas	are particularly cheap.
Manchester United	have won all of their matches.	The team	is doing really well.

Another pattern is where the rheme of a sentence contains elements which then become the themes of following clauses[3]:

> There are two methods you can use to feed your puppy: free feeding and scheduled feeding. Free feeding is when dry food is left out all day and the dog eats as it wishes. Scheduled feeding gives the dog food at set times of the day, and then takes it away after a period of time, such as a half hour.
>
> (http://www.k9web.com/dog-faqs/new-puppy.html)

Here the rheme of the first sentence has two elements: *free feeding* and *scheduled feeding*. Both elements then individually become the theme of following clauses. This can be represented in the following diagram:

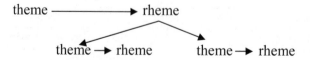

4.5 THEME AND RHEME, FOCUS OF INFORMATION AND GIVEN AND NEW

As we have mentioned previously, theme is 'the point of departure of the message', it is 'that which locates and orients the clause within its context' (Halliday & Matthiessen, 2004: 64) and the remainder of the clause is the rheme 'the part in which the theme is developed' (Halliday & Matthiessen, 2004: 64). *Theme/rheme* is a system belonging to the textual metafunction (see Chapter 2), because it is to do with how the information in the clause and the text in general is packaged. In addition to theme/rheme, there is another important textual system, referred to as *information focus*. Information focus, or simply *focus*, indicates what is most important or most newsworthy with regard to the information in the clause. It is indicated phonologically – how a clause may be spoken or read. It is where the main stress and pitch movement is placed in the *tone group* – the phonological units into which the information in the clause is packaged – referred to as the *tonic*. The tonic is placed on the key part of the newsworthy element of the clause, which typically comes towards the end. Thus in our earlier example, *The American president visited China,* the newsworthy information is *visited China* and, within that, the most newsworthy is *China*, and this is therefore where the tonic would occur, that is to say, the focus.

What is considered to be newsworthy in the clause is referred to technically as *new* and what is not considered not to be newsworthy – because it has already occurred in the text or is knowledge shared by writer and reader or speaker and hearer – is referred to as *given*. From this, we can see that new information is likely to occur in the rheme (because at the end of the clause) and given information in the theme (because at the beginning of the clause), although it is important to keep in mind that theme/rheme and given/new belong to different systems and that, as we shall see in the next section, given/new can be manipulated so that it does not correspond to theme/rheme.

4.6 THEME IN OTHER DECLARATIVE PATTERNS

So far we have looked at simple clause patterns following subject + verb + object/complement (with or without an adjunct) in our examples illustrating theme. The grammar of English provides quite a wide range of structures, however, which allows speakers and writers to manipulate what they make the theme of a clause.[4] If we take the example given earlier, *The American president visited China,* we can make a list of variations on this pattern, as follows (themes in italics):

1. *The American president* visited China.
2. *China* was visited by the American president.
3. *It was the American president* who visited China.
4. *It was China* that the American president visited.
5. *What the American president did* was visit China.
6. *The country the American president visited* was China.
7. *China, the American president* visited it.

Each of these clauses contains the same easily identifiable proposition; the basic information conveyed of the American president visiting China is identical in each case. However, the implication of each of these examples is different. In clause 1, for example, the attention is on where the president visited, China, while in clause 2, a passive clause, the attention is more on the person doing the visiting, the American president. In clause 3, while the attention is still on the American president, the effect is one of insisting or contradicting; it was the American president and not someone else who visited China. The other patterns suggest further distinctions in meaning. The grammar of English, thus, allows us to use theme/rheme and given/new as devices for adjusting the particular meaning we wish to apply to a given proposition and to foreground or background information, attitude and logical relationships.

Some of the patterns illustrated in this set of examples have special names: examples 3 and 4, for example, are usually referred to as *cleft* sentences; example 5 is technically referred to as a *pseudocleft*; example 7 is referred to as an *absolute theme*, because it is not actually a part of the clause. The function of these patterns is to divide up information into clause segments that can easily be moved around as theme or rheme, thus facilitating getting the right information as theme/ given early and rheme/new as late.

4.7 THEME IN PASSIVE CLAUSES

Example 2 above is a passive structure. In the active voice, the subject of the clause and therefore the experiential theme is usually the *agent*, or doer, of the action. The use of the passive allows other elements other than the agent, which in active clauses would be part of the rheme, to be introduced as theme. This is a very useful resource in certain situations in the ongoing discourse. Compare the following two clauses, the first in active voice and the second in passive, where the active voice theme is *The Normans* and the passive voice theme is *Rabbits*:

> *The Normans* introduced rabbits to Britain.
> *Rabbits* were introduced to Britain by the Normans.

These two clauses have the same experiential meaning, but, in certain contexts, one form is more suitable than the other. For example, look at the following text extract, which consists of three clauses, with the three themes: *rabbits, they* and *rabbits*. The use of the passive in the second clause, *they were introduced*, allows this continuity to be created.

> Rabbits originate from the western Mediterranean. They were introduced to Britain by the Normans in the 12th century to provide meat and fur. Rabbits are now widespread throughout Britain and Ireland.
>
> (http://www.mammal.org.uk/index.php?option=com_content&id=226)

If this second clause had been written in active voice, *The Normans introduced rabbits to Britain,* this continuity would not have been possible.

So far we have only considered declarative clauses (statements). But what about the two other main types of clause in English: interrogatives (questions) and imperatives (orders)?

4.8 INTERROGATIVE THEMES

Interrogative is the basic grammatical pattern for asking questions. A question presumes that there is something that the speaker wants to know. As Halliday and Matthiessen (2004: 75) state, therefore, the natural theme of a question is what the questioner wants to know and the use of interrogatives involves selecting an element that indicates the sort of answer that the questioner requires and placing it at the beginning of the clause.

There are two types of interrogative questions: yes/no, or open, questions (polar interrogatives) and closed questions (wh- interrogatives). In both cases, the theme includes the word that indicates what the speaker wants to know, as in *are you, did you, do you, can you, have you.*

*   *Are you* American?
*   *Do you* love me?
*   *Shall we* dance?

- *Didn't he* do well?
- *Could you* move over?

In these examples, in addition to the auxiliary verb, we have italicised the subject which follows it as also part of the theme, because the auxiliary verb on its own does not carry any experiential meaning. In yes/no questions, therefore, the theme includes both the auxiliary verb and the following subject.

With closed question themes, in contrast, the wh- question word does refer to an experiential element of the clause (to what the speaker wants to know) and so the wh- question word alone or the nominal group in which the wh- questions occurs (if it is part of a nominal group) constitutes the theme:

- *Where* do you live?
- *Who* do you want to talk to?
- *How many eggs* do you need?
- *How big* is your house?
- *Why* didn't she pay for her meal?

Questions are more frequently found in spoken interaction than in written text, but the following is an internet posting that employs a lot of questions (themes in italics):

Philosophers have always been interested in art and aesthetic value. *But[5] what* is art anyway? *How* should we define the notion of art? *And what* is it that distinguishes art from non-art? *How about* aesthetic value … *Is aesthetic value* something that resides in the object itself? *Or does it* have more to do with a kind of feeling, judgment, or sense of satisfaction had by an observer? *Do the intentions of the artist* play a role here? *Should art* have a purpose, such as evoking pleasure or conveying truth?

4.9 IMPERATIVE THEMES

Imperative clauses are used when you want someone to do something. So it is natural that the starting point, the theme, should be the action in question:

- *Open* the door.
- *Give* me the money.
- *Stay* back.
- *Mind* the gap.

In negative imperatives, the starting point is the negative auxiliary verb, *don't*. As with yes/no interrogatives, because the auxiliary verb does not carry any experiential meaning, the main verb is also included as part of the theme.

- *Don't leave* me.
- *Don't stop* work yet.
- *Don't take* too long.
- *Don't rush*.

A second form of imperative (inclusive imperatives) is when you want someone to join you in some action. Such imperatives have the verb preceded by *Let's*. The *'s* (us) in *Let's* is analysed as the subject of such clauses and, as the first experiential element of the clause, is considered to be part of the theme.

- *Let's* dance.
- *Let's* have another coffee.
- *Let's* play tennis tomorrow.
- *Let's* take a break.
- *Don't let's* get into a fight.
- *Don't let's* argue.

It is also possible to have imperative clauses which take a marked theme, with some form of adjunct.

- *After lunch, come to* see me.
- *To see it better, put on* these glasses.
- *Out you* get.

These patterns are said to be marked, because their more typical forms would be as follows:

- *Come* to see me after lunch.
- *Put on* these glasses to see it better.
- *Get out.*

4.10 EXCLAMATIVES

A final type of clause pattern to analyse for theme is that of exclamatives. Exclamatives are similar in structure to wh- interrogatives and can be analysed in the same way, with the wh- group as theme.

- *How lovely* to see you again!
- *What a big boy* you are now!

4.11 ELLIPTICAL THEMES

Especially in spoken language, themes (and rhemes) may be elliptical. This occurs because an element of the discourse may be carried over from a previous element or may be considered to be common knowledge to the speaker and hearer. Here are some examples from spoken discourse:

a) Would you like tea or coffee?
    [*I* would like] tea please.
b) Are you British or American?
    [*I'm*] American.
c) [*That* was a] Fantastic shot!

Here are two examples from written text:

a) *He* writes music and [*he*] plays it on his guitar.
b) *They* sang and [*they*] danced all night.

And here is an internet posting from a 13-year-old schoolgirl (ellipsed themes added in square brackets):

I get up around 5:30 to 6:00 in the morning and [/] eat breakfast and (/) get dressed and [/] do my hair and [/] put my shoes on and [/] brush my teeth and [/] leave!

(http://pbskids.org/itsmylife/school/you_said_it.html?ysiTitle=morning_routine)

It is worth pointing out that a criticism of earlier (and some more recent) English language teaching course books was that they required students too often to use complete sentences, insisting that learners begin their answers to questions with a subject/theme when ellipsis would be more natural.

4.12 EXISTENTIAL *THERE* AS THEME

Clauses such as *There's a cockroach in the kitchen, There are some left-overs to be eaten up, There was an earthquake in Turkey,* are referred to as existential clauses. There is disagreement over what should be accepted as theme in such clauses. Halliday and Matthiessen (2004) argue for *there* as theme, while Thompson (2004) prefers *there + be*. The important thing from a discourse perspective is that what is referred to as existing (the *existent* in Systemic Functional Linguistics) is placed in rheme, where new information is typically presented. As Lock (1996: 238) notes, existential *there* is often used to introduce new participants into the discourse, after which they may be picked up as themes in new clauses, as given information.

a) *While there are* sharks in Greece, most species are harmless.
b) *Although there are* 10,524 cameras in London a lot of these are very old …
c) *There are* nine languages in Eritrea. Tigrinya (50 per cent) and Arabic are the working languages.
d) *There are* 18,000 parking lot attendants in the USA with college degrees. *There are* 5,000 janitors in the USA with *PhDs*. In all, some 17 million college-educated Americans have jobs that don't require their level of education.

As Lock (1996) points out again, different kinds of learners tend to over- or under-use this pattern. He gives as an example the following **There are a lot of foreign students live in this building*, where *there are* is appended to the beginning of the clause without changing it to an embedded clause.

4.13 MULTIPLE THEMES

Some clauses (as we have seen with marked themes) will contain more than one element other than the subject brought to front place. When we have more than one element as part of a theme, we can refer to this as a multiple theme. These additional thematic elements will be either *interpersonal* (expressing some sort of attitude towards a statement) or *textual* (to do with how the text is held together). Interpersonal and textual themes are considered to be additional to the experiential theme and they precede it. There will always be an experiential theme; there may or may not be additional textual and interpersonal themes.

Interpersonal themes express the speaker's/writer's attitude to what is being said or his or her relationship with the interlocutor. They may be modal adjuncts or vocatives (addressing people by name). Here are some examples with interpersonal themes:

a) *Personally, I* think there is a very good chance he will join Manchester United.
b) *Perhaps he* will pay you a visit.
c) *Darling, I'*m waiting for you.

Here are some clauses with textual themes:

a) *Finally, they* finished their drinks.
b) *But I* don't want to wash the dishes.
c) *Moreover, your idea* would be impractical.

Textual themes tend to precede experiential themes, as these examples demonstrate. They perform a linking function, connecting two clauses together. In the above examples they are conjuncts, linking with clauses that have come before.

With some notable exceptions, such as *but, and, so, if* and *when*, interpersonal and textual elements do not necessarily have to be part of the theme. They may follow it, as in the following examples (textual elements: *however, nevertheless*; interpersonal elements: *possibly, naturally*).

a) *This huge wave of sympathy for Obama* **possibly** is just a refusal of McCain, to a large part.
b) *Hence, therefore, it* must **naturally** turn round the south coast of Ireland.
c) *John,* **however,** has made as good an attempt at this task as anyone could be expected to do.
d) *The answer,* **nevertheless,** is obvious.

In some multiple themes, there may be both an interpersonal and a textual element, in addition to the obligatory experiential theme. Elements functioning as interpersonal and textual themes fulfil the role of showing how the content fits in coherently with the surrounding text (Thompson, 2004: 158). It follows, Thompson writes, that these elements 'therefore naturally tend to gravitate towards the beginning of the clause, which is the structural slot (the Theme) where "fitting-in work" is done' (p. 158).

a) *Well, really, you* can use any kind of drinks can.
b) *So, actually it* is just a phone that plays mp3s and has a browser.
c) *On the other hand, fortunately, advances in the science of education* have given us the opportunity of improving our methods of instruction.

Where there is both an interpersonal and a textual theme, the textual theme will usually come first, as the above examples demonstrate. This is because of the linking function of textual themes with what has come before in the text. This is not a hard and fast rule, however, especially in speech. Here are some counterexamples from Google:

a) *Fortunately, on the other hand, I* have a PhD.
b) *Necessarily, therefore, the basic assumption of Egyptian civilization* was that it was a social order as eternal as the granite of its monuments.
c) *Happily, finally, one of those deadlines* didn't slip.

4.14 ANTICIPATORY *IT*

A particular type of clause, similar to some of the other variations on the unmarked declarative subject + verb + object clause, is the so-called *anticipatory it* clause (Hewings & Hewings, 2002). Hewings and Hewings (2002) classify these anticipatory *it* themes into four categories. Here are some examples:

1. Hedges:
    a) It is likely that …
    b) It could be argued that …

2. Attitude markers:
    a) It is of note that …
    b) It is worth pointing out that …

3. Emphatics:
    a) It follows that …
    b) It is apparent that …

4. Attribution:
    a) It has been proposed that …
    b) It is estimated that …

Note how these themes (which include the whole clause, not just *it*) are all interpersonal in nature, expressing the attitude or evaluation of the speaker/writer. This type of hedging is very frequent in academic discourse. It can present a problem to learners who are required to study through or work with the medium of English because, as Hewings and Hewings (2002: 368) point out, many languages have no counterpart to anticipatory *it* clauses. It is worth noting, also, that existential *there* is used in hedging as a counterpart to anticipatory *it*. So, as an alternative to, *it is possible that, it is likely that, it is probable that*, and so on, we might have *there is a possibility that, there is the likelihood that, there is the probability that.*

4.15 THEME IN CLAUSE COMPLEXES

Sometimes a sentence will consist of more than one clause. Gee (2011a) points out that there are three basic types of such patterns:

1. Two clauses can be conjoined (for example, 'Mary loves John and John loves Mary.').
2. One clause can be embedded as a participant inside another clause (for example, 'Mary thinks that the child loves her.').
3. One clause can be subordinated to another by use of grammatical words such as *as, while, because, so* (for example, 'Mary loves John because he is nice.').

With the first type, the two clauses are treated as main clauses and thus have two themes (*Mary* and *John*). With the second type, embedded clauses, the two clauses are treated as one main clause with one theme (*Mary*). With the third type, while each clause can be analysed as having its own theme (*Mary* and *he*), the clause that comes first can be analysed as the theme of the whole sentence. If we are interested in extended text, as we are in Discourse Analysis, then the latter approach will usually be more appropriate. Here are some more examples of this third type:

a) *Susan left her job at the university because she* wanted a change of career.
b) *While the children slept, their parents* played cards.
c) *Although the film was well reviewed by the critics, it* was not popular with the public

Notice how in these examples, by reversing the order of the main and subordinate clauses, by changing the themes, in other words, we change the meaning. Thus, with the first example, as it stands, the emphasis is on the reason for Susan leaving her job (she wanted a change of career). Leaving her job, as theme, is the framework for what the speaker/writer wants to say. Wanting a change of career, as rheme, is the main focus of the sentence. If we change this to *Because she wanted a change of career, Susan left her job at the university*, the reason is put into the background, as the framework of the sentence, the theme, while the action, leaving the job, as rheme, comes into the foreground. Similar transformations could be effected with examples 2 and 3. Another way of looking at this is to say that when these patterns are reversed, the first of the two clauses become marked themes and so are likely to be signalling a shift in orientation to the field, as is the commonly the case with marked themes.

4.16 THEMATIC DEVELOPMENT IN TEXTS

So far, our perspective on theme has been 'bottom-up', that is, looking at how theme behaves in individual clause patterns. This approach has been adopted because that is how the field has developed. There has historically been more research into theme at the clause level – in grammar – than at the level of the text. If we now take a more 'top-down' approach, that is, considering how theme develops in text, we arrive at a rather different picture. If we consider thematic choices in the context of the text and its social situation, then we can see theme as a resource for orienting to the field of discourse, to what the text is about. Theme, according to this perspective, provides a means of developing and orienting the new information in the text as it unfolds to what has already been given, or established (Martin & Rose, 2007).

Because they represent different subject matter and different perspectives on that subject matter, different registers will exhibit different patterns of thematic development or *methods of development*, to use a term coined by Fries (1981). Certain types of text may tend to prefer one type of theme–rheme relationship over another, while other texts will be more varied. In conversation, personal pronouns tend to dominate as theme (Halliday & Matthiessen, 2004). Here is an extract of conversation between two London teenagers talking about playing truant (or 'bunking off') at school (notice, as well as the personal pronouns as themes, ellipsis of certain pronominal themes, as mentioned earlier in the chapter):

Alphie:	I've been away about thirty.
Tony:	You have?
Alphie:	Yeah.
Tony:	Same here.
Alphie:	But on top of at least Christine
Tony:	D'y know that we was same way, maybe I'm a I'm a bit more <unclear>. I'm holding the record for most days off.
Alphie:	I've bunked off on Fridays.
Tony:	What bunked actually?
Alphie:	Actually bunked
Tony:	Walked out?
Alphie:	Well, like, pretended
Tony:	Most times <unclear> in class <unclear>
Alphie:	To go home. Wh= er see that my sis=. A lot of the time my my sister like, okay my mum would phone up and go walk her walk to school with Alphie on Friday, and actually, I'm I think He might try something. Anyway I pretend to take ages in the toilet

(Stenström *et al.*, 2002: 55)

As far as writing is concerned, young children or beginning L2 learners may rely on simple patterns to begin with. If we look back at the *parrot* text in Chapter 2, written by the primary school pupil, we already noted there the consistent pattern with the parrot or a body part of the parrot (referred to respectively as *he* or *his*) functioning as theme of most of the clauses.

The following (slightly adapted) descriptive text follows a consistent rheme–theme pattern, where the rheme of clause (a) (or a semantically related item) becomes the theme of clause (b) (themes in italics, rhemes in bold):

At Pacific Coffee Company, we choose only the best **Arabica beans** from around the world. The *Arabica trees* grow at altitudes between 3,000 to 6,000 feet and produce a **'hard bean'** **with more concentrated flavors.** *Coffee beans* grown at such altitudes require very careful cultivation with just **the right climatic conditions.** The *colder climate* encourages a slower maturing bean and the beans are harder, denser and of superior quality.

(http://in.pacificcoffee.com:8088/eng/product/ps_bea.html)

The following biographical text uses the theme and theme pattern as a consistent organising principle, that is, the same theme tends to be reiterated across clauses (relations shown in Table 4.1).[6]

First we give the text and then the thematic analysis in tabular form (Table 4.1).

Unable to work
Alex Webster

The lance Sergeant served in the Scots Guards for 10 years between 1990 and 2000. He was sent to Iraq for the first Gulf War and completed three tours of Northern Ireland, where he was hospitalised for 18 months by a crash. In 2002, however, he joined the Territorial Army and was deployed to Afghanistan where his vehicle was hit by a rocket grenade. He has ongoing surgery on his back, flashbacks, anxiety and temper problems. He has now set up a project to help similarly affected servicemen and women.

(*Independent on Sunday*, 1 August 2010: 29)

What Table 4.1 shows clearly is how the person who is the focus of the article, Alex Webster, the lance sergeant, is introduced as theme right at the beginning, in keeping with the notion of theme as 'point of departure', and then reappears as theme in various forms (*he* [five times], elliptical *he* and *his*).

The following text, a newspaper news article, is more varied in its thematic development:

View from the lanes of Pompeii

Google's Street View cars have driven hundreds of thousands of miles so people in 23 countries can see their home – and most other people's – on the web, writes Tim Bradshaw.

Table 4.1   Thematic development of a biographical text

Marked theme	Textual theme	Experiential theme	Rheme
		The lance Sergeant	served in the Scots Guards for 10 years between 1990 and 2000.
		He	was sent to Iraq for the first Gulf War
	and	(elliptical *he*)	completed three tours of Northern Ireland
	where	he	was hospitalised for 18 months by a crash.
In 2002	however	he	joined the Territorial Army
	and	(elliptical *he*)	was deployed to Afghanistan
	where	his vehicle	was hit by a rocket grenade.
		He	has ongoing surgery on his back, flashbacks, anxiety and temper problems.
		He	has now set up a project to help similarly affected servicemen and women.

The service began with five US cities in 2007, before expanding to Australia and Europe in 2008. *Oddball locations in its database* include the Palace of Versailles, Pompeii and Stonehenge.

Google's early images revealed the identities of the drivers and pedestrians who happened to be in the street when its cars drove by. *After concerns were raised by privacy campaigners* Google blurred faces and number plates in 2008. *Individuals* can also request to have their house fuzzed out, although the German service is the first to offer an opt-out before going live.

(*Financial Times* 22 August 2010)

In this text, the themes are *Google's Street View cars, the service, oddball locations in its data-base, Google's early images, after concerns were raised by privacy campaigners* and *individuals*. The second theme, *the service,* can be seen to pick up on the rheme of the preceding clause, which has described what the *service* consists of; *oddball locations in its database* is a new theme, although it relates back to the rheme of the previous clause in so far as that rheme referred to locations. *Google's early images* is a new theme, which depends on our understanding that Google is creating images; *after concerns were raised by privacy campaigners* is a marked theme (temporal adjunct), while *individuals* is a new theme.

Certain registers and genres may be recognisable by their thematic development. Biographies, as the text above about Alex Webster illustrates, tend to favour the reiterated theme pattern. Narratives, similarly, may reiterate the same theme (the protagonist) frequently. Here is a joke (a form of narrative) which follows this pattern:

A postal carrier is working on a new beat. *He* comes to a garden gate marked BEWARE OF THE PARROT! *He* looks down the garden *and, sure enough, there's* a parrot sitting on its perch. *He* has a little chuckle to himself at the sign and the parrot there on its perch. *The mailman* opens the gate *and* walks into the garden. *He* gets as far as the parrot's perch, *when suddenly, it* calls out: 'REX, ATTACK!'[7]

(www.pricelessparrots.com/parrot-jokes.htm)

Instruction manuals and recipes are other genres which favour reiteration of a constant theme, in this case imperative themes. The following is a recipe for omelettes.

- *Put* the pan on to heat with a little of the oil in it (not too much, about 2 tbspns max).
- *Break* the eggs into a dish and *whisk* them with a fork until well mixed; *add* a little salt and pepper.
- *When the oil has blue huey smoke rising from it pour in* the whisked egg, *have* a fork or flat wooden spatula ready, *and as the egg mix starts to bubble keep bringing* the cooked parts gently into the centre. This gradually allows the omelette to set into a pancake style consistency.
- *Carefully tap* the pan so that the cooked omelette moves and slightly overlaps the pan edge.
- *Gently fold* this overlap in toward the centre; *it* should only go one third distance.
- *Now arrange* your chosen filling in the centre of the omelette *and fold* the other edge in towards the middle.

© Ian Jenkins

(http://www.accessentertainment.co.uk/Eatingin/Recipes/Omelettes.htm)

Virtanen (cited in Hasselgård, 2010) shows how marked themes with temporal and spatial adjuncts can be used as a text-organising device in certain genres. Temporal adjuncts as marked theme are used in such a way in the following text from a stock market report (temporal adjuncts in italics):

Turnover in recent weeks has come close to a standstill *and for this year* has not approached the 500 million-a-day shares traded which is reckoned to be needed for securities houses to break even. In fact it has come nowhere near it.

Last week, the daily volume of equity trades peaked at 381 million and *on Monday this week* it had sunk to 267 million. *Yesterday* it recovered to paltry 281 million and *throughout December* it rose above 499 million shares a day on only five occasions.

In current conditions, market makers are keeping their books completely flat, reluctant to take on stock from sellers in case the market plunges. The last thing they need is surplus stock in a falling market. *In these sensitive times,* even buyers are unwelcome in case, by some miracle, peace breaks out and a short position has to get filled in at a higher price.

So far, though, the impact on the City broking houses has been surprisingly small. Some people have left in dribs and drabs but there has not been anything like the mass cuts which some had predicted.

(cited in Hasselgård, 2010: 81)

Similarly, marked themes, this time spatial adjuncts, are typical of the guide book genre, as illustrated in the following extract:

In the entrance to the gallery is a copy of Adrian de Vries's bust of Rudolf with his distinctive profile. *Here too* is Hans von Aachen's portrait of this Maecenas, with his fleshy Habsburg lips. He is magnificently dressed in damask decorated with peacock feathers, and wears the Order of the Golden Fleece. Note also here the works of Bartholomeus Spranger and Cornelius van Haarlem, both important Mannerists. *On the left* is Adrian de Vries's Adoration of Christ.

(cited in Hasselgård, 2010: 81)

More creative writers prefer to vary thematic development and sometimes play with it. Here is the opening paragraph to Barack Obama's autobiography (Obama, 1995: 3).

A few months after my twenty-first birthday, a stranger called to give me the news. *I* was living in New York at the time, on Ninety-Fourth between Second and First, part of that unnamed, shifting border between East Harlem and the rest of Manhatten. *It* was an uninviting block, treeless and barren, lined with soot-colored walk-ups that cast heavy shadows for most of the day. *The apartment* was small, with slanting floors and irregular heat and a buzzer downstairs that didn't work, so that visitors had to call ahead from a pay phone at the corner gas station, where a black Doberman the size of a wolf paced through the night in vigilant patrol, its jaws clamped around an empty beer bottle.

Notice how, in this opening paragraph, Obama begins not with the first person pronoun, *I*, – this is held back until the theme of the second sentence – but with a marked theme (temporal adjunct) *A few months after my twenty-first birthday* and a mysterious experiential theme, *a stranger*. Notice too, how the sentences are long, which means that the themes are far apart. The third theme, *it*, refers to Obama's *apartment*, although that has not been mentioned before, so it is a new theme, although it could be interpreted as a meronym, a part of the larger whole that is the area of New York referred to in the second sentence. The fourth theme, *the apartment*, again, is a meronym, this time of the larger unit that is the *uninviting block* that is the rheme of the previous clause.

4.17 HYPERTHEME AND MACROTHEME

Martin and Rose (2007) extend the analysis of thematic development to the level of the paragraph, arguing that an initial clause or clause complex can act as theme (referred to as *hypertheme*) of the whole paragraph (rather like a topic sentence in traditional accounts). This is rather different to the types of theme analysed so far, as it refers to the general topic of a stretch of text, not a part of a clause. Where we have a hypertheme, there will, in addition, be the other methods of development going on. Nevertheless, hypertheme establishes what Martin and Rose (2007), as mentioned earlier, refer to as the *field* of a stretch of text (its subject matter; what it is about) and may affect the method of development accordingly.

If we look at the following text (the first three paragraphs of H.P. Lovecraft's horror story, *The Shunned House*), the hyperthemes are indicated in bold. The first of the three hyperthemes introduces the idea of irony as horror and the rest of the paragraph elaborates on this notion. The second hypertheme, *Now the irony is this,* uses the cataphoric demonstrative pronoun *this* to point forward to the elaboration of what *this* refers to in the rest of the paragraph. The third hypertheme refers to the attraction of the house for the curious and the rest of its paragraph shows how this is the case, through a description of the prospect and location of the house.

> **From even the greatest of horrors irony is seldom absent**. Sometimes it enters directly into the composition of the events, while sometimes it relates only to their fortuitous position among persons and places. The latter sort is splendidly exemplified by a case in the ancient city of Providence, where in the late forties Edgar Allan Poe used to sojourn often during his unsuccessful wooing of the gifted poetess, Mrs. Whitman. Poe generally stopped at the Mansion House in Benefit Street – the renamed Golden Ball Inn whose roof has sheltered Washington, Jefferson, and Lafayette – and his favorite walk led northward along the same street to Mrs. Whitman's home and the neighboring hillside churchyard of St. John's, whose hidden expanse of Eighteenth Century gravestones had for him a peculiar fascination.

> **Now the irony is this**. In this walk, so many times repeated, the world's greatest master of the terrible and the bizarre was obliged to pass a particular house on the eastern side of the street; a dingy, antiquated structure perched on the abruptly rising side hill, with a great unkempt yard dating from a time when the region was partly open country. It does not appear that he ever wrote or spoke of it, nor is there any evidence that he even noticed it. And yet that house, to the two persons in possession of certain information, equals or outranks in horror the wildest fantasy of the genius who so often passed it unknowingly, and stands starkly leering as a symbol of all that is unutterably hideous.

> **The house was – and for that matter still is – of a kind to attract the attention of the curious**. Originally a farm or semi-farm building, it followed the average New England colonial lines of the middle Eighteenth Century – the prosperous peaked-roof sort, with two stories and dormerless attic, and with the Georgian doorway and interior panelling dictated by the progress of taste at that time. It faced south, with one gable end buried to the lower windows in the eastward rising hill, and the other exposed to the foundations toward the street. Its construction, over a century and a half ago, had followed the grading and straightening of the road in that especial vicinity; for Benefit Street – at first called Back Street – was laid out as a lane winding amongst the graveyards of the first settlers, and straightened only when the removal of the bodies to the North Burial Ground made it decently possible to cut through the old family plots.
>
> (http://www.classicreader.com/book/3801/1/)

Martin and Rose (2007) also refer to a level above that of hypertheme, *macrotheme*. Macrothemes are simply higher levels of text organisation than hyperthemes. A macrotheme introduces a whole text or larger stretch of text, previewing the hyperthemes which will follow. Macrothemes are typical of certain registers, such as academic writing, where clear organisation is highly valued. Not all registers employ macrothemes. As Martin and Rose (2007) point out, some registers prefer chaining ideas together, without employing a hierarchical structure of hyperthemes and macrothemes. Other registers employ a mixture of hierarchical ordering and chaining, rather like the interplay between the different methods of development of the clause level themes.

One register which does prefer a hierarchical structuring of macrothemes and hyperthemes is that of academic writing. In a study of the use of hyperthemes in student writing of history and management essays, Ravelli (2004: 104) argues that 'The student who (through the use of hyperthemes) can successfully predict where they are going, flag where they are, and reiterate where they have been, is more likely to be able to convince through their writing than the student who cannot.' Ravelli's study also noted significant disciplinary differences in the linguistic resources used to signal hyperthemes, an important factor to bear in mind in any application to the teaching of academic writing.

4.18 APPLICATION TO PEDAGOGY

Theme is fundamental to text construction, both spoken and written. Effective control of thematic development develops gradually over time. Indeed, it has been noted that, for L1 users of the language, in writing, it continues to develop right up to tertiary level (Christie & Derewianka, 2008: 21). And this is also probably true of speaking, although theme in spoken language has not received as much attention in the literature.[8] Hewings and North (2006) studied how British undergraduate students used marked themes in academic essays in the disciplines of history of science and geography. In both disciplines the amount of marked themes used increased from the first to the third year of study and greater use of marked theme correlated with higher marks awarded. However, within these trends there were significant disciplinary differences, the history of science essays demonstrating 47 per cent more use of marked themes than those in geography, thus confirming the need for teachers to encourage not only greater use of marked themes, but also the need for variation in thematic development across registers.

If proficient use of theme and what Fries (1995) calls the *method of development* is problematic for L1 users, then it is likely to be even more so for L2 learners. In spite of this, however, it is paid scant attention in English as a second language course books and other teaching materials, Australian genre pedagogy being the exception (see Chapter 8).

As Lock (1996: 228) comments, first priority should be the unmarked word order for declaratives, interrogatives and imperatives. But, as learners develop, they need to add more variety to their speech and writing. Unrelieved use of unmarked themes in writing may be monotonous and seem immature. The following is a text written by an adult learner of English, downloaded from a language learning website called correct-my-english (themes italicised):

> *I* wake up with the lark then *i* take bath, after taking bath *i* take brakefast *then i* go out side the home *there's* my van driver waits for me *i* board in the van and reach at office, then *i* start my work, Basically *i* am a System Support Engineer that's why *i* check my mail and reply them or do some other work if needed at 1 o'clock *i* take lunch then *i* take siesta, after taking siesta *i* start doing my work, in evening *i* go to my institute where *i* teach to my students after taking 3 classes of 1 hour each *i* go back to my home, then *i* again take bath and have my dinner after taking dinner *i* conversate with my siblings and parents then sometimes *i* play a little guitar and then *i* hit the hay stack.
>
> (http://www.mail-archive.com/correct-my-english@googlegroups.com/
> msg00515.html)

Although it might partly be the topic of daily routine which encourages the reiteration *I* as theme here – firstly because it is a rather juvenile topic/genre and secondly because autobiographical writing does indeed encourage use of this pattern – the unrelieved repetition of *I* as theme is monotonous and sounds rather childish. More variation in thematic development would undoubtedly improve this text.[9]

In speech, lack of facility in the manipulation of theme (and the associated patterns of given and new) may disadvantage L2 users when in interaction with more proficient speakers. Failure to use some of the marked clause patterns in speech (as illustrated in the section above on theme in declarative clauses) will disadvantage learners in spoken interaction; they will not be fluent, may sound stilted, may not be able to introduce new topics when they want to or recognise topic shift and turn-taking on the part of their interlocutors. For example, let us take just one of the marked patterns illustrated in the earlier section, *It was the American president who visited China.* (technical term *it-cleft*). This pattern would be invaluable if a speaker wanted to contradict the interlocutor, for example,

A: The American president visited Japan.
B: No, *it* was China that was visited by the American president.

Many languages do not have structures such as these and so they present a challenge for learners. Other languages, for example, French, have similar structures, but French does not have the same pitch patterns that typically accompany these marked themes to mark the particular element which is the focus.

Control of textual themes is important for connecting text together, for giving it *texture*, although there is a danger of overuse, as a number of studies on the use of conjunctions have shown (for example, L. Flowerdew, 1998) and as is evident if we look again at the student text about a golf course previously cited in Chapter 3.

As golf playing is a popular sport in the world, **however**, we have only a few courses in the area, **therefore** in order to promote tourism and recreation, it is the time for us to construct a private golf course.
    The present situation of Shalo is a small village and it is only connected by a footpath. **Moreover**, most of the areas surrounding it are abandoned fields, grassland and woodland. **In view of the above**, we find that the inconvenience caused to the surrounding area is minimal. **Besides**, the resource of land will be better utilized as most of the area is abandoned land. **Moreover**, after initial contact with the villagers of X, all of them accepted our proposed compensation.

(author's data)

Control of interpersonal themes, on the other hand, is important for the expression of subtle distinctions of meaning to do with attitude and evaluation, such as those exemplified in the section above (section 4.14) on anticipatory *it*.

Different languages deploy theme and rheme patterns differently. As Lock (1996: 227) writes, for example, in Japanese, theme is marked by the particle *wa*. In Chinese, as in many languages, although a subject + verb + object pattern is the unmarked one, other constituents can be more freely thematised than in English, in addition to frequent ellipsis of the subject. It is common in Chinese for adjuncts and adverbial clauses to precede the main clause to prescribe the topic and setting. This means that learners may tend to overuse absolute theme in English and produce clauses such as:

And played the table-tennis I am very bad (Chan, cited in Chen, 2010)
(And I am very bad at playing table-tennis)

Hong Kong in the year 2047, it will have (…) (Chan, cited in Chen, 2010)

(In the year 2047, Hong Kong will have …)

Such learners may not be aware that marked theme in English is reserved for discourse functions such as topic shift, contrast, textual organisation and according to generic conventions (Chen, 2010).

English, indeed, is unusual in requiring so much reiteration of theme in the method of development as it does. In Spanish, for example, what would be translated as pronominal theme in English is encoded in the verb – *escribo/I write, escribes/you write, escribe/he/she/it writes*, and so forth. So it is not unusual to hear Spanish speakers come out with something like, *Is good to practise a lot*, with omission of the thematic *it*. Similarly, when beginning a clause with a marked theme, where English would require an experiential subject, the Spanish speaker of English may follow with a verb, for example, *In the morning, eat my breakfast.*

When it comes to interpersonal themes, cultural factors may enter into the picture. Mur Dueñas (2007), for example, has shown that in the high-stakes game of academic publishing, Spanish researchers tend to use a more impersonal style than their English-speaking background peers when they write for international publication, one manifestation of this being less frequent use of the first-person pronoun as theme, which is sometimes preferred by the L1 English writers in Mur Dueñas's (2007) study.

In another study, Fung and Carter (1999) found that Hong Kong Chinese learners of English used many fewer interpersonal discourse markers, such as *really, say, sort of, I see, you see, well, right, actually* in their speech than did their native-speaker peers. Fung and Carter (1999: 434) recommend the following teaching procedure:

Willis and Willis (1996: 64) suggest that a teaching process can start with activities raising awareness and sensitivity in which learners are encouraged to notice particular features of the language, to draw conclusions from what they notice and to organize the view of language in the light of the conclusions they have drawn, through analytical strategies such as highlighting, questioning, explaining, identifying, comparing with mother tongue, etc. (cf. LoCastro, 2003). The language awareness based III (Illustration–Interaction–Induction) approach proposed by McCarthy and Carter (1994), mediated through activities like language observation, problem-solving, and cross-language comparisons, can be illuminating in bringing out the meaning and usage of various DMs [discourse markers].

While there is no space to go into exercise typologies to deal with the teaching of theme, one obvious way of focusing on it is through the use of cloze exercises, where various aspects of theme could be highlighted through selective deletion, instead of the more random deletion of every *n*th word (McCarthy &Carter, 1994: 76).

4.19 QUESTIONS FOR DISCUSSION

1. Look at the set of examples in section 4.6. Discuss what you think the possible implications are for each of the examples. Do they all answer the same question? Would the speaker who produced these utterances have made the same assumptions about the listener's knowledge of the event described?
2. Using some of the patterns in section 4.6., change the position of the theme in the following clause and discuss in what ways your changes affect the meaning.

Miranda is angry with her boyfriend.

3.   Identify the themes in the following examples: (a) say if they are simple or multiple themes; (b) if multiple themes, identify the experiential, interpersonal and textual themes.

   1.   He went into his office.
   2.   The politicians and their aides entered the parliament.
   3.   Established in 1984, City University of Hong Kong is a modern, hi-tech institution committed to providing a quality learning environment for its students and the community.
   4.   On the one hand, I want to enjoy my food, but, on the other hand, I'm afraid of getting fat. (two examples)
   5.   Yesterday, the army suffered a serious defeat.
   6.   There are a lot of people waiting to come in.
   7.   Don't wait outside!
   8.   Open this door immediately!

4.   Identify all of the experiential, textual and interpersonal themes in the text below. What is its pattern of thematic development?

   Established in 1984, City University of Hong Kong is a modern, hi-tech institution committed to providing a quality learning environment for its students and the community. The University currently has a student enrolment of over 17,000 (excluding sub-degree students), of which over 5,900 are postgraduates. Its programmes provide a wide range of learning opportunities from undergraduate and postgraduate studies to continuing education. For more information about the University and its academic and supporting units, please visit our website (http:// www.cityu.edu.hk).

   (City University of Hong Kong Research Degrees Handbook)

5.   Take a part of a text you have written or read recently and analyse it in terms of its thematic development.
6.   Find a text which has clear hyperthemes. Say what register it belongs to. Mark the hyperthemes with a highlighting pen or by underlining. Say how the rest of the paragraph relates to its respective hypertheme.
7.   Look at this piece of student writing. How could you improve it by adjusting the thematic choices/development?

   Terrorist movements are extremely horrific. Some serious terrorist acts do upset people world-wide. Terrorists, in order to achieve their potential aims or force a government to do something, use violence, especially murdering, kidnapping and bombing.
      Very often, embassy officers are their targets. They take political leaders as hostages and keep them until their demands are met. In order to come to a mutual agreement, a government needs to negotiate with the terrorists. Efficient use of negotiating skills and time available are very essential concerns in the process of negotiation.

   (author's data)

8.   Think of some consciousness-raising activities to develop awareness of thematic development.

4.20 FURTHER READING

Martin and Rose, 2007; Ravelli, 2004; Thompson, 2004.

CHAPTER 5

Speech acts

5.1 SPEECH ACTS AND PRAGMATICS

Pragmatics is to do with how language is used in context and the relationship between language use and language form. It deals with various aspects of non-literal meaning, aspects of meaning which are not taken into account by the code/conduit model of communication referred to in Chapter 1. These aspects of non-literal meaning are dealt with under designations such as: speech acts; conversational implicature; the Cooperative Principle, politeness and relevance. In this chapter we will focus on speech acts; we will deal with the other topics in the next chapter.

5.2 DEFINITION OF SPEECH ACTS

An early discourse analyst, Labov (1972: 121), stated that '[t]he first and most important step in the formalisation of Discourse Analysis is to distinguish what is said from what is done'. Discourse Analysis should thus fundamentally be concerned with the functional rather than the formal features of language. The term 'functional' is suggestive of 'language functions', as in 'functions' and 'notions' in language teaching, if you are already familiar with the field. Indeed, this is what we will be talking about here, although we will use the more usual term in Linguistics and Pragmatics of 'speech acts'. With speech acts, then, we are concerned with the functional, or communicative, value of utterances, with language used to perform actions – actions such as greeting, inviting, offering, ordering, promising, requesting, warning, and so forth.

5.3 FORM AND FUNCTION

Sentences can be accounted for in terms of form or function. Consider the following three sentences:

I need help.
Can you help me?
Help me!

In terms of grammatical form, these sentences would be labelled declarative, interrogative and imperative, respectively. However, given the right circumstances, they might share the same function of seeking help. So form and function are different. The same function may be performed by a variety of forms. Conversely, the same form may express (given the right situation) a variety of functions. Consider the utterance 'Can you help me?', which is an interrogative. In some circumstances, this might be interpreted as a request for help. In other circumstances, it might be a question about my ability to help the speaker. Traditionally, the three grammatical forms of declarative, interrogative and imperative are presented in language teaching materials as equivalent to, respectively, statements, questions and commands. The above examples demonstrate that this is somewhat misleading. Consider some possible ways of requesting a light for a cigarette.

> Do you have a light?
> Got a light?
> Do you have a match?
> Got a match?
> A light please!
> A light!
> Give me a light please!
> Could you give me a light?
> Could you give me a light please?
> I'm out of matches.
> My cigarette needs lighting.
> I was wondering if you had a light.
> I wonder if you have a light.

These are just some of many possibilities. Some are interrogatives and others are not. Now consider some ways of issuing a command:

> Be quiet!
> Will you be quiet?
> You must be quiet!
> You are requested to be quiet.

The first of these commands is an imperative, but the other three are not.

5.4 WHY STUDY SPEECH ACTS?

Speech acts are important for us for two reasons. First, they can be seen as a basic unit in Discourse Analysis, just as sentences or clauses are the basic unit in grammar; as Searle *et al.* (1980: vii) put it:

> the minimal unit of communication is not a sentence or other expression, but rather the performance of certain kinds of acts, such as making statements, asking questions, giving orders, describing, … etc.

Second, the use of speech acts, or functions, again like sentences in grammar, can be used as an organisational principle for language teaching.

5.5 PERFORMATIVES

Austin (1962), in his book '*How to Do Things with Words*', and Searle (1969, 1975, 1976), with his work on 'speech acts', considered the nature of what they called 'performative' utterances[1]. Austin started by identifying a special type of verb in which the uttering of the verb is also the doing of the action:

I name this ship the Queen Elizabeth.
I bet you fifty dollars.
I order you to leave.
I suggest you work harder.

These verbs are called *performatives*. Austin informally estimated there to be somewhere between one and 10,000 performatives, based on a perusal of a dictionary, a point we will return to later.

According to Austin, as can be seen from the above examples, performative utterances are expressed with a performative verb in the simple present tense and active voice, prefaced by the first-person singular pronoun, *I*. They can also be expressed in the first-person plural – *We promise to pay you back* – and in the second-person passive – *You are requested not to smoke*. Performative utterances may furthermore be prefaced by *hereby* to emphasise the performative nature of the utterance – *I hereby resign from this committee*.

5.6 ILLOCUTIONARY FORCE

From the identification of performative verbs, Austin moved on to note that there are other ways in which performative meanings can be expressed.

With Performative	Without Performative
You are requested to leave	Please leave
I insist that you come	Do come
I promise to pay you back	I will definitely pay you back
I suggest you do it again.	Why don't you do it again?

These types of meaning are referred to as *illocutionary forces*, or *illocutionary acts*, the speaker's intention in making an utterance.[2] The language forms used to signal the performance of a speech act, such as *please* in requests or *do* in insists, may be referred to as illocutionary force-indicating devices (IFIDs) (Levinson, 1983). Certain speech acts may be conventionally associated with certain IFIDs. Requests, for example, are often realised by modals such as *would you/could you* and the word *please*. Warnings are often accomplished with the negative imperative *don't*, as in *Don't step on my blue suede shoes!* Suggestions are often performed by means of *Why don't you?*, as in the example above, *Why don't you do it again?* Advice is often given using the conventional pattern *Have you ever thought of ...?*

This conventionalised nature of many commonly used speech acts presents a challenge for language teaching and raises questions about the traditional associations between the three sentence types and their stereotypical functions of stating, questioning and commanding. Typically, declarative forms are used to to make statements, interrogatives are used to ask questions and imperatives are used to issue commands. However, these functions (speech acts) are not always expressed by their most closely associated forms. Questions may be realised by rising intonation. Commands may be realised by the modal verb *will* and emphatic stress: You *will* go to work today! This is a further reminder of the lack of one-to-one fit between form and function, as noted in section 5.3, above.

5.7 INDIRECT SPEECH ACTS

Another challenge to traditional assumptions about the relation between form and function is presented by what are referred to as *indirect speech acts*. Indirect speech acts are 'cases in which one illocutionary act is performed indirectly by way of performing another' (Searle, 1975: 60). If we take as an example the utterance, 'Can you pass the salt?', this is simultaneously a question about the hearer's ability to pass the salt and a request to pass the salt. The second meaning is the indirect speech act. There are two types of indirect speech act: conventionalised and non-conventionalised. Conventionalised speech acts make use of conventional forms which are recognised by the speech community as typically associated with a given speech act, as in *Can you pass the salt* (requesting), *Would you like to* (inviting), *Why don't you* (suggesting). Non-conventional speech act realisations depend more on the specific context for their interpretation. Thus, in a very hot room, an utterance such as *It's too hot in here* might be intended as a request (to turn on the air conditioner), or, at a concert, an utterance such as *The music is about to start* might be intended as a request to stop talking.

As you will be aware from our examples of the relation between form and function in section 5.3 above, it is possible to phrase speech acts in many different ways. The choice of realisation will depend on the relationships between the interlocutors and the degree of imposition involved.[3] If you have a close relationship with your interlocutor, then, in general, you can be more direct. If, on the other hand, the imposition is great, even if your interlocutor is a friend or relative, you will need to be more indirect.

Look at the range of possibilities for complaining about a meal in a restaurant.

Waiter, get the manager immediately.
Waiter, I insist on seeing the manager.
Waiter, I want to see the manager.
Waiter, I'd like to see the manager please.
Waiter, if it's not too much trouble I'd like to see the manager.
Waiter, I don't suppose I could see the manager, could I?

(from Carter *et al.* 2001)

Both conventionalised and non-conventionalised speech acts can pose difficulties for second-language learners, but the conventionalised ones are specifically more problematic in second-language contexts, for the reason that learners may not be aware that certain language forms are conventionally associated with particular speech acts. Thus learners may not realise that 'Would you like to do the washing up?' can serve as a request or even, as in my own childhood, a command, and is not a question about whether one would enjoy doing the washing up or not. Or they may not realise, if they are French, for example, that the conditional, *si on* (if you), is not used to make a suggestion in English, unlike in French. Thus a French-speaker intending a suggestion with an utterance in English such as, 'If we went to the cinema' ('Si on allait au cinéma', in French), might be misinterpreted, more appropriate verbalisations being 'Would you like to go to the cinema?' or 'Let's go to the cinema'.

However, non-conventional speech acts can also pose problems, in so far as, although they are not conventionalised in terms of the specific language patterns employed, they may be conventionalised in terms of the conditions in which they are performed. Thus in Arabic it is conventional that if you compliment someone on some article of clothing or other personal belonging, it is customary for them to offer the item in question as a gift. In Arabic cultures, it is therefore not a good idea to compliment people very much on their personal belongings or they will feel obliged to offer them to you. To take another example, in certain French-speaking cultures, an appropriate way to ask someone if they want to use the toilet is to ask if they want to wash their hands. This is not a recognised convention in Anglo cultures, where one is more likely to ask if one wants to use the bathroom or toilet (in fact there are variations between American and British culture on this issue too). Visitors to France may thus be perplexed by their hosts continually asking them if they want to wash their hands.

5.8 FELICITY CONDITIONS

How is it that we recognise when a particular speech act is being peformed? According to Austin (1962), certain logical conditions, referred to as *felicity conditions*, need to apply for this to happen. Felicity conditions are thus the logical conditions or expected circumstances necessary for the (felicitous/'happy') performance of a given speech act. The g*eneral condition* applies to all speech acts and requires that the participants in an exchange understand the language and that they are serious in what they are doing. The *propositional content condition* specifies the content of an utterance; for example, a request must be about a future act by the hearer, while a promise must be about a future act by the speaker. The *preparatory condition* sets out the conditions which must hold prior to the performance of the speech act. For example, a request assumes that the speaker believes the hearer is able to perform the requested action and that the hearer would not do it without being asked; a promise assumes that the action will not happen by itself and that it will have a beneficial effect. The *sincerity condition* requires that, for a request, the speaker genuinely wants the hearer to do the act; for a promise it requires that the speaker genuinely intends to do what s/he says s/he intends to do. The *essential condition* refers to what the utterance counts for; with a request, the utterance counts as an attempt by the speaker to have the hearer perform an action; a promise counts as a commitment on the part of the speaker to do something.

5.9 SPEECH ACT TAXONOMIES

A lot of research has gone into classifying speech acts (illocutionary forces). This is important for language teaching, because a systematic classification of speech acts offers a way of organising a language teaching syllabus. There have been two possible approaches to classifying speech acts. The first way, based on Austin's concept of performative verbs, is to group them together according to semantically similar classes. Thus speech acts such as *state, contend, insist, deny, remind, guess* could be labelled as *expositives* (that is, expounding something), while *promise, guarantee, refuse, decline* could be labelled as *commissives* (that is, committing the speaker to some course of action), and *order, request, beg* and *dare* could be grouped together as *exercitives* (that is, exercising of powers, rights or influences). The five categories which were put forward as a tentative framework by Austin (1962) are as follows:

1. verdictives – the giving of a verdict, as by a jury or umpire – for example, estimate, reckon, appraise;
2. exercitives – as mentioned above, the exercising of power, rights or influence – for example, appoint, vote, order, urge, advise, warn;
3. commissives – for example, promising or otherwise undertaking – promise, contract, undertake;
4. behabitives – a miscellaneous group, having to do with attitudes and social behaviour – for example, apologise, congratulate, commend;
5. expositives – the clarifying of reasons, arguments and communications – for example, reply, argue, concede, assume.

The second way of classifying speech acts is Searle's (1976) approach. Searle used a number of criteria to classify speech acts, the main ones of which are as follows:

•   *Illocutionary point*: the purpose of the speech act; for example, the purpose of a request is to get someone to do something for you; the purpose of a promise is to undertake to do something in the future; the purpose of description is to present a representation of something.

- *Direction of fit*: to make the words match the world, for example, a description, or to make the world match the words, for example, a promise.
- *Speaker's psychological state* (also referred to as the *sincerity condition*) – a description expresses a belief about something; a promise expresses an intention to do something; an apology expresses a regret about something.

Using these criteria, Searle came up with five categories of speech act, as follows:

1. Representatives – they relate to states or events in the world – assert, swear, define, report, etc.
2. Directives – they attempt to get the hearer to do something, e.g. command, request, invite.
3. Commissives – they commit the speaker to doing something in the, e.g. undertake, promise, threaten.
4. Expressives – the speaker expresses feeling regarding a state of affairs that the expressive refers to, e.g. thank, congratulate, welcome.
5. Declarations – Austin's performatives; acts which in their uttering change the world, e.g. I declare you man and wife.

Searle's taxonomy, in spite of critiques, has been the one that has been the best received and most applied.

5.10 SPEECH ACT TAXONOMIES IN LANGUAGE TEACHING

Speech act taxonomies have been developed specifically for language teaching syllabus design (van Ek & Alexander, 1989; Wilkins, 1976). Wilkins (1976), in his work on *Notional Syllabuses*, presented a framework similar to that of Austin, as follows:

1. judgement and evaluation – for example, approving, disapproving, estimating;
2. suasion – for example, persuading, commanding, warning;
3. argument – for example, reporting, asserting, rejecting;
4. rational enquiry and exposition – for example, comparing, defining, explaining;
5. personal emotions – for example, pleasure, displeasure, sorrow;
6. emotional relations – for example, greeting, flattering, thanking.

The following is the set of categories developed by the Council of Europe for the Threshold syllabus (van Ek & Alexander, 1975), a syllabus designed to be applied to the teaching of the languages of the various Council of Europe member countries.

- imparting and seeking factual information (e.g. identify, report, correct, ask);
- expressing and finding out intellectual attitudes (e.g. agree, disagree, deny, accept, offer, express capability);
- expressing and finding out emotional attitudes (e.g. express pleasure/displeasure, surprise, hope, satisfaction);
- expressing and finding out moral attitudes (e.g. apologise, forgive, approve, regret);
- getting things done (suasion) (e.g. suggest, request, invite, advise, warn, instruct);
- socialising (e.g. greet, introduce, take leave, attract attention).

Using this taxonomy as a framework, the Council of Europe applied it to anticipate particular linguistic realisation patterns that might be expected of learners at this Threshold Level of learning (it was targeted primarily at 16-year-olds), stating that they are selected according to the 'most likely and urgent needs' (van Ek & Trim, 1998: 27) of the target learners. Figure 5.1 shows the

1	**Imparting and seeking** factual information	**1.4.2.2**	**Please (can you) tell me +** **subordinate clause/ + NP** Please can you tell me the way to the station?
1.1	**Identifying (defining)**		
1.1.1	**(With suitable gesture) this (one),** **that (one), these, those**	**1.4.3**	**Seeking information** (person) who? Who is that?
1.1.2	**It is + me, you, him, her, us, them**		(possession) whose + NP? Whose gloves are these?
1.1.3	**the + be + NP/this, that, these, those** This is the bedroom.		(thing) what? Which + NP? What is this? Which suit will you wear tonight?
1.1.4	**I, you, he, she, it, we, they + be + NP** He is the owner of the restaurant.		(event) What happened?
1.2	**Reporting (describing and narrating)**	**1.5.1**	**(for confirmation)** Yes, No (+ tag)
1.2.1	**Declarative sentences** The train has left.		Yes, I he is. No, I he isn't
1.2.2	**NP + say, think + complement clause** He says the shop is shut.	**1.5.2**	**(for information)** Declarative sentences, clauses Phrases and single words
1.3	**Correcting**		(You work hard.)
1.3.1	**As 1.1 and 1.2, with contrastive stress** This is the bedroom. The train has left.	**1.5.2.1**	**(time) (When will it happen?)** At 6 p.m. Yes, I we do.
1.3.2	**(correcting a positive statement)** (for example, Valetta is in Italy.) **No (+ tag)**	**1.5.2.2**	**(place) (Where's my box?)** On the table.
	No it isn't. (degree) How far/much/long/hot, etc.? How far is it to York?	**1.5.2.3**	**(manner) (How do you drive?)** Not very fast.
	(reason) why? Why did you say that?	**1.5.2.4**	**(degree) (How far is it?)** Not very far.
1.3.3	**Negative sentences** Valetta isn't in Italy.	**1.5.2.5**	**(reason) (Why are you here?)** (because +) declarative sentence Because I am a member.
1.3.4	**(Correcting a negative statement)** (for example, We didn't go to London.) **Yes (+ tag)** Yes you did.	**1.5.3**	**(seeking identification)** See 1.1.
1.3.5	**Positive statements (with intensifying do)** You did go to London.	**2**	**Expressing and finding** **out attitudes** factual: agreement, etc.
1.4	**Asking**		
1.4.1	**(for confirmation)**	**2.1**	**Expressing agreement with a** **statement**
1.4.1.1	**Interrogative sentences** Did you see him?	**2.1.1**	I (quite) agree.
1.4.1.2	**Decclarative sentences with** **high-rising intonation** You saw him?	**2.1.2**	That's right.
		2.1.3	That's correct.
1.4.1.3	**Statement and question tag** They lost the match, didn't they?	**2.1.4**	Indeed
1.4.2	**For information**	**2.1.5**	Exactly
1.4.2.1	**wh- questions** (time) when? When will the guests arrive? (place) where? Where is my purse? (manner) how? How do you make an omelette?	**2.1.6**	**(with a positive statement)**
		2.1.6.1	**Yes (+ tag)**
		2.1.6.2	Of course.

Figure 5.1 Specification of speech acts and their possible realisation patterns for imparting and seeking factual information (van Ek & Trim, 1998: 28–29, adapted). NP, noun phrase.

specification of speech acts and their possible realisation patterns (referred to also as exponents) for imparting and seeking factual information.

The Threshold approach to language teaching subsequently fed into the design of the widely used Council of Europe Common European Framework of Reference for Languages (CEFR). As stated on the Council of Europe website (http://www.coe.int/t/dg4/linguistic/dnr_EN.asp), Threshold level approaches help make the textbooks more motivating and facilitate the development of more realistic and transparent evaluation systems.

5.11 CROSS-CULTURAL AND INTERLANGUAGE PRAGMATICS

Considerable work has been done on how speech acts are performed across languages and cultures. Some of this work focuses on native speaker performance on a given speech act (referred to as *Cross-cultural Pragmatics*), while other work (referred to as *Interlanguage Pragmatics*) focuses on how learners acquire the ability to perform a given speech act in a target language. Speech acts which have been the focus of most intensive study in both approaches are requests, refusals, apologies and compliments.

Olshtain and Cohen's (1983) work on native speaker realisations of apologies is typical of the cross-cultural approach. Olshtain and Cohen (1983) specify the felicity condition of the speech act, that is, that the speaker has said or done something for which s/he feels the need to make amends. Five strategies, together with typical linguistic realisations, are identified, as follows:

1. An expression of an apology

     • An expression of regret   *I'm sorry.*
     • An offer of apology   *I apologise.*
     • A request for forgiveness   *Excuse me.*

2. An expression or account of the situation   *The bus was late.*
3. An acknowledgement of responsibility:

     • Accepting the blame   *It's my fault.*
     • Expressing self-deficiency   *I wasn't thinking.*
     • Recognising the other person   *You are right.*
        as deserving apology
     • Expressing lack of intent   *I didn't mean it.*

4. An offer of repair   *I'll pay for the broken vase.*
5. A promise of forbearance   *It won't happen again.*

(cited in Ellis, 2008: 176)

The premise underlying this research is that, where the realisation patterns of speech acts across cultures and languages vary, there is a danger of transfer, of applying patterns from the L1 to the L2. Descriptions of individual speech act realisation patterns provide teachers and learners with the information they need (suitably presented, of course) to discover where the target language and the L1 overlap and, therefore, where positive transfer is likely and – where there are differences – where negative transfer is likely.

In the example just cited, there are actually two levels of knowledge required to understand or express an apology: the choice of an appropriate strategy (listed form 1–5, with substrategies in some cases) and the actual language used to realise the strategy. Leech (1983) and Thomas (1983) refer to these two types of knowledge as *sociopragmatic* and *pragmalinguistic*. The failure to master either or both can result in what Thomas (1983) refers to as *cross-cultural pragmatic failure*.

Paltridge (2005/2006) gives examples of both types of failure. For sociopragmatic failure he gives the example of a Thai worker being criticised in front of his co-workers by a foreign manager for being regularly late for work. In Thai culture, this would be inappropriate, as it would result in loss of face. A Thai manager would be more likely to talk about the problem of lateness in general terms or would talk to the individual concerned in private.

Paltridge's (2005/2006) example of pragmalinguistic failure is that of an English speaker failing to attach an address form such as *chan* or *san* to someone's name when speaking to a person in Japanese. In Anglo cultures, address forms tend to be less formal than in some cultures such as that of Japan. Indeed, many Chinese people adopt English names to be used when communicating with Westerners to avoid being addressed by their original Chinese given name (which they consider to be too informal for a relative stranger and should be reserved for family members and close friends). Another example of pragmalinguistic failure is the example above of a French learner of English who, transferring a pattern from French, might say 'if we went' as a suggestion.

Pragmatic breakdown is not limited to different cultures. There was a notorious criminal trial in the UK in the 1950s, involving two men, Derek Bentley and Chris Craig. Bentley, who was under arrest by the police, shouted to Craig, who had a gun, 'Let him have it, Chris!' Upon hearing this utterance, Craig shot and killed a policeman. The utterance is, of course, ambiguous, either meaning 'shoot him' or 'hand over the gun'. The prosecution claimed that the former was the intended meaning, while the defence argued that it was the latter. The judge sided with the prosecution and Bentley was sentenced to death as an accessory to murder and executed, only to be pardoned many years later.

The best-known work representing the second of the approaches to Contrastive Pragmatics mentioned above, Interlanguage Pragmatics, is the Cross-Cultural Speech Act Realization Project (CCSARP) (Blum-Kulka *et al.*, 1989a, b; Kasper and Blum-Kulka, 1993). This large-scale project focused specifically on requests and apologies across different languages and cultures, using primarily discourse completion tests (questionnaires which ask informants to write down how they would realise a given speech act in a given situation). The aim was to find out cultural differences between native and non-native speaker performance of requests and apologies at both sociopragmatic and pragmalinguistic levels. Languages and language varieties studied included American English, Australian English, British English, Canadian French, Danish, German, Hebrew and Argentinean Spanish.

The work of Olshtain and Weinbach (1993) is a good example from this project. Olshtain and Weinbach (1993) conducted three studies: a study of the performance of complaints by native speakers of Hebrew, a cross-cultural comparison of complaining by native speakers of Hebrew and of British and American English, and an interlanguage study, comparing complaint realisation by non-native speakers of Hebrew at intermediate and advanced proficiency levels with that of native speakers. The cross-cultural comparison displayed highly consistent response patterns across the three native-speaker groups. However, learners' complaints differed from those of the target group on all the measures employed in the study. Learners produced longer complaint utterances, chose more severe complaining strategies, and used more softeners and more intensifiers. Strategy choice was influenced by interlocutors' relative status, social distance and the hearer's obligation to have avoided the offensive act. The learners also produced longer utterances when the hearer's obligation was implicit, and they opted for more severe strategies than the native speakers when an explicit obligation had been violated. The non-native-speaker learners also displayed greater variability in their responses, indicating that they were not yet accustomed to target conventions.[4]

5.12 INSTRUCTED PRAGMATICS

As well as research on Cross-cultural and Interlanguage Pragmatics (speech acts), work has been conducted in a field which has been referred to as *Instructed Pragmatics*, the investigation of speech act development in instructional contexts. Rose and Kasper's (2001) *Pragmatics in Language Teaching* is a landmark text in this field. This volume investigated the teaching and assessment of second-language pragmatics in various contexts.

A notable recent study in this context and typical of the sort of empirical work which is going on in instructed speech act research is that of Taguchi (2012). Taguchi's longitudinal study asked two questions: (1) What patterns of pragmatic development can be observed among different pragmatic functions and attributes in a second language (L2)? (2) In what ways do individual differences and learning context affect the course of pragmatic development? Forty-eight Japanese college students studying English in an immersion setting in Japan participated in the study and were asked to complete a pragmatic speech act task (requests and opinions). Results revealed a profound increase in the low-imposition speech acts, but a slow development of high-imposition speech acts. Qualitative findings revealed that learners' history of participation and socialisation related to their speech act development.

A number of studies have investigated speech act development in study abroad contexts. A monograph by Barron (2003) investigated the development of social formulas, on the one hand, and the speech acts of offering and refusing, on the other, among Irish learners of German. In another monograph, Schauer (2010) examined the interlanguage pragmatic development of German learners of English at a British university, studying not only their pragmatic development, but also their pragmatic awareness.

Of a more practical nature, Bardovi-Harlig and Mahan-Taylor (2003) produced a set of lesson plans for the teaching of pragmatics, while Cohen and Ishihara (2005) also made available online speech act teaching and background material, but aimed at the teaching of Spanish and Japanese.

5.13 METHODS FOR RESEARCHING SPEECH ACTS

We mentioned above that discourse completion tests were used to collect data in the speech act research discussed. Clark and Bangerter (2004: 25) identify the various methods used in the literature in collecting speech act data. They identify three approaches: *armchair*, *field* and *laboratory*. Jucker (2009) subclassifies these approaches as follows: *armchair* is subdivided into philosophic and interview; *field* is divided into diary, philological, conversation analytic and corpus; while laboratory is divided into discourse completion task and role play.

Armchair (the term is often used in a disparaging way) involves imagining examples of language use and making decisions relating to their appropriateness. Field research involves going out into the real world and collecting naturally occurring data. These data may be stored as field notes by the researcher in a diary, or, if conversational, they may be recorded and transcribed; with this latter method the language realising the given speech act must be extracted using various corpus tools (O'Keeffe *et al.*, 2011). With the laboratory method, data are elicited in 'laboratory' conditions and participants in the research are asked to complete discourse completion questionnaires or to participate in role-plays. Each of these methods has its strengths and weaknesses (see Jucker, 2009, for discussion). The armchair method is the easiest, but it may not be reliable, being based on intuition; native-speaker intuition about language, it has frequently been shown, may be faulty. The field method has the advantage of using authentic data, but is extremely time-consuming and hence insufficient data may result from this method.[5] Laboratory methods have the advantage of being suitable for the collection of large amounts of data (large numbers of participants may be asked to complete the questionnaire or perform in role-plays); however, because the data are elicited in artificial conditions, they may not correspond to naturally occurring language.

As stated by Jucker (2009: 1633):

the ideal research method for the investigation of speech acts ... does not exist. ... There is not even a method that is in a general way better than all the others. An assessment of a particular method always depends on the specific research question that the researcher tries to answer because the different methods vary enormously in their suitability for specific research questions.

5.14 CRITIQUE

5.14.1 My earlier critique

In an early article (Flowerdew, 1990), I discussed a number of problems in applying speech act theory to language teaching. Briefly, these issues can be listed under six headings, as follows:

1. How universal are speech act categories?

All languages and cultures have speech acts, but they may not be the same. As Wierzbicka (1987: 10) points out, Aboriginal languages do not have verbs that correspond to *thank* and *apologise*, but they have verbs for speech acts which have no names in English. On the other hand, Polish has two verbs which correspond roughly to English *promise*, but neither of which means exactly the same thing. Hymes (1962) claimed that the names of its repertoire of speech acts encode a culture's view of its most relevant forms of talk. This view would seem to lend support to the idea of learning English based upon its set of speech act verbs. There is one important caveat, here, though. It needs to be acknowledged that the cultural rules that apply in all societies that use English are likely to vary. Those societies where English is a non-native institutionalised variety (for example, Nigeria, Singapore), in particular, are likely to have their own 'interpretation of the world of human action and interaction', to use a term from Wierzbicka (1987). Care needs to be taken to avoid cultural imperialism in the application of speech act theory to language teaching. Learners may wish to maintain their L1 cultural identity (LoCastro, 2003). Special care needs also to be taken where English is being used as a lingua franca between speakers from different cultural backgrounds.

2. How many speech acts are there?

If we take the number of performative verbs in English as indicative of the number of speech acts, then readers will recall that Austin (1962) estimated there to be somewhere between one and 10,000 performatives. Wierzbicka's (1987) dictionary of speech act verbs contains just 231 entries, but this is not a comprehensive list. Similarly, based on a survey of the *Longman Dictionary of Contemporary English*, Wen (2007) estimated there to be 230 speech act verbs in English. This must be an underestimation, however, and is probably due to the fact that the *Longman Dictionary of Contemporary English* is a learners' dictionary. Gozzi (1991), based on a supplement to *Webster's Third Unabridged Dictionary*, calculated that there were 75 new speech act verbs added to English in just one quarter-century, from 1961 to 1986. Given that there must be a very large number, at any rate, from a language teaching perspective, the question is how to handle such a large number. One approach is to apply Searle's (1976) taxonomy of basic categories and then select what may be considered to be the most important ones. This is not an empirical approach and is based on intuition. The Council of Europe tried to make this process more empirical by starting with the framework of categories, loosely based on Searle, and illustrated earlier in this chapter. This is still introspective, but this framework was fleshed out by then conducting a needs analysis among the target learners to find out what they consider to be the most important things they want to be able to do in the foreign language (Richterich & Chancerel, 1980).

3. The contrast between specific and diffuse acts

de Beaugrande and Dressler (1981) point out that there is a great difference between what they call 'relatively well defined' (p. 117) speech acts such as promising or threatening and 'extremely diffuse' (p. 117) speech acts such as stating, asserting or questioning. Individual illocutionary acts, as we have seen, have been defined in terms of the conditions that must pertain for their performance. However, the conditions pertaining for the performance of the more diffuse acts are not specifiable in the same way as are those for the well-defined acts such as promising or threatening. For this reason, no doubt, most of the work on individual speech acts is limited to a relatively narrow range of the more easily definable acts, such as requests, apologies, compliments, thanking, and so forth. What this means for the application of speech act theory is that a large part of what people actually do with language in performing the more diffuse acts is not susceptible to analysis in terms of speech acts.

4. The size of speech act realisation forms

Although writers on speech acts acknowledge that the formal manifestation of a speech act does not necessarily correspond to the single sentence[6], there is nevertheless a tendency to take the sentence as the standard speech act unit. A single act can be realised by less than a sentence (for example, agreement can be expressed by a simple *yes*), or more than one sentence (for example, a promise in the form of a formal oath might take many sentences). On the other hand, one sentence can express more than one act. Thus a student who asks the teacher, 'Would you speak more slowly please?' is simultaneously requesting action, asserting that the teacher speaks too quickly, and reporting difficulty (Richards & Schmidt, 1983: 126). Furthermore, an act is not necessarily limited to one speaker turn (Schmidt & Richards, 1980: 132; Brown & Yule, 1983: 233), but may be constructed over a number of turns (Thomas, 1983).

Obviously, as far as application of speech act theory is concerned, this question of size is a serious one. How is it possible to recognise in a spoken or written text, or specify in a syllabus inventory, the linguistic realisation of a given speech act, if the possible size of that realisational form cannot be specified? One approach that mitigates this problem is to focus on larger units of discourse, using Conversation Analysis (see Chapter 7) (see, for example, Huth & Taleghani-Nikazm, 2006; Liddicoat & Crozet, 2001; Walters, 2007).

5. Discrete categories versus scale of meaning

As was pointed out earlier, Austin (1962) based his estimate of the number of speech acts on the number of performative verbs in English. He thus assumed that speech acts and performative verbs are in a one-to-one relationship. This assumption has been criticised by Leech (1981, 1983) and others (Edmondson, 1981; Wierzbicka, 1985) on the grounds that there is no reason to believe that distinctions made in our vocabulary necessarily exist in reality. Searle was aware of this when he stated that 'the verbs "announce", "hint" and "confide" do not mark separate illocutionary points but rather the style or manner of performance of [the same] illocutionary act' (Searle, 1975: 28).

Leech (1981) argues that speech acts are indeterminate and exist along a scale rather than belonging to distinct categories. For example, it is difficult to say where the border might lie between a request and an order. In language teaching, therefore, is a sentence such as 'Open the door please' to be presented to the learner as a request or an order?

What the scalar, as opposed to the categorical, nature of speech act categories means for application to language teaching is that exact specification or assignment of speech act realisation forms will be problematic.

6. Empirical versus introspective data

We have reviewed the advantages and disadvantages of how to collect speech act data above. Ideally, we would want to base a syllabus on the most authentic data we could find. As Boxer and Pickering (1995: 52) stated, 'The teaching of speech acts should first and foremost be based on spontaneous speech in order to capture the underlying social strategies of the speech behaviour being studied.' This approach has been made much easier with the advent of easily searchable electronic corpora (see Chapter 9) (Ishihara & Cohen, 2010). A number of studies have used corpora to investigate speech act behaviour (for example, Jiang, 2006; Koester, 2002; Schauer & Adolphs, 2006). Some studies have compared the language of given speech acts in English teaching course books with authentic data (for example, Jiang, 2006).

5.14.2 Grundy's critique

Much more recent than my critique of speech act approaches to pedagogy, as summarised above, is one by Grundy (2012: 121), in a review of Ishihara and Cohen (2010). The list in Figure 5.2 presents what Grundy sees as the methodological stance of the book, with his own (contrary) view (in parentheses).

Grundy's conclusion is that Ishihara and Cohen's book 'uses native-speaker pragmatic norms as a way of determining a socioculturally inspired learn-in-order-to-use language teaching

---

1. Teaching and Learning Pragmatics accepts the concept of intrinsic cultural difference in which foreign language learners find themselves at cross-cultural variance with native speakers.
    (English as a Lingua Franca learners need to establish a common culture, at least for the purpose of linguistic encounters with others, which will therefore be intercultural.)

2. Contexts are presumptive and prescribe appropriate linguistic routines.
    (Contexts are made relevant or even perhaps created by the way language is used, and are not therefore predetermined.)

3. Appropriate linguistic routines are best characterized as speech acts whose form is revealed through DCTs which enable model utterances to be determined.
    (The vast majority of utterances are highly context-sensitive and cannot be reduced to a set of formulas. Trying to do this is tantamount to endorsing the contradictory notion of a decontextualized Pragmatics.)

4. Model utterances can be presented to learners as targets and discussed metalinguistically.
    (Such a product-oriented approach overlooks the processes that speakers undertake in finding an optimal form for a meaning and that hearers undertake in finding an optimal meaning for a form.)

5. Explicit metapragmatic awareness and declarative knowledge are crucial to the development of L2 pragmatic competence.
    (Implicit metapragmatic awareness and procedural skill are at the heart of all normal language use.)

Figure 5.2   Contrasting methodological stances on speech act approaches in language pedagogy (Grundy, 2012: 121). DCTs, discourse completion tests.

methodology' (pp. 121–122). This is in contrast to his own approach, in which 'English is regarded as a plural system and in which a speaker's identity is revealed in their own distinct pragmatic and metapragmatic choices'.

5.15 APPLICATION TO PEDAGOGY

Our discussion throughout this chapter has been within a context of pedagogic application. In this section, we will focus on some general principles for a pedagogical approach to speech acts. Clearly there is a need to go beyond the simplistic matching of communicative functions (speech acts) with social contexts and realisation forms. There is a need to develop awareness of the subtleties of context in affecting sociopragmatic and linguistic choice and meaning. This means a more consciousness-raising approach rather than memorisation of sociopragmatic and pragmalinguistic norms. Murray (2012) describes activities which might be involved in such an approach, as follows:

> awareness-raising activities that prepare learners for noticing and include: focusing on speech acts in the performance of which deviation from the L1 norm is most critical to meaning and interpersonal relations; engaging learners in discourse completion tasks; using authentic materials; encouraging learners to become their own ethnographers and observe how speech acts are realised in the L2 in particular contexts of use and to contrast this with the L1; and incorporating native-speaker role plays into classroom activities as a focus of student observation.

Such activities might be incorporated into the sort of analytic model proposed by Barraja-Rohan (2000: 71) for the teaching of sociopragmatics, as in Figure 5.3.

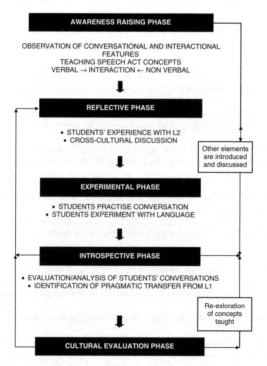

Figure 5.3   A framework for developing pragmatic (speech act) competence (Barraja-Rohan, 2000: 71, adapted from Conversation Analysis to speech acts)

At the same time as developing the sort of awareness we have described, learners need to develop an understanding of their particular role with regard to the cultural context within which they are likely to operate. To what degree, if any, do they want to assimilate to another culture? As Ishihara (2010) puts it:

> While it is important to ensure in instructional contexts that learners acquire receptive prag- matic competence to understand their interlocutors' intended meaning in the L2, teachers are advised not to expect learners to necessarily accommodate to perceived L2 norms. Instead, teachers could encourage learners to predict and observe the consequences of their pragmatic choices, that is, to critically analyze the sociocultural implications of their own language, as well as those of community members in terms of how identity, social practices, power structures, and affiliation with the community are constructed and negotiated.

There is thus a role for a critical approach to the development of speech act competence. Learners need to be encouraged to develop what might be referred to as *critical pragmatic aware- ness*.[7] Crozet *et al.* (1999: 181) refer to the understanding that will be derived from such awareness as 'a third place'. This third place consists of a space between the learner's native culture and the target culture, a space between the self and the other, or – where English is used as a lingua franca and is not the L1 of either interlocutors – a space between the learner's culture and the interlocu- tor's culture, neither of which may necessarily be what might be described as 'Anglo'.

5.16 QUESTIONS FOR DISCUSSION

1. Say if the verbs in the following utterances are performatives or not.

    1. You are reminded not to smoke in this office.
    2. I suggest you come back tomorrow.
    3. I declare this conference open.
    4. I can't ask him to do it again.
    5. I love you.
    6. The room is cooled by the air conditioner.

2. The following is ambiguous regarding its status as a performative: explain why.

    I bet 50 dollars on that horse.

3. Think of possible language forms for realising the following speech acts:

    1. identify
    2. agree
    3. apologise
    4. request
    5. attract attention

4. Look again at the range of possibilities for complaining about a meal in a restaurant in section 5.7. Write down a set of realisation patterns like this for:

    (a) asking someone out on a date;
    (b) borrowing some money from a friend.

    Put them in the order you might grade them according to difficulty in a language course.

5. Make a list of possible realisation forms from the speech act of requesting in English and in

another language you know. Which forms are the same and which are different? What does this suggest for teaching?

6. What are some of the advantages and disadvantages of a functional (speech act) syllabus as compared as to one organised along grammatical lines?

7. Consider the concept of *critical pragmatic awareness*, as explained in section 5.15. What form might this take in your own experience of second-language learning? Compare your view with that of others.

5.17 FURTHER READING

Barron, 2012; Grundy, 2012, Ishihara and Cohen, 2010; van Ek and Trim, 1998; Wilkins, 1976.

CHAPTER 6

The Cooperative Principle and Politeness

6.1 INTRODUCTION

In the previous chapter, we referred to Searle's concept of the indirect speech act. The phenomenon of indirect speech draws attention to the fact that there is not necessarily a one-to-one relation between what we say and the meaning of the sentences we use when their literal meanings are taken in isolation. Searle was first a philosopher before he was a linguist. Another philosopher of language, who came before Searle, was Grice. In this chapter, we will be talking about Grice and his concept of conversation (and other forms of language) as the cooperative interaction of two parties in the development of a common set of purposes. Grice referred to this as the 'Cooperative Principle' (CP). Following this discussion of the CP, the chapter will move on to consider the related phenomenon of politeness, another essential aspect of human interaction. We will consider how politeness relates to the CP, the conventions which are followed in order to maintain 'polite' behaviour, and different conceptions of how politeness might best be modelled and analysed.

6.2 THE COOPERATIVE PRINCIPLE

In participating in an interaction, Grice assumed that participants observe the following principle:

> Make your conversational contribution such as is required, at the stage at which it occurs, by the accepted purpose or direction of the talk exchange in which you are engaged (Grice, 1989 [1967]: 26).

Grice broke down this general principle into a number of subprinciples, which he referred to as maxims, as follows:

Quantity
- Make your contribution as informative as is required (for the current purposes of the exchange).
- Do not make your contribution more informative than is required.

Quality
- Do not say what you believe to be false.
- Do not say that for which you lack adequate evidence.

Relation (or relevance)
- Be relevant.

Manner
- Avoid obscurity of expression.
- Avoid ambiguity.
- Be brief (avoid unnecessary prolixity [verbosity]).
- Be orderly.

An example of observance of the principle and maxims would be in the following exchange:

A: What's the capital of Venezuela?
B: Caracas.

In this interaction, B has clearly told the truth (quality), has provided no more and no less information than was required (quantity), has fulfilled A's request for information (relation) and has done so in a clear and brief manner (manner).

Grice considered his maxims as not only something that all people observe, but as 'not merely something that all or most do *in fact* follow but as something that it is *reasonable* for us to follow, that we *should not* abandon.' (p. 29). So, if the CP and the maxims are rational, then we might expect them to be applicable in aspects of non-linguistic behaviour, and indeed they are. In his explication of Grice, Levinson (1983: 103) gives the following example:

> Consider, for example, a situation in which A and B are fixing a car. If the maxim of Quality is interpreted as the injunction to produce non-spurious or sincere acts (a move we need to make anyway to extend the maxim to questions, promises, invitations, etc.), B would fail to comply with this if, when asked for brake fluid, he knowingly passes A the oil, or when asked to tighten up the bolts on the steering column he merely pretends to do so. Similarly, A would fail to observe the maxim of Quantity, the injunction to make one's contribution in the right proportion, if, when B needs three bolts, he purposely passes him only one, or alternatively passes him 300. Likewise with Relevance: if B wants three bolts, he wants them *not* half an hour later. Finally, B would fail to comply with the maxim of Manner, enjoining clarity of purpose, if, when A needs a bolt of size 8, B passes him the bolt in a box that usually contains bolts of size 10. In each of these cases the behaviour falls short of some natural notion of full co-operation, because it violates one or another of the non-verbal analogues of the maxims of conversation.

This example from Levinson clearly shows that the maxims do indeed apply to all kinds of cooperative exchanges that operate in a rational sort of way.

6.3 IMPLICATURE

As mentioned above, in the previous chapter, we referred to Searle's concept of the indirect speech act. As already mentioned, again, the phenomenon of indirect speech acts draws attention to the fact that there is not necessarily a one-to-one relation between what we mean when we say something (an utterance) and the meaning of the sentences we use when they are taken in isolation. Utterances do not always carry their literal meaning. According to Grice, non-literal meaning must be inferred from context and the CP in a special type of inference he called *implicature*.

How does this work? Let us take the following exchange:

A.   Can you come to see me tomorrow?
B.   I've got a meeting.

B's reply might not immediately be interpreted as being related to A's question. However, since A has asked a question and an answer 'yes' or 'no' is expected to a question, then B's reply is here accepted as a negative answer. B has *violated* the maxim of relevance, that speakers normally give replies that are relevant to questions; but A can use this same maxim to work out the implicature that B cannot come to the meeting.

Grice states that to work out a conversational implicature, the hearer must rely on the following information:

1.   the conventional meaning of the words used, together with the identity of any references that may be involved;
2.   the CP and its maxims;
3.   the context, linguistic or otherwise;
4.   other items of background knowledge;
5.   mutual awareness of 1–4.

Here is another example, this time with the maxim of manner:

(at the end of a radio discussion of the British finance minister's performance)
(A) Interviewer: In a word should he [the finance minister] resign?
(B) Opposition politician: Well, I think he himself must see the untenability of his position.

In this exchange, B's reply is not as clear as it could be, thereby violating the maxim of manner. A, realising that B is violating the maxim of manner, is therefore able to derive the appropriate implicature, that the finance minister should resign.

The mechanics of implicatures such as these are thus that if, in making an utterance, the speaker does not appear, on a literal level, to be observing the maxims, the addressee nevertheless assumes the speaker to be observing them and thereby infers the implicature.

What these examples show is that, by observing the CP, interlocutors are able to work out what is meant from what is said. Hearers realise, according to Grice's theory, that literal meanings are not being employed (that the maxims are being violated) and infer additional meaning (implicatures) to make up for this.

6.4 FLOUTING THE MAXIMS

Examples such as those above are referred to by Levinson (1983) as *standard implicatures*. Grice also talked about another type of implicature, which he called *flouts*. A flout is when someone deliberately and ostentatiously contravenes a maxim. This may be considered to be a *major violation*. When a speaker is assumed by a hearer to be observing a maxim, then this is a case of *standard implicature*, as we have seen. If the speaker is assumed not to be observing the maxims, on the other hand, then this is on another level and is classed as a flout.

6.4.1 Flouting the quantity maxim

Grice gives the example here of someone writing a testimonial who only writes a couple of lines. In a normal situation, much more than a couple of lines would be required for a testimonial. The writer is ostentatiously breaching the quantity maxim, allowing the reader to infer the implicature that the writer does not have a high opinion of the person in question.

6.4.2 Flouting the quality maxim

Grice gives the examples of irony, metaphor, meiosis (understatement), and hyperbole. In such cases, speakers are not being truthful in the literal sense of the term. This being obvious to hearers, they infer further meaning, according to the context. An example of irony might be when someone says 'Great shot' in tennis, when they completely miss the ball. Utterances which contain metaphors, such as 'You're a pain in the neck', or 'He's a pillar of strength', clearly flout the maxim of quality. Similarly, understatement, such as 'I was a little bit lucky' after winning a huge prize, and hyperbole, such as 'I paid a fortune' (for something that was a little bit expensive) clearly also flout this first maxim, that is to say, they are not the literal truth. Here is an authentic example from a news report headline.

Arsène has his gloves on.

In order to understand this utterance you first of all need to know that Arsène is the manager of Arsenal Football Club (Arsène Wenger). But you also need to realise that this is not a literally true statement. You furthermore need to know that there are various purposes for gloves: to keep out the cold, to use while gardening, to use in surgical procedures, to protect boxers. Finally, you need to know that the news article up to this point had been discussing the struggle for the English Premier League championship. With this contextual information, it is possible to work out the implicature – not that Arsene is cold (which might be the most obvious one out of context), but that he is ready for a fight.

Another example of flouting the maxim of quality is the famous utterance by Princess Diana in an interview about her marriage to Prince Charles:

There were three people in this marriage …

Clearly, to say that three people are in a marriage is not truthful, as only two people can be married (in Christian societies at any rate). It is thus flouting the maxim of quality. The hearer is thereby led to the implicature that, although three people were not actually in the marriage (in the sense of being married to Charles and Diana), a third person (Charles's lover, Camilla Parker Bowles, now the Duchess of Cornwall and Charles's second wife), was involved.

6.4.3 Flouting the maxim of relation

The example Grice gives here is that of a tea party where A says 'Mrs A is an old bag.' After a moment of silence there is a complete change of topic such as 'The weather has been quite delightful this summer.' In this example, B implicates that A's statement should not be discussed by blatantly refusing to provide a relevant response.

Much humour is based on flouting the relevance maxim:

Army Officer:	Name?
Neddy Seagoon:	Neddy Seagoon
Army Officer:	Rank?
Neddy Seagoon:	Private
Army Officer:	Sex?
Neddy Seagoon:	Yes, please

(*The Goon Show*, BBC)

In this exchange Neddy Seagoon flouts the maxim of relevance by interpreting the information question 'sex' (that is to say, what is your sex?) as an invitation to have sex and not the more relevant interpretation that he is required to say whether he is male or female.

Here is a similar example of wilfully misinterpreting the relevance of a statement from an old-fashioned comedy routine:

Man outside a boarding house. Landlady looks down from window:
Landlady: What do you want?
Man: I want to stay here
Landlady: Well, stay there

6.4.4 Flouting the maxim of manner

An example here would be when a speaker is intentionally ambiguous. Advertisers often exploit the maxim of manner in this way. The old slogan 'Go to work on an egg' (that is to say, either have an egg before you go to work in the morning or start to eat an egg) is a good example. Or, as another example, speakers may wish to be obscure in their speech to avoid third parties understanding what they are saying. Parents often do this to avoid their children understanding what they are saying. Thus one parent might say to another: 'Let's go to that place we talked about yesterday' to avoid actually naming the place.

6.5 CONFLICTING MAXIMS

Sometimes, speakers will exploit a maxim and create an implicature because of a clash with another maxim. Grice (1989 [1967]) gives the following example (p. 32):

A: Where does C live?
B: Somewhere in the South of France

B is flouting the maxim of quantity here, in not fulfilling A's need for adequate information. This can be explained by supposing that B is aware that to be more informative would be to infringe the maxim of quality and not to provide a truthful answer. B accordingly implicates that he does not know the actual town where C lives.

6.6 HEDGES

As well as exploiting the maxims by obvious flouting, speakers may indicate that they are opting out of a maxim by using a special kind of what are called *hedges*, words or phrases telling hearers to disregard one of the maxims (this is not in Grice, but is discussed in various treatments of Grice, for example, Brown and Levinson, 1978, 1987; LoCastro, 2003; Yule, 1996). Here are some examples taken from the Michigan Corpus of Academic Spoken English (MICASE) corpus of lectures and student-advising sessions at the University of Michigan. They illustrate how speakers are metapragmatically aware of what they are saying.

Quantity
i don't want to qualify everything that i say, out, of existence, <LAUGH> uh but needless to say
(I'm going to contravene the quantity maxim even though I don't need to)

maybe i don't need to say this but i will say it anyway
(I may be going to contravene the quantity maxim)

Quality
um there was an article in the New York Times, sometime, last spring *i believe* …
(that is to say, what I'm telling you may or may not be true)

it's *probably* at least fifty years old *i would imagine*
(that is to say, it may not be that old and I am only guessing)

Relation
i don't want to get into this cuz i know you have somewhere else to go with this but
(I'm about to contravene the maxim of relation)

these children descriptors *may not necessarily be relevant*
(I may be contravening the maxim of relation)

Manner
i guess i'm not uh very clear, i don't know much about this history
(I'm aware that I have been flouting the maxim of manner – be clear – in discussing 'this history')

(following a complicated explanation) *this is all confusing i know*
(as in the previous example, but with regard to the previous explanation)

6.7 INFRINGING THE CP

Another way of failing to fulfil the maxims not referred to by Grice, but discussed in, for example, Thomas (1995: 74) is rather confusingly referred to as *infringing*. Infringing a maxim or maxims in this specialised meaning is when someone unintentionally generates an implicature. This category is very important from a second-language perspective because it may come about when a speaker (or writer) has inadequate command of the language.

Other situations where infringing is at stake are when someone is physically or cognitively impaired (for example, because the person is nervous or drunk or unable to develop a logical argument in conformity with the maxims). President George W. Bush, who was notorious for his 'misspeaking', provides many examples of illogical comments which can be interpreted as infringements. Here are just a few.

My job is a decision-making job. And as a result, I make a lot of decisions.
Most Americans feel overtaxed, and I promise you the Democrat Party is going to field a candidate who says I'm going to raise your tax.
I will try to the best of my ability to help those who lost life and property.
(http://www.dubyaspeak.com/polls/past)

6.8 VIOLATING THE CP

We said that the CP is the norm and we have seen that speakers may follow it to the letter, may set up standard implicatures by clearly not following it, may ostentatiously exploit it through flouting, may mitigate it through the use of hedges, or may infringe it because of some form of incapacity. In some cases, however, speakers may not tell the truth at all. In such cases, they disregard the CP without indicating to hearers that they are doing so. This is referred to as a *violation* of the CP and, although mentioned by Grice, is not developed by him. Flagrant lying would be the most obvious example of violation of the maxims, although sometimes speakers produce *white lies*, where they say something they know to be false, but for reasons which may be harmless or beneficial. For example, you might tell someone you have done something you have not in fact done, so as not to hurt the person's feelings. What is blameworthy or not is subject to cultural relativism, however.

6.9 LIMITATIONS OF GRICE'S THEORY

Various authors have pointed out limitations of Grice's theory. Before getting into these limitations, it might be said that, ironically, Grice was not the clearest of writers and that there is a degree of confusion in the literature regarding what he actually said and what has been stated by others. The main theoretical limitations that have been held against the CP can be listed as follows.

1.   Grice does not deal with interpersonal meaning.
2.   The CP does not allow for variation according to activity/genre and culture.
3.   There may be overlap in the maxims.
4.   The maxims are different in nature.
5.   There may be a range of possible interpretations of the maxims.
6.   There are better competing models.

We will take them one by one.

1.   Various authors have criticised Grice on the grounds that, in his concern to present a 'rational' model, the CP only deals with the exchange of information, with ideational meaning, and neglects the important interpersonal dimension. Indeed, some authors have expanded Grice's model to include politeness (most notably Leech, 1983), as we shall see below. Others have gone further and emphasised how, in some cultures, the interpersonal dimension of meaning may take precedence over the ideational. The anthropologist Rosaldo (1982), for example, has shown how the Ilongots of the Philippines use language primarily to establish and negotiate relationships rather than exchange information. To be fair to Grice, however, he does state that:

      There are, of course, all sorts of other maxims (aesthetic, social, or moral in character), such as 'Be polite,' that are also normally observed by participants in talk exchanges, and these may also generate nonconventional implicatures (Grice, 1989 [1967]: 28).

      Limitation to the ideational aspect of meaning can thus at best be seen as a limitation of Grice's theory, not a flaw.

2.   Various authors have also criticised Grice for failing to consider how operation of the CP might vary according to genre and culture. Indeed, if the CP is applied to different genres and cultures, then variation in its application is likely to follow. We already saw in the example above of the political interview extract concerning the British finance minister that the politician in this extract seemed to be applying the maxim of manner in a way that might be specific to politicians in interview situations; in other speech situations a more straightforward answer might be expected. To take a cultural example, in some cultures, the maxim of quality might be applied differently to others. In some cultures, for example, for reasons of face, if you are invited to a social function, it is appropriate to accept an invitation, even if you do not plan to attend. Thus,

while this might be considered a violation of the quality maxim in some cultures, in others it might be interpreted (accompanied by other discreet signals, perhaps) as an implicature. This is again a limitation rather than a shortcoming, because, first, Grice only professed to be dealing with conversation, and, second, although there may be cultural variation in their application, this does not mean that the maxims do not apply at all.

To take account of cultural relativity, Clyne (1994) has suggested adapting the CP by rewording three of the four maxims and adding a fifth (interestingly, he does not suggest any changes to the relation maxim). The maxims of quantity, quality and manner are reworded as follows:

Quantity
'Make your contribution as informative as is required for the purposes of the discourse, within the bounds of the discourse parameters of the given culture.'

Quality
'Do not say what you believe to be in opposition to your cultural norms of truth, harmony, charity, and/or respect.'
'Do not say that for which you lack adequate evidence.'

Manner
Clyne retains the overall maxim of clarity, but adds the following submaxims.
'Do not make it any more difficult to understand than may be dictated by questions of face or authority. Make clear your communicative intent unless this is against the interests of politeness or of maintaining a dignity-driven cultural value, such as harmony, charity or respect.'
'Make your contribution the appropriate length required by the nature and purpose of the exchange and the discourse parameters of your culture.'
'Structure your discourse according to the requirements of your culture.'

To these three revised maxims and the unchanged relation maxim, Clyne adds a fifth:

'In your contribution, take into account anything you know or can predict about the interlocutor's communication expectations.'

Clyne's revised model is particularly valuable for intercultural communication, allowing as it does for different cultural applications. As White (2001: 66) comments, such variability is very valuable when concerns such as informativity, length, truthfulness, harmony and dignity-driven values are in play.

3. Grice's examples are carefully selected to demonstrate unambiguously individual maxims in operation. But in many cases there may be overlap and more than one maxim may apply to a given utterance. Thomas (1995) criticises Grice on these grounds, although, to be fair to Grice, he does acknowledge this possibility (p. 40), but without exemplifying it. Thomas (1995: 92) gives the following example from Shakespeare's *Hamlet*.

Polonius: What do you read, My Lord?
Hamlet: Words, words, words.

In this example, Hamlet flouts the maxim of quantity in not giving enough information to Polonius, but he also flouts the maxim of relevance in not giving the sort of answer that would be required for such a question. Indeed, Thomas claims that the maxim of relevance is always in operation, because if you do not assume that an utterance is relevant, you will not look for an implicature (see more on relevance below). This does not mean that the other maxims do not come into play, however; merely that the relevance maxim may be seen to subsume the others. As Cutting (2008: 41) has written, the quantity maxim can be reworded as 'give the right amount of relevant information'; the quality maxim can be restated as 'give sincere relevant information'; and the maxim of manner can be modified as 'give unambiguous relevant information'. This may be seen as a shortcoming of Grice (see also Wilson & Sperber, 2004), although, when it comes to application, as we shall see, having the four maxims to consider can be useful.

4. The four maxims do not seem to operate at the same level. As just mentioned, the maxim of relevance can be seen to be operating all of the time. Thomas (1995: 91) claims that the maxim of quality is the most straightforward, arguing that an utterance is either true or not, but how does one measure to what degree an utterance is sincere? The maxims of quantity and manner are again imprecise. How does one judge what is the right amount of information or what is the right level of clarity and brevity? This is indeed a limitation for any application of the CP, but, again, it does not undermine it altogether.

5. Grice's theory requires that hearers can clearly recognise when an implicature is intended. This is not always the case, however. There may be a range of possible interpretations for a given utterance. Take the following example. A student came to my office for the first time for a consultation. Above my desk is a notice board with two sets of postcards of famous paintings pinned to it: one of Italian Renaissance depictions of the Madonna and child and the other of works by Picasso in his cubist style. After the consultation, the student got up to leave and said, 'I like those Italian paintings'. What was the intention of her remark? Was she following the maxims of quality and quantity and telling me the truth and the whole truth or was she contravening these two maxims and intending an implicature, by not telling me the whole truth, that she liked the Italian paintings, but did not like the ones by Picasso? There is no way that I can tell without directly asking her.

6. Many writers have suggested adapting, extending or simplifying Grice's model due to perceived inadequacies. With regard to simplification, there has been much interest in an alternative theory of implicature to that of Grice put forward by Sperber and Wilson (1995) in the form of *Relevance Theory*. Briefly, at the risk of oversimplification, Sperber and Wilson argue that Grice's model of inference can be reduced to one single maxim, that of relevance, which makes the other maxims superfluous. Wilson and Sperber (2004: 9) claim that '[h]uman cognition tends to be geared towards the maximisation of relevance', a concept which they refer to as the *Cognitive Principle of Relevance*. The term 'relevance' is used in a technical sense, to mean something like *communicative efficiency*. Any information has the potential to be more or less relevant to individuals. Given the tendency to maximise relevance, individuals will only attend to a stimulus that is relevant enough. The process is thus rather like a cost–benefit analysis, with individuals choosing to process those stimuli which require the least effort.

Relevance theory is thus a theory of communication that posits a selection from available inputs and that these inputs carry with them signals of their own relevance which allow the audience to determine which are the most important. Sperber and Wilson's model is, like Grice's model, an inferential one, in that speakers provide evidence of their intention to convey meanings and that these meanings are inferred by hearers based on the evidence provided. But instead of Grice's four maxims, Sperber and Wilson's theory requires only simple principle, that of relevance.

There are a number of advantages of Sperber and Wilson's theory over that of Grice, although the two approaches do not necessarily need to be seen to be in competition with each other. Sperber and Wilson's model is itself not without its critics, but it does allow certain problems with Grice to be overcome. For example, instead of hearers having to apply a maxim enjoining them to be relevant, all utterances are unavoidably relevant (to a greater or lesser extent). Instead of comprehension as a process of first processing literal meaning and then working out inferences, all processing involves inference. The notion of flouting is also not necessary, because, again, all input is relevant. Finally, the problem of universality with regard to Grice is avoided with relevance theory, because relevance varies according to context; indeed, it varies between individuals.

Sperber and Wilson's theory of relevance has many implications for language pedagogy, although, to date, there are few concrete applications. A website with relevant bibliography is: http://www.ua.es/personal/francisco.yus/rt.html#second.

To sum up this discussion on Grice, in spite of the limitations just listed, Grice's model offers a useful heuristic for figuring out what is going on in verbal interaction. It also offers, as we shall see below, a useful heuristic for guiding learners in text comprehension and production (whether it be spoken or written), on the one hand, and for evaluating learner texts, on the other.

6.10 AN EXAMPLE OF APPLICATION OF THE CP TO PEDAGOGY

In his, in many ways, excellent book, *Discourse Analysis for Language Teachers* (McCarthy, 1991), Michael McCarthy, in his preface, writing about the CP, states as follows:

> In a decade of language teaching, since they first came to my notice, I have never met an occasion where the maxims could be usefully applied … Grice, therefore does not figure in this book.

In this section, I will explain why I am not in agreement with McCarthy regarding the applicability of Grice.

To begin with, I will refer to a short article by White (2001), entitled 'Adapting Grice's maxims in the teaching of writing'. In this article, starting from the premise that Grice's CP applies to writing as well as speaking, White shows how the CP can be adapted to the teaching of the former 'by providing both teachers and writers with a way of understanding successful and unsuccessful written correspondence in mono- and cross-cultural settings'. White's claim is that readers expect clarity, brevity and sincerity in writing and that writing which fails to meet these criteria is likely to be unfavourably received. He demonstrates his case by means of a business letter written by a Polish undergraduate student and reactions from a small sample of UK business people. Most of the UK business people felt that the communicative purpose of the letter had not been achieved and the shortcomings of the letter were interpreted in terms of Grice's maxims.

Rather than present the letter in question in White's article, I will here reproduce a letter I received some years ago by e-mail and which I have used productively in my MA Discourse in Language Education course (Figure 6.1).

Before getting into a detailed analysis of the letter, there are two things that can be said. First, as White points out in his article, there are cultural issues at stake here. The universality of Grice's maxims, or, rather, the universality of the degree to which they apply across cultures, needs to be questioned, as, in fact, was done above (criticism 2). Second, different people may have different notions as to how well or badly the maxims are being applied. For this reason, the analysis presented here can be considered as a joint production of myself and my students, but, as in all Discourse Analysis, it is still only one possible analysis.

The analysis will consider the letter as it relates to each of the four maxims in turn.

6.10.1 Quantity

In the first three paragraphs of the letter too much time seems to be spent on justifying the request (paragraphs 1 and 2) and praising the addressee (paragraph 3), thereby flouting the maxim of

1. Dear Mr Flowerdew
2. I am writing to ask if you can grant me a favour.
3. I am a candidate for Master of Art in Beijing Normal University, studying
4. linguistics. Since I began to work on my thesis, I have been searching for the
5. materials on Winter's Functional Vocabulary – which you have studied
6. comprehensively. Yet months have passed, and even Beijing Library, the
7. largest library in China, also disappoints me by the lack of relevant books and
8. journals.
9. Therefore, after reading your article published in TESOL News, (Vol. 15, no.
10. 2) named Functional Vocabulary in Applied Linguistics, I have considered over
11. and over, and finally decided to write to you for help. I may be so bold as to do
12. so, however, I am really anxious to get the two functional vocabulary lists of
13. both Hargreaves and Spencer. Otherwise, the reliability of my thesis will be
14. extremely reduced.
15. The report of your study is soundly data-based and is enlightening to anyone
16. who takes an interest in this domain. No doubt, it will also help me much in
17. my thesis writing. But as my subject will be restricted to Chinese people writing
18. business reports in English, the result of my research is expected to differ
19. greatly from yours. I am looking forward to the honour of informing you of my
20. conclusion as early as possible.
21. Thank you in advance for your consideration for my request – the two lists of
22. functional vocabulary.
23. Yours sincerely

Figure 6.1   Letter received by the author.

quantity. Arguably, this request could have been made in just one sentence: *Would you be so kind as to send me a copy of your article*?

6.10.2 Quality

In a number of places, the sincerity of the writer can be questioned, especially bearing in mind that the requested article was in fact a very short piece of just a few paragraphs in a newsletter.

> – l. 4–5, 'since I began to work on my thesis, I have been searching for the materials'
> – l. 13–14, 'the reliability of my thesis will be extremely reduced'
> – l. 15–16 'the report of your study is soundly data-based and is enlightening to anyone who takes an interest in this domain'

Is the writer showing sincerity, one wonders, in showing how extremely keen he or she is in to obtain the article in question? And is the article really that important and significant, considering that it is only a short newsletter piece (although the writer might not have realised this)?

6.10.3 Relation

In spite of the fact that the letter starts off very directly, succinctly and to the point (l. 2 'I am writing to ask if you can grant me a favour.'), the writer then does not follow up on this promising start. We have an example here of what Scollon and Scollon (1995) and others refer to as 'delayed topic', a typical feature of Chinese discourse style (although that is not to say that it does not occur in 'Western' discourse). Clues are given (l. 12, the need to get the vocabulary lists; l. 16–17, explanation that the article will help with thesis writing), but it is not clear until right at the end (and even then only indirectly) that the writer is requesting that the addressee send him or her a copy of the vocabulary lists (or complete article, it is not clear which): 'my request – the two lists of functional vocabulary'.

6.10.4 Manner

The question here is whether the text is clear, concise and unambiguous or not. My students and I are of the opinion that this is not the case. We have already mentioned the indirectness and the delay in getting to the topic, both of which can be considered as violations of the CP.

In concluding this brief analysis, we can see how powerful the CP is in working out what is going on in this message. Watts (2003: 208) refers to Grice's CP as 'a set of rational injunctions on how to be a good rhetorician'. In the context in which Watts wrote this, it was intended as a critique, but in this context here we can see that the CP offers a powerful heuristic for evaluating a piece of writing.

6.11 POLITENESS

If we look at the letter analysed above again, we might see that a lot of what was analysed as flouting the maxims of the CP can be related to politeness, the use of language (and behaviour) in such a way as to encourage good relations between participants. At the same time as not following the maxims, the writer might be interpreted as being overly polite. This suggests that we might add another maxim to the CP: 'Adopt an appropriate amount of politeness!' (It also suggests, as previously mentioned, that there is an intercultural issue here.)

6.11.1 Lakoff's and Leech's models of politeness

As suggested above, some writers have extended Grice's CP to include politeness. Lakoff (1973) has politeness as one of her two basic rules of pragmatic competence, the two rules being 'Be clear' (that is to say, follow Grice's CP) and 'Be polite'. There are three subrules of 'Be polite': 'Don't impose', 'Give options' and 'Be friendly'. The whole model is shown in Figure 6.2, although this figure could be slightly misleading, because Lakoff states that, depending on circumstances, the second rule (politeness) can override the first rule (the CP).

Leech (1983) has a more complicated model than Lakoff, but also sets a politeness principle alongside Grice's CP. Leech has seven submaxims coming under his politeness principle. These submaxims are: tact, generosity, approbation, modesty, agreement, sympathy and phatic.

6.11.2 Brown and Levinson's model of politeness

Probably the most influential model of politeness, however, is that of Brown and Levinson (1978, 1987), which we will now consider in some detail. Brown and Levinson start with the concept of *face*, which they borrow from the sociologist Goffman (1971).

Following Goffman, for Brown and Levinson, face is 'the public self image that every member wants to claim for himself' (1987: 61). Face consists of two desires which interactants attribute to one another in communication: the desire to be unimpeded (negative face) and the desire to be approved of (positive face) (Brown and Levinson, 1987: 62). An important feature of Brown and Levinson's model is that, in addition to acting according to their face wants, in conformity with Grice's

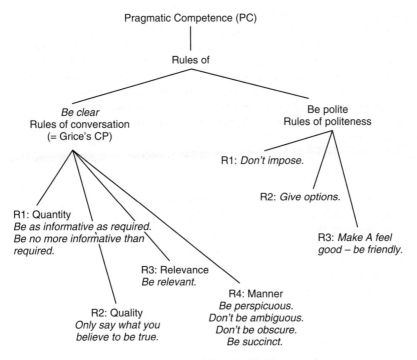

Figure 6.2   Lakoff's rules of pragmatic competence (Watts, 2003: 60, adapted).

CP, interactants are assumed to be guided by rationality, that is to say, they will work towards their rational purposes. Face wants and the application of rationality together result in particular types of linguistic behaviour which Brown and Levinson refer to as positive and negative politeness: positive politeness to show solidarity and indicate closeness and intimacy; negative politeness to show non-encroachment and social distance.

In Brown and Levinson's model, positive and negative politeness only come into play in the performance of speech acts which are intrinsically face-threatening (face-threatening acts or FTAs). FTAs are acts which threaten addressees' self-image, which embarrass them or make them feel uncomfortable. Positive politeness strategies would include compliments and expressions of solidarity. Negative politeness strategies would include indirectness, hedging, minimisation of imposition, expressions of deference and apologies. In performing an FTA, speakers have five options, as shown in Figure 6.3.

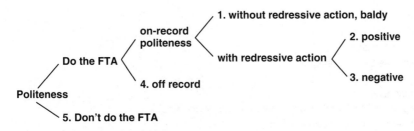

Figure 6.3   Options available when performing a face-threatening act (FTA) (Brown & Levinson, 1987: 69).

The speaker may perform the FTA off record (that is to say, indirectly) or on record (directly). If the latter, then this may be with or without redressive action (that is to say, positive or negative politeness). It is important to note that, in Brown and Levinson's model it is only where redressive action is concerned that positive and negative politeness come into play. Brown and Levinson provide an extremely detailed taxonomy of strategies which speakers use when expressing negative and positive politeness. Choice of strategy is determined by the estimated risk of loss of face to the speaker or hearer in the performance of a given speech act and by the relative power and social distance of interlocutors. Each of these strategies is illustrated with empirical examples by Brown and Levinson from three languages.

The following is the list of 15 positive politeness strategies (to show solidarity and indicate closeness and intimacy).

1. Notice, attend to H (hearer) (H's interests, wants, needs, goods).
2. Exaggerate (interest, approval, sympathy with H).
3. Intensify interest to H.
4. Use in-group identity markers.
5. Seek agreement.
6. Avoid disagreement.
7. Presuppose/raise/assert common ground.
8. Joke.
9. Assert or presuppose S's (speaker's) knowledge of and concern for H's wants.
10. Offer, promise.
11. Be optimistic.
12. Include both S and H in the activity.
13. Give (or ask for) reasons.
14. Assume or assert reciprocity.
15. Give gifts to H (goods, sympathy, understanding, cooperation).

Space precludes a consideration of all of these strategies, but examples of a few of the more easily illustrated ones, taken from Brown and Levinson, can be given.

Strategy 1:   Notice, attend to H: *Goodness, you cut your hair!*
Strategy 2:   Exaggerate: *What a fantastic garden you have!* (with exaggerated prosody)
Strategy 4:   Use in-group identity markers: *Help me with this bag will you luv/son/pal?*
Strategy 9:   Assert or presuppose S's knowledge of and concern for H's wants: *Look, I know you want the car back by five, so should(n't) I go to town now?*
Strategy 12:   Include both S and H in the activity: *Let's stop for a bite.*

Here is the list of negative politeness strategies (non-encroachment and social distance):

1. Be conventionally indirect.
2. Question, hedge.
3. Be pessimistic.
4. Minimise the imposition.
5. Give deference.
6. Apologise.
7. Impersonalise S and H: avoid the pronouns 'I' and 'you'.
8. State the FTA as a general rule.
9. Nominalise.
10. Go on record as incurring a debt, or as not indebting H.

And here are some example illustrations of the negative politeness strategies.

Strategy 1:   Be conventionally indirect: *Won't you come in?*
Strategy 2:   Question, hedge: *I suppose/guess/think Harry is coming?*
Strategy 3:   Be pessimistic: *I don't suppose/imagine there'd be any chance/possibility/ hope of you ...*
Strategy 4:   Minimise the imposition: *I just want to ask you if I can borrow a little paper.*
Strategy 7:   Impersonalise S and H: *It is regretted that ...*
Strategy 10: Go on record as incurring a debt, or as not indebting H: *I'd be eternally grateful if you would ...*

The subtitle of Brown and Levinson's volume is 'Some universals in language usage', so there is no doubt that Brown and Levinson consider their model of politeness to apply to all cultures. Their theory, however, has come in for considerable criticism on the grounds that it fails to take account of cultural variation (for example, Arundale, 2006; Gu, 1990, Ide, 1989; Mao, 1994; Matsumoto, 1988, 1989). Most of these critiques are with regard to East Asian politeness, in particular, and argue that Brown and Levinson's model is focused on the wants of the individual, that is to say it is *Western*, and fails to take into account the more social, community-oriented nature of Asian cultures. In spite of these critiques, Brown and Levinson (1987: 15), in the second edition of their volume, have defended their position, writing that:

> Such cultural differences [as those pointed out by their critics] doubtless exist and work down into the linguistic details of the particular face-redressive strategies preferred in a given society or group. Nevertheless, for the purposes of cross-cultural comparison developed here, we consider that our framework provides a primary descriptive format within which, or in contrast to which, such differences can be described.

More recently, Leech (2007) has updated his 1993 model and proposed a *Grand Strategy of Politeness*, which claims to be able to take account of both Eastern and Western cultures.

6.12 HOUSE AND KASPER'S MODEL OF FTA REALISATIONS

As we have seen with Brown and Levinson's model, politeness is closely associated with FTAs. Quite a lot of work was done by members associated with the Cross-Cultural Speech Act Realization Project referred to in the previous chapter in looking at politeness, as it is associated with specific FTAs. A good example of this work is that of House and Kasper (1981), who looked at the linguistic realisation patterns of politeness associated with the FTAs of complaints and apologies. Using role-play data of English and German interactions, House and Kasper found there to be considerable difference in the distribution of politeness markers associated with the two FTAs, with the German data being more direct than the English. House and Kasper developed a taxonomy of politeness markers to account for their data. The following are the categories used, divided according to two major classes: *downgraders* and *upgraders*. The former play down the impact an utterance is likely to have on the hearer and the latter increase the force of the impact an utterance may have.

Downgraders
1. politeness markers, for example, *please*;
2. play-downs (syntactic devices designed to reduce the force of an utterance) for example, past tense (*I wondered if ...*); durative aspect (*I was wondering ...*); negation (*Mightn't it be a good idea ...*); interrogative (*Mightn't it be a good idea*); modal (*Mightn't ...*);
3. consultative devices (structures which seek to involve the hearer cooperatively), for example, *Would you mind if ...* ;

4. hedges (adverbials which introduce an element of doubt into a proposition), for example, *kind of, sort of, somehow, more or less*;
5. understaters (adverbial modifiers which understate a state of affairs), for example, *a little bit, not very much*;
6. downtoners (sentence modifiers which modulate the impact of an utterance on the hearer), for example, *just, simply, possibly, perhaps*;
7. committers (sentence modifiers which reduce the level of commitment of the speaker), for example, *I think, I guess, I believe, I suppose*;
8. forewarnings (devices to forewarn the hearer and reduce the possible negative reaction, often in the form of a metacomment on the FTA itself), for example, *This may be a bit boring, You're a nice guy but …*;
9. hesitators (non-verbal hesitations and false starts), for example, *erm*
10. scope-staters (expressions of subjective opinion), for example, *I'm afraid you're in my seat, I'm not happy about the fact that you did P*;
11. agent avoider (syntactic devices designed to avoid expressing the agent of a proposition), for example, passives, impersonal constructions with *they, one*, etc.

Upgraders

1. overstaters (adverbial modifiers which over-represent the reality of a proposition), for example, *absolutely, purely, terribly, frightfully*;
2. intensifiers (adverbial modifiers which intensify certain elements of a proposition), for example, *very, so, such, quite, really*;
3. committers (sentence modifiers which indicate a heightened degree of commitment), for example, *I'm sure, certainly, obviously*;
4. lexical intensifiers (strongly negatively marked lexical items), for example, *swear words*;
5. aggressive interrogatives (devices to involve the hearer and therefore reinforce the impact of the utterance), for example, *Why haven't you told me before?*
6. rhetorical appeal (attempts to prevent the hearer from not accepting a proposition), for example, *You must understand that, Anyone can see that…* .

A number of things can be said about this taxonomy. First, the listing is very heterogeneous, with the profusion of categories nearly as varied as the linguistic items that may be used to realise them. Be that as it may, the list draws attention to the complexity of the task for any potential learner wanting to master the appropriate use of FTAs in a second language and the danger of what Thomas (1983) refers to as *cross-cultural pragmatic failure* at the pragmalinguistic level. This task is made the more challenging due to the fact that, as House and Kasper demonstrated, the choice of the different strategies varies across languages. This identification of the variation across languages further draws attention to a point that has been made already more than once with regard to earlier work on the CP and politeness, that is to say, the non-universality of the application of the principles or maxims identified. When one considers that English and German are closely related languages, one realises that the discrepancy is likely to be even greater for less closely related languages, especially languages with more complex politeness systems such as Japanese, Korean and Thai (Watts, 2003: 186). Each of the categories applies to both English and German, according to House and Kasper, but, with less closely related languages, it is likely that there will be categories which are not shared.

6.13 'POST-MODERN' APPROACHES TO POLITENESS

The approaches to politeness reviewed thus far have all been based on Grice's CP and speech act theory. This has been referred to as the 'classical' view of politeness (Terkourafi, 2005). Politeness, according to this view, is concerned with using particular linguistic devices/strategies according to universal rules/principles. More recently, another view has come to the fore, the so-called 'post-modern' view (Terkourafi, 2005). According to this view, politeness is not a universal given, but is contested across cultures and, importantly, within cultures. What constitutes polite behaviour is negotiated between speakers and hearers and cannot be predicted by a fixed model. Neither can it be found to reside in individual utterances, as was the assumption of the classical view, but is a relational, co-constructed phenomenon. In order to study politeness, according to the post-modern view, the analyst must study situated language and examine how politeness is constructed in ongoing discourse.

As an example of this, let's take the following extract of data cited by O'Keeffe *et al.* (2011). (The data are from the *Limerick Corpus of Irish English.*)

A: Does anyone want a mineral?
B: I'll have one.
A: Yeah?
B: **Make me a cup of tea.**
C: The kettle is boiled. He's dehydrated.
A: Do you want a cup of tea?
C: Does anyone want the cup before she goes?
D: Ok I will so.
C: Kettle is boiled anyway. Oh I'll have a cup too …
A: … do you take sugar?
B: Yes **please.**
A: How many?
B: One and a half.
A: Do you want [some chocolate]
B: **Please** yeah.
C: **You shouldn't give him anything.**

We can see here how politeness is negotiated in the ongoing discourse. B performs a bald on-record FTA (using Brown and Levinson's terminology), *Make me a cup of tea* (marked in bold), which would be interpreted as lacking in politeness according to the classical view. However, B later softens this tone by twice using *please* (marked in bold). So the initial assessment of politeness is revised as the discourse progresses.

We also see something else noted by the post-modern view in this extract, that participants have their own understanding of what constitutes polite behaviour. We can see this in C's final utterance (in bold) *You shouldn't give him anything*, which can be interpreted as a response to B's perceived impoliteness earlier, that is to say, B does not deserve a cup of tea.

Post-modern politeness theorists refer to lay interpretations of politeness as politeness1 and linguists' interpretations as politeness2 (Terkourafi, 2005). The politeness1 perspective (the lay one) allows us to interpret this situation according to one family's conception of what constitutes polite behaviour for them in this particular setting (O'Keeffe *et al.*, 2011: 78). Such conceptions of what is appropriate to a given situation are referred to by Watts (2003: 20) as *politic behaviour*. Politic behaviour is defined as 'that behaviour, linguistic and non-linguistic, which the participants construct as being appropriate to the on-going social interaction.' People may have their own values regarding politeness and do not always think of it as a good thing (Terkourafi, 2005: 241). Use of politeness markers such as those analysed by, for example, Brown and Levinson and House and Kasper may not necessarily be considered as necessarily positive, but may be evaluated as either positive or negative.

If we take another corpus extract, this time from Stenström *et al.* (2002), we can further note how people have their own views of what is polite behaviour (politeness1), but notice how in this extract, involving an inner-city teenager and her younger sister, the actual tone of the language is 'rather aggressive and challenging', to use Stenström *et al.*'s words (2002: 59):

> (Dawn is talking to her younger sister, Courneyde)
> Dawn: Courneyde. Take that thing out your mouth.
> Courneyde: No
> Dawn: What? You don't tell me no. I'll box you.
> (...)
> Courneyde: I want a drink
> Dawn: (challenging) Ha?
> Courneyde: I want [a drink.]
> Dawn: [Not I] want! What is this then? **Could I have a drink please**?
> Courneyde: A drink **please**?
> Dawn: (challenging) Ah?
> Courneyde: A drink **please**?

In another example of data from Stenström *et al.* (2002: 96), we can again see the abrupt tone used by working-class inner-city teenagers. This language would be seen as highly lacking in politeness, according to the classical view, but, as other data from Stenström *et al.* (2002) show, between the teenagers in question, this is the normal way of interacting.

> Jack: How do you reckon you did in that French thingie [test of some sort] today?
> Elliot: **Crap**.
> Jack: It was quite difficult actually wunnit?
> Elliot: Mm.

Stenström *et al.* (2002: 60) contrast this sort of aggressive interaction style with data from a more middle-class (the label is Stenström *et al.*'s) mother and child, showing much greater use of politeness strategies (in bold, added).

> Mother: Hi **darling** ...
> Norah: erm Esmee's here, erm, **can we just** go up to Kilburn? To get some, pens and stuff and **I need to get some money out of my**
> Mother: why didn't you do it on the way home?
> Norah: cos **I need to get some money out** [to get]
> Mother: [oh okay]
> (...)
> Mother: alright **darling**, please **don't be long will you**?
> Norah: no, what time shall I be back by?
> Mother: tea won't be any longer than an hour, an hour and a half, shops shut at five, five thirty
> Norah: okay, I'll go straight to my account and then to Woolworth's or something, saw nanny in Kilburn.

So, again, in this extract, we see how what is considered as an appropriate level of politeness (politeness1) is specific to a particular context.

One other issue to be developed in more recent work on politeness is its counterpart, impoliteness (Bousfield, 2007; Bousfield and Locher, 2008; Culpeper, 2011). If politeness is a question of degree, then polite and impolite language are two opposite poles of the same thing, not necessarily discrete items. Here is another example of data from Stenström *et al.*'s (2002: 170–171) corpus of inner-city teenage talk:

Kenneth: So have you got anything new since I've been away?
Cliff: Dunno
Kenneth: Got any new games for your computer?
Cliff: No. It's fucked innit? You must have fucked it up.
Kenneth: Why what's the matter with it?
Kenneth: You know the little box that goes into the back of the telly?
Cliff: Yeah.
Kenneth: He pulled the wires out.
Cliff: Who did?
Cliff: Rob
Kenneth: Why?
Cliff: He's a prick.

Such language would be considered impolite, to say the least, by traditional measures. Stenström *et al.* (2002: 170) describe the use of *It's fucked innit?* as 'not to invoke politeness, but the opposite, namely to "aggressively boost the force of a negative speech act"(Holmes, 1995: 80)'. However, this sort of language is normal for the teenagers in question, so in terms of politeness1, it must be considered as an acceptable level of (im)politeness that has been negotiated by this group of speakers for the situation in which they find themselves. In fact, Stenström *et al.* (2002) see this type of language as a marker of solidarity and group identity of the inner-city teenagers who use it and as a counterdiscourse to that of the older generation. It therefore has a positive value for the teenage users concerned. This again shows how politeness is a negotiable concept.

Clearly, from a second-language perspective, it is important to know about how to be impolite, just as it is to be polite. Or, taking a 'post-modern' view of politeness as negotiable, it is important to know what degree of politeness/impoliteness is appropriate in a given context – what the interactants consider to be politic, to use Watts's term. As Mugford (2008: 375) has written, teachers typically envisage their role as that of 'cement[ing] relationships, creat[ing] common understanding, and encourag[ing] intercultural tolerance'. Mugford (2008: 375) argues, however, that this 'Pollyanna EFL [English as a foreign language] world' is unrealistic and that learners need to learn how to deal with unpleasant transactional contexts as well as pleasant ones. 'By not teaching impoliteness', Mugford (2008: 389) claims, 'teachers are potentially allowing learners to be dominated by TL [target language] users'.

Finally, mention can be made to the concept of *overpoliteness* (Culpeper, 2011; Watts, 2005), which has not been researched much to date (Culpeper, 2011). However, overpoliteness, like impoliteness, can be perceived negatively by interlocutors and may also lead to cross-cultural pragmatic breakdown.

6.14 APPLICATION TO PEDAGOGY

In considering the CP and politeness with regard to pedagogy, it might be argued that these phenomena are universal and can therefore be carried over from learners' L1s. However, as has been indicated in several places in this chapter, while the notions of implicature and politeness may be universal, they are subject to linguistic and cultural variation with regard to their application. In a large-scale empirical study, Bouton (1999) tested the ability of non-native English-speaking international students (NNSs) (in the USA) to interpret implicatures in English as American native speakers do. The results demonstrated that, on arrival in the USA (depending on the type of implicature), the NNSs involved in the study failed to recognise implicatures 16–21 per cent of the time. Following a pedagogical intervention, Bouton found that, for formulaic implicatures – which were the most problematic for the NNSs – a mere 6 hours of formal instruction, followed by informal follow-up over a 6-week period and based on the same test items, brought the learners very nearly up to the same level as the Americans. Clearly, there is a role for cross-cultural teaching with regard to the CP.

While accepting that there is a role for the teaching of the sort exemplified in Bouton's study, which focuses on individual items and the matching of individual forms and functions, Murray (2010) argues that such a methodology can be complemented by a more process-oriented consciousness-raising approach. Such an approach involves presenting the general principles of the CP, the application of which can be explored further by learners as they progress. The method recommended by Murray (2010) is one of regular and guided classroom discussion rather that of an itemised syllabus. Rather than presenting the maxims of the CP in their raw form, in a bottom-up way, Murray (2010: 297) suggests eliciting them through guided questions such as: *During conversation, what do you think are some of the things that influence what we say and how we say it?* Possible answers might include:

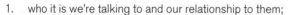

1.　who it is we're talking to and our relationship to them;
2.　where the communication's taking place;
3.　the feelings of the other person;
4.　the impression we want to give of ourselves;
5.　the kind of image we want to project.

These answers might be followed up by the teacher with a question such as *How do these things affect what we say and how we say it?* Students' responses might include:

1.　They sometimes affect the amount we say.
2.　They may affect how direct we are.
3.　We might not say exactly what we feel.
4.　We may lie or be dishonest.
5.　Our language might be more formal or more casual.
6.　We may be vague or deliberately unclear.

These responses might in turn be followed up by teacher prompts such as:

1.　Why are we sometimes indirect in the way we say things?
2.　What happens when we use very informal language in formal situations?
3.　Why might the amount we say be important?
4.　Why might we say more than we need to say?
5.　Why might we say less? Can you think of any specific examples?

Once students start to consider issues of informativity, directness, relevance and conciseness such as these and to discuss specific examples of language use, then, inevitably, questions of cultural relativity will arise and students will be in a position to develop further their ability to recognise contrasts in speech act realisation patterns and how the CP (and principles of politeness, one might add) operate differently in the target language and their L1. In addition, although Murray does not make this point, the same principles can be found to be at work across different genres and activity types in the L1 and the target language and awareness of this phenomenon can be similarly developed. Such an emphasis would be particularly relevant to English for Specific Purposes courses.

Just as bottom-up and top-down approaches to pedagogy are both relevant and have their value with regard to the application of Grice's maxims, so are they with regard to politeness. The classical view, with its inventories of items, suggests a more bottom-up approach, dealing with the various categories systematically one by one. The post-modern view, on the other hand, with its more global approach, suggests a top-down methodology, raising awareness of how politeness develops over stretches of discourse and is co-constructed by the participants as the discourse progresses. Both approaches have their merits and an eclectic view to pedagogic application for both the CP and for politeness has much to recommend it.

6.15 QUESTIONS FOR DISCUSSION

1. Consider the following in light of the CP and implicature:

    A.
    Teacher: Okay students. If anyone thinks they can't speaking English well, please stand up.
    (A student, Bridget, stands up)
    Teacher: Why are you standing up Bridget? Your English is very good.
    Bridget: I know. I just didn't want you to be the only one standing up.

    B.
    Lawyer: Did you ever stay all night with Mr Jones in New York?
    Witness: I refuse to answer that question.
    Lawyer: Did you ever stay all night with Mr Jones in Chicago?
    Witness: I refuse to answer that question.
    Lawyer: Did you ever stay all night with Mr Jones in Miami?
    Witness: No.

    C.
    A parent phones home and speaks to his young son, Alex, who has a friend visiting, Rupert.

    Alex: Do you want to speak to Rupert?
    Parent: OK.
    Rupert: Hello.
    Parent: Hello Rupert. What are you doing?
    Rupert: I'm speaking to you on the telephone.

    D.
    Palestinian leader Yasir Arafat: We are trying to get our people to stop shooting from Area A.
    Israeli General Giorta Elland: Does that mean there is permission to continue shooting from other areas?

    E.
    Exam question: Analyse the noun groups in the following passages:
    Introduction of student answer: In a passage, noun group is a basic element. Without noun group, it cannot form a passage. It, thus, is necessary to analyse the noun group of the two texts.

    F.
    A message left on a Hong Kong answering machine, notifying the husband of a patient that his wife had passed away:

    This is Queen Mary Hospital. Your wife is dead already.

2. Grice has been criticised for failing to consider how the operation of the CP might vary according to genre and culture. Think of some different genres and cultures and consider to what extent the application of the CP and the maxims do or do not exhibit generic/cultural specificity.

3.   Say if each of the following demonstrates positive or negative politeness:

   a. Thanks a lot mate.
   b. That'll be two bucks.
   c. You are kindly requested not to smoke.
   d. Would it be all right if I borrow your car?

4.   Think of a language other than English. Does it have any ways of indicating politeness that are not found in English?
5.   It is claimed that the maxims of conversation and politeness vary across languages/cultures. Can you think of any situations in your own experience which support this view?
6.   'Post-modern' approaches to politeness claim that politeness conventions vary according to situation. Can you think of any situations where politeness is: (a) more exaggerated than in most contexts; and (b) less pronounced than in other contexts?
7.   Record a piece of spoken interaction and transcribe it. Analyse it for its features of politeness. Use any of the models of politeness you prefer.
8.   What approach would you prefer for teaching politeness – according to the 'traditional view', in a bottom-up (deductive) fashion, or in a 'post-modern way', in a more top-down (inductive) fashion? Give your reasons.

6.16 FURTHER READING

Brown and Levinson, 1978, 1987; Grice, 1989 (1967); Leech, 1983; Thomas, 1983; Watts, 2003; White, 2001.

CHAPTER 7

Conversation Analysis

7.1 INTRODUCTION

In this chapter, we will consider the approach to spoken interaction known as Conversation Analysis (CA). There are strong reasons for focusing on conversation in Discourse Analysis, because, as noted by Levinson (1983: 284), 'conversation is clearly the prototypical kind of language usage, the form in which we are all first exposed to language – the matrix for language acquisition.'[1] CA was developed within the context of sociological enquiry and was pioneered by a breakaway group of American sociologists, sometimes also referred to as *ethnomethodologists,* under the leadership of Harold Garfinkel and followers such as Harvey Sacks, Emanuel Schegloff and Gail Jefferson. Given their sociological background, these researchers were interested in studying how language was employed in social interaction rather than developing linguistic theory. Instead of applying some overarching theory concerning social structure, however, they worked inductively with empirical data in the form of recordings of naturally occurring talk, which was transcribed in a detailed fashion. The aim was, and remains to this day in ongoing work, to describe social interaction in terms of the actions it is used to perform, not from the outside, but from the inside, from the perspective of the user (referred to as an *emic* perspective).

According to CA, conversation is conceived of as speech actions which build together to create coherent social interaction. CA does not apply any model of speech acts such as those reviewed in Chapter 4 (indeed, it does not use the term *speech act*). Rather, true to their ethnomethodological approach, conversation analysts use, as far as possible, categories employed by the participants involved in interaction themselves. Actions that they are interested in include asking, answering, disagreeing, offering, contesting, requesting, teasing, finessing, complying, performing, noticing, promising, and so forth (Schegloff, 2007: 7). Working inductively from the bottom up with categories such as these, CA has been able to reveal a rich body of facts about conversation and demonstrate that it follows an elaborate, but systematic, set of rules, or architecture.

7.2 METHODOLOGY AND TRANSCRIPTION SYSTEM

The methodology of CA involves the meticulous transcription of naturally occurring audio- or video-recorded talk (Jenks, 2011). The repeated playing of the recording in order to make the detailed transcription means that the analyst becomes increasingly familiar with the data. The analysis normally proceeds through a number of stages. First, a particular conversational phenomenon is identified – for example, a linguistic token, a particular social action or sequence. Second, a preliminary collection of the selected phenomenon is assembled. Third, this is broken down into subsets and the most significant subset is singled out for analysis. Fourth, the clearest examples of this subset are analysed. Fifth, less clear examples are analysed. Sixth, and finally, any deviant cases are considered

(Wilkinson & Kitzinger, 2008). There is also another approach for more targeted analysis, referred to as 'single case analysis' (Hutchby & Wooffitt, 2008), in which 'the resources of past work on a range of phenomena and organizational domains in talk-in-interaction are brought to bear on the analytic explication of a single fragment of talk' (Schegloff, 1987: 101).[2]

Because of the need for a very detailed written record, a special transcription system was developed by Jefferson (2004). A glossary of some of the major symbols of Jefferson's model is as follows (developed by Hutchby & Wooffitt, 2008).

(0.5)	The number in brackets indicates a time gap in tenths of a second.
(.)	A dot enclosed in a bracket indicates a pause in the talk of less than two-tenths of a second (also referred to as a micropause).
=	The 'equals' sign indicates 'latching' between utterances.
[ ]	Square brackets between adjacent lines of concurrent speech indicate the onset and end of a spate of overlapping talk.
.hh	A dot before an 'h' indicates speaker in-breath. The more h's, the longer the in breath.
hh	An 'h' indicates an out-breath. The more h's, the longer the breath.
(( ))	A description enclosed in a double bracket indicates a non-verbal activity. For example ((banging sound)). Alternatively double brackets may enclose the transcriber's comments on contextual or other features.
soun–	A dash indicates the sharp cut-off of the prior word or sound.
sou:::nd	Colons indicate the speaker has stretched the preceding sound or letter. The more colons, the greater the extent of the stretching.
!	Exclamation marks are used to indicate an animated or emphatic tone.
( )	Empty parentheses indicate the presence of an unclear fragment on the tape.
(guess)	The words within a single bracket indicate the transcriber's best guess at an unclear utterance.
word.	A full stop indicates a stopping fall in tone. It does not necessarily indicate the end of a sentence.
word,	A comma indicates 'continuing' intonation.
word?	A question mark indicates a rising inflection. It does not necessarily indicate a question.
↑↓	Pointed arrows indicate a marked falling or rising intonational shift. They are placed immediately before the onset of the shift.
a:	Less marked falls in pitch can be indicated by using underlining immediately preceding a colon.
a:	Less marked rises in pitch can be indicated by using a colon which is itself underlined.
Under	Underlined fragments indicate speaker emphasis.
CAPITALS	Words in capitals mark a section of speech noticeably louder than that surrounding it.
° °	Degree signs are used to indicate that the talk they encompass is spoken noticeably quieter than the surrounding talk.
Tha(gh)t	A 'gh' indicates that the word in which it is placed had a guttural pronunciation.
> <	Inward chevrons indicate that the talk they encompass was produced noticeably faster than the surrounding talk.
→	Arrows in the left margin point to specific parts of an extract discussed in the text.
[H:21.3.89:2]	Extract headings refer to the transcript library source of the researcher who originally collected the data.

One thing that immediately strikes the reader of talk transcribed using this system, as will be seen from the transcribed examples of talk included in this chapter, is how much it diverges from folk beliefs about talk. Talk does not occur in complete sentences, as is often believed to be the case, for one thing. Talk does not occur in discrete turns, either, but with quite a lot of overlapping. In addition, words do not always occur in discrete units, but are frequently assimilated together. Furthermore, speech is often interspersed with non-verbal *ums*, *ers* and *ahs* (referred to as *continuers*), which are only noticed with a very careful transcription. Many of these features are often ignored in language-teaching materials, already demonstrating the potential value of CA for language teaching.

7.3 TURN-TAKING

Even advanced learners of a second or foreign language are likely to have experienced the difficulty of gaining and holding the floor, especially in multiparty talk. This is because of a lack of command of the turn-taking system. Turn-taking is, in fact, the starting point for CA. CA begins with the unremarkable observation that conversation takes place with one speaker following another taking turns at talk. In a seminal paper, Sacks *et al.* (1974/1978) outlined how speakers organise turn-taking in conversation. Turn boundaries are marked when one speaker stops talking and another takes over. During this exchange of turns there may be some gap between turns or some overlap, but this is usually minimal.

Turns are made up of what are referred to as *turn construction units* (TCUs) TCUs consist of various linguistic units which include sentential, clausal, phrasal and lexical constructions. They may also contain, or, indeed, be uniquely made up of, non-verbal elements such as silence, laughter, continuers, and bodily and facial movements. Liddicoat (2007) gives the following example to show the diversity of TCUs, drawing attention to 'at', which is a lexical unit, but which is recognised as a TCU in the fourth turn by the mother, who responds to it. In this example, we also see sentential, phrasal, lexical and non-verbal elements contributing towards TCUs.

```
1        Ther:    What kind of work do you do?
2        Mother:  Food service
3    →   Ther:    At?
4
5        Mother:  (A) / (uh) post office cafeteria downtown main post office on Redwood
6        Ther:    °Okay°
```

(Liddicoat, 2007: 55)

Each speaker has the right to complete one TCU and then the next TCU is up for negotiation, that is to say, there is the *possibility* of another speaker taking over (see below). In some cases – stories, for example – more than one TCU is possible per turn. In the above example, however, each turn corresponds to one TCU.

How do interlocutors know when a turn has finished, or is about to finish? Three criteria come into play here: syntax, intonation and pragmatics. A turn may be recognised as complete if it represents a syntactically complete unit, that is, a sentence, a clause, a phrase or a lexical item. A TCU may be recognised as complete according to its intonational pattern. More critically, a TCU may be recognised as such if it represents a recognisable pragmatic or social action (in some cases more than one). A further criterion that has been posited for TCUs is that of non-verbal behaviours, especially gaze (Goodwin, 1981), although, as Liddicoat (2007: 59) points out, this must be less important than the other features, as TCU completion is still possible where visual cues are not present, for example, telephone conversations.

Interlocutors have the ability to project possible completion points of turns. This is evidenced by overlapping talk, as in the following example.

```
1        Joe:     B't he wannid the] dawg dih bite iz wife.
2                 (0.5)
3        ( ) :    [ ] °ehhh°
4        Joe:     [ ] So ↑he come[s ho:me one]   night   ] =
5        Carol:   [heh heh heh]   heh he]   h =
6    →   Joe:     = the sonofa] bitch [bit hi:m.]
7    →   Carol:   = heh hehw]        [bit hi:m,]
```

(Liddicoat, 2007: 56)

In this example, Carol is able to complete Joe's TCU with him, clearly indicating that she has anticipated how it will be completed.

Places where TCU completion is possible are referred to as *transition relevance places*. Transition relevance places are not fixed at the end of a TCU because of interlocutors' ability to project the completion of TCUs. Schegloff (2007: 4) refers to the transition relevance place as 'the span that begins with the immanence of possible completion'.

7.4 RULES FOR TURN-TAKING

The rules for the allocation of turns, following the principle of transition relevance, were set out by Sacks *et al.* (1974/1978) as follows:

1. At the transition–relevance place of a turn:

A. where the next speaker is selected by the current speaker:
    the current speaker must stop talking and the next speaker must take over

B. where the next speaker is not selected by the current speaker:
    any speaker may, but need not, self-select, with first speaker acquiring rights to a turn.

C. where the next speaker is not selected by the current speaker:
    the current speaker may, but need not, continue if no other speaker self-selects.

2. Whichever choice has been made, then 1. A–C come into operation again.
(adapted from Sacks *et al.*, 1974/1978: 13).

It is not claimed that these 'rules' are consciously applied or even known by interactants, but that they are naturally acquired, implicitly understood and automatically employed each time interaction takes place. The rules are deceptively simple, but are general enough to apply to different settings, numbers of participants, sets of relationships, topics and contexts (Hutchby & Wooffitt, 2008: 51). Some institutionalised contexts, nevertheless, vary. The ordering of turns in debates, for example, is pre-allocated, and other institutionalised speech events such as committee meetings, school class-room lessons and trials also have their own turn-taking rules. There is also the possibility that the rules may differ across cultures. In Burundi, for example (presumably in formal settings), the order in which individuals speak in a group is strictly determined by seniority of rank (Albert, reported in Levinson, 1983: 301). In spite of this evidence for cross-cultural diversity, Levinson (1983: 301) claims that there is 'good reason' for thinking that for 'informal, ordinary kinds of talk' the rules are valid for all cultures. Hatch (1983: 133), whilst agreeing that the turn-taking system itself 'may well be universal', cites studies which indicate that pause length, which often indicates the place for turn-taking, does vary across language groups. Certain North American Indian tribes, for example, tolerate much longer pause length. Indeed, in a well-known study, Scollon and Scollon (1990) have shown how, in intercultural interactions, Athabaskans in Alaska tend to observe longer pause lengths between turns than do their American and Canadian counterparts, resulting in miscommunication, due to the fact that the Americans and Canadians interpret these longer pauses as a desire not to speak.

7.5 ADJACENCY PAIRS

Focusing now on the relation between pairs of turns, it has been noted that certain classes of turns are closely related to others. Closely related pairs are referred to as adjacency pairs. Pairs which be identified in the literature include:

> accusation–denial/confession;
> announcement–response;
> apology–acceptance/refusal;
> assertion–agreement/dissent;
> boast–appreciation/derision;
> challenge–response;
> closing–closing;
> complaint–apology/denial;
> compliment–acceptance/rejection;
> greeting–greeting;
> insult–response;
> invitation–acceptance/refusal;
> offer–acceptance/refusal;
> question–answer;
> request–acceptance/rejection;
> summons–answer;
> threat–response.

Adjacency pairs are defined by Schegloff (1972, 2007) and Schegloff and Sacks (1973) as having the following features:

1. two-utterance length;
2. adjacent positioning of component utterances;[3]
3. different speaker producing each utterance;
4. relative ordering of parts (that is, first pair parts (FPPs) precede second pair parts (SPPs));
5. discrimination relations (that is, the pair type of which an FPP is a member is relevant to the selection among second pair parts).

7.6 CONDITIONAL RELEVANCE

The key point in the definition of adjacency pairs above is point 5, which accounts for how one utterance circumscribes the utterance which follows. This notion is developed further by the concept of conditional relevance (Schegloff, 1972: 76). According to the principle of conditional relevance, one utterance provides for the relevance of a following type of utterance by setting up an expectation of what is likely to follow. If the expected type of utterance does not occur, then it is 'an event' and is deemed to be 'officially', or 'notably' absent (Schegloff, 1972: 76). It is important to note the difference between this type of rule and the rules of syntax. In syntax, sequencing rules are prescriptive

– for example a subject is followed by a verb – but with adjacency pairs this is not the case. In fact, it is those situations where an anticipated SPP does not occur which demonstrate the robustness of the concept of conditional relevance.

7.7 PREFERENCE ORGANISATION

A refinement to the concept of conditional relevance is provided by the further notion of preference. Some adjacency pairs have only one central type of SPP. Greetings and farewells are examples of such pairs. For example, a greeting such as Hi! may have various return greetings, such as, Hi! Hi there! or Hello!, but the return greeting is the only type of SPP. Such reciprocal pairs (farewells are another example) are the exception, however. Most adjacency pairs have more than one possible type of SPP. For example, the expected response to an invitation is either an acceptance or a refusal. Similarly, a request may be granted or rejected. But the members of these pairs of responses are not equal in value; they are not 'symmetrical alternatives' (Schegloff & Sacks, cited in Schegloff, 2007: 59); one is 'preferred' over the other, which is said to be 'dispreferred'.

Preference is not a psychological characterisation, but a structural one; preferred responses are typically simpler, whilst dispreferred responses tend to be marked by various kinds of complexity, including delays, prefaces and accounts, (Pomerantz, 1984; see also Levinson, 1983: 334–335 for details and examples). Preference can thus also be thought of as an action that is played out structurally in various ways.

Compare the following two extracts. The first is an invitation and straightforward (preferred) acceptance, while the second is another invitation, but this time followed by a (dispreferred) decline.

Invitation – accept
1 Amy: w' d yuh like tuh come over t'morrow night
2 Jane: yea:h.= that' d be nice.

[Liddicoat, 2007: 110]

Invitation – decline
1 Harry: I don' have much tuh do on We : nsday
2   (.)
3   w' d yuh like tuh get together then.
4   (0.3)
5 Joy: huh we : : I lhh I don' really know if yuh see
6   i's a bit hectic fuh me We : nsday yih know
7 Harry: oh wokay

(Liddicoat, 2007: 110)

In the second of these examples, with the dispreferred SPP decline, we can see a number of delaying tactics and, in fact, there is no direct rejection at all. Dispreferred declines can be seen as rude or hostile, so extra conversational work is required in their performance.

The next example of an SPP decline is simpler, but it is still mitigated and attenuated; it is not a direct decline:

A: Is it near Edinburgh?
B: Edinburgh? It's not too far.

(Schegloff, 2007: 64, modified)

Because agreement is preferred over disagreement, (dispreferred) disagreement may be presented as if it were (preferred) agreement:

A: How about friends. Have you friends?
B: I have friends. So-called friends. I had friends. Let me put it that way.

(Sacks, cited in Schegloff, 2007: 66, modified)

In this pair, B's answer is shaped initially as an agreement, *I have friends*, but this apparent agreement is then mitigated as it becomes clear that s/he does not in fact have any friends, with the addition of *So-called friends* and the past tense *I had friends*.

As well as overall preference for agreement, where possible, there is preference for contiguity (Sacks, 1987). While it is possible for question-and-answer turns to contain extra information, there is a preference for FPPs and SPPs to come immediately next to each other. It only tends to be FPPs followed by dispreferred SPPs that are not contiguous. Such FPPs followed by dispreferred SPPs may contain a gap in between them, with the silence representing a gap in the continuity of the two parts; or the SPP may be prefaced with a delay, such as *uh*, a hedge (*I dunno*) or some other discourse marker such as *well*, or *anticipatory accounts*, as in the following example, where there is a combination of a turn initial marker (*well*), a hedge (*I don't know*), and an account (*I got a lot of things* …).

A: Yuh comin down early?
B: Well, I got a lot of things to do before getting cleared up tomorrow. I don't know. I w– probably won't be too early.

(Schegloff, 2007: 69, modified)

7.8 EXPANSION SEQUENCES

Adjacency pairs may be expanded in various ways. They may be prefaced by *pre-expansions*; they may be extended by *post-expansions*; and they may be expanded by *insert expansions*, where a sequence is inserted between the FPP and SPP of a base adjacency pair. Because these expansions are usually sequences in their own right, they are also referred to as *pre-sequences, post-sequences* and *insertion sequences*. Although they are sequences in their own right, however, they are treated as expansions of base adjacency pairs because they combine together with a base adjacency pair in the performance of a particular basic action.

7.8.1 Pre-expansions

Pre-sequences prepare the ground for what is to follow. They may be specific to particular actions, for example, pre-invitations ('I've got two tickets for the rugby match …'), pre-requests ('Are you busy right now?'), and pre-announcements ('You'll never guess!'). In addition, they may be generic, designed to project forward to any form of talk.

For reasons of space, we will only look at pre-invitations of the specific types, followed by the generic class. Schegloff divides pre-invitations into three types: *go-ahead, blocking* and *hedging*.

The go-ahead type promotes progress for the recipient to proceed with the base FPP which the pre-invitation is projecting. Clara's acceptance in the following example (l. 7, *Yeah*) is thus foreshadowed by Nelson's pre-invitation (l. 4, Watcha doin' .).

1   Clara: Hello
2   Nelson: Hi.
3   Clara: Hi.

```
 4   Nelson:  F_pre  →   Watcha doin'.
 5   Clara:   S_pre  →   Not much.
 6   Nelson:  F_b    →   Y'wanna drink?
 7   Clara:   S_b    →   Yeah.
 8   Nelson:             Okay.
```

(Schegloff, 2007: 30)

In the blocking type of pre-invitation, the pre-invitation raises the possibility that the invitation, if tendered, will be declined and thereby discourages, or blocks, the invitation in the first place. Thus, in the next example. Judy's *Well, we're going out* (l. 12) blocks John from following up on his pre-invitation FPP *Ha you doin – <say what 'r you doing.*

```
 1                      Ring
 2   Allen:             Hello?
 3   John:              Yeah, is Judy there?
 4   Allen:             Yeah, just a second.
 5                      ((silence))
 6   Judy:              Hello,
 7   John:              Judy?
 8   Judy:              Yeah,
 9   John:              John Smith.
10   Judy:              Hi John
11   John:   F_pre  →   Ha you doin –<say what 'r you doing.
12   Judy:   S_pre  →   Well, we're going out.
```

(Schegloff, 2007: 30)

In the third type of pre-invitation, the hedging pre-invitation, a full response is contingent on what the invitation is going to be. Thus Judy, in the next example, gives grounds for not proceeding to the invitation (l. 3 *We're going out*), then follows with a hint that the answer might change her response (l. 3 *Why*).

```
 1   Judy:              Hi John.
 2   John:   F_pre  →   Ha you doin–<say what 'r you doing.
 3   Judy:   S_pre  →   Well, we're going out. Why.
 4   John:          →   Oh, I was just gonna say come out and come over
 5                  →   here and talk this evening, [but if you're going=
 6   Judy:                                          ['Talk,' you mean get
 7                      [drunk, don't you? ]
 8   Judy:              =[out you can't very] well do that.
```

(Schegloff, 2007: 31)

It is to be noted that a block or hedge may or may not result in the invitation sequence occurring, but it is still classified as a pre-sequence even if it does not occur; 'It was done as a pre-invitation, in order to accomplish that action; it was heard that way and responded to that way as accomplishing that action' (Schegloff, 2007: 34).

Turning now to the generic type of pre-expansion, this is a sequence that is not designed to prepare for any particular type of action, but rather to gain the attention of an interlocutor in order to initiate any form of talk. It takes the form of summons–answer. A very common context for summons–answer is in conversational openings. Before it is even possible to begin a conversation, it is necessary to gain the attention of the chosen interlocutor. In the following example, in fact, the summons is repeated, presumably because it was not heard the first time:

```
1        C: Anne
2    →   A: ((Silence))
3    →   C: Anne
4        A: What
```

(Nofsinger, 1991, cited in Liddicoat, 2007: 127)

So, in this example, we have two adjacency pairs: first a summons–answer in lines 1 and 2, and then a greet–greet in lines 3–4.

Summons–answer sequences are not limited to conversational openings, however. They may also be found in ongoing talk where it is necessary to gain the attention of the intended interlocutor – 'where an intended recipient is currently engaged in some other activity, such as talking to a third participant, where the recipient has temporarily left the room, or where the intended recipient is not currently one's recipient in a multi-party conversation' (Liddicoat, 2007: 128). Levinson provides a simple example, presumably from a dinner-table setting:

```
A:   John?
B:   Yeah?
A:   Pass the water wouldja.
```

(Levinson, 1983: 310)

The FPP in the summons–answer sequence takes a variety of typical forms. It may be the name or title of the addressee, a politeness marker such as *Excuse me*, or physical contact (Schegloff, 2007: 127). SPPs may be performed by the addressee redirecting eye gaze to the summoner and with verbal forms such as *what*, or *yes/yeah* (Goodwin, 1981).

As with other pre-expansions, as well as go-ahead devices (as in the previous example), the summons–answer sequence has various blocking and hedging variations. Blocking may be effected by non-response to the summons, while hedging may involve some sort of forestalling or delay to further talk, such as 'I'm busy,' 'Just a moment,' 'Be right there,' 'I'm in the bathroom' and 'Leave me alone!' (Schegloff, 2007: 51).

With all pre-expansions, it is important to bear in mind that, although they are sequences in their own right, they are not complete. It is only in their relevance to what is to come next in the following base pair that they achieve their coherence, in projecting forward that some further talk will follow.

7.8.2 Post-expansions

Post-expansions follow and extend a preceding base adjacency pair. They may consist of a single turn or of a pair of turns. Single turns of this type are referred to as minimal post-expansions and are also called *sequence-closing thirds* (SCTs). SCTs typically take the form of particles or combinations of evaluative particles such as *oh* and *okay*, as in the following example.

```
1        Harry:   I don' have much tuh do on We:nsday.
2                 (.)
3                 w' d yuh like tuh get together then.
4                 (0.3)
5        Joy:     huh we::llhh yuh see things a bit hectic fuh
6                 me We:nsday yih know I don' really know
7    →   Harry:   Oh wokay
```

(Liddicoat, 2007: 157)

They may also take the form of evaluative lexical items such as *good* or *great*, as in the following sequence:

```
1        Annie:   we were wondering if if you' n Fra:nk w' d like
2                 to come over Sat' day night for a few drinks.
3        Sue:     Yeah we c' d do that.
4    →   Annie:   Goo::d.
```

(Liddicoat, 2007: 156)

Where a post-expansion takes the form of a pair of turns, its function is not to evaluate and close the base pair it is attached to, as was the case with the SCTs, but, on the contrary, to create a context for further talk. This is often the case when there is perceived to be some sort of trouble with an SPP and some form of repair is required. In the following sequence, for example, Nick, in his second turn, repeats part of what Sasha has just said [*sixth*], and this is confirmed by Elvis [*yeah*]. The initial adjacency pair is thus extended with a further (post-expansion) pair:

```
Nick:     on– [ which] day' s your anniversary?
Sasha:    Sixth. June.
Nick:     the sixth,
Elvis:    yeah,
```

(Liddicoat, 2007: 159)

7.8.3 Insert expansions

Insert expansions, also called *insertion sequences*, are adjacency pairs which expand other pairs by being inserted, or nested inside them. The function of the insert expansion is to clarify something on the part of the addressee before responding to the FPP, as in the next example.

```
1   I:    how would you descri:be (.) yourself
2         and your appearance and so on
3         (.)
4   R:    describe my appearance,
5   I:    Yeah
6         (1.0)
7   R:    su– su– slightly longer than average hair
          ((goes on to describe appearance))
```

(Hutchby & Wooffitt, 2008: 169)

Here, R's first turn in reply to I's FPP question is what Hutchby and Wooffitt (2008: 169) refer to as a 'question-seeking clarification/confirmation'. A response to this FPP is required, (I. 0) (*yeah*), before R provides the SPP to the initial question of the first turn.

In fact, there may be multiple nesting, referred to as *expansion of expansions* (Schegloff, 2007: 109), such that it may take a long time before the conditional relevance of an FPP is confirmed by the occurrence of its SPP (see Schegloff, 2007: 111–113 for a long example).

7.9 TOPIC MANAGEMENT

So far, we have seen how CA has looked at turns and pairs of turns (adjacency pairs), and also at various types of expansions. In all of the examples of data we have looked at thus far, however (except for the embedded insertion sequences), the sequences have been relatively short. Some-times, sequences are longer than those we have been looking at. In order to manage such longer turns, conversational participants need to be able to manage topics. This means being able to initiate topics, develop topics once they have been initiated, shift from one topic to another and terminate topics when a conversation reaches a close. The brief account of topic management which follows is based on that of Wong and Waring (2010).

7.9.1 Topic initiation

Topic initiation may occur at the beginning or end of a conversation, following a series of silences, or after the termination of a prior topic. There is a range of devices for initiating topics, including topic initial elicitors (for example, *What's new? How are you doing?*), specific news enquiries (*When are we going to get that new three-piece suite?*), news announcements (*I went to the ballet last night*), pre-topical sequences (*What do you do for a living? Where do you live?*), setting talk (*Nice weather we're having, This train is taking a long time to get here*).

7.9.2 Topic pursuit

It is not always the case that topic initiations are taken up. Where this is the case, participants may further insist on pursuing the introduced topic. In the following example, Maggie has elicited a topic with *What have you been up to?*, but Lawrence is not very responsive. Maggie, accordingly, follows up with a topic initial elicitor (specific news enquiry), *You're still in the real estate business Lawrence?*

```
1   Maggie:          .h What have you been up to.
2                    (0.5)
3   Lawrence:        We:ll about the same thing. One thing
4                    Anoth [er. I should
5   Maggie:    →           [You're still in the real estate business
6                    Lawrence?
```
                                (Button & Casey, cited in Wong & Waring, 2010: 113)

7.9.3 Topic shift

Topic shift occurs within a given topic sequence when one of the participants proposes that they move to another topic. It may happen in one of two ways: disjunctive topic shift and stepwise topic shift.

The following is the list of disjunctive markers provided by Crow (cited in Wong & Waring 2010: 116). These markers are used when a participant wants to mark a move into a new topic as abrupt or not highly relevant to the ongoing conversation.

- Anyway;
- All right;
- Oh;
- Speaking of X;
- That reminds me of;
- Oh say;

- I tell you what;
- One more thing;
- Listen, there's something I've gotta tell you;
- You know what?
- Before I forget;
- By the way;
- Incidentally.

The following is a good example of disjunctive topic shift, with the use of the marker *anyway*:

```
1  Lesley:        He had a good innings did [n't he.
2  Mum:                                     [I should say so:
3                 Ye:s
4                 (0.2)
5  Mum:           Marvelous,
6  Lesley:   →   .hhh Anyway we had a very good evening on
7                 Saturda:y …
```

                                    (Drew, cited in Wong & Waring, 2010: 118)

Stepwise topic shift is a smoother way than disjunctive topic shift of moving from one topic to another. It is smoother because a transition, rather than a break, is marked between the two topics. In the following example, the three examples of *Okay* both at the same time refer to the topic in progress, in signalling agreement, and prepare the way for new topical activity. Furthermore, in the first example, there is a semantic link between the two topics, as represented by *Jill*, who is a participant in both of them:

```
1  C:         I guess the ba:nd starts at ni:ne.
2  D:         Oh really?
3  C:         Yah from what Jill told me.
4  D:    →   Okay when's Jill gonna go.
5  C:         Same time (0.2) we're gonna meet her there.
6  D:    →   Okay um (0.5) so you wa:nt to take your car
7  C:         We can take your car if you wa:nt.
8  D:         .hhh hhh I mean you want– you wanna have your
9             car there so you can le:ave.
10 C:         Yeah I think that's be a better idea.
11            Okay.
12            (0.5)
13 D:    →   Okay hhhh we;; what what time is it now °I don't
14            have my watch on.
15 C:         Six o'clock.
```

                                (Beach, 1993, cited in Wong & Waring, 2010: 121)

7.9.4 Topic termination

Topics can be closed down by pre-closing items such as *well* or *okay*. *Assessment tokens* such as *great, good, that's good, oh splendid,* and *lovely* are typically used to close off topics and whole conversations, as in this next example, with the pre-closings *okay* and *well* and the assessment token *lovely*, which is the final topic of the conversation:

```
1   Ed:         I think she'd like to.
2               (0.2)
3   Les:   →    Hm:hn– [Okay then. [Right [well
4   Ed:                [So–        [(yes) I ['ll see you on–
5               on Thursday at six thirty then.
6   Les:   →    Lovely
7   Ed:         I(   )
8   Les:        [] Bye bye then,
9   Ed:         Bye:,
```

(Antaki, cited in Wong & Waring, 2010: 126)

7.10 STORIES

An important frequent manifestation of longer turns is when individuals tell a story. Stories do not happen in isolation, however, and, in studying stories, it is important to consider the interactional context in which they occur. Speakers need to create a space within the ongoing action in which to insert the story and to establish the fact that they are going to take a longer turn. And recipients need to indicate their understanding of the ongoing talk as they listen, by the use of continuers, which indicate that they are forgoing the opportunity to take a complete turn. They also need to do this at the end of a story, to indicate their understanding that the story has been completed, show their appreciation of its meaning and its potential to generate further talk.

We can see how these features function by taking an example of story-telling from Hutchby and Wooffitt (2008: 127).

```
1    L:   Are you not feeling very [we:ll,
2    J:                            [°(  )°
3         (.)
4    J:   No I'm all ri:ght
5         (.)
6    L:   Yes.
7         (0.6)
8    J:   °Ye:s I'm all right, °
9    L:   °Oh:. ° .hh Yi–m– You know I– I– I'm broiling about
10        something hhhheh[heh . hhhh
11   J:                   [Wha::t.
12   L:   Well that sa:le. (0.2) At– at (.) the vicarage.
13        (0.6)
14   J:   Oh ye[:s,
15   L:        [.t
16        (0.6)
17   L:   u (.) ih Your friend 'n mi:ne was there:re
18        (0.2)
19   J:   (h[h hh)
20   L:     [mMister:, R:,
21   J:   Oh y(h)es, °(hm hm)°
22        (0.4)
23   L:   And em: .p we (.) really didn't have a lot'v cha:nge
24        that (.) day becuz we'd been to Bath 'n we'd been:
25        Christmas shoppin:g, (0.5) but we thought we'd better
```

```
26        go along t'th'sale 'n do what we could, (0.2) we
27        hadn't got a lot (.) of s:e– ready cash t'spe:nd.
28        (0.6)
29   L:   In any case we thought th' things were very
30        expensive
31   J:   Oh did you.
32        (0.9)
33   L:   AND uh we were looking round the sta:lls 'n poking
34        about 'n he came up t' me 'n he said Oh: h:hello
35        Lesley, (.) still trying to buy something f'nothing,
36        .tch! .hh[hahhhhhhh!
37   J:            [.hhoonnnn!
38        (0.8)
39   J:   Oo[: : :[ : L e s l e y]
40   L:     [OO:. [ehh heh heh ]
41        (0.2)
42   J:   I:s[ n 't ]      [he
43   L:      [What] do y[ou sa:y.
44        (0.3)
45   J:   Oh isn't he dreadful.
46   L:   °eYe::s.°
47        (0.6)
48   J:   What'n aw::ful ma[::n
49   L:                    [eh heh heh heh
50   J:   Oh:: honestly I cannot stand the man it's just
51        (no[:     )
52   L:      [I thought well I'm gon' tell Joyce that, ehh heh
```

(Hutchby & Wooffitt, 2008: 124–125)

In this example, the story begins with a preface. Following the canonical structure of story prefaces, the preface we have in this story is a three-part structure of: (1) story preface: *You know, I'm broiling about something*; (2) a request to hear the story on the part of the recipient: *What?* and (3) the beginning of the story itself, with the recipient suitably prepared for the story: *Well, that sale at the vicarage*. As the story progresses, we see how, although transition relevance points occur and the recipient of the story is given plenty of opportunities to take the floor, these opportunities are not taken up, the recipient merely indicating that she is orienting to the story with, for example, *oh yes* (l.14), *oh did you* (l.31), *yes* (l. 46), and *no* (l. 51) and with non-verbal acknowledgements (for example, 1.19, l.39, l.49). As indicated by Hutchby and Wooffitt (2008), there is a lot more going on in this extract, but these are perhaps the points of most interest with regard to a CA approach to stories. One feature not discussed by Hutchby and Wooffitt (2008), however, with regard to this story, is the ending. We can note how the recipient, J, in line 50–51, indicates that she has understood that the story has come to an end, *Oh:: honestly I cannot stand the man*, another important role of the recipient in the joint negotiation of stories.

7.11 REPAIR

Repair refers to the suspension of ongoing talk, in order to deal with some sort of *trouble*, where trouble refers to hearing, production or understanding. Repair is not a negative phenomenon, indicative of some deficiency, but a natural self-regulating device which is prevalent in all talk.

Indeed, repair plays an important role in maintaining the overall coherence of talk and making total breakdown the very rare occurrence that it is.

There are four main types of repair (see, for example, Wong and Waring (2010) for further sub-categories): (1) self-initiated self-completed; (2) self-initiated other-completed; (3) other-initiated self-completed; and (4) other-initiated other-completed.

7.11.1 Self-initiated self-completed

The speaker himself or herself identifies the cause of the trouble and resolves it:

```
1        Olive:   Yih know Mary uh:::: (0.3) oh:: what was it.
2    →             Uh:: Tho:mpson.
```

(Schegloff et al., 1977: 363, modified)

7.11.2 Self-initiated other-completed

The speaker himself or herself identifies the cause of the trouble, but the recipient resolves it.

```
1        A:   He had dis uh Mistuh W— whatever k— I can't think of his first name, Watts
             on, the one thet wrote I/ that piece,
2    →   B:   Dan Watts.
```

(Schegloff et al., 1977: 364, modified)

7.11.3 Other-initiated self-completed

The recipient of the trouble identifies it and resolves it himself or herself.

```
1        A:   Hey the first time they stopped me from selling cigarettes was this morning.
2    →   B:   From selling cigarettes?
3        A:   From buying cigarettes. They // said uh
```

(Schegloff et al., 1977: 370, modified)

7.11.4 Other-initiated other-completed

The recipient of the trouble identifies it and the speaker resolves it.

```
1        Joy:    Kerry's no good. She's haven a fight with Sally.
2    →   Harry:  Yih mean Sarah dontchuh. Those two are always fightin'
```

(Liddicoat, 2007: 190, modified)

It is important to note that there is a general preference for self-initiated over other-initiated repair (Schegloff et al., 1977).

Repair is clearly a significant topic for language teaching. Both teachers and learners need to be made aware that repair is a natural part of linguistic interaction and that self-correction and other correction are an intrinsic part of the negotiation of meaning. Such knowledge can, indeed, be liberating for learners.

7.12 INSTITUTIONAL TALK

So far, in our account of the major patterns identified in CA, we have taken examples from everyday conversation, which was the original focus of CA and remains today the canonical form. Levinson (1983: 318) wrote as follows, 'there are … many kinds of talk – for example, courtroom or classroom interrogation – which exhibit features of conversational activity like turn-taking, but which are clearly not conversations'. It was not soon after CA began, in fact, that attention began to be turned to other more institutional forms of talk such as the courtroom and classroom mentioned by Levinson.[4]

Institutional talk is investigated by taking everyday conversation as the benchmark and looking for distinctive features of the institutional talk in question (Hutchby & Wooffitt, 2002: 140). Institutional talk is not fundamentally different from everyday talk, but involves either a reduction in the turn-taking options available in everyday talk or a specialisation of the range of practices taken up (Hutchby & Wooffitt, 2002: 140). Furthermore, institutional talk can be categorised into two types: formal and non-formal. The formal type includes courts of law, many kinds of interview and 'traditional' teacher-led classrooms. Non-formal types, which are more loosely structured than the formal types, include doctor consultations, counselling sessions, social work encounters, business meetings, service encounters and radio phone-ins (Hutchby & Wooffitt, 2002: 140).

In the formal category of institutional talk, participants orient to a specific turn-taking format, referred to by Atkinson and Drew (1979) as *turn type pre-allocation*. In the types of institutional interaction in question, institutional participants ask the questions and the lay participants, whether they be witnesses, pupils or interviewees, are expected to provide the answers. The following example, which is taken from a rape trial, clearly shows this pattern:

```
 1  A:  You have had sexual intercourse on a previous
 2      occasion haven't you.
 3  B:  Yes.
 4  A:  On many previous occasions?
 5  B:  Not many.
 6  A:  Several?
 7  B:  Yes.
 8  A:  With several men?
 9  B:  No.
10  A:  Just one?
11  B:  Two.
12  A:  Two. And you are seventeen and a half?
13  B:  Yes.
```

(Levinson, cited in Hutchby & Wooffitt, 2008: 142)

Traditional classroom teaching, another type of institutional talk, also has its own preferred pattern of turn type pre-allocation, commonly referred to as *IRF* (initiation–response–feedback/follow-up),[5] as in:

```
Teacher:  What's the capital of France?
Pupil:    Paris
Teacher:  Yes, good.
```

In non-formal institutional talk, as already stated, the constraints are less rigid than with the formal type. Although there might be a general orientation towards institutional goals, there is much more room for variation in the turn-taking patterns. This permeability between the institutional and everyday domains presents a challenge for the analyst. One way to deal with this challenge, as mentioned earlier, is to take everyday talk as the benchmark and examine to what extent the non-informal type deviates from the everyday. With regard to the medical interview, Maynard and Heritage (2005: 431) have commented as follows:

> interactional practices through which persons conduct themselves elsewhere are transported from the everyday world into the doctor's office. Accordingly, studies of the medical interview draw upon the plenitude of previous CA research concerned with ordinary conversation.

Thus, studies of the various phases of the medical interview, including its opening, its closing, its history, physical exam, diagnosis, and treatment recommendations have all drawn on similar patterns in everyday talk (Maynard & Heritage, 2005). Heritage (1997: 164) lists six areas where the 'institutionality of interaction' might be investigated:

1. turn-taking organisation;
2. overall structural organisation of the interaction;
3. sequence organisation;
4. turn design;
5. lexical choice;
6. interactional asymmetries.

With regard to pedagogy, CA approaches to various types of institutional talk are clearly relevant to work in English for Specific Purposes (ESP) (Bowles & Seedhouse, 2007). CA's emphasis on the permeability of the interface between everyday and institutional talk is an important one for ESP, with potential for a more sophisticated approach to the question of specific versus general approaches to teaching.

7.13 CA ACROSS CULTURES

CA studies of talk across cultures can provide the basis for comparison of L1 and L2 norms, with its potential for application to pedagogy (see Schegloff et al., 2002, for references). Schegloff et al. (2002) argue that CA may offer a broader conception of Interlanguage Pragmatics than the current model (see Chapter 5); where Interlanguage Pragmatics is limited to the single speech act as its unit of analysis, CA can offer sequential organisation.

As a first example of how this might work, Paltridge (2005/2006: 116) reports a study by Béal (1992) of workplace English involving French and Australian speakers of English. The Australians in the workplace in question were frustrated when, in response to their greeting of *Did you have a good weekend?* their French counterparts gave what they considered to be over-lengthy accounts of their activities. The Australians did not realise that these accounts could be explained by the fact that *Did you have a good weekend?* is not a normal way to open a conversation for French speakers and that it was interpreted as a real request for information. This example shows how FPPs and their corresponding SPPs can differ across cultures.

As a second, lengthier, example, the results of a monograph by Cheng (2003) contrasting Hong Kong Chinese (HKC) and Native English speakers of English (NESs) and using a CA framework also demonstrated differences in how these two groups perform certain sequences. Cheng had five major findings in the conflict management situations she studied.

1. HKC employed a greater number of instances of and more elaborate redressive language in their disagreements than did the NE speakers.
2. HKC responses to compliment ranged from no verbal response or a continuer to outright rejection of the compliment, while NES responses were always in the form of accepting the compliment. (Cheng explains this finding in terms of the Western notion of minimising or avoiding self-praise [Pomerantz, 1984] and the contrasting Chinese politeness notion of 'self-denigration' and 'other elevation' [Gu, 1990]).
3. HKC preferred a 'one-at-a-time' model to turn-taking, while the NESs favoured more overlapping of turns.
4. HKC were more likely to initiate topics than NESs.
5. HKC preferred an inductive style of sequencing information as compared to the more deductive style of the NESs.

These findings clearly have significance for intercultural communication and language teaching.[6]

7.14 CRITIQUE

One of the challenges to CA is the difficulty of doing it. Wilkinson and Kitzinger (2008: 69) describe this challenge as follows:

> CA work is extremely demanding of the researcher. It is very time-consuming and labour-intensive – from initial transcription (which is a pre-requisite for analysis), through the various phases of analysis itself. It is also extremely complicated, and requires extensive training in concepts and techniques before it can be used effectively.

From a theoretical perspective, CA has been critiqued on a number of counts. First, it has been criticised for its lack of systematicity (Eggins & Slade, 2005). There is no finite set of adjacency pairs and there is no set of criteria for recognising them. In addition, CA is not a quantitative approach (for the most part). There is no way of comparing the relative frequencies of the various units of analysis (Eggins & Slade, 2005). Furthermore, CA has been criticised for its failure to take account of context or the psychological motivation of the participants in turn-taking, as is the case in alternative theories, such as Critical Discourse Analysis (CDA) or ethnography (see Waring *et al.*, in press for review). Based on these criticisms, there have been various calls to combine CA with other social research methodologies, such as CDA or ethnography (for example, Stubbe *et al.*, 2003).

Notwithstanding these critiques, CA offers a theory and methodology which allow us to understand how talk is used in interaction in both everyday and institutional practices. It offers a clear and replicable methodology and a body of research findings against which ongoing studies can be bench-marked.

Specifically regarding foreign- and second-language learning contexts, contrastive work offers the possibility of highlighting differences in how talk is organised across cultures, with its potential for feeding into syllabus and materials design. More broadly, CA offers a powerful model of talk which can serve as a target for learning and for understanding and intervening in classroom interaction.

7.15 APPLICATION TO PEDAGOGY

7.15.1 CA and research in second-language acquisition

Until the late 1990s, Chomsky's rationalist theory of universal grammar had been predominant in second-language acquisition (SLA) research. Since then, however, in line with a more social view of learning (also referred to as *socially distributed learning*) and along with other recent sociolinguistic and sociocultural approaches (for example, Kramsch, 2000; Lantolf & Pavlenko, 2001), CA has begun to take up a place in SLA research and theory building.[7]

While the Chomskyan approach is theory-driven, based on the idea that research is conducted to test the theory (in the case of SLA, Chomsky's theory), as we have seen, CA is based on a more social, participant-relevant account. The argument for CA for SLA (more recently referred to as CA-SLA) is that the microanalytic methodology, based as it is on participant behaviour, allows researchers to reveal the detailed features of interaction and develop an account which has the potential to elucidate how and when learning comes about or fails to come about.

As with mainstream CA, the focus of CA-SLA is on sequence organisation, turn-taking, repair, the structure of speech events and integration of speech with gesture.[8] This focus, in common with mainstream CA, is achieved through the examination of detailed transcriptions of collections of cases of ordinary or individual cases of (classroom) practices (Brouwer & Wagner, 2004). One particular aspect of this developing focus is a move towards more longitudinal studies, given SLA's interest in language development (Brouwer & Wagner, 2004; Markee, 2008).

Typical findings of CA-SLA are to be found in the work of Markee (2000). Markee has highlighted, for example, the interactional differences between teacher-fronted and small-group second-language interactions; he has also shown how, in second-language interactions – in common with first-language interaction – there is a preference for self-initiated repair over other-initiated repair; he has, furthermore, shown how learners may cannibalise TCUs that occur in prior interactions in order to recycle them in novel, complex ways (Markee, 2000). Other specific findings of CA in SLA that are worthy of mention include those of Wagner (2004), who has shown how teachers and learners orient to different participant frameworks and shift their orientation as an interaction progresses. Further interesting findings are provided by Ohta (2001), who has demonstrated how, in the IRF pattern of classroom interaction, material which recurrently appears in the teacher's follow-up turns eventually emerges in students' production, thus demonstrating the teaching potential of the IRF pattern. As a final example, Waring (2009) has demonstrated how certain participation structures create speaking opportunities for fellow participants in learner–learner interactions.

An important limitation of CA in SLA is that it is often not possible to identify successful learning, because there is no external behaviour to demonstrate it. Only a relatively small part of SLA is thus observable through talk, but CA is nevertheless a powerful tool with which to examine what there is (Markee, 2008).

7.15.2 CA and teaching and learning

An appreciation of the principles and practices of CA can develop awareness on the part of teachers of the nature of talk, which is the target of the teaching of speaking and listening skills in both first- and second-language contexts. More than this, though, in its focus on what Heritage and Atkinson (cited in Kasper, 2006: 86) refer to as 'the competences that ordinary speakers use and rely on in participating in intelligible, socially organized interaction', CA provides a goal for teaching and learning. In second-language research, these competences are referred to together as *interactional competence* and, according to Markee (2000), they include three practices: sequential organisation, turn-taking and repair. Kasper (2006) breaks interactional competence down further, into the following capacities:

- to understand and produce social actions in their sequential contexts;
- to take turns at talk in an organised fashion;
- to format actions and turns, and construct epistemic and affective stance, by drawing on different types of semiotic resources (linguistic, non-verbal, non-vocal), including register-specific resources;
- to repair problems in speaking, hearing and understanding;
- to co-construct social and discursive identities through sequence organisation, actions-in-interaction and semiotic resources;
- to recognise and produce boundaries between activities, including transitions from states of contact to absence of contact (interactional openings, closings) and transitions between activities during continued contact.

How might this operate in practice? To take an example, awareness of the intricacies of the turn-taking practices of the target culture can help learners communicate more effectively and avoid cross-cultural pragmatic failure (Thomas, 1983). Familiarity with the typical wordings of certain types of turn, to take another example, can similarly assist in the development of interactional competence. As Wong and Waring (2010: 125) put it, '[l]ittle words and phrases such as *actually*, *anyway*, or *by the way* carry nuanced interactional meanings'. Understanding of the importance of recipient design and the importance of continuers in story-telling is another salient example of how the findings of CA can benefit learners. Awareness of the conventions of topic shift and of repair is similarly invaluable in developing oral proficiency.

Insights from CA can help textbook writers in designing more authentic learning materials, as is increasingly being recommended (for example, Thornbury, 2005b). Too often, textbook dialogues fail to represent what talk is actually like (Wong, 2002, 2007). This is a problem from the very beginning of learning, where, for example, there is a lot of emphasis on opening a conversation. CA has placed a lot of emphasis on examining this crucial stage of spoken interaction. Unfortunately, the findings are too rarely applied by materials designers.

Bowles and Seedhouse (2007) present a model for applying CA findings to the classroom in Languages for Specific Purposes (LSP) contexts. The model consists of two stages. In a first stage, a CA description is created of the target interaction. This then forms the basis for the second stage, which applies the description to develop pedagogical methods and materials. Following Basturkmen and Crandell (2004), Bowles and Seedhouse (2007) call for analysis on the part of learners of CA transcripts, arguing that this can have positive effects on students' perception of appropriacy and bring them closer to native speaker targets. At the same time, they critique Basturkmen and Crandell (2004) for not providing a detailed enough transcript in their article, arguing that the omission of pause length marks, for example, makes the transcript resemble a Pinter play rather than a genuine conversation. For Bowles and Seedhouse (2007), a detailed transcript is essential if *interactional* competence is to be the goal and not just *pragmatic* competence.

Bowles and Seedhouse (2007) argue that, for LSP, interactional competence will be specific to each institutional domain, although they add that the same principles can be applied to general-purposes language teaching. In LSP, the approach can be to compare transcripts from general and institutional contexts. Bowles and Seedhouse (2007) give the example of Wong (2007), who showed the importance of focusing on particular practices that have been identified by CA as significant in the target domain, in Wong's case the problematic feature of 'moving out of closings', where signalling procedures are essential for successful conversational closure.

Bowles and Seedhouse (2007) also have specific recommendations for classroom activities with transcripts. Following Burns *et al.* (1997), they recommend listening and transcription completion exercises for identifying particularly significant interactional features. In addition, transcripts can be the focus of classroom discussion, which might include comparison of successful and less successful interactional features of conversations. Furthermore, Bowles and Seedhouse (2007) suggest comparing authentic transcriptions with published learning materials and highlighting the reality observable in the authentic data *vis-à-vis* the inadequacies of the published materials. Another recommended classroom activity is the comparison of L1 and L2 transcripts (Burns *et al.*, 1997).

Bowles and Seedhouse (2007) sum up their discussion by noting that 'there is now a growing body of LSP classroom methods and activities which can make use of CA results in order to provide the interactional focus we are advocating for LSP materials'. Most of these activities, it might be argued, are equally applicable in non-specific, general language teaching.

Wong and Waring (2010) highlight the relevance of CA findings in three areas of instructional practices: repair, task design and management of participation. For repair, they show how CA descriptions provide for a wider range of alternatives for dealing with problematic learner contributions. For task design, they demonstrate how analysis has shown that the most authentic tasks in the language classroom often turn out to be the off-task talk. This is because, when off task, learners can be engaged in solving real-life problems. Wong and Waring argue, therefore, for the relevance and usefulness of off-task activity. For the management of participation, they argue that teachers need to consider how their actions affect learner participation. For turn design, for example, teachers can encourage participation by, for example, leaving their turns incomplete or leaving the F (feedback/follow-up) slot empty in the IRF sequence.

CA clearly has a lot to offer language pedagogy, both in terms of providing goals for learning and in terms of specific classroom practices.

7.16 QUESTIONS FOR DISCUSSION

1. Think about what might be the challenges in teaching everyday conversation. Make a list of five such challenges.
2. Consider the rules for turn-taking in section 7.3. Write a similar set of rules for the interaction in a typical university seminar.
3. Look at the list of adjacency pairs in section 7.5. Select the five pairs that might be most useful for a beginners' course.
4. Write short dialogues for language learning, illustrating: (a) pre-sequencing; and (b) insertion sequencing.
5. Why is topic management important in conversation?
6. Why is repair important in language learning? What are the differences, if any, between L1 and L2 repair?
7. Can you think of any cross-cultural differences relating to conversation, such as those reported by Béal and Cheng in section 7.13?
8. Look at the dialogues in a language learning course book. To what extent do they correspond to authentic conversational patterns? If they are different, what are these differences and what are the possible drawbacks and advantages of this?
9. What do you consider to be some of the most important insights from CA for language learning and teaching? List five.

7.17 FURTHER READING

Liddicoat, 2007; Schegloff, 2007; Sidnell, 2010; Wong and Waring, 2010.

CHAPTER 8

Genre Analysis

8.1 INTRODUCTION

The term 'genre' can be traced as far back as Aristotle; it means 'kind' or 'form' and was used by the Greek philosopher in his *Poetics* to refer to major types of literature: poetry, drama and the epic. These divisions have expanded considerably, but the notion of genre as a particular type of literature has lasted into the present era. At the same time, it has been extended to refer to more popular cultural forms: soap opera, film noir, western, thriller. These are terms which have entered into the popular consciousness and which are studied in the fields of cultural and media studies. In the field of Applied Linguistics and Educational Linguistics, however, the term 'genre' is used rather differently and refers to different communicative events which are associated with particular settings and which have recognised structures and communicative functions. Examples of genres according to this conceptualisation would be business reports, academic lectures, news articles, recipes, religious sermons, political speeches, curriculum vitae, and more recent 'virtual' genres such as various types of e-mails, text messages, instant messages, tweets and Facebook pages.

Given the distinctive features of individual genres, they are amenable to pedagogic exploitation; systematic descriptions of the distinguishing features of genres, of how they are produced and how they are received provide targets for learning. In first-language contexts, some genres are acquired naturally in the home, but many have to be taught through the formal education system. In second-language contexts, especially those where there is little or no exposure to first-language contexts, all genres may need to be taught to a greater or lesser extent.

8.2 GENRE AND REGISTER

In the literature, as pointed out in note 1 in Chapter 2 on register, there is sometimes confusion between the terms 'genre' and 'register'. It is important to differentiate the two, although there will inevitably be some overlap. In Chapter 2, we defined register as a type of language associated with a particular field of activity or profession. Given genres may also be associated with particular fields of activity or professions, but, as characterised in the previous section, in this book, they are specific communicative events. Instruction manuals (a type of genre) may be used in the field of aviation, by airline pilots, but they are also used in many other fields and by many other professions. Lectures are another example of a genre mentioned in the previous section. Lectures are attended by students of mathematics, but they are also attended by students in other fields. Lectures, therefore, represent a genre, but not a register. Another way of pinpointing the distinction between register and genre is in terms of communicative purpose. Register is a type of language associated with a particular field or profession, but this language may be used for various purposes. Communicative purpose, on the other hand, is a distinctive feature of genres. Martin (1993: 2), indeed, defines genre as 'a category that describes the relation of the social purpose of text to language structure'. The purpose of a lecture is didactic; the purpose of a news article is informative; the purpose of a news commentary is persuasive.

Although communicative purpose may be considered as a defining characteristic of genres and a key one in distinguishing it from register, to define it simply in these terms is not sufficient. Indeed, various linguists have identified limitations to communicative purpose as a defining characteristic. Askehave and Swales (2001) note that it is often difficult to ascribe purposes to texts, thus making it difficult to consider purpose as a defining criterion: 'If communicative purpose is typically ineffable at the outset, or only establishable after considerable research, or can lead to disagreements between "inside" experts and "outside" genre analysts, or indeed among the experts themselves, how can it be retained as a "privileged" guiding criterion?' (p. 197). Bhatia (1993, 2004) talks about how writers have what he calls 'private intentions' in addition to more transparent socially recognised communicative purposes when they create a text/genre. They may seek to manipulate the generic characteristics for their own personal motives. A book review may have evaluation of the object of the review as its recognised communicative purposes, but a reviewer might at the same time seek to criticise the author for personal reasons. Similarly, a question asked in a conference may have the recognised purpose of eliciting information from the speaker, but may, at the same time, seek to undermine the speaker's credibility or demonstrate the questioner's knowledge.

8.3 OTHER CHARACTERISTIC FEATURES OF GENRE

There are a number of other features, in addition to purpose, which have been cited as distinguishing genres.

8.3.1 Staging

First, and this is perhaps the most easily recognised feature of many genres, they are staged. By staged, we mean that a genre has a specific sequential structure (which it follows more or less strictly). We can exemplify this if we consider *instructions* as a genre. Instructions typically follow a series of stages as in the following simple example (Figure 8.1), noted in a guest house (Alishan International Guest House) kitchen during a recent visit to Australia. Each stage in this text/genre, reading down each column and starting on the left, represents a different instruction or prohibition.[1] The three sets of instructions are organised under the three headings of 'SAY THE KITCHEN', 'FOOD ITEMS' and 'SAFETY ISSUES'.

8.3.2 Communities of practice

Another characteristic feature of genres is that they belong to particular communities of users (Bhatia, 1993, 2004; Swales, 1990, 2004). Lectures, for example, are engaged in by teachers and students. News articles involve journalists and newspaper readers. People who do not belong to such *discourse communities* or *communities of practice* may find it more or less difficult to participate in the relevant genres. Clearly, it takes a lot of expert knowledge to write an academic article in a given field. As Bhatia (2004: 25) notes, established members of a given professional community are likely to have a much better understanding of a genre than apprentices or outsiders. Outsiders are easily identified as such by members of discourse communities. On the other hand, certain genres are familiar to most people. The instruction genre exemplified in Figure 8.1 is a good example

Alishan

International Guest House

I am happy for you to cook and use my utensils but you must follow my rules.

SAY THE KITCHEN	FOOD ITEMS	SAFETY ISSUES
I am happy for you to cook and use my utensils but you must follow my rules	*Mark your name or room number on all your food items.	*Never put the HOT pots and pans on the countertops as it will burn the tops.
*You make a mess – You clean it up	*Once a week the cupboards and fridge will be cleaned, any food items without markings will be removed.	*Never leave the burners or the toaster on unattended. If you need to get something, ask someone else to watch over your burner or the toaster.
*You use them – You wash them		
*You wet them – You dry them		*In case of a small grease fire, DO NOT use water, this will only spread the fire without putting it out. Use the lid of a pot or fire blanket to over the area.
*You remove them – You put them back If you think these rules are too tough please do not use the kitchen!		*If your activity in the kitchen area activates the fire alarm the $530 Fire Brigade callout fee will be charged to you.

Figure 8.1   Instructions text.

of a genre that many people would be familiar with. Swales (1990) argues that casual conversation and narrative ('genres' with which we are all familiar) are outside the purview of Genre Analysis, being somehow prior to more institutionalised and specialised genres and classing them as 'pre-genres'.[2] This claim is debatable, however. Eggins and Slade (2005), for example, have broken down 'conversation' into a range of 'sub-genres' for the 'macro-genre' of conversation, as follows:

narrative;
anecdote;
exemplum;
recount;
observation/comment;
opinion;
gossip.

This question of 'pre-genres' and professional genres is an important one for pedagogy. If genres are only located in professional discourse, they may best be dealt with within the context of English for Specific Purposes (ESP) programmes. If they extend beyond specialised fields, then they can legitimately claim a place within the 'general English' curriculum.

8.3.3 Conventionalised lexicogrammatical features

A further characteristic ascribed to genre is that of conventionalised lexicogrammatical features (for example, Bhatia, 1993, 2004; Swales, 1990).[3] If we look at our example of instructions in Figure 8.1 above, we can note a certain number of typical lexicogrammatical features. For example, the use of parallel grammatical structure for many of the instructions and the use of material process verbs (for example, *make a mess, clean up, use, wash, wet, dry*) is easily recognised as a feature of this particular genre. On the other hand, we can see a certain individual creativity in this particular example of the instructions genre, for example, the rather quirky heading *SAY THE KITCHEN*, and how the instructions in the left-hand column are presented as oppositional pairs – *You make a mess/You clean it up, You use them/You wash them*. Furthermore, most of the instructions in the left-hand column are not worded as imperatives, as is more typically the case with instructions (and as we find in the right-hand column), but with what might be called reduced conditionals *([If] you make a mess, you [must] clean it up, [If] you use them, you [must] wash them)*. Some genres are more conventionalised than others. Oaths of office, marriage vows and formal written invitations, for example, tend to be quite formulaic. Kuiper's (2009) book, *Formulaic Genres*, deals with weather forecasts, livestock auctions, the chanting of tobacco auctioneers, supermarket check-out talk, pump aerobics, square-dancing and engagement notices, among other genres), all of which are classed as formulaic by Kuiper.

8.3.4 Recurrent nature of genres

We have noted how genres are conventionalised to a greater or lesser extent in terms of their communicative purposes, their staging, their lexicogrammatical patterning and how they are conventionally used by particular communities. Conventionality is an important feature when we come to consider how genre knowledge is acquired. Genre knowledge develops through repeated exposure and practice. Knowledge acquired through repeated exposure is stored in the form of what psychologists refer to as *schemata* (singular, *schema*), which are mental representations used to store information. These representations create expectations which are invoked when individuals participate in the performance of genres. If some generic feature meets our expectations in terms of our model of a given genre, then it is stored in memory as belonging to that genre. If a generic feature does not meet our generic expectations, then it is stored separately. This is how genre knowledge is built up over time and through repeated exposure. We can thus say that its *recurrent* nature is another important feature of genre.

8.3.5 Genre as a flexible concept

Given the hedging and provisos which have been given for each of these features in the above discussion (the 'more or less' nature of each of the features discussed), a 'flexible' rather than a 'static' view is required (Paltridge, 2005/2006: 89). Indeed, a number of scholars have argued that genre is beyond definition. Swales (2004), for example, prefers to talk about metaphors rather than definitions with respect to genres, on the grounds that definitions are not 'true in all possible worlds and all possible times' (cited in Paltridge, 2006: 86). Similarly, Paltridge (2006: 89) argues for genres to be considered as *prototypes* rather than defining features:[4]

> There may be typical ways in which they are organised at the discourse level, typical situations in which they occur, and typical things they 'aim to do'. It is not always the case, however, that these will necessarily be the same in every instance, even though they may be in the majority of cases.

Finally, Kress (2003: 101) has rather eloquently written about the tension around the claimed conventional features of genre, referring to:

> the fundamental tension around genre, hovering uneasily between regularity and replicability on the one hand ... and the dynamic for constant flux and change on the other hand.

8.3.6 Genre relations

Increasingly, genre scholars have come to acknowledge that, in order to conduct an adequate analysis, it is necessary to take into account other genres with which the target genre interacts (Bhatia, 2004; Swales, 2004). We can use the umbrella term *genre relation* to refer to the range of different ways individual instances of a genre can relate to other genres. Devitt (1991) uses the term *genre set* to refer to a range of text genres which a professional group uses in the course of their daily routine, for example, a conference presentation, a poster and a research article in the case of academics. Bazerman (1994: 97) talks about *systems of genres*. A genre system, for Bazerman, is a full set of genres which constitute a complete interaction (for example, a complete exchange of letters).

Raisanen (2002) refers to genre sets and genre systems, but she also considers *genre chains*, which are chronologically related sequences of genres in a given interaction. The following is a simplified version of the genre chain for a conference paper, as illustrated by Raisanen (2002) (also reproduced in Swales, 2004: 19), showing how other genres precede and follow the conference paper itself.

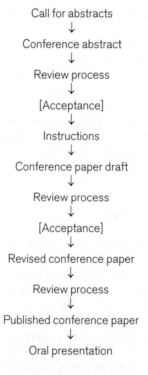

Call for abstracts
↓
Conference abstract
↓
Review process
↓
[Acceptance]
↓
Instructions
↓
Conference paper draft
↓
Review process
↓
[Acceptance]
↓
Revised conference paper
↓
Review process
↓
Published conference paper
↓
Oral presentation

My study of public discourse in the lead-up to and following the change of sovereignty over Hong Kong from Great Britain to the People's Republic of China (Flowerdew, 2012a), is interesting for its involvement of a genre chain. The study focused on the post-colonial government's promotion of Hong Kong as a world-class city. This promotion involved a quite complex genre chain involving genres from the genre set used by many governments: public forums and exhibitions, focus group discussions, presentations to statutory and advisory bodies, a website, consultation documents, information leaflets and other publicity materials, including consultation digests, information leaflets and videos.

One might think that a consultation would follow a systematic sequence in a genre chain, if not a tight sequence, then a general direction in which these genres serve first to generate the ideas, then to present them to the public for feedback, then to generate a report based on this feedback, before promotional genres are produced to promote the idea to the Hong Kong public and the world at large. In actual fact, however, because the Hong Kong government ultimately controlled this 'consultation', the study showed, the promotional texts preceded the completion of the consultation. This is a very clear example of how the elements in a genre chain should interact, the meanings in one text influencing the meanings in the next member of the chain. But in this case, the flow was disrupted, suggesting that the so-called consultation was cosmetic, the Hong Kong government having decided what it wanted to do before conducting the consultation.

Uhrig (2011) brings together the notions of genre set and genre chain (he uses the term 'genre network') in his depiction of the genres an MBA student needed to participate in, leading up to an assessed oral presentation (Figure 8.2). As Figure 8.2 indicates, before students were able to perform the presentation, they had to participate in a range of other genres, including reading a business case, writing a recommendation based on the case, listening to lectures, reading textbooks and participating in classroom interaction.

A further notion we can classify under the umbrella of genre relations, in addition to genre set, genre system and genre chain, is that of *disciplinary genre* (Bhatia, 2004: 54). Disciplinary genres include all those genres associated with a profession or discipline (not just those involved in a particular individual's sphere of activity (genre system) or specific activity (genre set and genre chain).[5] Disciplinary genre refers to a more abstract concept than the preceding three, in so far as it may not relate to the life world of individuals. But the concept is significant in so far as it can identify all of those genres which an individual *might* engage in in a particular domain, and which might, therefore, serve as an organising principle for a language programme. Table 8.1 sets out each type of genre relation identified here.[6]

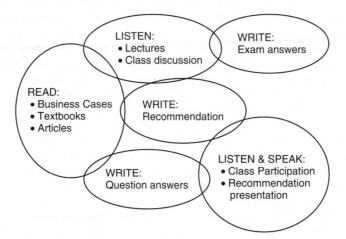

Figure 8.2   Genres leading up to a recommendation presentation in an MBA course (Uhrig, 2011: 6, adapted).

Table 8.1   Types of genre relations

Types of genre relations	Definition	Source
Genre set	A range of genres which a professional group uses in the course of their daily routine	Devitt (1991)
Genre system	A full set of genres (spoken or written) which are involved in a complete interaction	Bazerman (1994)
Genre chain	A chronologically related sequence of genres in a given interaction	Raisanen (2002)
Disciplinary genres	All those genres associated with a profession or discipline	Bhatia (2004)

Each of the four different manifestations of genre relations listed above highlights how genres interconnect one to another. This is very important for Genre Analysis, because it demonstrates how an analysis of a given genre may be missing a lot if it is taken in isolation from other members of its set of relations. Genre relations are also very important for genre-based pedagogy. The genre set allows the learner to see the similarities and differences in move structure and linguistic realisation patterns across different genres in a particular field. The genre system allows the learner to see the similarities and variations in move structure and linguistic realisation patterns within one particular interaction. The genre chain also focuses on one interaction as it develops over time through different genres. Disciplinary genres allow the learner to see the full range of genres, move structure and realisation patterns in which they may be involved at some point in the future. Furthermore, participation in a set of genre relations may also aid in developing genre knowledge of individual genres within that set of relations (Tardy, 2009). Working with sets of genre relations is, of course, closer to real life than dealing with individual instances of genres and may be closer to the target activities of a language curriculum than dealing with individual genres in isolation.

8.3.7 Intertextuality

In an educational context, working at the level of genre relations highlights the role of intertextuality – how there are references in one text to other texts (Kristeva, 1980; Bakhtin, 1981, 1986) (see Chapter 1). Intertextuality may take various forms. Fairclough (1992a: 117) distinguishes between *manifest intertextuality* – quotation, citation and paraphrase – and *constitutive intertextuality* – (generic) features which do not leave an obvious trace from the source. Devitt (1991) distinguishes three types of intertextuality: referential, functional and generic. Referential intertextuality is when one text refers directly to another one; it is close to Fairclough's manifest intertextuality. This may be quite easily recognised. Functional intertextuality is when a text is part of a larger system of texts dealing with a particular issue (Bazerman's genre set). Generic intertextuality is when a text draws on similar texts created in a similar situation (Fairclough's constitutive intertextuality). Table 8.2 sets out each type of intertextuality identified here.

In two studies I conducted with Alina Wan (Flowerdew & Wan, 2006, 2010), focusing on tax computation letters and audit reports, respectively, each type of Devitt's three categories of intertextuality was noted. Taking the later of these two studies as an example, referential intertextuality was noted in the audit reports in the way that they cited data from the company which was under audit's accounting documents. Functional intertextuality was present because the audit reports were part of the whole audit process involving many different genres, most notably perhaps the company's account documents, but also meetings and e-mails between the auditors and the company's accountants and discussions among members of the audit team. Generic

Table 8.2 Types of intertextuality

Type of intertextuality	Definition	Source
Manifest intertextuality	Quotation, citation and paraphrase	Fairclough (1992a)
Constitutive intertextuality	(Generic) features which do not leave an obvious trace	Fairclough (1992a)
Referential intertextuality	When one text refers directly to another one	Devitt (1991)
Functional intertextuality	When a text is part of a larger system of texts dealing with a particular issue	Devitt (1991)
Generic intertextuality	When a text draws on similar texts created in a similar situation	Devitt (1991)

intertextuality was a very notable feature of the audit reports, because the auditors followed very closely the format of earlier reports, in fact using templates. As a result, each audit report looked extremely similar.

It is worth mentioning here that generic intertextuality varies according to contexts. In workplace settings, there is a much greater tolerance for generic intertextuality, very often sections of one document being incorporated into another to the extent that, as noted in my studies with Alina Wan (Flowerdew & Wan, 2006, 2010), templates may be used. In other contexts, creative writing classes in schools and universities, for example, much greater value is placed on originality and creativity and copying or borrowing from other texts is frowned upon and classed as plagiarism. There is a fine line between generic intertextuality and plagiarism, however, which may be hard for learners to grasp.

All of these aspects of intertextuality are important for learning, in both mother-tongue and second-language contexts. There is clearly work to be done by the curriculum developer and the learner in raising to consciousness these features of genre, especially the more 'hidden' constitutive variety, which may not be obvious. Much genre-based pedagogy focuses on individual texts and this notion of intertextuality is lost.

8.3.8 Intercultural nature of genres

Given their grounding in communities of practice and the fact that communities of practice are likely to vary across cultures, it follows that genres are likely to be subject to intercultural variation. In early work, Kaplan (1966) noted differences in the way different cultures structured academic essays, making the strong claim that this was due to different cultural thought patterns. Kaplan has since withdrawn his strong cognitive claim and various writers have been at pains to avoid overgeneralising cultural differences across genres, preferring to see differences in terms of 'the differences or preferences in the pragmatic and strategic choices that writers make in response to external demands and cultural histories' (Kubota, 1997, cited in Paltridge, 2006: 96).

Notwithstanding the possible causes of generic differences, various researchers have noted significant contrasts. In one interesting study, Garcés-Conejos Blitvich and Fortanet-Gómez (2008) compared two corpora of peninsular Spanish and American English job résumés targeting multinational corporations. In spite of the fact that both corpora emanated from communities which shared what the authors, following Scollon and Scollon (2012), refer to as the Western *utilitarian discourse system* and that they shared the same communicative purpose, a number of differences were noted both at the level of assessments by members of the two communities of practice and at the level of rhetorical structure. One significant difference, for example, was that, while both groups of résumé writers mitigated possible threats to face by means of impersonalisation, résumés in the American subcorpus accomplished this by means of omission of all first-person pronouns or determiners, while résumés in the Spanish subcorpus preferred to perform this same function by means of nominalisation. In terms of pedagogic application, Garcés-Conejos Blitvich and Fortanet-Gómez (2008: 70) concluded that '[i]n an increasingly globalised world, it becomes essential for ESP practitioners to learn more about résumé writing practices and their assessments by members of the same community of practice in different cultures to avoid miscommunication and misperceptions that may end in an unsuccessful job search'.

8.4 APPROACHES TO GENRE PEDAGOGY

Approaches to genre in Applied Linguistics and Language Education have developed differently in the diverse contexts of North America, Great Britain and Australia, most notably. In North America, genre theory has taken a more sociological approach, while in Great Britain and Australia the approach to genre has been more linguistic. In all three domains, genre theory has been applied in pedagogic practice, with differing emphases. In a much-quoted article, Hyon (1996) categorised genre study according to three approaches, or schools: the ESP school, the Sydney school, and the New Rhetoric (more recently Rhetorical Genre Studies [RGS]) school. We will discuss these three approaches one by one.

8.4.1 The ESP school

8.4.1.1 Key concepts

To begin with the ESP school, this work was started by Swales (1990) and Bhatia (1993), the former investigating academic genres (primarily the research article) and the latter more interested in business and legal genres. The focus of this work was pedagogic, the idea being that good genre descriptions could feed into ESP materials development and pedagogy more generally. The basic idea is to establish systematic links between communicative purposes and properties of texts. Communicative purposes, it is argued, are expressed in characteristic ways in texts by particular discourse communities – the people who regularly participate in a given genre and who share similar communicative purposes. Communicative purposes are expressed in a staged or sequenced manner, a text being built up systematically through a series of what are called moves and steps (as we have already seen in our instructions text (Figure 8.1), for example. These moves and steps may be obligatory or optional, may vary in their sequencing, may be repeated, and may be embedded one within another (Swales, 1990: 58).

Perhaps the best-known model of generic staging is Swales's (1990: 141) CARS ('Create A Research Space') structure, which he posits for academic research article introductions. The model indicates how scholars support and promote their contribution to the field by first identifying the field of enquiry and summarising previous research, then identifying a gap in the existing work, and finally summarising how they will fill this gap. The three stages of the model, with submoves, or steps, are as follows:

> Move 1. Establishing a territory:
>   Step 1. Claiming centrality
>   and/or
>   Step 2. Making topic generalisation
>   and/or
>   Step 3. Reviewing items of previous research.

Move 2. Establishing a niche:
      Step 1A. Counterclaiming
          or
      Step 1B. Indicating a gap
          or
      Step 1C. Question-raising
          or
      Step 1D. Continuing a tradition.

Move 3. Occupying the niche:
      Step 1A. Outlining purposes
          or
      Step 1B. Announcing present research
      Step 2. Announcing principal findings
      Step 3. Indicating research article structure.

As another example of schematic structure, Bhatia (1993) offers the following model of seven typical moves for the genre of sales letters:

1. establishing credentials;
2. introducing the offer;
3. offering incentives:

    a. offering the product/service;
    b. essential detailing of the offer;
    c. indicating value of the offer;

4. referring to enclosed documents;
5. inviting further communication;
6. using pressure tactics;
7. ending politely.

These moves and steps are not all obligatory, it should be emphasised again, nor do they necessarily follow the sequence given, and, in some cases, they may be repeated, or recursive.

As well as having a prototypical schematic structure, the various communicative functions of a genre exhibit typical conventionalised verbalisation patterns, or realisations, which are again recognised as such by the discourse community. The following are examples of authentic realisations of the first step of the first move of Swales's research article introductions, 'claiming centrality', as cited by Swales (1990: 144):

- *Recently, there has been a spate of interest in how to …*
- *In recent years, applied researchers have become increasingly interested in …*
- *The possibility … has generated interest in …*
- *Recently, there has been wide interest in …*
- *The time development … is a classic problem in fluid mechanics.*
- *The explication of the relationship between … is a classic problem of …*
- *Many investigators have recently turned to …*

It is important to stress that there is no one-to-one relation between move and realisation pattern (unless a genre is extremely conventionalised, such as vows at a wedding, or the oath at a public swearing-in), but, in many institutional genres, there is a good possibility of typical verbalisation patterns occurring, such as these presented here by Swales. In the examples just cited, for example, we can immediately note the recurrence of *recently/in recent years, interest[ed] in* and *classic problem*, along with the use of the present perfect tense in more than one instance.

Knowing how to perform a genre, according to this ESP view, involves knowing both its schematic structure, or staging, on the one hand, and the specific form–function correlations of each stage, on the other. Someone participating in a genre who does not have a command of these specific patterns and the limits to their possible variability is quickly recognised as either incompetent or an outsider, an important consideration from the L2 perspective, where non-native speakers may need to compete with native speakers in academic and professional contexts.

Since their original book-length treatments of genre, both Swales (2004) and Bhatia (2004) have developed their insights further, both indicating how there is greater complexity to genre than perhaps suggested in their original coverage of the topic. Bhatia (2004), for example, contrasts what he characterises as the relative simplicity of the 'ideal world' of his original analysis with the greater complexity of what he calls the 'real world' of his later conception. The 'real world' view incorporates three main insights. First, that genres occur in relation to other genres and should not be considered in isolation. Second, that genres are dynamic and have a propensity to develop and be exploited in their composition by expert users. Third, that there are disciplinary differences in genres, a feature which had been underestimated in the earlier approach.

In more recent years, attention has been turned on the part of some ESP practitioners to the application of Corpus Linguistics techniques to Genre Analysis. Corpus techniques have proved to be powerful tools in highlighting typical lexicogrammatical patterns functioning with and across generic moves (Biber *et al.*, 2007; Flowerdew, 1993a; L. Flowerdew, 2005, 2008a, b; Flowerdew & Forest, 2009; Gavioli, 2005; Gledhill, 2000; Lee & Swales, 2006; Partington, 1998)

At the same time, as A. M. Johns (2003: 206) has noted, ESP 'is becoming increasingly context-driven, and the overlap between the New Rhetoric [RGS] … and the ESP research and theory, becomes greater every year'. A focus on context as much as text was always in fact a part of ESP Genre Analysis. Take, for example, the seven stages Bhatia (1993: 22–36) recommends for Genre Analysis, as follows, five of which (1, 2, 3, 5, 7) are to do with context.

1. placing the given genre-text in a situational context;
2. surveying the existing literature;
3. refining the situational/contextual analysis;
4. selecting a corpus;
5. studying the institutional context;
6. levels of linguistic analysis;
7. consulting with specialist informants.

It is just that, in practice, much of the focus in ESP has been on the linguistic level, stage 6. Some ESP approaches employing a more contextual approach would include studies by, for example, Boswood and Marriott (1994), A. M. Johns (1997, 2002a), Paltridge (2004, 2008), and Swales and Luebs (1995) (see also the discussion in A. M. Johns *et al.*, 2006).

8.4.1.2 *Application to pedagogy*

Application of ESP genre theory has focused on tertiary-level contexts, helping students to prepare for both undergraduate and postgraduate study. A very popular textbook in universities throughout the world is Swales and Feak's (2012) *Academic Writing for Graduate Students*, a volume which incorporates many of the findings of ESP Genre Analysis conducted by Swales and Feak and their collaborators.

In his 1990 volume, Swales indicated how a genre-based pedagogy can be developed as part of a task-based approach. He provided an example of the genre of request letters for academic papers. The learning activity is broken down into four tasks, as follows, based on a set of genre samples (in this case, request letters).[7]

1. analysing the similarities and differences in the subject and purpose of the samples;
2. describing what changes might be made to increase the effectiveness of the samples;
3. A. examining extracts of the letters for their lexicogrammatical features and their appropriateness to the situation;
   B. drafting a letter;
4. collecting examples of correspondence received by students in the form of short letters and sharing with classmates.

Swales's approach represents a fairly conservative application of genre theory to a concrete pedagogical situation. The procedure is one of familiarisation with the genre and its generic features, consciousness raising *vis-à-vis* the social and lexicogrammatical dimensions of the genre, hands-on practice in producing a genre and critical reflection on the whole process.

One of the most influential applications of the results of ESP genre has been Swales's CARS model and adaptations to various contexts. Baker's (2010) recent description of his pedagogic application of the CARS model in the Chilean context is fairly typical. Baker describes how the following steps of reading, speaking, noticing and writing were applied to a given academic article:

1. Students read the article outside class.
2. The students' reaction to the article is discussed in class.
3. Students underline citations, rhetorical phrases, lexis and signpost language.
4. The rhetorical use of the underlined language is then discussed.
5. A three-paragraph reader response is written.

Results from the discussion recorded by Baker include the following:

1. The first person '*I*' can be used.
2. '*You*' is never used to address the reader.
3. Introductions include the three-move 'CARS' model (Swales, 1990).
4. Contractions are not used.
5. Modals are used to soften claims (hedges) and mark degrees of certainty.
6. Citations are a prominent feature and positively affect the writer's credibility.
7. Conclusions are short, precise and restate the aims of the article.
8. Passive voice is a prominent feature.
9. Formal vocabulary is used.
10. Noun phrases (nominalisation) often replace verbs.
11. Phrasal verbs are rarely used.
12. A rich variety of rhetorical phrases is used to achieve cohesion and coherence.
13. Sentence length, word order and word choice affect the writer's 'voice'.
14. Impersonal language is seen as objective and unbiased.
15. Unsupported claims negatively affect the writer's credibility.

Since Swales's (1990) initial work on ESP genre, ESP researchers and practitioners have been mindful of accusations of overgeneralisation and prescriptivism in the application of genre descriptions to pedagogy. Thus, Swales (1990: 213) already suggested 'consciousness-raising' rather than overt teaching. Similarly, while Dudley-Evans (1997: 62) writes that 'the main argument in favour of the use of genre analysis in teaching ESP is that it provides non-native speakers with the linguistic and rhetorical tools they need to cope with the tasks required of them', and that '[o]f course, the linguistic forms are important', he nevertheless argues that 'one should make apparent *the range of possibilities* for expressing a move or other units constituting a genre' (emphasis added). I myself argued that, in certain circumstances, a 'process' or 'educational' approach to the teaching of genres (Flowerdew, 1993b) is to be preferred to a more prescriptive 'training' model and that understanding of the principles underlying generic patterning is more important in developing generic competence than specific features of individual genres.

In a recent monograph, Tardy (2009) conducted a study of the development of genre knowledge on the part of a group of graduate students in a North American university. Tardy's findings provided answers to three fundamental questions in her study. The first of these questions was: 'How do writers move toward expert genre knowledge?' Tardy concluded that six main resources and strategies are drawn upon in this enterprise: (1) prior experience and repeated practice; (2) textual interactions; (3) oral interactions; (4) mentoring and disciplinary participation; (5) shifting roles within a genre network; and (6) resource availability. Tardy's second question was: 'What impacts the shape of genre learning?' Tardy identified three factors: the individual, the community and the task. The third question was: 'Can genres be taught?' Tardy's response was affirmative, although she noted that proficiency in genre performance cannot be exclusively developed in the context of the classroom.

In order to promote effective genre learning, Tardy offered three principles for pedagogy.

1. Build a genre-rich environment which provides students with a range of strategies and resources.
2. Help student learners develop complex and dynamic views of texts, while at the same time allowing that texts may sometimes need to be simplified.
3. Consider genres in the context of their networks.

8.4.2 The Sydney school

8.4.2.1 Key concepts

This approach to genre is referred to as the *Sydney school* because it developed out of work conducted at the University of Sydney, among followers of the systemic functional linguist (SFL) Halliday, under the leadership of Martin. Martin and Rose (2012: 1) explain that the term *Sydney school* was first used by Green and Lee (1994), although it became more popular following the paper published by Hyon (1996), referred to above. The Sydney school employs a methodology derived from Hallidayan SFL, a model which, as shown in Chapter 2, is particularly powerful in identifying the close correlations between form and function which are a characteristic of particular linguistic situations.

To remind ourselves of this model, as presented in Chapter 2, Halliday posits three parameters of context, or *context of situation*. These are *field*, which is the subject matter and activity type of the text; *tenor*, which corresponds to the relation between the participants in the text; and *mode*, which refers to the rhetorical channel and function of the discourse – what part the text is playing (for example, Halliday & Matthiessen, 2004). These three contextual parameters are associated with their respective macrofunctions, or purposes: *ideational* (conveying factual information), *interpersonal* (expressing the speaker's attitude and indicating and maintaining social relations) and *textual* (creating texts which are coherent and cohesive within themselves and which fit the situation in which they are created).

As defined in Chapter 2 and in this chapter, above, register is a particular language variety, usually associated with a particular group of people or activity. As noted in Chapter 2, Halliday is ambivalent about the role of genre in his model and it is not a part of his habitual metalanguage.

Some of Halliday's fellow systemicists, however, have devoted considerable attention to the notion of genre and how it might fit into an SFL model. For Martin (1992: 505–506), most notably, following Gregory and Carroll (1978), communicative purpose, as the motivation of genre, is integral to all components of a text's meaning – ideational, interpersonal and textual. It therefore merits a separate level to register. Genres, for Martin, as the unfolding of communicative purposes, create different permutations of ideational, interpersonal and textual meaning, or register. Two genres, such as live commentary and newspaper story, may typically unfold differently – the commentary starts at the beginning and the news story with the result – but may belong to the same register, sports.

Just as the Sydney school shares with the ESP school the notion of communicative purpose as essential to genre, so do they share the notion of staging. Terms used to refer to this feature in the SFL tradition are *schematic structure* or *structural formula* (Hasan, 1977, 1979, 1985; Martin, 1992; Martin & Rose, 2012; Ventola, 1987). So, the Sydney school conception of genre is in accordance with the distinction made at the beginning of this chapter between register and genre, in emphasising communicative purpose and staging as the distinctive features of the latter. Bringing together the notions of communicative purpose and schematic structure, Martin (1984: 25) thus defines genre as 'a staged, goal-oriented, purposeful activity'.

Paltridge (2002) highlights an important difference between the Sydney school and the ESP approach to genre, making a distinction between *genre* and *text type*. Genres can be recognised according to external criteria and are named by their users. Laboratory reports, research articles, lectures and tutorials are examples of genres. Following Swales (1990), these, or their component parts, are the focus of ESP Genre Analysis. Text types, on the other hand, are rhetorical modes that follow systematic internal discourse patterns. Problem–solution, exposition and argument are examples of text types. Text types, referred to as *elemental genres*, are the main focus of the Sydney school. *Elemental genres*, or text types, combine together to create what are called *macro-genres* (e.g. laboratory reports, essays) by the Sydney school.

Martin (1992) traces the notion of schematic structure back to Mitchell (1957), who, like Halliday, was greatly influenced by the British linguist, Firth. Mitchell, although not using the term 'genre', specified the following elements for shop transactions as they are conducted in Libya, where he did his research.

1.   salutation;
2.   enquiry as to the object of sale;
3.   investigation of the object of sale;
4.   bargaining;
5.   conclusion.

Later, as an example of SFL genre work on schematic structure, Ventola (1987) proposed the following prototypical set of moves for service encounters.

1.   greeting;
2.   attendance allocation;
3.   service bid;
4.   service;
5.   resolution;
6.   goods handover;
7.   pay;
8.   closing;
9.   goodbye.

Table 8.3 shows the schematic structures of key elemental genres, as developed by the Sydney school (Lock & Lockhart, 1998, cited in Hyland, 2004: 33).

Table 8.3 Schematic structures of key elemental genres as developed by the Sydney school (from Lock & Lockhart, 1998, cited in Hyland, 2004: 33)

Genre	Stages	Purpose
Recount	Orientation ^ Record of events ^ (Reorientation)	Provides information about a situation Presents events in temporal sequence Brings events into the present
Procedure	Goal ^ Steps 1–n ^ (Results)	Gives information about the purposes of the tasks – in title or intro Lists activities needed to achieve the goal in correct sequence Presents final state or 'look' of the activity
Narrative	Orientation ^ (Complication) (Evaluation) ^ Resolution	Gives information about characters' situation Presents one or more problems for characters to solve Evaluates the major events for the characters Sorts out the problems for the characters
Description	Identification ^ Aspect n ^ (Conclusion)	Defines, classifies, or generalises about a phenomenon Describes attributes of each category of the phenomenon Sums up the description
Report	Problem ^ Reason n ^ (Conclusion) ^ Recommendations	Identifies a problem Gives possible reasons for or consequences of the problem Makes suggestions for solving the problem Presents measures to be adopted as a result of the report

^ = is followed by; ( ) = optional stage; n = stage may recur.

Figure 8.3 shows the secondary school genres mapped in terms of their social purposes.

To show how schematic structure and form–function correlations interact, interesting work has been done by Coffin (2006). Coffin shows how the school genre of *historical account* typically develops according to the three stages of *background*, *account sequence* and *deduction*. In

Figure 8.3   Map of genres in school (Martin and Rose, 2012: 110).

the account sequence stage the writer chronicles events as they unfolded in past time. Instead of being simply presented as following one from another, however, events play an *agentive* role in producing subsequent events (p. 211). This is realised in the grammar by means of nominalisations (the use of nouns, where more usually verbs would be used) in initial clause (*thematic*) position. This form–function relation of nominalisation realising event as agent is illustrated in the following text, where the nominalisations are 'belief', 'abuse', 'period', and 'resistance' respectively.[8]

> As a result in their **belief** in 'terra nullius', from 1788 onwards the English began to occupy sacred land and use Aboriginal hunting and fishing grounds. This **abuse** by the new British government soon led to Aborigines becoming involved in a physical struggle for power. The first main **period** of Aboriginal resistance was in the Sydney area from 1794 to 1816 when the Eora people, under the leadership of Pemulwuy, resisted the Europeans through guerrilla warfare. This **resistance** resulted in the colonisers using different methods of control.

8.4.2.2 *Application to pedagogy*

In contrast to ESP, with its pedagogic focus on tertiary-level contexts, Sydney school genre theory has been developed primarily within the context of Australian primary schools (also in secondary and indigenous contexts), where it has been used as a tool for developing a fully fledged pedagogy (Martin & Rose, 2012). This started with work by Martin and Rothery (Martin & Rose, 2012; Rothery, 1996, cited in Feez, 2002: 54), who categorised primary school text types, or genres (Feez, 2002: 54), resulting in five major 'genre families' of *stories*, *histories*, *reports*, *explanations* and *procedures*, each characterised by distinctive schematic structures, which were in turn characterised by typical lexical, grammatical and cohesive patterning (Martin & Rose, 2008, 2012). This taxonomy was then developed into a 'language-based approach to teaching and learning' (Martin & Rose, 2012; Rothery, 1996, cited in Feez, 2002: 54) which, in particular, sought to give less-privileged children access to genres which are highly valued in the society at large. A teaching–learning cycle was developed, which drew on Vygotsky's (1986) dialogic model of learning, with the teacher providing *scaffolding to* help learners participate in the joint construction of learning tasks (Martin & Rose, 2012).[9]

The text-based syllabus upon which the genre pedagogy model was developed (Feez & Joyce, 1998) is presented to learners by means of a multistage model of classroom interaction on the lines of that presented in Chapter 2, for register, and consisting of: (1) building the context; (2) modelling and deconstructing the text; (3) joint construction of the text; (4) independent construction of the text; and (5) linking related texts (Feez, 2002; Feez & Joyce, 1998; Martin & Rose, 2012). Perhaps surprisingly, Sydney school genre-based pedagogy has not been greatly employed in ESP settings (although see Flowerdew, 2002; and Jones, 2004).

This methodology can be incorporated into a model of course design, as developed by Burns and Joyce (cited in Hyland, 2004: 92), as follows:

1. Identify the overall contexts in which the language will be used.
2. Develop course goals based on this context of use.
3. Note the sequence of language events within the context.
4. List the genres used in this sequence.
5. Outline the sociocognitive knowledge students need to participate in this context.
6. Gather and analyse samples of texts.
7. Develop units of work related to these genres and develop learning objectives to be achieved.

In school contexts, this model might effectively be used with the curriculum map illustrated in Figure 8.3 above. Such a map can be used to indicate to teachers how to select and analyse texts within the context of their overall programmes (Martin & Rose, 2012).

Less well known than their work on writing, Sydney school linguists have applied their genre model to the teaching of reading (Martin & Rose, 2012). This is very noteworthy, because most applied genre work has focused on writing (although see Hyon, 2002, for a notable exception). Martin and Rose's approach to reading works with the same sequential phase approach of their descriptive work. The description of the generic stages, or *phases*, as they are now referred to, is used to inform the preparation before reading; the teacher is able to paraphrase the text which is about to be read. Martin and Rose (2012: 131) describe this procedure as follows:

> This type of preparation summarises the sequence of phases identified in the analysis above, in terms that all students can understand, including its key events, and using many of the words from the passage. It also starts by relating the passage to the preceding events. Such a preview gives students a map of how the text will unfold, including a series of signposts so that they will recognise key elements as they occur. No student will struggle to comprehend what is happening at each step, so all will be able to follow the words closely as they are read. If the text is read aloud, weaker readers need not struggle to decode unfamiliar words as it is read to them. If students are likely to find the text comparatively easy to follow, the preview can be brief, as in the chapter preparation above. If the text is more challenging, the preview can be more detailed, summarising its phases.

8.4.3 The Rhetorical Genre Studies school

8.4.3.1 Key concepts

Viewed from the perspective of RGS, the ESP and Sydney schools have more in common with each other than sets them apart. It is true that, in directing their attention to schematic structure, on the one hand, and form–function correlation at the level of the clause, on the other (and also the interaction of the two), the ESP and Sydney schools are both linguistic in approach, setting a lot of store on the relationship between communicative function and linguistic form.

RGS scholars – few, if any, of whom have a background in linguistics, as A. M. Johns (2002b) tells us – have a much more social way of looking at genre (for example, Freedman & Medway, 1994a, b), seeing the linguistic orientation of the ESP and Sydney schools as too deterministic and simplistic. The linguistic approach of the ESP and Sydney schools, these researchers argue, tends to reify genre, in not allowing for the fact that genres are all the time evolving (see, for example, Bazerman, 1988; Yates, 1989). The linguistic approach, they argue, also fails to take account of the multiple purposes of genres; of the different purposes of reader and writer or speaker and hearer; and of how purposes develop as a genre progresses (A. M. Johns, 2003). The linguistic approach, according to these RGS scholars, also overemphasises the conventional nature of form–function relations at the clause level and thereby neglects the potential for creativity within genres. The linguistic view, furthermore, fails to take account of the intertextual nature of genres (Bakhtin, 1981, 1986; Kristeva, 1980), the RGS school contends, of how each unfolding of a genre draws on participants' previous experience of that genre and related genres; finally, according to RGS, the linguistic approach fails to take account of the hybrid nature of genres, of how they intertwine with each other and how some elements are more easily recognisable as generic than others (Berkenkotter & Huckin, 1995: 17).[10]

If the above are the negative aspects of the linguistic approach for the RGS scholars, what are the features of genre which they themselves emphasise? Hyon (1996: 698) tells us that RGS focuses more on situational context than linguistic forms and that it emphasises social purposes and the *actions* resulting from these purposes within specific situations. In a seminal paper for RGS, Miller (1984: 151), one of the most influential members of the RGS group, claims that a definition of genre should be focused on the action it is used to accomplish rather than its substance or form.

An important outcome of this emphasis on action is that Genre Analysis methodology needs to be ethnographic rather than linguistic; it must focus on the attitudes, beliefs, activities, values and patterns of behaviour of the discourse community engaging in the genre or genres which is/are the focus of study. There is, therefore, a need to go beyond what Luke (1994: ix) refers to as the mere 'broad brush-stroke references to the importance of "context of situation"' of more text-oriented researchers. Or, as Coe (2002: 199) puts it, '[g]enres are not just text types; they imply/invoke/ create/(re)construct situations (and contexts), communities, writers and readers (that is, subject positions'. A good example of this social approach would be Schryer's (1993) account of the attitudes of clinicians and researchers towards the manuscripts they write and read. Another example would be Casanave's (1992) study of a graduate student in sociology and how the types of writing she was required to do alienated her from the discipline, because they seemed remote from the reason she had been drawn to it, to help the underprivileged. Further examples would be Artemeva's account of how novice engineers learn their professional genres (Artemeva, 2006) or Smart and Brown's (2006) study of professional writings of students placed as interrns in various professional contexts.

Because, for the RGS school, genre focuses on action, it must be related to cognition, since cognition and action are related one to the other (Bawarshi & Reiff, 2010: 79). Bawarshi and Reiff (2010: 79–80) draw on Berkenkotter and Huckin (1995), leading RGS theoreticians:

> Genre knowledge (knowledge of rhetorical and formal conventions) is inextricably linked to what Berkenkotter and Huckin refer to as procedural knowledge (knowledge of when and how to use certain disciplinary tools, how and when to inquire, how and when to frame questions, how to recognize and negotiate problems, and where, how, and when to produce knowledge within disciplinary contexts). Genre knowledge is also linked to background knowledge – both content knowledge and knowledge of shared assumptions, including knowledge of *kairos*, having to do with rhetorical timing and opportunity. As forms of situated cognition, thus, genres enable their users not only to communicate effectively, but also to participate in (and reproduce) a community's 'norms, epistemology, ideology, and social ontology.'

At the same time, perhaps because of its social nature, RGS stresses the fluidity of genres, how they are ever changing and may be manipulated by their participants (Schryer, 1993, refers to 'stabilised-for-now' structures of genres). One ramification of this fluidity is that even conventionalised genres may be open to change when manipulated by particularly influential or powerful individuals. Bazerman (1988), for example, shows the powerful effect Newton and Edison had in shaping the scientific research article. Genres have also undergone much more sudden and striking changes and development with the advent of new technology-dependent genres such as blogs and podcasts.

Returning now to the role of the individual in genre creation, every time someone engages in a genre, the question arises as to how much they should rely on the prefabricated patterns and routines, the standardised generic features, which have been made available to them from previous repeated encounters with the genre and how much they should be creative and innovative by choosing non-standard forms. To a degree, this choice will depend upon the extent to which a genre is conventionalised. A genre such as a wedding ceremony, coronation or presidential swearing-in leaves little, if any, room for choice. But a dinner-table conversation, a poem or a personal letter all provide room for individual creativity; indeed, one's performance of genres such as these may be judged according to how creative and original one is. An important part of an individual's genre knowledge is thus knowing when and how to follow the conventions, on the one hand, and when and how to be creative, on the other.

Given the dichotomy of genre as at one and the same time fluid and yet conventionalised, genre may be open to contestation and struggle. These two opposing generic forces of fluidity and stability were referred to by Bakhtin (1986), the precursor of contemporary writing on genre, as *centripetal* and *centrifugal* forces, forces which he saw as fundamental in language use. With contestation and struggle within genre studies we enter into the realm of language power and the potential for a critical Genre Analysis, an approach aimed at the 'revealing of unseen players and unmasking of others', as Freedman and Medway (1994a: 2) put it.

Another feature of genre from the RGS perspective is its reflexivity: how, on the one hand, society reflects generic structures, because generic structures are there before society can make use of them, but how, on the other hand, generic structures reflect society, because they are continually modelled and remodelled by society, their users. An important implication of this view for Genre Analysis is, again, that it needs to be dialectic; it needs to study both the society which is using the genre or genres which are the focus of study, but at the same time it needs to study the generic structures themselves. Analysis must thus be a constant to-ing and fro-ing between context and text, text and context.

A final feature of work in RGS we can mention here is how it is often complemented with other theories, such as activity theory, situated learning theory, theories of distributed cognition, Giddens's structuration theory and Bourdieu's social theory of practice (Artemeva & Freedman, 2006a).

Although we have highlighted the salient features of the RGS approach and contrasted it with the ESP and Sydney school approaches, to conclude, it is worth stressing that these different approaches have more in common than what sets them apart (Flowerdew, 2011), especially as far as pedagogy is concerned. As Freedman (2006: 104) has written:

> As explicated in their theoretic formulations, these two approaches [ESP and Sydney school, on the one hand, and RGS, on the other] have much in common. Both insist on the limitation of traditional conceptions of genres which focused only on recurring textual features. Both stressed the need to recognize the social dimensions of genre … Both approaches emphasize the addressee, the context, and the occasion. … It is not so much in their theoretic formulations, but rather in their realization within research, that the differences between these two approaches are most salient.

8.4.3.2 Application to pedagogy

RGS has been mainly confined to North America and has primarily focused on genres in academic and professional contexts. A lot of RGS research has focused on the acquisition of genres by novices in new communities of discourse (Artemeva & Freedman, 2006b: 2). However, as A. M. Johns (2002b: 10) has written, 'many proponents [of RGS] are sceptical about genre pedagogies, about the ways in which schooling might assist students in acquiring, critiquing, and using genres for their own purposes'. This is because genres, for RGS, are always situated in real contexts and involve real participants and audience. These situations cannot be recreated in the classroom, but can only be acquired in those situations through a process of what Lave and Wenger (1991) call 'legitimate peripheral participation'. As Adam and Artemeva (2002) put it: 'People learn at home, at work or in a community without explicit instruction'. That is not to say that RGS has nothing to say to the teacher. As A. M. Johns (2003: 210–211) has written, again:

> Certainly ESL/EFL composition instructors should acquaint themselves with the literature in RGS, if for no other reason than to provide cautions against reductionist pedagogies that

portray text descriptions as fixed templates instead of opportunities for studying evolving, negotiated, situated discourses.

The approach to pedagogy for RGS is an apprenticeship-based model combined with a familiarisation on the part of learners with the target contexts and related genres (Freadman, 1994). Freedman (sic) (1987) insists that learning a genre can only be done by practising it: 'full genre knowledge (in all of its subtlety and complexity) only becomes available *as a result of having written*' (p. 207). She has a model for acquiring new genres, which duly emphasises this minimalist approach (p. 102).

1. The learners approach the task with a 'dimly felt sense' of the new genre they are attempting.
2. They begin composing by focusing on the specific content to be embodied in this genre.
3. In the course of the composing, this 'dimly felt sense' of the genre is both formulated and modified as (a) this 'sense', (b) the composing processes, and (c) the unfolding text are interrelated and modify each other.
4. On the basis of external feedback (the grade assigned), the learners either confirm or modify their map of the genre.

In spite of scepticism such as that of Freedman, some RGS scholars have addressed more overt pedagogical issues, even producing textbooks (for example, Bullock, 2005; Devitt *et al.*, 2004; Trimbur, 2002). One favoured approach is to develop what Bawarshi and Reiff (2010: 192) refer to as *meta-genre awareness*, an awareness which stresses the interaction between genre and context. Bawarshi and Reiff (2010: 193–194), describe how (with Devitt) they developed such a model in a textbook (Devitt *et al.* 2004), adopting the following activity stages:

1. Collect samples of the genre.
2. Identify the scene and describe the situation in which the genre is used:

    a. setting;
    b. subject;
    c. participants;
    d. purposes.

3. Identify and describe patterns in the genre's features.
4. Analyse what these patterns reveal about the situation and scene.

Other RGS researchers have described how researchers can combine research and pedagogy, as, for example, in Smart and Brown's (2006) study, cited above, of a group of workplace professional writing student interns, where the researchers combined research and pedagogy and assisted the student interns in developing their generic competence, not just in their specific context, but for a range of workplace settings that they would be likely to encounter in their future careers. Furthermore, Artemeva (2006), in her study on novice engineers, also cited above, shows how her participants developed professional genre knowledge through academic, as well as workplace, experiences.

8.5 CRITIQUE

When we consider critique of genre theory, we really need to deal with each of the three schools discussed in this chapter separately. If we consider, first, the conception of language, of the two 'linguistic' schools, the ESP school is rather eclectic in its approach, while the Sydney school works with a well-developed linguistic theory and descriptive model. The former is easier to apply, while the latter is more detailed, but requires training in the theory and analysis. On the other hand, the RGS school does not have a model of language *per se*. One problem with all of the schools is that the term *genre* is rather slippery and difficult to define. This presents problems of application, it goes without saying. We reviewed above the main problems that RGS has with the two linguistic approaches – the issue of the multiple purposes of genres, claimed overemphasis on the conventional nature of form–function relations at the clause level, claimed neglect of the potential for creativity within genres, and claimed failure to take account of the intertextual and hybrid nature of genres. These 'problems', on the other hand, would probably be refuted by the two linguistic schools, although they remain issues worthy of consideration, whatever one's perspective. The main critique on the part of the two linguistic schools of the RGS school would be that it neglects the important focus on language and form. Those working in ESP and SFL are more concerned with teaching non-mainstream populations, making language and form especially important, perhaps.

Moving now to critiques of genre-based pedagogy, Paltridge (2001: 122–126) discusses a number of what he calls 'limitations' of the approach in general. The first of these is the difficulty in assigning texts into specific genre categories, already mentioned as a problem in genre theory in the previous paragraph. Another problem of the genre-based approach for Paltridge is the difficulty for teachers who are working in communities where the target language is not in widespread use. In such contexts, there may be a difficulty in gaining access to examples of appropriate spoken and written genres, especially if the context for teaching is a foreign-language classroom. A further issue for Paltridge is the question of creativity: to what extent should learners be taught the conventional features of genres and to what extent should they be encouraged to develop an independent voice? As one unidentified contributor to a well-known blog wrote (http://rsa.cwrl.utexas.edu/node/5649), 'ESL students learn a few sentence structures really well and deploy them repeatedly rather than attempt to try anything novel. Trying something novel, after all, risks failure. It is better to write monotonously without error than adventuresomely and risk error'. This issue of convention versus invention applies to all three schools, not just the two linguistic ones. A final issue concerned with teaching in a foreign language mentioned by Paltridge is the difficulty for the teachers of finding suitable texts and a potential lack of familiarity with the particular features of the target genres. At the same time, learners in such contexts may have difficulty in finding an authentic audience for their English-language communications, although developments with the internet have opened up more opportunities in this regard.

8.6 APPLICATION TO PEDAGOGY: GENERAL PRINCIPLES

We have already discussed pedagogic application throughout this chapter and in our discussion of each of the three schools of genre pedagogy above. Here we will limit ourselves to a consideration of some general principles in support of a genre-based approach. A number of advantages of genre-based teaching are mentioned by Paltridge (2001: 7). First, for Paltridge, genre-based teaching, following Bhatia (2002), develops the acquisition of *generic competence*, 'that is, the ability to respond to new and recurring genres'. This does not just mean the development of linguistic and communicative competence, for Paltridge. In a genre-based approach, learners develop not only language and discourse skills, but also skills to interpret and apply knowledge about culture, circumstances, purposes and motives that prevail in particular settings (Paltridge, 2001: 7).

Second, for Paltridge, genre-based pedagogy offers the advantage of providing access to genres which have high cultural capital, that is, genres which are highly valued by society. This idea is controversial (see, for example, Luke, 1996, and below under 'critique'), but many educators feel that it is essential that students should be given the opportunity to access these genres which may be essential for full participation in social life. Gee (1997, cited in Paltridge, 2001: 9), for example, believes that genre awareness is essential so that learners learn 'the purposes that different genres serve in society and culture'. Similarly, Martin and Rose (2012: 5) are strongly in support of this view,

invoking a UNESCO document which argues for 'full and equal opportunities for education for all …
to advance the ideal of equality of educational opportunity'.

A third advantage of genre-based teaching for Paltridge is that it allows for the inclusion of the
best aspects of other syllabus types, acting as an overarching framework incorporating grammar,
vocabulary, functions and notions, tasks, situation types and content areas.

Hyland (2004: 10–11) lists seven advantages of genre-based writing instruction (all of which
can also be applied to the other skills of reading, speaking and listening), as follows.

Genre teaching is:

1. *Explicit.* Makes clear what is to be learned to facilitate the acquisition of writing skills;
2. *Systematic.* Provides a coherent framework for focusing on both language and contexts;
3. *Needs-based.* Ensures that course objectives and content are derived from student needs;
4. *Supportive.* Gives teachers a central role in scaffolding student learning and creativity;
5. *Empowering.* Provides access to the patterns and possibilities of variation in valued texts;
6. *Critical.* Provides the resources for students to understand and challenge valued discourses;
7. *Consciousness raising.* Increases teacher awareness of texts to confidently advise students on
   their writing.

This list provides a fittingly positive note with which to end this chapter.

8.7 QUESTIONS FOR DISCUSSION

1. Write down the names of five genres with which you are familiar. What are the communicative
   purposes of each of these genres?
2. Think of a genre and design a genre chain or network to show the other genres with which it
   interacts.
3. Think of, or find examples of, a written genre in your L1 and your L2. What similarities and differences do you notice in the generic features of each?
4. What are the advantages and disadvantages of a genre-based approach to teaching?
5. Of the three approaches to genre pedagogy – RGS, ESP and Sydney school – which one do
   you prefer? Give your reasons.
6. Based on Bawarshi and Reiff's ideas about developing *meta-genre awareness*, choose a genre
   and then:

   1. Collect samples of the genre.
   2. Identify the scene and describe the situation in which the genre is used:

      a. setting;
      b. subject;
      c. participants;
      d. purposes.

   3. Identify and describe patterns in the genre's features (schematic structure and lexico-
      grammatical features).
   4. Analyse what these patterns reveal about the situation and scene.

8.8 FURTHER READING

Bawarshi and Reiff, 2010; Bhatia, 1993, 2004; Flowerdew, 1993a, b; Hyland, 2004; Hyon, 1996;
   A. M. Johns, 2002a; Paltridge, 2001; Swales, 1990.

CHAPTER 9

Corpus-based approaches

9.1 WHAT IS A CORPUS?

A *corpus* (plural *corpora*) is a large collection of language, usually held electronically, which can be used for the purposes of linguistic analysis. The earliest known corpora were compiled by hand and consisted of biblical texts. In the modern era, an early electronically stored corpus was the Brown corpus, developed at Brown University, USA, in the early 1960s, and consisting of one million words. Other notable, more recent, corpora are the Bank of English, developed by COBUILD at Birmingham University, UK, which consists of well over 500 million words, the British National Corpus (BNC), consisting of 100 million words and the Corpus of Contemporary American English (COCA), consisting of over 425 million words and still growing.

A number of corpora have been constructed specifically with educational/academic applications in mind. These include the Michigan Corpus of Academic Spoken English (MICASE), the Michigan Corpus of Upper-Level Student Papers (MICUSP), their British counterparts, the British Academic Spoken English Corpus (BASE) and the British Academic Written English Corpus (BAWE), and the Test of English as a Foreign Language (TOEFL) 2000 Spoken and Written Academic Language Corpus.

At the same time, there are innumerable small corpora consisting of as few as 100,000 words or less, developed for specialist purposes. There are also parallel corpora, which consist of two or more corpora that have been sampled in the same way for different languages, usually of texts that have been translated. In addition to these corpora, the worldwide web can also be used as a corpus, either by using a search engine such as Google or Yahoo! or via specialised interfaces, for example: http://www.webcorp.org.uk/live/.

To put the size of these corpora into perspective, as Gavioli and Aston (2001: 238) have noted, even the very large corpora consist of less language than will be encountered by average humans in their daily life. In addition, the composition of these corpora is different to what the individual experiences in real life, many, if not most of them consisting of written language. Furthermore, in real life, certain texts may be experienced more than once, while they will only occur once in a corpus.

While some corpora are kept in a 'raw' state, others are *annotated*, or *tagged*, for parts of speech, or other information such as who is speaking or when the speaker has changed, a process which can be done automatically.

9.2 WHAT IS CORPUS LINGUISTICS?

Corpus Linguistics is the application of computational tools to the analysis of corpora, in order to reveal language patterns which systematically occur in them. The rationale for such an analysis is that, on the one hand, large amounts of text can be analysed automatically – much more than would be humanly possible manually – and that, on the other hand, patterns may be revealed by the computational tools which may not be obvious to the naked eye. Corpus techniques are capable of providing information about various features of language, including lexis, multiword phrases, grammar, semantics, pragmatics and textual features.

Corpus analysis can provide a combination of the frequency of all the words or phrases and a record of all of the verbal environments in which these words occur (known as a *KWIC* [*key word in context*] *analysis* or *concordance*). Figure 9.1 shows a concordance of a single word based on a small corpus. It is to be noted that the concordance can be ordered in various ways from left and right of the keyword or phrase to reveal different collocational and grammatical patterns.

In addition to raw frequency data and KWIC concordances, there are a number of other phenomena which corpus tools can capture. One such is *dispersion*, the rate of occurrence of an item or feature in a corpus or individual file within a corpus; this can be displayed visually by means of a *dispersion plot*. Another thing corpus tools can provide data about is *keyness*, the significance with which a word or phrase occurs more or less frequently in a particular text or domain-specific corpus as compared to a *reference corpus*, that is to say, another corpus – which is usually larger – made up of a larger number of text types. Typical reference corpora for English would be those given as examples in section 9.1.

The results of Corpus Linguistics to date have been impressive and many insights, both large and small, about language have been arrived at through its application. Furthermore, many of the findings have fed into language teaching resources and materials and, even, as we shall see, had a not insignificant influence on teaching methodology.

9.3 SOME FUNDAMENTAL INSIGHTS ABOUT DISCOURSE FROM THE CORPUS PERSPECTIVE

A key insight of corpus linguists is the phraseological nature of language, how language is (at least partly) made up of more or less prefabricated multiword chunks, for example, *on the one hand, by the way, today I'm going to*. Sinclair (1991) referred to this tendency as the *idiom principle*. The idiom

Hit	KWIC
341	ensures, that whilst large social changes are noted, the individua
342	mple example for the large social changes which he accredits to th
343	determinants of the large social group sizes of geladas: <list>Ab
344	port cohesion within large social groups. The issue preliminarily
345	the individual and larger social changes in our understanding of
346	re reform. Overall lasting social policy reform involves the gover
347	lessness relates to a less social status. From analysing conversat
348	in the job world, but like Social work a job in this ever expandin
349	have been born into a low social class, but marry a man from a hi
350	ciation with groups of low social status. (Holmes, 2001). An examp
351	f language while the lower social class would be comfortable with
352	ved by other people. Lower social classes generally have a wider v
353	hat more speakers in lower social classes had a higher rate of not
354	e used by members of lower social classes. In 1966 William Labov p
355	es as opposed to the lower social classes. This can be proved by t
356	red to speakers from lower social classes who dropped ninety-six p
357	mber of [h] and the lowest social group omits the most number of [

Figure 9.1   Concordance of *social* sorted by first word on the left, first word on the right and then second word on the right.

principle can be contrasted with the *open-choice principle*, which has traditionally informed linguistics, whereby the speaker has many word-for-word options in building up discourse, that is to say, that many words possibly fit into any given slot, as long as they are grammatical.

In putting more emphasis on vocabulary with the idiom principle, Sinclair reversed the traditional roles for grammar and lexis. Grammar does not govern lexis, he argued, but, the other way round: lexis governs grammar. A focus on the structure of lexical chunks can lead to an understanding of grammar and discourse and not the other way round.

The idiom principle has important ramifications for Language Education, because it suggests that language might be taught, at least partly, in chunks rather than according to the more traditional slot and filler grammatical approach (Lewis, 1993, 1997). In support of the idiom principle, research in L1 acquisition studies has shown that children first acquire chunks and, only after this, generalise from chunks to grammatical rules (Wray, 2002, cited in Granger, 2011). If fluent speakers of a language acquire a huge stock of prefabricated patterns in order to communicate effectively, then learners need to develop a stock of such chunks, in order to develop fluency in the language as much as, if not more than, knowing grammatical rules which enable them to perform using the slot and filler approach.

The lexical approach was already argued for by Nattinger and de Carrico (1992: 32), who wrote as follows:

> It is our ability to use lexical phrases that helps us to speak with fluency. This prefabricated speech has both the advantages of more efficient retrieval and of permitting speakers (and learners) to direct their attention to the larger structure of the discourse, rather than keeping it narrowly focused on individual words as they are produced.

The lexical approach was later taken up and popularised by, most notably, Lewis (1993, 1997), who coined the slogan, 'language is grammaticalised lexis, not lexicalised grammar' (Lewis, 1993: 89).

Hoey developed Sinclair's idiom principle further in his theory of *lexical priming*. According to this theory, individuals are 'primed' (through their experience of previous encounters with vocabulary items) to expect words to occur in particular combinations. These combinations may involve other lexical items (collocation), grammatical items (*colligation,* see below), or textual environments (*textual colligations*). Lexical priming occurs when a vocabulary item is acquired and 'it becomes loaded with the contexts (linguistic, generic and social) in which we repeatedly encounter it, such that we subconsciously expect and replicate these contexts when we read, write, hear and speak' (http://lexicalpriming.org/). Lexical primings are tied to context and it cannot be assumed that primings functioning in one given context operate in the same way in other contexts. So, a word may be primed one way in, say, medicine or the news and in another way in, say, law or casual conversation (Hoey, 2005).

9.4 FEATURES OF ANALYSIS

Given the above insights from corpus linguistic theory and their relevance for Language Education, what are some of the features that Corpus Linguistics can analyse?

9.4.1 Word frequency

This is the most fundamental feature that can be analysed by means of corpus techniques. Most corpus software, such as Antconc and Wordsmith Tools (probably the two most popular publicly available packages – the former being downloadable for free), can produce frequency lists (which can be ordered alphabetically or by frequency). Used in conjunction with a concordancer (also a

Table 9.1   The 20 top nouns in the COBUILD corpus and in a biology corpus (Flowerdew, 1993a: 236, adapted)

COBUILD corpus	Biology corpus
time, people, way, man, years, work, world, thing, day, children, life, men, fact, house, kind, year, place, home, sort, end	cell, cells, water, membrane, food, plant, root, molecules, plants, wall, energy, concentration, organism, cytoplasm, animal, stem, structure, body, part, animals

basic feature of corpus software), frequency lists can also be created for multiword sequences (also referred to variously as *n-grams*, *clusters*, *prefabs* and *lexical bundles*, or just *bundles*).

The power of this application for language pedagogical purposes is in the potential for contrasting data from different corpora and obtaining information about register variation according to field of discourse. In an early study (Flowerdew, 1993a), for example, I discovered that there were striking differences in the frequency of nouns in two corpora I was working with, a general corpus (COBUILD) and a corpus of biology text created from lectures and readings in a university biology course (Table 9.1). The pedagogical implications of such a finding are many, but the main one is that students studying in the register of biology at the university in question need to learn a different set of lexis to that required in everyday life.

9.4.2 Collocation

Collocation is the combination of lexical words with one another. The word *fast* is likely to collocate in a large general corpus with words like *train* and *food*, as in *a fast train* and *fast food,* but is unlikely to be found together with *meal,* or *sleep*; *quick*, on the other hand, is likely to be found with *shower* and *meal*, as in *a quick* shower and *a quick meal,* but not with *train* or *food.*

Collocates are identified by *concordancers*, which display the node word in the centre of the screen, allowing for identification of their collocates on both the left and the right. If words immediately following the node word to the right are ordered alphabetically, then it is easy to identify those items which most typically collocate with the node. This analysis can be repeated at subsequent intervals from the node word to the right and to the left (that is to say, one two, three, four words to the right etc. and one, two, three, four words to the left, etc.). Normally collocates are identified at up to four or five words to the right or left and what constitutes a collocate is normally determined by statistical measures (L. Flowerdew, 2012).

As mentioned above, one feature of collocation is recurrent multiword patterns. Such patterns can be recovered automatically by corpus software. They occur in sequences of two, three, four and even more words, frequency decreasing with the length of the sequence. Some sequences are meaningful, while others are not. A feature of registers and genres is that they manifest distinctive patterns of these units.

According to Hoey's (2005) theory of lexical priming, there is also *textual collocation*, how words are primed to occur in particular cohesive relations. 'Every word is primed to participate in, or avoid, particular types of cohesive relation in a discourse; these are its textual collocations' (p.13). An example of this from Hoey (p. 119) is that over 80 per cent of occurrences of the word *army* in his corpus are as part of cohesive chains, whereas words such as *asinine, blink* and *particularly* are independent of such chains.

9.4.3 Colligation

Colligation refers to the grammatical, as opposed to lexical, environments in which a word occurs. Hoey uses the word *consequence* to demonstrate colligation. Analysing a large corpus of data from the *Guardian* newspaper, his corpus investigation found that *consequence* has a very low likelihood of appearing as the object of a clause, in contrast to *preference* and *use*, which do occur frequently in such a position. While we find many sentences such as: *The homeless are asked if **they have a preference*** and *The minister called on schools to **make more use*** *of the colleges' vocational experience*, Hoey argues, based on his corpus data, sentences like the following are rare: *Unfortunately it also **had this tragic consequence*** *that the baby became grossly bloated.*

While colligation refers to the grammatical associations of a word in a sentence, *textual colligation* refers to the position where the word tends to occur within a discourse. 'Every word is primed to occur in, or avoid, certain positions within the discourse; these are its textual colligations,' Hoey (2005: 13) writes. *Consequence,* for example, tends to occur in sentence-initial position, as either part of an adjunct or as part of the subject. The plural form of consequence, *consequences,* on the other hand, while not favouring an initial position in the sentence, does tend to occur in the first sentence of paragraphs.

9.4.4 Semantic prosody

Semantic prosody refers to the meaning associations that words carry with them by virtue of their typical collocations with sets of semantically related words. Louw (1993: 157), who popularised the term, defined semantic prosody as a 'consistent aura of meaning with which a form is imbued by its collocates'. Louw gave the words *utterly, bent on* and *symptomatic* as examples of negative aura, or semantic prosody. The process by which semantic prosody is created is described by Stewart (2010: 1), as follows: 'Semantic prosody is instantiated when a word such as CAUSE co-occurs regularly with words that share a given meaning or meanings, and then acquires some of the meaning(s) of those words as a result. The acquired meaning is known as semantic prosody.'

Semantic prosodies tend to be either negative or positive. By reading the concordances of the word *cause* in the COBUILD corpus, Stubbs (1996: 173–174) found that, in common with Louw's examples of *utterly, bent on* and *symptomatic,* in more than 90 per cent of cases, the lexical environments of *cause* were negative. *Cause* collocated with words like *accident, cancer, concern, damage, death, disease, pain, problems* and *trouble.* In contrast, a word like *provide* had a positive semantic prosody, typically collocating with words like *aid, assistance, care, employment, facilities, food, funds, housing, jobs, money, opportunities, protection, relief, security, services, support* and *training* (Stubbs, 1996: 173).

Semantic prosody is thus a type of pragmatic meaning, communicating a speaker's or writer's positive or negative attitude towards what s/he is saying. An important consideration with regard to semantic prosodies is that they are not accessible to intuition; they can only be identified by means of a corpus (McEnery & Hardie, 2012: 136). Indeed, Hunston (2007) has demonstrated that semantic prosodies vary according to register and the particular phraseologies in which a word occurs.

9.4.5 Semantic preference

Related to semantic prosody is *semantic preference*. Here, the concern is not with pragmatic value, but with sets of words semantically related, according to the systems of synonymy, meronymy and antonymy we looked at in Chapter 3 or which are typically associated with particular registers or genres. Words belonging to such sets can typically be found to collocate in corpora. Such sets can be given a gloss to label the semantic preference. Example semantic preferences might thus be 'measurement' or 'causality' or 'history' or 'medicine' or 'research articles'. Semantic preference is thus like semantic prosody, in that it refers to the meaning relations attaching to collocating sets. Unlike semantic prosody, however, it does not carry with it any sense of attitudinal meaning.

From the point of view of application to, say, syllabus design, one might wonder what the difference is between deriving semantic sets from a corpus and through intuition or from a thesaurus. The answer is that the corpus will give only those items which occur in the corpus; it may not include some items that can be derived from intuition. On the other hand, the corpus will provide frequency data, allowing the syllabus designer to select more frequent items and to prioritise items in the syllabus.

9.5 MULTIDIMENSIONAL ANALYSIS

The approach to Corpus Linguistics we have been focusing on in the above sections is sometimes referred to as Firthian or neo-Firthian, because it followed the meaning-focused approach to language initiated by the British linguist Firth (L. Flowerdew, 2012; McEnery & Hardie, 2012). Rather a different approach to corpora has been developed in the USA by Biber and his followers, referred to as *multidimensional analysis*. Biber's distinctive approach was developed in his work published as *Variation Across Speech and Writing* (Biber, 1991). Biber's purpose was to distinguish various named registers in term of their configurations of linguistic features.

The starting point was a set of registers and a set of linguistic features. Twenty-three registers were employed, including press reports, biographies, official documents, academic prose, various types of fiction, personal and professional letters, face-to-face and telephone conversations, interviews and spontaneous speeches, to mention just some of those included. Sixty-seven linguistic features were used in the analysis. Most of these linguistic features were syntactic (for example, tenses, relative clauses, adverbials), although lexical features (for example, lexical classes, mean word length) and semantic features (for example, different types of modals, place and time adverbials) features were also utilised.

The corpus was tagged automatically to identify the various features and the frequencies of each of the features were counted. The co-occurrence of various features across the different registers was then computed using factor analysis and these features were classified according to the following functional parameters:

* involved versus informational production;
* narrative versus non-narrative concerns;
* elaborated versus situation-dependent reference;
* overt expression of persuasion;
* abstract versus non-abstract style.

On this basis, Biber was able to characterise any register according to the degree to which it exhibited the various parameters and to compare registers in terms of these same parameters. One of the main conclusions of Biber's study was that variation does not occur in terms of all or nothing, but rather in terms of degree, along a cline. Another conclusion was that the various named registers do not adequately represent the different text types of English. As measured on the five dimensions, some registers are closer to each other than would be expected based on their names. Thus, for example, in terms of the involved versus informational dimension, personal letters were closer to face-to-face conversation than they were to official documents. The differences between spoken and written registers cannot be characterised simply in terms of speech and writing, therefore, but need to be considered in terms of more subtle distinctions.

Although none of the features employed by Biber in his analysis could be described as discourse features, in the sense that they are all sentence-level phenomena, multidimensional analysis does show up distinctive features of registers and to that extent can be seen as a contribution to Discourse Analysis. The features used in the analysis are primarily formal categories, but they come together, through factor analysis, in terms of their communicative functions.

Biber's analysis was used in one of the first corpus-based grammars of English: the *Longman Grammar of Spoken and Written English* (Biber *et al.*, 1999). An innovative feature of this grammar is the frequency data which are provided for the various grammatical features across registers.

In a later application of Biber's multidimensional analysis, the number of variables has been extended in the model. In particular, stance markers and lexical bundles have been added to the variables.

Of particular interest to readers of this book is Biber and colleagues' work on university registers (Biber *et al.*, 2002; Biber, 2006). The idea of the project was to describe the registers that students typically encounter in their university life. To this end, they created a 2.7-million-word purpose-built corpus consisting of ten university registers. Registers represented in the corpus included class sessions, office hours, study groups, on-campus service encounters, textbooks, course packs, and university catalogues and brochures. One of the major findings of the project was the tremendous amount of variation across the dimensions identified in the study, as represented by the different registers. On this basis Biber *et al.* (2002: 41) concluded that:

> [s]udents must deal not only with informationally dense prose but also with interactive and involved spoken registers. They must handle texts with elaborated reference as well as those that rely on situated reference, and texts with features of overt persuasion as well as texts that lack those features. They must understand discourse that uses an impersonal style with many passives as well as discourse that tends to avoid passives.

Another major finding of Biber *et al.*'s study was that, contrary to what was found in the earlier study of speech and writing reported above, different registers tended to be polarised along the various dimensions. That is to say, the written registers featured informationally dense prose, a very non-narrative focus, elaborated reference, few features of overt persuasion and an impersonal style, while spoken registers were characterised by features of involvement and interaction, situated reference, more overt persuasion and fewer features of impersonal style (Biber *et al.*, 2002: 41).

In more recent work, Biber and colleagues (Biber *et al.*, 2004, 2007) have applied a multidimensional approach to discourse structure, using computerised techniques known as TextTiling. TextTiling is a technique that identifies stretches of discourse (referred to as *vocabulary-based discourse units* [VBDUs]) that are maximally dissimilar in their vocabulary, the assumption being that different sets of words will be used in different types of VBDU. Figure 9.2 is an example of two VBDUs, where the distinctive words in each VBDU are shown in bold.

Biber *et al.* (2004: 55) summarise the steps in the VBDU analysis procedure, as follows:

1. Identify all VBDUs in a large, multiregister corpus, using TextTiling.
2. Analyse the linguistic characteristics of each VBDU, using multidimensional analysis.
3. Identify and interpret the basic VBDU types, using cluster analysis.
4. Analyse the preferred VBDU types in each register.
5. Analyse the structure of particular texts as sequences of VBDU types.

The approach can be applied to any register. In their first study, for example, Biber *et al.* (2004) analysed three registers: classroom teaching, textbooks and academic research articles. In a subsequent study by Biber *et al.* (2007), research articles and university class sessions were the focus of analysis. This approach to discourse structuring offers a novel way of text segmentation. It can be viewed as a complementary approach to move analysis, as applied in Genre Analysis (see below). Indeed, Biber et al (2007), in a number of contrastive studies, compare and contrast this method of move analysis with the more top-down approach used in Genre Analysis.

VBDU BOUNDARY

it's all **relative** to the individual **culture. of course** our **culture today** is **breaking apart.** it's really **very difficult** to **say** we **have a culture today. we have just** the **collection of some cultures. so** really we **ought to say** that **what's right** is **relative** to the **subculture.** but **then subcultures probably are** not as **homogeneous** as we **tend** to **think** we **are.** we're **all individuals** and **so even if I am a member** of a **subculture I'm probably going to disagree on certain issues. so where does** that **put us** ? whether it's **right** or **wrong** is **relative too. there are no standards** that **are valid beyond** the individual **person. if I think something** is **right, then** it is **right for me. if I think something** is **wrong,** it is **wrong for me. if I think** it's **right** and you **think** it's **wrong, then for me** you it is **wrong, for me** it is **right.**

VBDU BOUNDARY

and that's as **far** as we **can go.** that's **radical** individual **relativism.** and **many social commentators in** the **United States these days see such radical** individual **relativism as a rampant disease** that's **about** to **destroy** our **society** and is **usually thought by philosophy professors.**... or **people in cultural studies any more.** uh **somehow we've survived,** but uh we're not really **interested in** that we're **interested** whether it's a **correct theory** or not. and we're not really **this semester interested** whether it's a **correct theory, talk about** that **next semester.** uh this **semester** we're **interested in** whether or not **Sartre should be called** a **relativist.** and it **certainly looks like** it.

VBDU BOUNDARY

Figure 9.2   Example of text extract from classroom teaching, showing the location of vocabulary-based discourse unit (VBDU) boundaries (Biber *et al.*, 2004: 56–57).

9.6 CORPUS-ASSISTED DISCOURSE ANALYSIS

To the extent that Corpus Linguistics is concerned with patterns of language above the level of the sentence, as we have seen, it can be considered as an approach to Discourse Analysis. In mainstream Corpus Linguistics, however, the results of the analysis are arrived at automatically by means of the computer and analysts do not usually concern themselves with the contexts of the data which they derive. Mainstream Corpus Linguistics, arguably, therefore, does not concern itself with language in its context of use (unless, of course, the corpus itself is considered to be the context) (but see below on this question of context).

A distinguishing feature of discourse approaches to corpus analysis (sometimes referred to as Corpus-Assisted Discourse Analysis [CADS]) is that analysts are concerned to consider not only the corpus-derived data, but also the texts and contexts from which these data are derived. While Corpus Linguistics is essentially a quantitative approach to language, concerned with the frequency of occurrence of various language patterns, CADS introduces an additional, qualitative dimension to analysis. In addition, where mainstream corpora may consist of samples of texts, corpora used in CADS will more likely be made up of complete texts. Corpus approaches to discourse (or, to put it the other way round, discourse approaches to corpora) are becoming more and more popular.

Baker (2006) discusses a number of advantages of a corpus-based approach to discourse, as follows. First, because corpus tools can provide many examples of a given linguistic phenomenon, they can provide a greater degree of objectivity than can a qualitative analysis, that may be limited to a single text or small number of texts. As Baker (2006: 12) writes, '[it] becomes less easy to be selective about a single newspaper article when we are looking a hundreds of articles – hopefully, overall patterns and trends should show through'. Baker does acknowledge, however, that bias can in no way be removed completely and that corpus researchers, if they have such a disposition, can be as biased as anyone (p. 12).

Second, Baker notes that a corpus-based approach can identify what he refers to as 'the incremental effect of discourse', by which he means how discourses (with a small D) are built up over time, even though particular items might not occur that frequently. Corpus tools can identify how such discourses are created incrementally. He gives the example of the following sentence: 'Diana, herself a keen sailor despite being confined to a wheelchair for the last 45 years, hopes the boat will encourage more disabled people on to the water.' We may argue here, following Baker, that in spite of this sentence appearing to construct disabled people in a positive way, the use of the phrase *confined to a wheelchair*, and the way that the coordinator *despite* is used here, prompt the reader to infer that the disabled are not expected to be keen sailors. So, which Discourse does this sentence represent: the positive one or the negative one? By applying corpus tools to a large general corpus of British English, Baker is able to ascertain that the items *confined* and *wheelchair* have a tendency to co-occur and that *wheelchair* also tends to co-occur with coordinators such as *despite* and *although*. Baker concludes from this analysis that the original sentence about Diana is not an isolated case and that it belongs to a Discourse which negatively constructs people in wheelchairs.

A third advantage of a corpus-based approach to discourse noted by Baker is the opposite of the incremental argument, that is to say that the use of a particular linguistic feature identified in a single text, which might lead the analyst in a particular direction, may not be corroborated in a corpus of texts. The corpus thus here serves as a check on the analyst.

A fourth advantage of Corpus-based Discourse Analysis for Baker is the opportunity that it provides for triangulation (the use of multiple methods of analysis). Discourse Analysis of individual texts represents one mode of enquiry, while corpus-based study represents another, both supporting each other and making the analysis more reliable.

9.7 CORPORA AND CONTEXT

Widdowson (1998b) critiqued corpus approaches on the grounds that, while a corpus can provide examples of language, it does not tell us anything about the context in which those examples were produced. Meanings identified based on concordance lines do not tell the whole story, Widdowson argued, claiming that 'reality does not travel with the text' (p. 711). While some corpus linguists (for example, Stubbs, 2001; Tognini-Bonelli, 2001) have argued, contra Widdowson, that elements of social meaning can be identified through recurrent patterns occurring in a corpus (see L. Flowerdew, 2008a for discussion), this is a strong argument for introducing elements of the context into the analysis. In fact, as indicated in the previous section, there are now numerous examples of studies incorporating contextual features with corpus analysis, especially in academic and professional contexts.

At one level, many corpora allow users to click on individual corpus lines to see the whole text within which the concordance extract occurs. Corpora can thus enable users to view context. At another level, context can be introduced into a corpus through tagging it (by hand) according to relevant sociolinguistic variables. This is the case with the MICASE corpus of academic speech, for example. MICASE allows the user to view the original transcript of the (spoken) text within which a given concordance occurs by simply clicking on it. Each transcript is coded for a number of sociolinguistic variables, including native speaker status, speaker sex, speaker L1 background and speaker disciplinary field. Thus the viewer can obtain this sociolinguinguistic information for any concordance line. In addition, concordances can be grouped according to these variables via the search function. It is thus possible to obtain sets of concordances, for example, which only include native speakers, or which only include men or women, or which only include transcripts involving speakers from a particular language background or from a particular discipline.

Where specialised corpora are concerned, additional contextual information can be gained using other research methods, such as interviews and focus groups with those whose language is included in the corpus. An example of this is Hyland's (2000) study of *Disciplinary Discourses*, where he combined interviews and focus group discussions with users of the genres, triangulated with corpus-based analysis, in order to understand the relationship between the cultures of academic communities and their discourses. The analysis allowed Hyland to move from differences in such minutiae in the corpus as reporting verbs across disciplinary subcorpora (engineers tend to 'report', while philosophers tend to 'argue' and biologists to 'describe'), for example, to explanations for such minutiae in terms of the academic cultures to which the participants belong.

In the field of business discourse, in an approach not unlike that of Hyland, Handford (2010) used interviews to triangulate his corpus data of business meetings with the perspectives of the participants. In this way, he was able to relate textual patterns to discursive, professional and social practices.

Prior to Handford, Bilbow (1997, 1998, 2002) created a corpus of intercultural business meetings at an international airline in Hong Kong and involved the participants in the meetings through interviews and focus group discussion. Bilbow was able to use the differing cultural perspectives of the participants on the data (in the form of speech act realisation patterns) for the purposes of cross-cultural training in the company concerned.

Also in the business field, Stubbe and colleagues (2003) went so far as to involve the participants whose language made up their corpus in setting the research agenda for their study. Stubbe and colleagues also gave the participants ownership of the data, to be used for communication training purposes. In return, the participants allowed the researchers to work alongside them as collaborators in the research endeavour.

Finally, in the field of healthcare, a team at Nottingham University has combined communication studies in healthcare encounters with corpus approaches (Adolphs *et al.*, 2004). The approach is illustrated with an analysis of a corpus of telephone calls combined with conversation analytic techniques. The analysis reveals how health advisors position callers as the subjects of the interaction, how they give credibility to the advice they give and how they terminate the encounter with what the researchers refer to as a 'convergence coda'.

More and more integrated studies such as those just mentioned are now being conducted. Typically, these approaches are very much applied and involve a training goal, feeding back the findings to the participants. Another feature that many of these approaches have in common is that they are qualitative in nature or incorporate a qualitative dimension, using relatively small amounts of data, not designed to make statements about language in general.

An early account along these lines from a pedagogical perspective was that of Tribble (2002), who suggested a combination of corpus and contextual analysis in familiarising learners with a particular genre they might need to write in an academic context. In addition to using corpus tools to interrogate a corpus made up of texts belonging to the target genre, Tribble suggested a number of contextual questions that could be asked of the text. The corpus and contextual questions that learners could be invited to consider are set out in Table 9.2.

9.8 MOVE ANALYSIS

Another relatively recent development in discourse-focused corpus analysis has been to look at the distinctive features of generic moves. Biber *et al.*'s (2007) book, *Discourse on the Move*, referred to earlier, combines chapters which, on the one hand, use bottom-up VBDU analysis to identify discourse moves, as discussed above, while on the other hand, using top-down (manual) tagging to

Table 9.2   Analytic framework incorporating contextual and corpus-based features (Tribble, 2002: 133)

Contextual analysis	
Name	What is the name of the genre of which this text is a part?
Social context	In what social setting is this kind of text typically produced? What constraints and obligations does this setting impose on writers and readers?
Communicative purpose	What is the communicative purpose of this text?
Role	What roles may be required of writers and readers in this genre?
Cultural values	What shared cultural values may be required of writers and readers in this genre?
Text context	What knowledge of other texts may be required of writers and readers in this genre?
Formal text features	What shared knowledge of formal text features (conventions) is required to write effectively in this genre?
Linguistic analysis	
Lexicogrammatical features	What lexicogrammatical features of the text are statistically prominent and stylistically salient?
Text relations/textual patterning	Can textual patterns be identified in the text? What is the reason for such textual patterning?
Text structure	How is the text organised as a series of units of meaning? What is the reason for this organisation?

identify moves. A range of other studies have followed this latter approach (L. Flowerdew, 2008a, b, c; Flowerdew & Forest, 2009; Upton & Connor, 2001). In my own study, with Richard Forest, using Discourse Analysis techniques, we identified and annotated the moves in a corpus of PhD literature reviews. We then identified the salient features of each of the moves, using a computerised keyword technique, and discovered that three words – *research, study* and *studies* – correlated with particular moves and in particular phraseological patterns.

9.9 SMALL CORPORA

The research reported above in section 9.7 made use of relatively small corpora. The type of research in that section did not seek to make any broad generalisations about language, as is done with larger reference corpora, but it provided information about particular genres, that is to say research articles (Hyland, 2000, 2004), business meetings (Bilbow, 1997, 1998, 2002; Handford, 2010) and telephone service encounters (Adolphs *et al.*, 2004). What is considered to be small is being frequently reinterpreted as computers become more powerful (Sinclair, 2001: xiii). A decade or more ago a small corpus might have been somewhere around 100,000 words. Nowadays, however, a million words would not be considered to be very large at all. So it is difficult to define what a small corpus is exactly. An important variable is whether the data are written or spoken. Written data are easily managed and can often be downloaded directly from the internet. Spoken data, on the other hand, take a long time to transcribe. So a small corpus of spoken data is likely to be smaller than a small corpus of written data. As Sinclair (2001: xiii) notes, however, 'there is no special virtue in being small', except that smaller is more manageable. So, other things being equal, the larger the amount of data, the better, because more generalisations about the corpus will be possible. The more data we have, the more confident can we be about the 'descriptive adequacy' of our findings (Meyer, 2002: 3).

One danger if a corpus is too small is that of not having enough examples. Any corpus has half of its words occurring only once (Sinclair, 2001: x), but in corpus work we need multiple examples, not only of words, but of pairs or more of words occurring together, to get representative examples of grammatical usage, collocations or prosody. On the other hand, if working with restricted registers and genres, the likelihood of new words being added when the size of the corpus is increased is less (Meyer, 2002: 39). If we are applying the corpus to language pedagogy – for example, syllabus design or classroom materials – then what we want is the typical, not the atypical, so a smaller corpus is likely to be more acceptable.

Having identified the issue of size as a potential problem, there are three main advantages to using small corpora which we can list here. The first advantage is that small corpora are relatively easy to create, often being constructed by teachers and curriculum developers themselves. As a consequence, they can quickly be exploited. Sinclair (2001: x) refers to large corpora as being designed for 'late human intervention' (because of the time and effort it takes to create them) and small corpora as being designed for 'early human intervention' (because they can quickly be created and used).

The second advantage of small corpora is that the data can be limited to a particular genre in a particular setting and so salient features of the genre are not drowned out by data from other genres and/or settings.

The third advantage is that small corpora can be processed by readily available software packages such as AntConc and Wordsmith Tools or web-based tools.

These three advantages of small corpora make them ideal for application in many language-teaching situations and, in particular, in specific purpose contexts. Sinclair (2001: xii–xiii) sets out the advantages of small corpora for language teaching as follows.

> corpus evidence can illuminate language teaching from many different angles; as well as … comparisons [across languages and genres], there is the accurate description of structure, reliable models of usage, how words and phrases are actually translated [with parallel corpora], what are the essentials in a syllabus, what are the characteristic errors of learners etc.

Gavioli (2005) provides a book-length treatment of corpora in English for Specific Purposes (ESP), highlighting the use of small corpora.

9.10 LEARNER CORPORA

Learner corpora are systematic collections of learner language data. The aim of learner corpora is to compare learner usage with native, or expert, usage. A given learner corpus may also be compared to other learner corpora. Most learner corpora are collected from learners of a particular language background, so that the distinctive interlanguage of those speakers (or writers) is represented and can be compared with expert usage or from other L2s.

Probably the best known collection of learner corpora is the *International Corpus of Learner English* (ICLE), created by Granger with her students and colleagues. This collection originally consisted of written language (argumentative essays), but there is now also a suite of spoken language corpora. In addition, there is a comparable corpus of L1 data. Apart from ICLE, more and more learner corpora are being created worldwide. These developments include diachronic learner corpora, which track learners over a period of time (for example, the in-progress *Longitudinal Database of Learner English* project by the Centre for English Corpus Linguistics, University of Louvain, Belgium).

Learner corpora are usually annotated for features of learner interlanguage (errors). Comparison of learner and expert corpora can reveal inappropriate use and also over- and under-use of given features on the part of learners. Findings from learner corpus analysis can be applied to dictionaries, grammars and the design of syllabuses. For the classroom teacher, learner corpora can be used to help test teachers' intuitions about whether a particular target language feature is difficult or not (Granger, 2002: 22). Learner corpora can also be created by teachers from their regular classes of students for immediate pedagogical use (Granger, 2004). Such data have the advantage of being more relevant and motivating, as the producers of the data are also the users (de Cock, 2010: 132).

One issue of concern with learner corpora is that, in focusing on error, there is a danger of a deficit model of learning developing, where the emphasis is on student failure rather than success. This can be overcome by focusing on positive features of interlanguage, what learners have already mastered correctly (de Cock, 2010: 132). Diachronic corpus evidence would be particularly useful in this regard.

9.11 APPLICATION TO PEDAGOGY

In discussing the application of Corpus Linguistics to Language Education, a distinction can be made between direct and indirect approaches (Flowerdew, 2009; Frankenberg-Garcia, 2012; Leech, 1997; Römer, 2010; Stubbs, 2004). Indirect approaches are concerned with the use of corpus research methods in the production of dictionaries, grammars and teaching materials, while direct applications involve the actual use of corpora or corpus outputs in the classroom.

9.11.1 Indirect applications

Corpus methods and findings provide a solid basis for developing language learning resources of one sort or another. As Frankenberg-Garcia (2012) points out, 'many teachers have been using corpus-based materials such as dictionaries, grammars and textbooks for some time without actually knowing what a corpus is.' The results of corpus-based input into these resources are immense, however.

9.11.1.1 Dictionaries

The area in which corpora have had the greatest impact is in the creation of dictionaries. In fact, lexicography provided much of the impetus for Corpus Linguistics as a discipline of enquiry. Corpus findings can enrich dictionaries by providing frequency data, authentic examples for citations and empirically based information about grammatical usage and register and genre variation. Most dictionaries nowadays incorporate corpus findings, *Collins COBUILD English Dictionary*, created under the guidance of Sinclair, being the precursor of others produced by publishers, including Longman, Macmillan, and Oxford and Cambridge University Presses. Hoey (undated), chief adviser on the *Macmillan Dictionary of English for Advanced Learners*, in a discussion of this dictionary, suggests that there are five questions that linguistics (and learners) need to ask about any word (and that are included in his dictionary), as follows.

1. What does the word mean?
2. What words does it associate with?
3. What meanings does it associate with?
4. What grammatical functions does it associate with?
5. What positions in the text does the word favour?

Astute readers will note that, with the exception of perhaps the first, these questions relate to lexical features identified by corpus linguists, as discussed above in this chapter, namely semantic

preference (question 2), semantic prosody (question 3), colligation (question 4) and textual colligation (question 5); even question 1, in part, is relevant to the discussion of this chapter, because the
meaning of a word is partially determined by the company it keeps with other words (it was Firth
[1957: 11], Sinclair's teacher and mentor, who declared that 'You shall know a word by the company
it keeps').

9.11.1.2 Grammars and grammar resource books

Corpus-informed dictionaries were followed by reference grammars, Sinclair again being the pre-
cursor, with the *Collins COBUILD English Grammar* (Sinclair *et al.*, 1990). This has been followed
by the *Longman Grammar of Spoken and Written English* (Biber *et al.*, 1999) and the *Cambridge
Grammar of English* (Carter & McCarthy, 2006). With regard to grammar resource books, again,
Collins, under the leadership again of Sinclair, was the first, with an extensive series called *Collins
COBUILD English Guides*. Titles focused on linguistic features such as *Determiners* (Berry, 1996),
Linking Words (Chalker, 1996) and *Reporting* (Thompson, 1993).

9.11.1.3 Course books

In my state-of-the-art chapter on corpora in language teaching for *The Handbook of Language
Teaching* (Flowerdew, 2009), I referred to Nattinger (cited in Richards & Rogers [2001: 133–134]),
who, as early as 1980, put forward the idea of organising a syllabus according to prefabricated patterns, as follows:

> Perhaps we should base our teaching on the assumption that, for a great deal of the time
> anyway, language production consists of piecing together the ready-made units appropriate
> for a particular situation and that comprehension relies on knowing which of these patterns
> to predict in these situations. Our teaching, therefore, would center on these patterns and the
> ways they can be pieced together, along with the ways they vary and the situations in which
> they occur.

> Instead of being organised in terms of grammatical forms, the syllabus can be designed around
> the most important recurrent patterns (Sinclair & Renouf, 1988; Willis, 1990; Willis & Willis, 1988).
> This type of syllabus is referred to as a lexical syllabus. Willis and Willis (1988) wrote an early com-
> mercial course book to be organised along phraseological lines, although further applications have
> been slow in coming. An exception is the *Touchstone* multilevel course book series (McCarthy *et
> al.*, 2005).

9.11.1.4 Specialised indirect applications

As well as in commercial applications, corpora have been used by practitioners 'in the field'. Flowerdew (1993a) describes how an ESP syllabus and set of course materials can be designed using
input on frequency and concordance data derived from a corpus of lectures and readings. A resource
which is being widely applied in the field of English for Academic Purposes (EAP) is Coxhead's
(2000) academic word list, a corpus-derived list. The list consists of 570 word families that are not
among the most frequent 2,000 words of English, but which are frequent in academic registers. The
list can be used in the preparation of EAP courses. More recently, lists have been created based on
lexical phrases, or bundles (for example, Simpson-Vlach & Ellis, 2010).

9.11.2 Direct applications

With direct corpus approaches to pedagogy, we enter a field referred to as *data-driven learning* (DDL). DDL was developed by T. Johns, the idea being that students themselves become linguistic researchers (T. Johns, 2002). T. Johns also used the metaphor of 'language detective' and the slogan 'Every student a Sherlock Holmes!' (T. Johns, 1997: 101) to describe the role of the learner in DDL. With DDL, the student works directly with corpora or corpus outputs. The student is thus immersed in an environment of authentic language, sometimes referred to as 'real' language – as opposed to artificial language – by proponents of DDL.[1] In DDL, learners need to seek answers to questions that can be found by means of corpus queries and/or concordance lines. They need to conduct searches, analyse recurrent patterns to be found in concordance lines and make their own generalisations. Learners may do this by working on concordance print-outs (T. Johns's preferred method) or directly with the computer and the corpus (Gaskell & Cobb, 2004; Gavioli, 2001; Meyer *et al.*, 2000). As well as presenting learners with authentic language use, DDL may have a corrective function, in allowing learners to compare their output with that of expert writers or by consulting a learner corpus that has been tagged for errors (Gilquin & Granger, 2010: 359).

Hoey (undated) has suggested that a phraseological approach might be best suited to advanced learners and that DDL might be especially appropriate with this group.

> Collocations and idioms are of the greatest importance to the language learner; one of the things that distinguishes an advanced learner's language from that of a native speaker is that advanced learners often manifest grammatical correctness but collocational inappropriateness.

This is a valid point, but it raises a fundamental issue concerning the role of the 'native speaker' as the target for leaning. The suggestion here is that the target for learning is 'native-speaker' English (notwithstanding that, elsewhere, Hoey (2005) presents a more critical view of the native-speaker construct).[2] While 'native-speaker' English might be a valid target for many, some applied linguists have critiqued this view, some of them arguing that lingua franca English should be the target, not 'native-speaker' English, and others arguing that world Englishes might also be an alternative target (see Flowerdew, 2012b, for discussion). With an eye on this issue, some applied linguists and practitioners prefer to refer to *expert,* as opposed to *native-speaker* corpora.

With DDL, the corpus becomes (at least partly) the teacher; or, to put it another way, the teacher becomes a guide who helps the learner interrogate the corpus and interpret the corpus findings. This is a new role for teachers and, in some contexts, may take some adapting to; teachers who see themselves as facilitators rather than purveyors of knowledge are likely to be better suited to this approach. On the other hand, if a teacher is not an L1 speaker of the language (or even if s/he is, in many cases) the corpus can replace the dictionary, the grammar book or native-speaker informant, because the corpus takes on these roles. A problem with this, though, is that, with a dictionary, a grammar or a native speaker, one is dealing with 'agreed' knowledge.[3] With the corpus, the user needs to exercise judgement, in terms of probability and tendencies, rather than 'right or wrong'.

9.11.3 Language education and lexical priming

Hoey's (2005) theory of lexical priming has particular implications for language teaching. In a concluding section of his book, devoted to implications for learners of a second language, he writes that, following his theory of priming, when the vocabulary of the first language is acquired, it is learned for the first time. When a second language is learned, however, the learner will likely already have the primings from the first-language vocabulary, which will be superimposed on the primings of the new language. In the early stages of learning, this might be an aid, Hoey claims, but later, when more subtle meanings are at stake, Hoey's theory implies that a whole new field of 'false friends' will come into play, that is to say words that have the same meaning in two languages but which are primed differently in terms of collocation, colligation, semantic prosody and semantic preference.

Given that the range of primings in any language is infinite, the theory presents a major challenge in terms of methodology. Where the first-language user builds up primings over a lifetime in authentic contexts of use, second-language learners need to do this over a limited timescale and usually in the context of the classroom. Rather than teaching lists of words and their primings, a better strategy for the teacher is likely to be one that teaches – based on corpus data – noticing and learning strategies that assist learners in developing what might be called their 'priming literacy'.

9.12 CRITIQUE

The *critique* section has been delayed until last in this chapter, because critique needs to be considered in relation to both Corpus Linguistics as an approach to language and as an application to Language Education. This is not the result of a desire to end on a negative note, far from it.

9.12.1 Criticisms of Corpus Linguistics as an approach to language

A fundamental aspect of Corpus Linguistics in the context of this chapter and this volume is that, in focusing on phraseology, Corpus Linguistics is not really Discourse Analysis; it only tells us about phrasal phenomena, not language use above the level of the sentence, which is the domain of Discourse Analysis. In the course of this chapter we have seen how this might be responded to.

First, one might argue that phraseologies are sensitive to register and genre. On the one hand, as we have already explained in this chapter, phraseologies tell us a lot about registers and genres; on the other hand, knowledge about registers and genres can inform our understanding of phraseologies.

Second, it is possible to employ corpus techniques to look at suprasentential phenomena, not just phraseologies. We have seen this with Biber's VBDUs. Other studies of suprasentential features that we could cite are Partington's (1998) and Flowerdew's (2003a) studies of how abstract nouns operate across sentences, or the chapters in Flowerdew and Mahlberg (2006), which consider various features of lexical cohesion, or Aijmer's (1996) study of conversational routines. Having said that, it must be conceded that there are many suprasentential features of discourse that are not amenable to corpus analysis – for example, theme–rheme patterns or pronoun referents, and other cohesive links (Biber *et al.*, 1998). The computer can identify surface features of text, but not underlying semantic relations (unless these are first of all tagged) (Thornbury, 2010: 275).

Third, as we have seen in the sections on Corpus-assisted Discourse Analysis and corpus and context, many approaches now employ multiple methods, integrating corpus tools and other qualitative methods associated with Discourse Analysis.

Baker (2006) mentions some other potential drawbacks of Corpus Linguistics, two of which we can mention here. The first of these is that corpus analysis, in spite of the appearance that it gives of objectivity, is still subjective – subjective in terms of the items selected for analysis and in terms of the interpretation put on the data by the analyst. Corpus Linguistics findings are thus susceptible to abuse and disagreement, according to this view. Of course, the same criticism might apply to any qualitative research methodology, but the issue does highlight the fact that Corpus Linguistics is not just a quantitative approach, but both a quantitative and a qualitative one.[4]

The second of Baker's concerns is that corpus data may go out of date. Language is evolving all the time and so researchers need to be aware that, if they want to represent contemporary usage, their corpora need to be up to date. A good example of this problem is the *British National Corpus*.

This corpus was collected in the mid-1990s. It is thus questionable to what extent it represents – now that we are well into the twenty-first century – contemporary British usage, which was the intention of the corpus. One part of the corpus, the BNC Colt corpus, is devoted to teenage language. One may ask to what extent the data in this subcorpus conform to the way British teenagers use English today, given the rapid rate at which adolescent language evolves (Flowerdew, 2009).

9.12.2 Criticisms of corpus applications to Language Education

Turning now to criticisms of applications of corpus techniques to pedagogy, Guilquin and Granger (2010) and Granger (2011) discuss a number of potential problem areas for data-driven learning. Guilquin and Granger (2010) highlight four potential drawbacks.

The first of these is logistical, concerning money and time. The cost of acquiring and maintaining the necessary hardware and software may be beyond the budgets of schools and universities, even in sophisticated societies. In addition, it takes time, first of all, to prepare the materials to be used in DDL and, second, to prepare the students to use the materials, students who are likely to be unfamiliar with this form of learning.

The second drawback is from the teacher's point of view. Teachers will need in-service training to be able to develop DDL. In addition, teachers may find it difficult adapting to the particular requirements of DDL, an approach which assigns a less central role for the teacher than the individual may be accustomed to. Teachers may feel that they lose control with such an approach and, in traditional contexts, they may not feel comfortable in no longer being the main source of knowledge and expertise in the classroom, this passing, in part, to the computer.

The third potential drawback, for Guilquin and Granger (2010), is from the learner's point of view. Adapting to be able to learn through DDL requires time and effort. Learners need to develop 'corpus literacy' (Mukherjee, 2002: 179); they need to learn how to devise appropriate search strategies and make generalisations from search results. If they are deductive learners, they may have difficulty in adapting to the more inductive approach of DDL. It is important for learners that (a) the textual data they are asked to work with are at an appropriate level of difficulty and (b) they are given a task that using concordance data helps them perform.

The fourth potential drawback, for Guilquin and Granger (2010), is in terms of the content of learning. Teachers need to make sure that the data they are using are appropriate, correspond to the appropriate register, genre and level of difficulty of the learners, and represent contemporary usage. They need to make sure that the search output is appropriate, that there is neither too much nor too little, nor no relevant data at all. Data may be difficult to interpret for learners because of limited knowledge of the target language. Furthermore, teachers need to be aware that DDL may not be suitable for all language questions. Errors in prepositions, for example, may be more readily dealt with by DDL than articles, for example (Someya, cited in Guilquin & Granger, 2010: 367).

Granger (2011) adds two further issues of concern with regard to the lexical approach in general. First, if DDL becomes too dominant, the generative power of structural grammar may be ignored: 'it would be a foolhardy gamble to rely primarily on the generative power of lexical phrases', Granger argues. The piling-up in memory of a lot of chunks without the knowledge of how to put them together may be detrimental. Granger cites Wray, who argues for 'a balance between formulaicity and creativity'. Second, in a lexical approach, there is a lot of emphasis on the many patterns individual words can enter into; there is thus a risk of too much depth and not enough breadth in terms of the range of learning items.

A final danger to guard against with DDL, and not referred to by Guilquin and Granger (2010) or by Granger (2011), but mentioned by Swales (2002) is that DDL carries with it the risk of an emphasis on the decontextualised corpus line, at a time when applied linguists are still, after many years, struggling to get away from this approach to language teaching.

9.13 QUESTIONS FOR DISCUSSION

1. Which do you think is more important in language: the idiom principle or the open-choice prin-
    ciple? What implications might this have for teaching and learning a language?
2. Think of some words which have: (a) a broad range of collocates and (b) a narrow range of col-
    locates. Give examples of each type.
3. Think of some words which have (a) a negative and (b) a positive semantic prosody. If possible,
    use a concordancer, such as COCA (http://corpus.byu.edu/coca/) to test your intuition.
4. The following is the web address of MICASE: http://quod.lib.umich.edu/m/micase/. Go online
    and experiment with the social variables which are available for, for example, sex, native- versus
    non-native speaker, first language, and academic position. Note how a search for a given word
    or phrase will vary according to these variables.
5. What are the advantages and disadvantages of small and large corpora from the point of view
    of application to pedagogy?
6. What is your opinion regarding an appropriate target for learning: 'native-speaker' English, a
    variety of World Englishes, or lingua franca English?
7. Section 9.12.2 presents a series of possible drawbacks to corpus-based approaches to teach-
    ing and learning. Review these drawbacks and then consider the advantages. Which set of
    arguments do you think makes a more powerful case? Give your reasons.

9.14 FURTHER READING

Baker, 2006; Flowerdew, 2012b; McEnery and Hardie, 2012; O'Keeffe and McCarthy, 2010;
    O'Keeffe *et al.*, 2007; Sinclair, 1991.

CHAPTER 10

Critical Discourse Analysis

10.1 INTRODUCTION

Critical Discourse Analysis (CDA) is a transdisciplinary approach to discourse, drawing on social as well as linguistic theory. It has been influential not only in language studies, but also in other fields such as business, public health, organisational studies, media studies, accounting, and even tourism. It focuses on the ways social power is enacted through spoken and written text (and, more recently, through visual images, sound and other forms of semiosis), with a special emphasis on dominance, exploitation and resistance in various social contexts.

The approach followed by CDA differs from the other approaches dealt with in this book in that the starting point is a specific social issue or problem rather than particular linguistic features or phenomena. It investigates how such issues – for example, institutional power relations, racism, sexism, political exploitation – are instantiated in discourse, whatever form that discourse might take.

As mentioned in Chapter 1, in CDA, the term *discourse* may be used in a different way to that of the other chapters in this book. In previous chapters, we have used the term *discourse* to refer to language use in general. In CDA, the term *discourse* may be used to refer to a specific set of meanings expressed through particular forms and uses which give expression to particular institutions or social groups (Kress, 1989a). We can thus talk about 'the discourse of managerialism' or 'the discourse of advertising' or 'gay discourse' or 'Christian discourse'. This meaning derives from the work of the French philosopher, Michel Foucault (1982), for whom discourse refers more to a set of ideas or beliefs than to specific instances of language. Discourse is what *could be* said about something rather than what *is* said about it, according to Foucault. Following this reading, discourse comes close to ideology. In this meaning, *discourse* is a count noun and can be used in the plural; we can talk about different *discourses*. As mentioned in Chapter 1, again, this understanding of the term discourse is referred to by Gee (2011a) as big 'D' discourse, as opposed to the other meaning, which he labels with a little 'd'.

The antecedents of CDA are usually said to lie in *Critical Linguistics*, a movement developed at the University of East Anglia during the 1970s. Scholars working in this group, led by Fowler (for example, Fowler, 1991, 1996a), but also including names such as Kress, Hodge and Trew (for example, Fowler *et al.*, 1979) were concerned to develop a social approach to linguistics which recognised power relationships as a central theoretical issue and text as its main unit of analysis (Kress, 1989a). Five figures are generally seen as key in CDA: Norman Fairclough, Gunther Kress, Teun van Dijk, Theo van Leeuwen and Ruth Wodak, although Kress and van Leeuwen have not emphasised the critical element in their more recent work, having been more active in other areas,[1] particularly in Multimodal Discourse Analysis (for example, Kress & van Leeuwen, 1996). According to Wodak (2001a), this group of researchers came together at a meeting in 1991 organised by van Dijk in Amsterdam and which was seen as the 'formal' initiation of CDA. In addition, the group contributed articles to a special edition of *Discourse and Society,* in 1993, entitled *Critical Discourse Analysis.* That being said, it is important to emphasise that CDA has never been a 'school' in the strict sense of the term, each member of the group following his or her own approach.

Many social theorists, such as Bernstein, Bourdieu, Derrida, Gramsci, Foucault, Giddens and Habermas, have drawn attention to the key role of language in society. However, as Fairclough (2003a: 2), probably the most prominent theoretician in CDA, has pointed out, these theorists have not examined the linguistic features of text. CDA, on the other hand, has sought to bring together social theory and textual analysis. As in mainstream critical social theory, the aim of CDA is to uncover hidden assumptions (in the case of the latter, in language use) and debunk their claims to authority. Following Hegel, however, criticism is not simply a negative judgement, but has a positive emancipatory function. CDA thus has a specific agenda in bringing about social change, or at least supporting struggle against inequality (van Dijk, 2001a).

CDA views language (and other semiotic systems) as a form of social practice (Fairclough, 1989; Fairclough & Wodak, 1997; Wodak, 2001a). According to Fairclough (1989), 'using language is the commonest form of social behaviour'. If language is a form of social behaviour, then there is a need to relate theories of society to theories of language. As Chouliaraki and Fairclough (1999: 16) put it:

> We see CDA as bringing a variety of theories into dialogue, especially social theories on the one hand and linguistic theories on the other, so that its theory is a shifting synthesis of other theories, though what it itself theorises in particular is the mediation between the social and the linguistic …

Fairclough sees every instance of discourse as having three interrelated dimensions: as a text (spoken or written); as an interaction between people involving processes of producing and interpreting the text; and as part of a piece of social action. These three dimensions are seen as interacting (Figure 10.1).

Fairclough (1992a:10–11) writes with regard to a later version of this diagram that:

> The relationship between social action and text is mediated by interaction: that is, the nature of the interaction, how texts are produced and interpreted, depends upon the social action in

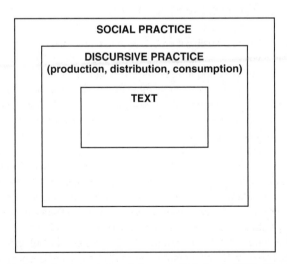

Figure 10.1   Fairclough's three-dimensional view of discourse (Fairclough, 1989: 25, adapted)

which they are embedded; and the nature of the text, its formal and stylistic properties, on the one hand depends upon and constitutes 'traces' of its process of production, and on the other hand constitutes 'cues' for its interpretation.

In addition to the above, CDA has a number of other commonly shared precepts. First, as already suggested, CDA views discourse and society as mutually constitutive, that is to say, a society is not possible without discourse and discourse cannot exist without social interaction. That is not to say, however, that all action is discursive. On the contrary, CDA allows for the interplay of discursive and material action (van Leeuwen [1996], in particular, emphasises this point).

Another precept of CDA is that, because it is interested in power relations and is emancipatory in nature, it typically examines specific discursive situations where dominance and inequality are to the fore. Analysis does not view discursive interaction as necessarily a question of *heroes* and *villains* (van Dijk, 1993; Wodak, 1999), however. Participants may not be aware of how powerful or powerless they are in discourse terms. Indeed, it is the role of CDA to reveal these relationships.

In fact, CDA may play a role in bringing about change in social practices and relationships in, for example, teacher development, the design of guidelines for non-sexist language or proposals to increase the intelligibility of news and legal texts (Titscher *et al.*, 2000). The related movement of *Critical Language Awareness* (CLA), developed by Fairclough and his associates at the University of Lancaster (Fairclough, 1992b) (see more on this below), argues for a systematic application of a critical approach to language along the lines of CDA in schools and in society at large.

A further commonly held precept is that CDA is open to multiple readings (although this has been critiqued: for example, Blommaert, 2005; Widdowson, 2004), as indicated by the following quotations from Fairclough (2003a: 14–15):

> we should assume that no analysis of a text can tell us all there is to be said about it – there is no such thing as a complete and definitive analysis of a text …

> Textual analysis is also inevitably selective: in any analysis, we choose to ask certain questions about social events and texts, and not other possible questions. … There is no such thing as an 'objective' analysis of a text, if by that we mean an analysis which simply describes what is 'there' in the text without being 'biased' by the 'subjectivity' of the analyst.

However, readings will be more plausible if grounded in the interplay of text and context (Fairclough *et al.*, 2011). Analysis involves a continual shunting between the microanalysis of texts and the macroanalysis of social structures and formations and power relations.

Contextual analysis may or may not include ethnographic analysis. Although Fairclough (2003a: 15) allows for an ethnographic dimension, this is not part of his personal practice. For Wodak, on the other hand, ethnography is essential to her method (see below; see also Blommaert, 2005). For both Fairclough and Wodak (Fairclough *et al.* 2011), an important dimension of context is intertexuality (Kristeva, 1980, following Bakhtin, 1986), how one text interrelates with other texts.

In the study of context, Fairclough *et al.* (2011) refer to the historical dimension – understanding the historical sociopolitical situation in which a text is produced. They use an analysis of an extract of an interview with Margaret Thatcher as an example of the importance of an understanding of this historical dimension – in this case, of what was going on in Britain in the 1940s.

As well as being historical, CDA can be historiographic, that is to say, it can play a part in the writing of history (Fairclough, 2001; Flowerdew, 2012a; Fowler, 1996b). Indeed, history is one of the most obvious disciplines which might make use of CDA as an analytical method (see articles in Martin & Wodak, 2003).

10.2 SOME MAJOR PROPONENTS

10.2.1 Fairclough

Fairclough has focused on discourse and power (Fairclough, 2001), on discourse and social change (globalisation, neoliberalism, knowledge economy) and on media discourse. He takes a theoretical approach, usually examining relatively small extracts of text in order to illustrate concepts such as orders of discourse, intertextuality, hybridity and voice. On the social side, he is influenced by the work of Foucault and the political economists Laclau and Mouffe (1985/2001), among others. In terms of political engagement, his book, *New Labour, New Language?* (Fairclough, 2000), is an attempt at a more popular contribution aimed at the general public, while his earlier edited collection *Critical Language Awareness* (Fairclough, 1992b) has argued for a systematic critical approach to language that can be carried over into schools and to the public at large.

A summary of one of Fairclough's later papers (2005) gives an idea of his approach. In this paper, Fairclough makes it clear that his is a specific version of CDA

> which is characterized by a realist and dialectical-relational theory of discourse, a methodology which is oriented to constructing objects of research through theorizing research topics in dialogue with other areas of social theory and research, and selecting methods which are in part inherent to this version of CDA and in part dependent upon the particular object of research.

In this particular study, Fairclough focuses on elements of political transition in Romania – the 'knowledge-based economy' – focusing on one discourse phenomenon – recontextualisation – how an element of discourse may be taken from a particular context and incorporated into another one, with a consequent change of meaning.

10.2.2 Wodak

In common with Fairclough, Wodak's research agenda focuses on the development of theoretical approaches to CDA. She combines elements of ethnography, argumentation theory, rhetoric and functional systemic linguistics, focusing on gender, language in politics, prejudice and discrimination. She is best known for her work on political discourse to do with antisemitism in Austria, where she developed, with colleagues, her *discourse-historical* method. She has also studied the discourse and politics of the European Union, focusing on issues including unemployment, NATO and neutrality in Austria and Hungary, the discursive construction of European identities, racism 'at the top' and parliamentary debates on immigration. In general, Wodak's approach is much more ethnographic than Fairclough's. She is also interested in the role of history in discourse (Martin & Wodak, 2003), labelling her approach the 'discourse historical method' (Wodak, 2001b).

10.2.3 van Dijk

Developing earlier work in the 1970s on the psychology of text processing with Walter Kintch (van Dijk, 1977b), van Dijk's contribution to CDA has been in developing a sociocognitive model, with a focus on the discursive reproduction of racism, in particular, by politicians, journalists, scholars and writers (which he refers to as the 'symbolic elites'), and in printed news media. van Dijk's sociocognitive approach attempts to bridge the gap between society and discourse. Working from a mental models approach, van Dijk sees discourse, processed via long- and short-term memory, as shaping our perceptions and understandings. Stereotypes and prejudice can occur when such models become overgeneralised. In relation to this work, van Dijk has been interested in developing theories of ideology and context. He founded the leading journal devoted to CDA, *Discourse and Society*, which he still edits.

10.2.4 Kress

Although, as already mentioned, in his later work, Kress has moved away from CDA, as one of the founding members of the group, his is an important contribution. Already, in earlier work, with Fowler (Fowler *et al.*, 1979) and Hodge (Hodge & Kress, 1979/1989), he was a leading theoretician for critical linguistics, focusing on ideology in news discourse. His later book, *Linguistic Processes in Sociocultural Practice* (Kress, 1989a), is significant in setting out some important principles for CDA, as is his contribution to the special edition of *Discourse and Society,* referred to above, 'Against Arbitrariness: The Social Production of the Sign as a Foundational Issue in Critical Discourse Analysis'. In this paper, as in his other contributions, Kress (1989b) argues that a fundamental understanding for a critical approach to discourse is the 'motivated' relation of the signifier and the signified, how producers and readers of signs are motivated by their backgrounds and social histories which make up the relevant context, including the social structures and the power relations existing therein. He also argues that a focus on 'bland' texts might be more productive than texts which are less obviously ideologically marked and for the intrinsically multimodal nature of texts.

10.2.5 van Leeuwen

van Leeuwen is influenced by his background in film and television and emphasises the overall semiotic nature of discourse (van Leeuwen, 2004), considering not just text, but acoustic and visual elements of discourse, as well as material action. With regard to CDA, and in accordance with his overall semiotic approach, van Leeuwen (1996: 33) has stated that:

> [t]here is no neat fit between sociological and linguistic categories and if Critical Discourse Analysis, in investigating for instance the representation of agency, ties itself in too closely to specific linguistic operations or categories, many relevant instances of agency might be overlooked.

van Leeuwen is well known for a large-scale project studying globalisation and discourse (Machin & van Leeuwen, 2003) and for his 2008 book *Discourse and Practice: New tools for CDA* (van Leeuwen, 2008).

10.3 SOME KEY ISSUES

10.3.1 Language and power

Indicative of the central role of power in CDA is the title of Fairclough's (1989) seminal collection of papers where he first published his ideas on CDA, *Language and Power*. CDA enables us to look into the discourse dimensions of power abuse, which leads to injustice and inequality. As one of the essential functions of text and talk is to persuade others to one's point of view, it is possible to analyse the linguistic structures and the discursive strategies of a discourse in order to uncover the power struggle, social inequality and other forms of social and political problems at issue (van Dijk, 1993). It follows, therefore, that the social, political and cultural organisation of dominance in the language structures of a discourse is constitutive of a hierarchy of power.

When applied to the analysis of social inequality, CDA accounts for how discourse structures – which are established through various linguistic patterns and structures – work in their specific ways to convey social cognitions (how people think) – which, in turn, contribute to the development of the social structures of inequality and injustice of power in society. The relationship between power and language is not seen as deterministic, however, but as variable, power influencing language and language affecting power. It is not possible, therefore, to 'read' power relations 'off the page' or text. That being said, particular linguistic forms may typically be used in the expression of power. An early insight is the distinction in many European languages between first and second pronouns (*tu/vous*) of Brown and Gilman (1960), whereby the *tu* form may be used by the more powerful person, but the *vous* form is required by the less powerful.

Access to specific forms of discourse – for example, those of politics, the media, science or education – is itself a power resource. Different resources are employed to exert different kinds of power. The military exerts power through force or the threat of it; the rich exert power through money; while parents and teachers exert power through authority or knowledge (van Dijk, 2008). Whatever type of power is at stake, however, it will be exercised, to a greater or lesser degree, through discourse.

10.3.2 Hegemony

Fairclough (2003a) relates CDA to Gramsci's (1971) notion of *hegemony*. Gramsci used the term 'hegemony' to refer to the exertion of power through implicit means rather than military force. This may be achieved through application of laws, rules and habits or may just be a matter of general consensus (van Dijk, 2008). For Fairclough (2003a: 92), hegemony is 'leadership as much as domination across the economic, political, cultural and ideological domains of a society'. Hegemonic struggle can be related to discourse in so far as social structures and discursive structures are in a mutually defining relationship. Social structure is manifested in its discursive practices and discursive practices are constitutive of social structure, in society's norms, conventions, relations, identities and institutions (Fairclough, 2003a: 64). This means that changes in society are reflected in changes in discursive practice and vice versa. In bringing hegemony and discourse together, one can talk of discursive hegemony. By this is meant, as Fairclough (2003a: 218) defines the term, 'the dominance and naturalisation of particular representations', how certain discourses come to prevail in given sociopolitical contexts, as a result of a struggle between the relevant political actors.

10.3.3 Identity

Another important concept in CDA is that of identity. Identity is a fluid construct that is subject to change. The person who I am now is different to the person I was ten years ago or even last week, or indeed yesterday, for that matter. At the same time, identity may be multiple. I have an identity as a man, as a professor, as a father, and as a husband, for example. Burgess and Ivanic (2010: 240) describe how identities in educational contexts are usually transitory.

> For most students, identities in education are transitory, mediating identities; hence, the practices in which they engage while attending courses may be for extrinsic purposes, not part of the identities to which they aspire for the rest of their lives. Students may be in an ambivalent relation with this identity: partially desiring and partially resisting being constructed as 'someone in education'. In the immediate present, however, this is an aspect of their identity that they cannot ignore.

Identity is important in discourse terms because one's identity is manifested in one's social practice, an important part of which is discursive practice. As well as individuals constructing their own identities, a large part of identity is constructed by others; by how we are perceived. Identity is therefore a binary construction. Kress (1989a) refers to this as 'projecting' identity on to others. He gives the example of the political leader whose role is to give definition to an entirely new group. It is the leader's role in such a situation to produce texts which bring together hitherto disparate discourses in a unified, coherent manner (Kress, 1989a: 15). In my book on the discourse of Hong Kong's transition from British to Chinese sovereignty (Flowerdew, 2012a), I showed how the outgoing British Governor projected a rather 'British' identity on to the Hong Kong people, while the incoming Hong Kong Chinese Chief Executive projected a much more 'Chinese' identity on to these same Hong Kong citizens.

Given the foregoing, identity is constructed through space and time (Flowerdew, 2012a). In discourse analytic terms, this means that an individual or a group's identity will to an important degree depend on the situational and historical context in which they are located. The situational aspect of context with regard to discourse identity is emphasised by Blommaert (2005). Blommaert notes how, as people shift from place to place, 'they frequently, and delicately, and each time in very minimal ways, express different identities' (Blommaert, 2005: 224). Wodak and colleagues (Wodak *et al.* 1999) have demonstrated the importance of place in the creation of national identity, how people identify with a particular country. Although identities are partly created by others and projected on to groups or individuals, there is no guarantee that the projected identities will be taken up by individuals. To quote Chiapello and Fairclough (2002: 195), 'a new discourse may come into an institution or organisation without being enacted or inculcated'.

10.4 METHODS AND TOOLKITS FOR CDA

In terms of methodology, Reisigl (2008) has listed a sequence of steps for the systematic critical analysis of political discourse (but which can equally be applied to other fields), as follows:

1. Consult previous knowledge about the sociopolitical problem that possesses linguistic aspects.
2. Collect (triangulated) discursive data for analysis.
3. Prepare and select specific data for analysis.
4. Formulate research questions and hypotheses based on rapid checking of data or part of it.
5. Pilot the analysis to adjust analytical instruments and further spell out research questions.
6. Develop detailed case studies; these can operate at macro or micro linguistic levels or at the level of context; they lead to an overall interpretation of the results of analysis, taking into account the social, historical and political context of the analysed data.
7. Formulate critique to reveal problematic discursive strategies, solve specific problems of communication, or improve communication; this is based on ethical principles such as democratic norms and human rights; it focuses on opaque, contradictory and manipulative relations among power, language and social structures and commits itself to cognitive and political emancipation (and improvement of communication).
8. Apply results, for example, publication of a book/articles and/or more widely disseminated outlets.

As well as his broad methodology, Reisigl (2008) lists a set of analytical categories:

1. How are social actors – either individual persons or groups – linguistically constructed by being named (nomination)?

2. What positive or negative traits, qualities and features are attributed to the linguistically con-structed social actors (predication)?
3. Through what arguments and argumentation schemes do specific persons or social groups try to justify or delegitimise claims containing specific nominations and predications (for example, claims of discrimination of others)?
4. From what perspective or point of view are these nominations, predications and argumenta-tions expressed (perspectivation)?
5. Are the respective utterances (nominations, predications, argumentations) articulated overtly, are they intensified or are they mitigated (mitigation versus intensification)?

In line with its eclectic approach, various other practitioners have presented 'toolkits' for doing CDA. The term 'toolkit' might not sound very scientific, but it is appropriate, given that the lists of features to look for in analysis are presented as suggestive rather than prescriptive, exhaustive taxonomies. Examples of these can be found in various sources.

To start with a simple one, van Dijk (2001c: 99) has suggested the following as features of text to examine:

- stress and intonation;
- word order;
- lexical style;
- coherence;
- local semantic moves such as disclaimers;
- topic choice;
- speech acts;
- schematic organisation;
- rhetorical figures;
- syntactic structures;
- propositional structures;
- turn-taking;
- repairs;
- hesitation.

In his early *Language and Power*, in Chapter 5, 'Critical discourse in practice: description', Fair-clough (1989) presented what he called a 'mini reference manual' (p. 106) in the form of a list of questions and subquestions to ask in a CDA study. The major divisions are as follows:

1. What experiential values do words have?
2. What relational value do words have?
3. What expressive values do words have?
4. What metaphors are used?
5. What experiential value do grammatical features have?
6. What relational values do grammatical features have?
7. What expressive values do grammatical features have?
8. How are (simple) sentences linked together?
9. What interactional conventions are used?
10. What larger-scale structures does the text have?

Each of these questions has a set of subquestions. For example, question 5 has the following:

1. What types of *process* and *participant* predominate?
2. Is agency unclear?

3.   Are processes what they seem?
4.   Are *nominalisations* used?
5.   Are sentences active or passive?
6.   Are sentences positive or negative?

Another list is that of Huckin (2005), entitled 'Some useful tools and concepts for Critical Discourse Analysis'.

Word/phrase level
- Classification, including names, labels;
- Connotations, code words;
- Metaphor;
- Lexical presupposition;
- Modality;
- Register, including synthetic personalisation;
- Politeness.

Sentence/utterance level
- Deletion, omission:
  - through nominalisation;
  - through agentless passive;
- Transitivity / agent–patient relations;
- Topicalisation/foregrounding;
- Presupposition;
- Insinuation, inferencing;
- Heteroglossia.

Text level
- Genre conventions;
- Discursive differences;
- Coherence;
- Framing;
- Foregrounding/backgrounding;
- Textual silences;
- Presupposition;
- Extended metaphor;
- Auxiliary embellishments.

General
- Central versus peripheral processing;
- Use of heuristics;
- Ideology;
- Reading position;
- Naturalisation, 'common sense';
- Reproduction–resistance–hegemony;
- Cultural models and myths; master narratives;
- Intertextuality;
- Context; contrast effects;
- Communicator ethos;
- Vividness;
- Repetition;

- Face work;
- Type of argument;
- Interests;
- Agenda-setting.

Finally, Jäger (2001: 55–56) has a further toolkit/list and Gee (2011b), who has much in common with CDA, although not normally being included in the group, has a whole book along the lines of a toolkit.

What all of these lists have in common is their emphasis on their indicative – as opposed to comprehensive – nature. One problem that they have, however, is that, although some of them include context, in their emphasis on textual features, they carry the danger of the user putting too much emphasis on textual features at the expense of context (see Blommaert, 2005, for a critique of CDA's heavy emphasis on text at the expense of context). Perhaps what is also needed is a toolkit to help in the analysis of context.

10.5 CDA AND SYSTEMIC FUNCTIONAL LINGUISTICS

A number of CDA practitioners have claimed allegiance to Systemic Functional Linguistics (SFL) and a number of commentators have claimed it to be a preferred method. Fowler (1996a: 12), for example, advocates a simplified model of Halliday's grammar (supplemented by concepts from Pragmatics). Fairclough (2003a: 5–6) adopts a similar approach, also mentioning the possible use of Pragmatics, Conversation Analysis and Corpus Linguistics. Wodak (2001a: 8), although not making consistent use of the model in her own work (see above), has stated as follows:

> Whether analysts with a critical approach prefer to focus on microlinguistic features, macrolinguistic features, textual, discursive or contextual features, whether their angle is primarily philosophical, sociological or historical – in most studies there is reference to Hallidayan systemic functional grammar. This indicates that an understanding of the basic claims of Halliday's grammar and his approach to linguistic analysis is essential for a proper understanding of CDA.

Of the commentators, we can cite Renkema (2004: 284):

> In Critical Discourse Analysis more and more attempts are being made to ground analyses and interpretations of power relations on systematic descriptions of discourse. A promising perspective was developed by the founding father of the socio-semiotic approach … Michael Halliday.

As we saw in Chapter 2, according to Halliday's SFL (Halliday & Matthiessen, 2004), language is conceived of as a resource for communication and making meaning rather than as a formal system, as is the case in many other forms of linguistics. Linguistic structures, in this model, are viewed as interrelated choices (systems) which are available for the expression of meanings in situational contexts. Any utterance will simultaneously express meanings according to the three 'macro-functions': the ideational function (language as an expression of the individual's experience of the world); the interpersonal function (how individuals relate to each other through language at the social level); and the textual function (how linguistic forms are used to relate to each other and to the situational context).

The case for SFL in CDA is put by Martin and Wodak (2003: 8):

> SFL provides critical discourse analysts with a technical language for talking about language – to make it possible to look very closely at meaning, to be explicit and precise in terms that can be shared by others, and to engage in quantitative analysis where this is appropriate.

There is no doubt there are many very good studies which make use of SFL (many of the analyses by Fairclough, for example, or the studies collected in Martin and Wodak [2003], or Martin's [2000] exemplificatory paper on how SFL can be used in CDA) and some of the systems and concepts within Halliday's framework, such as transitivity (categories of processes and participant roles), modality, thematic development and grammatical metaphor have been used in CDA studies in the 'precise and explicit' way that Martin and Wodak describe.

However, there would be a number of problems with this approach if it were to be adopted as the only framework for CDA (which, as already should be clear, is not the case). First of all, to understand the grammar fully, a lot of work is required. For example, in a talk a few years ago, Halliday (2006) stated that some 17,000 systems would be required to analyse fully the meaning potential of just one transitive verb. Similarly, Halliday's best-known work, *An Introduction to Functional Grammar* (Halliday & Matthiessen, 2004), extends to nearly 700 pages. This is why Fowler (1996a) states that this work 'offers both more and less than is required', 'more' in the sense that there is too much to absorb and 'less' in that it is not comprehensive enough to handle all the aspects of a text that one might want to analyse. Another problem with the SFL approach is that it is not designed to deal with pragmatic phenomena such as indirect speech acts and implicature. A third problem is that the model of context in SFL is relatively unexplored. None of these problems, however, implies that SFL cannot be employed in CDA along with other approaches. The other approaches may be desirable, however, because SFL is concerned with developing a systematic linguistic description according to a set of formal categories, but in any given text, there may be structures and functions which do not fit neatly into these categories (see van Leeuwen, 1996, for further discussion on this).

10.6 CDA AND CORPUS LINGUISTICS

Although slow to take off, critical discourse analysts are starting more and more to use corpus tools. Hunston (2002: 109–123) gives a summary of earlier CDA corpus-based work, while Baker (2006) and L. Flowerdew (2012) have more recent overviews. Probably the first CDA article to take a corpus approach was that of Hardt-Mautner (1995; see also Mautner, 2009a, b), while Morrison and Love (1996) and Flowerdew (1997) gave other early applications. More recent empirical studies of note are those of Baker *et al.* (2008) and Morley and Bayley (2009).

Hardt-Mautner (1995) lists four advantages of a corpus approach for CDA. First, a corpus approach allows the researcher to examine syntactic and semantic properties of key lexical items exhaustively. Second, it can serve as a heuristic, providing ideas for further qualitative investigation. Third, it produces 'results' in its own right; frequency of a certain form or of certain collocates may in itself be relevant for a critical point of view. Fourth (although perhaps this should come first), at the most fundamental level, the concordance is an extremely useful research tool, assisting the researcher in analysing the data more efficiently than would otherwise be the case.

Hardt-Mautner (1995) rightly emphasises that a corpus approach does not replace the more traditional qualitative analysis of CDA, but, instead, is a useful support. A further advantage of a corpus approach is that it may help to overcome criticisms of bias in more qualitative CDA analysis. Corpus findings may be based on large bodies of data, thereby making findings more representative and systematic (Baker, 2006).

While early corpus applications to CDA used quite simple concordancing techniques, more recent studies have used more sophisticated search and display tools, annotation systems and statistics, reflecting advances in mainstream corpus studies (Baker, 2006).

While, as we have seen in Chapter 9, teachers have embraced corpus techniques and developed data-driven learning, to date, reports are lacking of data-driven learning projects developed from a specifically critical perspective. No doubt such accounts will appear at some point, as this would seem to be a logical development.

10.7 POSITIVE DISCOURSE ANALYSIS

As a complement, or, indeed, antidote to CDA, Martin (1999), has suggested 'PDA', or *Positive Discourse Analysis*, as a possible development. 'The approach exemplifies a positive style of Discourse Analysis that focuses on hope and change, by way of complementing the deconstructive exposé associated with Critical Discourse Analysis' (Martin, 1999: 29). In a later paper Martin (2004: 197) has stated:

> I suppose it would be going too far to propose a 10 year moratorium on deconstructive CDA, in order to get some constructive PDA off the ground. But we do need to move beyond a preoccupation with demonology, beyond a singular focus on semiosis in the service of abusive power – and reconsider power communally as well, as it circulates through communities, as they re-align around values, and renovate discourses that enact a better world. Good question, of course, what better is! And how to achieve it? We can start to ask.

Instead of deconstructing a speech by Australian Conservative Prime Minister John Howard, Martin argues, work could be directed to the Australian Sorry Day and analysis could focus on Aboriginal Elders, the impact of their stories of being taken from their families, and its effect in turn on migrant children and their families.

In a similar vein, Luke (2002: 106) has also called for an emancipatory form of Discourse Analysis.

> I have argued that to move beyond a strong focus on ideology critique, CDA would need to begin to develop a strong positive thesis about discourse and the productive uses of power. To paraphrase Marcuse (1971), we would need to begin to capture an affirmative character of culture where discourse is used aesthetically, productively, and for emancipatory purposes.

One danger of proposals such as those of Martin and Luke, however, would be that of the enterprise turning into a form of propaganda on behalf of the status quo. Another argument against PDA is that it sets up a false opposition with CDA. The term 'critical' incorporates both negative and positive, deconstruction and construction. One might argue, therefore, that, in arguing for a better world, CDA already incorporates a positive element.

10.8 CRITIQUE

Perhaps ironically, given its name, CDA has attracted rather a lot of criticism (in the negative sense of the word) as an approach and method for Discourse Analysis. These critiques are too numerous to review fully, but we can mention some of them. Perhaps the most common criticism is that CDA is biased. Blommaert (2005: 31–32), for example, talks about what he calls 'the predominance of biased interpretations' in CDA, arguing that this raises questions about 'representativeness, selectivity, partiality, prejudice and voice (can analysts speak for the average consumer of texts?)'.

Another criticism of CDA is that it is too deterministic in its interpretations. According to Hammersley (1997: 244–245), CDA 'often involves the adoption of a macro-sociological theory in which there are only two parties – the oppressors and the oppressed – and only one relationship between them: dominance'.

A third criticism is that the interpretation of the lay reader is ignored (see, for example, Stubbs, 1994). Analysts may have different readings from the actual consumers of the texts analysed. This is Blommaert's (2005: 32) point in the above quotation, 'can analysis speak for the average consumer of texts?'

Each of these criticisms has been responded to by various CDA practitioners, although there is not space here to enter into this debate. The following, however, are relevant references for both sides of the argument (Billig, 2008; Blommaert, 2005; de Beaugrande, undated; Fairclough, 1996, 2008; Flowerdew, 1999/2007; Stubbs, 1997; Widdowson, 1995a, b, 1996, 1998a, 2004).

10.9 APPLICATION TO PEDAGOGY

When it comes to application to pedagogy, CDA is more concerned with raising general awareness on the part of learners of the role of language in society than directly improving their proficiency in the use of the language. In addition to learner awareness, CDA has an important role to play in teacher education and can be applied to the analysis of learning materials in order to analyse their ideological underpinnings; are the materials politically biased, sexist, and so forth?

10.9.1 Critical Language Awareness

CLA is a concept developed by Fairclough (1992b) and colleagues, building on the *Language Awareness* movement, which was itself started earlier by Hawkins (1984). CLA presupposes a critical conception of education and schooling (Fairclough, 1992c: 2) and, as such, can be related to the more familiar parallel movement of critical pedagogy, based on the work of Freire (1985).

Fairclough's case for CLA was based on three arguments (Fairclough, 1992c: 3). First, in the place where and at the time when it was developed (the UK in the late 1980s and early 1990s), there were changes taking place in the ways in which power and social control were exercised, changes in which language was deeply imbricated. Second, there were changes in the role of language in various types of work and in professional–client relationships, with a larger service sector and smaller manufacturing sector and quality of communication coming to be seen as part of the quality of service. Third, there were changes in language practices as an important element of the imposition of change, with language becoming less formal and professionals having to adapt their communicative styles to clients rather than vice versa.

As a consequence of these three changes, Fairclough claimed that 'people commonly have problems knowing how to act as professionals, clients, parents, children, managers, employees, colleagues; and part of the problem is not being quite sure how to talk, write, or interpret what others say or write' (p. 6).

Based on these premises, Fairclough argued that CLA was an urgently needed element in Language Education, 'a prerequisite for effective democratic citizenship' and that CLA should be 'an *entitlement* for citizens, especially children developing towards citizenship in the educational system' (p. 3, original emphasis).

Fairclough recommended that CLA should be developed using the same tools as those identified in Figure 10.1 above for CDA, namely *description* of formal aspects of language in texts; *interpretation* of interaction, that is what conventions are employed and how; and *explanation* of how processes of interaction relate to social action.

Elsewhere in the 1992 volume, Janks and Ivanic (1992) argued that simple 'language awareness', or 'raised consciousness', is not enough if CLA is to be truly emancipatory. They argue:

> It is a central tenet of this chapter that 'language awareness' or 'raised consciousness' is not liberatory enough. Only if CLA empowers people to successfully contest the practices which disempower them would we claim that it is emancipatory. Awareness needs to be turned into action (Janks and Ivanic, 1992: 305).

In his main contribution to the original volume on CLA – a chapter entitled 'The appropriacy of "appropriateness"' – Fairclough (1992d) critiqued the notion of appropriateness underlying thinking on

Language Education and language awareness at the time. His main target was Hymes's conception of communicative competence, as referred to in Chapter 1 of this volume, and Hymes's view that:

> [w]e have to account for the fact that a normal child acquires knowledge of sentences, not only as grammatical, but also as appropriate. He or she acquires competence as to when to speak, when not, and as to what to talk about, with whom, when and in what manner… There are rules of use without which the rules of grammar would be useless (Hymes, 1974: 15).

For Fairclough, this view was normative; imposing the 'rules of use' was to perpetuate the social status quo, a status quo which was tied to relations of domination and subordination. Hymes's notion of communicative competence, as taken up by educationists, was a reification and naturalisation of these unequal power relations in society, Fairclough argued. Because such a notion of appropriateness was widely taken up in educational contexts – unthinkingly, as common sense, in Fairclough's view – it was an important obstacle for CLA to overcome. The view of CLA put forward by Fairclough and colleagues 'stresses the mutually reinforcing development of critical understanding of the sociolinguistic order, and practice, including the creative practice of probing and shifting existing conventions' (Fairclough, 1992d: 53). Language awareness 'should not push learners into oppositional practices which condemn them to disadvantage and marginalization; it should equip them with the capacities and understanding which are preconditions for meaningful choice and effective citizenship in the domain of language' (Fairclough, 1992d: 54).

One of the examples Fairclough uses to illustrate what he refers to as 'sociolinguistic hegemony' is that of standard English and 'doctrines of correctness' (p. 51). It is a case of saying that only standard English is acceptable and other varieties are inappropriate. Fairclough had in mind the situation in the UK, but a similar argument is valid in countries where English in not the mother tongue and where governments and educational institutions impose standard English as the target second language and, in so doing, reject available local varieties.

10.9.2 Some examples of the application of Critical Language Awareness

It might seem that CLA is an activity more suited to L1 than L2 education, but this need not be the case, as some of the examples in this section will demonstrate.

In my own work (with Lindsay Miller) (Flowerdew & Miller, 2005), we have argued for a critical component to be incorporated into the second-language syllabus (specifically related to listening, but the same would apply to comprehension in general, including both listening and reading) for two reasons. First, such a component introduces a level of sophistication to language learning, where there is often a danger of trivialisation. Comprehension questions, particularly at the beginner's level, are very often at a rather inconsequential, surface level. Encouraging learners to be critical is more likely to exercise their analytical abilities and, at the same time, to be motivational. Second, echoing CLA, with a critical approach, language teaching has the opportunity of preparing learners for responsible citizenship. English is increasingly becoming an international lingua franca and it is appropriate that the learning of English should incorporate a (critical) international perspective on the world.

One example that Flowerdew and Miller (2005) use to illustrate how this might work, even at a beginner's level, is a television advertisement for Thai International Airlines. In this advertisement, a voice whispers the words 'smooth as silk'. This phrase is a commonly used idiom in English, but when used in this particular context it takes on a new meaning; smoothness does not refer to a surface here, but to the smooth ride one has with this particular airline and the smooth service – a distinctive feature of certain South-East Asian airlines – that is offered. If we consider the context of airline service, we may realise that this utterance has a political dimension that may not strike us on first hearing. 'Smooth as silk', in the context of the television advertisement, is accompanied by an image of a beautiful young female cabin crew member attending to a male passenger. It is not unreasonable to 'read' this image as suggesting that it is the woman, or one of her peers, who will make travel with Thai airways 'smooth'. There are gendered inequalities of power here in the suggestion that the female cabin crew member is expected to smoothen one's (men's) travel. What this might suggest for a model of listening (or reading) is a critical component that encourages learners to analyse the context within which what they hear is created and thereby deconstruct it so as to reveal the inequalities of power that the text reproduces. This may seem a demanding requirement best left to advanced students, but if we think about it, the utterance 'Smooth as silk', from a strictly linguistic point of view at any rate, is hardly complex. As such it could quite appropriately be used in teaching at the most elementary levels.

Turning now to other approaches to application, an early account of the application of CLA is that of Wallace (1992), who describes how she applied CDA to reading materials, arguing that a critical element is generally missing from textbooks, selected texts being on bland topics unlikely to be controversial, often in order to exemplify linguistic structures. Wallace developed a reading methodology which involves the questioning of ideological assumptions as well as 'general' reading comprehension. In this methodology, rather than emphasising right and wrong answers, questioning encourages a critical reading and asks learners to use language to explore and explain a text's ideological positioning.

In further early work, Clark and Ivanic (1997) developed a CLA approach to English for Academic Purposes courses at university level in writing. Their approach is summarised as asking students constantly to answer the following questions: 'Why are conventions/practices the way they are?', 'In whose interests do they operate?', 'What views of knowledge and representations of the world do they perpetuate?' and 'What are the possible alternatives?' (Clark & Ivanic, 1999: 66). Clark and Ivanic (1997: 217) seek to 'empower learners by providing them with a critical analytical framework to help them reflect on their own language experiences and practices, the language practices of others in the institutions of which they are a part, and the wider society within which they live'.

Janks (1999) discusses the use of student journals as a means of assessing the development of students engaged in a postgraduate course in CLA in South Africa. Janks demonstrates the multiple identities that are revealed through the journals and how these identities are transformed or conserved as learners enter a new discourse community. In addition, Janks raises the difficult question as to whether CLA increases students' agency and leads to transformative action or not.[2]

In a later development of her earlier work, Wallace (2009) describes an advanced reading course for foreign-language learners in London which allowed her to examine some key principles of CLA. Wallace argues for the need of a course such as the one she describes to draw attention to the ideological bases of discourses as they circulate both in everyday life and within specific texts. The course Wallace describes:

> directed students' attention to the manner in which literacy practices offer insight into power relations in everyday life, as well as, at the micro level, examining the manner in which specific texts reinforce or challenge relations of power through the patterning of linguistic choices (pp. 98–99).

Wallace's course description included the following goals for students (p. 109):

- Do you want to improve your critical reading skills in English?
- Do you feel that you would like a fuller understanding of the written texts which you encounter in your day-to-day life in Britain?

This class aims to help you:

- Read between the lines, that is, understand the hidden messages of written texts.
- Understand some of the cultural meanings in written texts.
- See how texts persuade us to behave or think in particular ways.
- Appreciate the ways in which texts are written for different audiences.
- See how texts may be read in different ways by different people.

The course included a wide range of different texts, including advertisements, newspaper texts, leaflets and forms, textbooks and magazines.

Wallace claims that there is a need to go beyond expert exegesis in CDA and examine how it might become an activity in which social groups can participate, with its potential to empower participants both in educational settings and in everyday life. This, she claims, is the great advantage of CLA, in so far as it can take place in a classroom, with 'a ready-made interpretative community' (p. 99). Another advantage of this group approach is that interpretation becomes negotiable, where in the CDA literature it is usually the work of 'the lone armchair critic' (Stubbs, 1994: 99), a complaint of critics of CDA, as noted above.

A very practical approach to using CDA in the language classroom is presented by Cots (2006). Cots does not use the term *CLA*, instead locating his approach in CDA theory, but it clearly is an instance of CLA. Cots (2006) contrasts what he considers to be two different approaches to discourse: a non-critical view and a critical view, as follows.

A non-critical view of discourse:
- a stretch of language perceived to be meaningful, unified, and purposive;
- different ways of talking / writing about (and structuring) areas of knowledge or social practice (for example, medical discourse, ecological discourse).

A critical view of discourse:
- ideologically determined ways of talking or writing about persons, places, events or phenomena;
- a mode of social practice that is both structured by society and, at the same time, contributes to structuring that same society.

This is followed by a comparison of critical and non-critical views of Discourse Analysis, as follows.

A non-critical view of Discourse Analysis:
- description of natural spoken or written discourse;
- study of what gives a stretch of language unity and meaning.

A critical view of Discourse Analysis:
- analysis of how texts work within specific sociocultural practices;
- explanation of how discourse is shaped by relations of power and ideology and, at the same time, is used to construct social identities, social relations, and systems of knowledge and belief.

Cots relates his pedagogical approach to Fairclough's model of CDA, as was shown above, with the stages slightly modified as *social practice, discourse practice* and *textual practice.*

From an analytical point of view, the model of CDA proposed by Fairclough (1989, 1992b) considers discourse as the result of three different types of practice: social, discursive, and textual. At the level of social practice, the goal is to discover the extent to which discourse is shaped by and, at the same time, influences social structures and the nature of the social activity of which it forms part. The discursive practice dimension acknowledges the specificity of the communicative situation, taking into account both material and cognitive aspects related to the conditions of textual production and interpretation (for example, intertextuality, presuppositions, etc.). Finally, the textual practice dimension focuses on formal and semantic features of text construction, such as grammar or vocabulary, which contribute to conveying/interpreting a specific message (p. 339).

When this model is applied to language users or learners:

[t]he 'critical' nature of the model is that it relies on the users'/learners' capacity to interpret a text within a specific communicative, social, and ideological context and react to it taking into account their personal experience and values.

Pedagogical exploitation of a given text, as exemplified by a piece about the Amish religious community in North America, follows the three stages of Fairclough's model. In the social practice phase of the activity, learners reflect upon the following aspects:

1   how the text contributes to a particular representation of the world and whether this representation comes into conflict with readers' own representations;
2   how the textual representation is shaped by the ideological position of its producer(s);
3   how the text contributes to reinforcing or changing the ideological position of its readers.

The following set of questions is suggested to help learners in their analysis in this social practice stage:

1.   Are the Amish typical American people? Why?
2.   In your opinion, who wrote the text? An Amish or a non-Amish person? Try to justify your answer.
3.   What do you think of the Amish after reading the text? Would you like to be an Amish?

The discourse practice phase of the activity centres on the specificity of the communicative situation of the text, taking into account material and cognitive circumstances such as the following:

1.   the discourse type or genre that the text can be classified into and the intertextual chains it enters into;
2.   the contribution of the different propositions in the text to the overall impression of coherence;
3.   the readers' knowledge of the world and experience of other texts that the author draws upon.

The following are suggested facilitating questions for learners for this discourse practice stage:

1.   Where can you find a text like this? What kind of readers is it addressed to? Is it written for Amish or non-Amish people?
2.   What is the 'point' of the text? What is the author trying to tell us? What do you remember from the Amish after reading the text?
3.   What do you know about New York or the USA? The Amish live near New York. Are they really 'an unusual community'? How does the author of the text try to show us that they are 'unusual'?

The third stage, the textual stage, focuses on the salient formal and semantic features of text construction. The following example questions focus on connectors, modality and vocabulary, respectively:

1.   What linking words connect the following ideas in the text:

Living near New York < > Lifestyle of the Amish
Using banks and going to the doctor's < > Having phones
Playing baseball and eating hot dogs < > Having TVs, radios, carpets …
Having churches < > Being very religious

2.   Are the ideas on both sides presented as paradoxical or contradictory?
3.   Look for examples in the text containing the verb can/can't. What can the Amish do? What can the Amish not do? Next look for examples containing the verbs *have to* and *allow*, expressing obligation. What are the Amish obliged to do?
4.   Fill in the 'you' column in the table below and say in each case if the word/phrase in question has a positive (+) or a negative (–) meaning for you. When you have finished, do the same to fill in the 'Amish' column according to what the text says.

Cots concludes his article with a checklist of questions for teachers (a) to approach language use with a 'critical' attitude, and (b) as a reference framework to plan how to present language use to learners. The list is as follows:

A   Social practice
A.1 What social identities does/do the author(s) of the text represent?
A.2 What is the relationship between the social identities the author(s) represent(s)?
A.3 What is/are the social goal(s) the author(s) has/have with the text?
A.4 To what extent is the text necessary to accomplish the goal(s)?
A.5 In what kind of social situation is the text produced? How conventional is it?
A.6 Does/do the author(s) represent or appeal to particular beliefs?
A.7 What are/may be the social consequences of the text?

B   Discourse practice
B.1 How conventional is the text taking into account its situation of use?
B.2 Does it remind us of other texts we have encountered either in its form or in its content?
B.3 Can we classify it as representative of a specific type?
B.4 Is the text more or less accessible to different kinds of readers?
B.5 Does it require us to 'read between the lines'?
B.6 Does it presuppose anything?
B.7 Who are the producer(s) and intended receiver(s) of the text?

C   Textual practice
C.1 If the text is co-operatively constructed (for example, a conversation), is it obvious in any way that one of the participants is more in control of the construction than the others?
C.2 How are the ideas represented by utterances, sentences, or paragraphs connected in the text?
C.3 Does/do the author(s) follow any rules of politeness?

The examples from Flowerdew and Miller, Wallace, Clark and Ivanic, Janks and Cots presented in this section are quite varied in their approaches. What they all have in common, however, is the goal of raising awareness on the part of learners of societal inequalities as argued for by Fairclough and what he claims as 'a prerequisite for effective democratic citizenship' and as 'an *entitlement* for citizens, especially children developing towards citizenship in the educational system', as cited above.

10.10 QUESTIONS FOR DISCUSSION

1. In section 10.1, it is stated that CDA 'typically examines specific discursive situations where dominance and inequality are to the fore'. Can you think of any situations where this is the case? In what ways is language used to enact dominance and inequality in these situations?
2. In section 10.1, it is stated, again, that 'Participants may not be aware of how powerful or powerless they are in discourse terms.' Can you think of any examples where this is the case? What are the reasons for this?
3. Think of a 'big D' discourse with which you are familiar. What are some of its linguistic characteristics?
4. Select a newspaper with which you are familiar. What sort of identity does this newspaper project on to its government or the government of another country? What are some of the linguistic/discursive features of this projection of identity?
5. Can you think of a discursive situation where a PDA study might be appropriate? What might some of the features of this discourse be?
6. In section 10.9, it is stated: 'When it comes to application to pedagogy, CDA is more concerned with raising general awareness on the part of learners of the role of language in society than directly improving their proficiency in the use of the language.' Do you think there is any benefit for language proficiency in a CDA approach? If so, how might this come about?
7. Do you agree that there is a role for CDA and CLA in schools and in society at large? If so, what is this role?
8. Wallace lists the following goals for a critical reading course:
    a) Read between the lines, that is, understand the hidden messages of written texts.
    b) Understand some of the cultural meanings in written texts.
    c) See how texts persuade us to behave or think in particular ways.
    d) Appreciate the ways in which texts are written for different audiences.
    e) See how texts may be read in different ways by different people.

    Find a text or texts which might be suitable for such an analysis. Then apply the stages that Wallace suggests to the text. How effective do you think this approach would be with a group of learners with whom you are familiar?

10.11 FURTHER READING

Cots, 2006; Fairclough, 1992b, 2003a, b; Fairclough *et al.*, 2011; Wodak, 2001a; Wodak and Meyer, 2001.

Answers to objective questions

CHAPTER 3

Question 1

1. *It* in the second sentence refers back to *skeleton* in the first sentence: anaphoric.
2. *It* in the second sentence refers back to *this property* in the first sentence: anaphoric.
3. *The (white wine)* in the second sentence refers back to *white wine* in the first sentence: anaphoric; *he* in the second sentence refers back to *He* in the first sentence: anaphoric.
4. *these* and *those* refer outside the text: exophoric.
5. *The* refers outside the text (unique reference): exophoric.

Question 2

a) Inappropriate substitution with *didn't*; the closest antecedent is *won't have anything to say'*, but this is unlikely to be the speaker's intention! More likely, *didn't* was intended to substitute for *don't go straight into politics*, which comes earlier.
b) *It* in *don't know it* seems to refer back to *have children*; presumably the writer meant *it* to refer forward to what comes later, *we have a nursery*.
c) A reference item, *they*, is missing after the second *as*.

Question 3

Holmes – man – He – his – his – him – he – he – his – him – his – him – him – he – his – him – his.

Question 4

rooms – (They) – bed-rooms – sitting-room – windows – apartments – surroundings
things – boxes – portmanteaus – property

CHAPTER 4

Question 3

1. *He*; simple, experiential.
2. *The politicians and their aides*; simple, experiential.

3. *Established in 1984, City University of Hong Kong*; complex, *Established in 1984* (textual), *City University of Hong Kong* (experiential).
4. *On the one hand, I*; complex, *on the one hand* (textual), *I* (experiential); *but on the other hand* (complex); *but* (textual), *on the other hand* (textual), *I* (experiential).
5. *Yesterday, the army*; complex, *Yesterday* (textual), *the army* (experiential).
6. *There* or *there are;* (both possible labellings are possible, depending on whether you follow Halliday and Matthiessen [2004]) or Thompson [2004]); simple, experiential.
7. *Don't wait*; simple, experiential.
8. *Open*; simple, experiential.

Question 4

Established in 1984, City University of Hong Kong is a modern, hi-tech institution committed to providing a quality learning environment for its students and the community. *The University* currently has a student enrolment of over 17,000 (excluding sub-degree students), *of which over 5,900* are postgraduates. *Its programmes* provide a wide range of learning opportunities from undergraduate and postgraduate studies to continuing education. *For more information about the University and its academic and supporting units,* **please** *visit* our website (http://www.cityu.edu.hk).

Key: *textual themes*; experiential themes; **interpersonal theme.**
Method of development: the theme of the first clause is picked up as the theme or an element of the theme of the second clause, and so forth.

CHAPTER 5

Question 1

1. Performative
2. Performative
3. Performative
4. Not performative
5. Not performative
6. Not performative

Question 2

Bet could be a performative here or it could be reporting a past action.

CHAPTER 6

Question 3

a. Positive politeness
b. Positive politeness
c. Negative politeness
d. Negative politeness

Notes

1 INTRODUCTION

1 Other approaches include *Inter-cultural Discourse Analysis*, which considers the ways different cultures go about performing discourse (discussed in various chapters of this book), and *Multi-modal Discourse Analysis*, which uses the techniques of Discourse Analysis to study other semiotic systems besides language, including visual and acoustic systems (referred to in Chapters 8 and 10). Jaworski and Coupland (1999), in the introduction to *The Discourse Reader*, in addition to those approaches mentioned here, include *ethnography of communication*, *interactional sociolinguistics*, *discursive psychology* and *narrative analysis*.

2 Because sentences can have different functions in different instances of use, discourse analysts often prefer the term 'utterance' to that of 'sentence', especially in the analysis of spoken text. An utterance is thus the use of a particular sentence (or longer or shorter stretch of language) at a particular time and in a particular context.

3 For more recent formulations see, for example, Bachman (1990), Canale (1983) and Celce-Murcia (2007).

4 There were two precursors to this model (Celce-Murcia, 1995; Celce-Murcia *et al.*, 1995).

2 SYSTEMIC FUNCTIONAL LINGUISTICS AND REGISTER

1 In the literature, there is often confusion about the terms *register* and *genre*. Halliday generally does not use the term genre, but when he does, it is used in an everyday meaning of the term as a type of literature or, more technically, represents a feature of mode which refers to the staged nature of the discourse structure. In this book, the term *genre* will be used to refer to complete, structured, staged language events (written or spoken). The conception of genre, here, is broader than that of Halliday; it is how a register may be instantiated in a particular language event. Genre will be dealt with in Chapter 8. For this reason, the present chapter saves for later the account of genre of Martin and colleagues in Sydney, Australia, and its pedagogic application, an account which might have been expected to figure more here otherwise.

2 Cohesion will be dealt with more thoroughly in Chapter 3.

3 Thematic development will be dealt with more fully in Chapter 4.

4 These are actually marginal instances, since neither has a corresponding verbal form.

5 Another way of calculating lexical density (and the one preferred by Halliday) is in terms of the number of lexical words per unembedded clause, so that a text with an average of five lexical words per unembedded clause would have a lexical density of five.

6 We are not devoting much attention to the textual metafunction in this chapter, as this will be dealt with in more detail in the next two chapters, on cohesion and thematic development, respectively.

3 COHESION

1 Text kindly provided by Lawrence Wong.

4 THEMATIC DEVELOPMENT

1 An adjunct, in grammar, is a word or phrase which, while adding to the meaning of a clause, does not affect its essential unmarked structure of subject + verb + complement. It is realised as an adverbial (word or phrase) or prepositional phrase. In *My aunt was given that teapot yesterday by the Duke*, there are two adjuncts: the adverbial *yesterday* and the prepositional phrase, *by the Duke* (Halliday and Matthiessen, 2004: 124).
2 However, see Berry (1995: 65) for a similar approach to ours.
3 This pattern, in fact, is an example of *a macrotheme*, a theme acting as point of departure for the whole segment of text, followed by two *hyperthemes*, themes which act as the theme of complete paragraphs (Martin and Rose, 2003). See below on hyperthemes.
4 Of course, in speech, the prosodic system works in conjunction with the grammar in signalling what is given and new.
5 *But* and later *and* and *or* in this passage are treated as part of the theme. Such themes are referred to as *textual themes* and will be dealt with in section 4.13. Textual themes function as part of *complex themes*, where there is a *texual* or *interpersonal* element.
6 As we saw in Chapter 3, this pattern would be referred to as an identity chain if we were analysing cohesive chains in this text.
7 You need to know that *Rex* is a common name for a dog in order to understand this joke.
8 Some educational researchers in L1 contexts (for example, Berry 1995) have made a distinction between *interactional thematisation*, which is associated with speech, and *informational thematisation*, which is associated with writing. They stress the importance of developing the latter in learners, on the assumption that the former will be naturally acquired. This may be true in L1 contexts, but in L2 situations, it can be argued, both need to be developed.
9 Thematic variation is not valued in all registers, it should be borne in mind. An injunction such as 'vary your sentence beginnings' might not be appropriate in all cases, scientific writing being one register where repetition is favoured and is not seen as repetitious.

5 SPEECH ACTS

1 See note 2 for a definition of the term 'utterance'.
2 Austin, in fact, distinguished three types of act in the performance of an utterance: the locutionary act – the expression of the literal or semantic meaning of the utterance; the illocutionary act – the intended meaning of the act, the speech act proper, such as greeting, inviting, offering, ordering and such like; and the perlocutionary act – how the act is received by the hearer (its uptake). In this chapter we are only really concerned with the illocutionary act, or the speech act proper.
3 Degree of imposition is defined by Brown and Levinson (1987: 77) as 'the degree to which they are considered to interfere with an agent's wants of self-determination or of approval (negative and positive face wants)'. See Chapter 6 for more on Brown and Levinson.
4 As summarised by Kasper and Blum-Kulka, 1993: 612–662.
5 In cases where plentiful data are available, attempts have been made to use corpus tools to identify speech acts. In the corpus method, search strings are developed that locate instances of a given speech act by identifying syntactic patterns or lexical items that are typical for the given speech act. As Jucker (2009) points out, however, it is an open question whether a given speech act is sufficiently standardised to allow such search techniques to be effective. A search may either retrieve many hits that on manual inspection turn out not to be examples of the target speech act, or it may fail to retrieve actual instances of the target speech act (Jucker, 2009).
6 In fact, speech acts are better discussed in terms of utterances rather than sentences (see note 2).
7 This applies not just to speech acts, but also to other pragmatics phenomena, as will be discussed in the next chapter.

7 CONVERSATION ANALYSIS

1 It is worth noting that many conversation analysts do not consider CA to be a form of Discourse Analysis, but as something entirely different.
2 See Waring (2009) for an explication of this approach.

3 Although this is not always the case (Schegloff, 2007), as we shall see.
4 A recent collection on institutional talk is Antaki (2011).
5 See Chapter 2 for a rather different approach to the analysis of IRF.
6 A collection of papers focusing on comparative features of talk in action is Sidnell (2009).
7 See, for example, the book-length treatments of Markee (2000), Lazaraton (2002) and Seedhouse (2004) and the special issues of *Applied Linguistics* (23(3), 2002) and *Modern Language Journal* (88(4), 2004).
8 http://www.tesol.org/s_tesol/sec_document.asp?CID=476&DID=2154.

8 GENRE ANALYSIS

1 It is worth noting that the communicative purpose of this genre is fairly easily determined, as to prohibit and prescribe certain actions or forms of behaviour.
2 Bhatia (1993, 2004) similarly insists on the institutionalised character of genres, stating that 'Genres are reflections of disciplinary and organizational cultures, and in that sense, they focus on social actions embedded within disciplinary, professional and other institutional practices' (2004: 23). Grabe (2002), on the other hand, takes an opposing view, arguing in favour of the teaching of two 'macro-genres': narrative and exposition.
3 In this feature we can see clearly the overlap between register and genre in terms of analysis.
4 How there are many types of bird or cup, say, each more or less different, but how we can easily recognise an unfamiliar bird or cup as such, even though we have never encountered that type before.
5 Swales (2004: 22) refers to this as genre network – 'the totality of genres available for a particular sector (such as the research world), as seen from any chosen synchronic moment'.
6 A further category identified by Bhatia (2004) is that of *genre colony*. Genre colonies are genres which share a particular communicative purpose, such as promoting, introducing or reporting. Genre colonies may intersect disciplines and professions. Genre colonisation comes about where communicative purposes associated with one domain influence another domain. An example would be how promotional purposes, which typically are a feature of advertising, come into academic genres, which are not traditionally associated by such purposes.
7 One thing that this activity shows is how genres develop over time (and sometimes even die). It is unlikely that apprentice academics would write letters in this day and age of the internet.
8 To avoid using systemic terminology I have simplified the explanation of this process as it is described by Coffin.
9 The concept of scaffolding is derived from Vygotsky's (1986: 188) idea that 'what the child can do in cooperation today he can do alone tomorrow'.
10 These issues have been developed in later ESP school work by Swales (2004) and Bhatia (2004).

9 CORPUS-BASED APPROACHES

1 The term 'real' in this context has been critiqued (see, for example, Carter, 1998; Cook 1998).
2 'So-called native speakers', Hoey (2005: 184) writes, 'are non-native in many contexts and all speakers are, according to the position I have been putting forward, in a permanent state of learning. … What distinguishes learners (or more accurately, types of learning) is not, therefore whether they are native or non-native but how the primings come into existence.'
3 Although it is not uncommon to encounter disagreement among native speakers regarding what is or is not appropriate usage.
4 McEnery and Hardie (2012: 141) also emphasise the qualitative nature of corpus in their discussion of semantic prosody and how interpretation is dependent on the intuition of the analyst.

10 CRITICAL DISCOURSE ANALYSIS

1 Although see van Leeuwen (2008).
2 Taking this a stage further, one might also ask the following question: 'May the strategies identified in a critical approach to language be turned around by those in power to further apply them in the promotion of power and dominance?'

References

Adam, C. & Artemeva, N. (2002). Writing instruction in English for Academic Purposes (EAP) classes: introducing second language learners to the academic community. In Johns, A. (Ed.) *Genre in the Classroom: Multiple perspectives* (pp. 179–196). Mahwah, NJ: Erlbaum.

Adolphs, S., Brown, B., Carter, R., Crawford, P. & Sahota, O. (2004). Applying Corpus Linguistics in a health care context. *Journal of Applied Linguistics*, 1(1): 9–28.

Aijmer, K. (1996). *Conversational Routines in English: Convention and creativity*. Harlow: Longman.

Antaki, C. (2011). (Ed.) *Applied Conversation Analysis: Intervention and change in institutional talk*. Basingstoke: Palgrave Macmillan.

Artemeva, N. (2006). A time to speak, a time to act: A rhetorical genre analysis of a novice engineer's calculated risk taking. In Artemeva, N. & Freedman, A. (Eds) *Rhetorical Genre Studies and Beyond* (pp. 188–239). Winnipeg, Manitoba: Inkshed.

Artemeva, N. & Freedman, A. (2006a). (Eds) *Rhetorical Genre Studies and Beyond*. Winnipeg, Manitoba: Inkshed.

Artemeva, N. & Freedman, A. (2006b). Introduction. In Artemeva, N. & A. Freedman, A. (Eds) *Rhetorical Genre Studies and Beyond* (pp. 1–8). Winnipeg, Manitoba: Inkshed.

Arundale, R. (2006). Face as relational and interactional: a communication framework for research on face, facework, and politeness. *Journal of Politeness Research*, 2: 193–216.

Askehave, I. & Swales, J. M. (2001). Genre identification and communicative purpose: a problem and a possible solution. *Applied Linguistics*, 22: 195–212.

Atkinson, J. M. & Drew, P. (1979). *Order in Court: The organization of verbal interaction in juridical settings*. London: Macmillan.

Austin, J. L. (1962). *How to Do Things with Words*. New York: Oxford University Press.

Bachman, L. (1990). *Fundamental Considerations in Language Testing*. Oxford: Oxford University Press.

Baker, P. (2006). *Using Corpora in Discourse Analysis*. London: Continuum.

Baker, T. (2010). Genre matters in academic writing. *International House Journal of Education and Development* 28. Retrieved from http://ihjournal.com/genre-matters-in-academic-writing.

Baker, P., Gabrielatos, C., Khosravinik, M., Krzyzanowski, M., McEnery, T. & Wodak, R. (2008). A useful methodological synergy? Combining Critical Discourse Analysis and Corpus Linguistics to examine discourses of refugees and asylum seekers in the UK Press. *Discourse and Society*, 19(3): 273–306.

Bakhtin, M. M. (1981). *The Dialogic Imagination: Four essays*. Austin, TX: University of Texas Press.

Bakhtin, M. M. (1986). *Speech Genres and Other Late Essays* (transl. McGee, V. W.). Austin, TX: University of Texas Press.

Bardovi-Harlig, K. & Mahan-Taylor, R. (2003). Teaching Pragmatics. Retrieved from http://exchanges.state.gov/englishteaching/.

Barraja-Rohan, A.-M. (2000). Teaching conversation and socio-cultural norms with conversation analysis. In Liddicoat, A. J. & Crozet, C. (Eds) *Teaching Languages, Teaching Cultures* (pp. 65–78). Melbourne: Language Australia.

Barron, A. (2003). *Acquisition in Interlanguage Pragmatics. Learning how to do things with words in a study abroad context.* Amsterdam: John Benjamins.

Barron, A. (2012). Interlanguage pragmatics: From use to acquisition to second language pedagogy. *Language Teaching*, 45(1): 44–63.

Basturkmen, H. & Crandell, E. (2004). Evaluating pragmatics-focused materials. *ELT Journal*, 58(1): 38–49.

Bawarshi, A. S. & Reiff, M. J. (2010). *Genre: An introduction to history, theory, research and pedagogy.* West Lafayette, IN: Parlor Press.

Bazerman, C. (1988). *Shaping Written Knowledge. The genre and activity of the experimental article in science.* Wisconsin: University of Wisconsin Press.

Bazerman, C. (1994). Systems of genres and the enactment of social intentions. In Freedman, A. & Medway, P. (Eds) *Genre and the New Rhetoric* (pp. 79–101). London: Taylor and Francis.

Beach, W. (1993). Transtitional regulatities for 'casual' 'okay' usages. *Journal of Pragmatics*, 19: 325–352.

Béal, C. (1992). Did you have a good week-end? Or why there is no such thing as a simple question in cross-cultural encounters. *Australian Review of Applied Linguistics*, 15(1): 23–52.

Beekman, J. & Callow, J. (1974). *Translating the Word of God.* Grand Rapids, MI: Zondervan Publishing House.

Berkenkotter, C. & Huckin, T. (1995). *Genre Knowledge in Disciplinary Communication: Cognition/culture/power.* Hillsdale, NJ: Erlbaum.

Berry, M. (1995). Thematic options and success in writing. In Ghadessy, M. (Ed.) *Thematic development in English texts* (pp. 55–84). London: Pinter.

Berry, R. (1996). *Determiners.* London: Collins.

Bhatia, V. K. (1993). *Analysing Genre: Language use in professional settings.* London: Longman.

Bhatia, V. K. (2002). Generic view of academic discourse. In Flowerdew, J. (Ed.) *Academic Discourse* (pp. 21–39). London: Pearson.

Bhatia, V. K. (2004). *Worlds of Written Discourse.* London: Continuum.

Bhatia, V. K., Flowerdew, J. & Jones, R. (2008). *Advances in Discourse Studies.* London: Routledge.

Biber, D. (1991). *Variation Across Speech and Writing.* Cambridge: Cambridge University Press.

Biber, D. (2006). *University Language: A corpus-based study of spoken and written registers.* Amsterdam: John Benjamins.

Biber, D., Conrad, S. & Reppen, R. (1998). *Corpus Linguistics: Investigating language structure and use.* New York: Cambridge University Press.

Biber, D., Johansson, S., Leech, G., Conrad, S. & Finegan, E. (1999). (Eds) *Longman Grammar of Spoken and Written English.* London: Longman.

Biber, D., Conrad, S. & Leech, G. (2002). *Longman Student Grammar of Spoken and Written English.* Essex: Longman.

Biber, D., Csomay, E., Jones, J. K. & Keck, C. (2004). A corpus linguistic investigation of vocabulary-based discourse units in university registers. In Connor, U. & Upton, T. A. (Eds) *Applied Corpus Linguistics: A multidimensional perspective* (pp. 53–72). Amsterdam: Rodopi.

Biber, D., Connor, U. & Upton, T. A. (2007). *Discourse on the Move: Using corpus analysis to describe discourse structure.* Amsterdam: John Benjamins.

Bilbow, G. T. (1997). Spoken discourse in the multicultural workplace in Hong Kong: Applying a model of discourse as 'impression management'. In Bargiela-Chiappini, F. & Harris, S. J. (Eds) *The Languages of Business: An international perspective* (pp. 21–48). Edinburgh: Edinburgh University Press.

Bilbow, G. T. (1998). Look who's talking: An analysis of 'chair-talk' in business meetings. *Journal of Business and Technical Communication*, 12(2): 157–197.

Bilbow, G. T. (2002). Commissive speech act use in intercultural business meetings. *International Review of Applied Linguistics in Language Teaching*, 40(4): 207–303.

Billig, M. (2008). The language of Critical Discourse Analysis: The case of nominalisation. *Discourse and Society*, 19(6): 783–800.

Blommaert, J. (2001). Context is/as critique. *Critique of Anthropology*, 21(2): 13–32.

Blommaert, J. (2005). *Discourse: An introduction*. Oxford: Oxford University Press.

Blum-Kulka, S., House, J. & Kasper, G. (1989a). (Eds) *Cross-cultural Pragmatics: Requests and apologies*. Norwood, NJ: Ablex.

Blum-Kulka, S., House, J. & Kasper, G. (1989b). Investigating cross-cultural pragmatics: An introductory overview. In Blum-Kulka, S., House, J. & Kasper, G. (Eds) *Cross-cultural Pragmatics: Requests and apologies* (pp. 1–34). Norwood, NJ: Ablex.

Boswood, T. & Marriott, A. (1994). Ethnography for specific purposes: Teaching and training in parallel. *English for Specific Purposes*, 13: 2–21.

Bousfield, D. (2007). *Impoliteness in Interaction*. Philadelphia: John Benjamins.

Bousfield, D. & Locher, M. (2008). (Eds) *Impoliteness in Language: Studies on its interplay with power in theory and practice*. Berlin: Mouton de Gruyter.

Bouton, L. F. (1999). Developing non-native speaker skills in interpreting conversational implicatures in English: Explicit teaching can ease the process. In Hinkel, E. (Ed.) *Culture in Second Language Teaching and Learning* (pp. 47–70). New York: Cambridge University Press.

Bowles, H. & Seedhouse, P. (2007). Interactional competence and the LSP classroom. In Bowles, H. & Seedhouse, P. (Eds) *Conversation Analysis and Languages for Specific Purposes* (pp. 305–330). Bern: Peter Lang

Boxer, D. & Pickering, L. (1995). Problems in the presentation of speech acts in ELT materials: The case of complaints. *ELT Journal*, 49(1): 45–58.

Brouwer, C. E. & Wagner, J. (2004). Developmental issues in second language conversation. *Journal of Applied Linguistics*, 1(1): 29–47.

Brown, R. & Gilman, A. (1960). The pronouns of power and solidarity. In Paulston, C. P. & Tucker, G. R. (Eds) *Sociolinguistics: The essential readings* (pp. 253–276). Oxford: Blackwell.

Brown, P. & Levinson, S. (1978). Universals in language usage. In Goody, E. (Ed.) *Questions and Politeness* (pp. 56–289). Cambridge: Cambridge University Press.

Brown, P. & Levinson, S. (1987). *Politeness: Some universals in language use.* (2nd Edition) Cambridge: Cambridge University Press.

Brown, G. & Yule, G. (1983). *Discourse Analysis*. Cambridge: Cambridge University Press.

Bullock, R. (2005). *The Norton Field Guide to Writing*. New York: W. W. Norton.

Burgess, A. & Ivanic, R. (2010). Writing and being written: Issues of identity across timescales. *Written Communication*, 27(2): 228–225.

Burns, A., Joyce, H. & Gollin, S. (1997). Authentic spoken texts in the language classroom. *Prospect*, 12(2): 72–86.

Butler, J. (2003). *Structure and Function: A guide to three major structural–functional theories. Part 1: Approaches to the simplex clause. Part 2: From clause to discourse and beyond.* Amsterdam and Philadelphia: John Benjamins.

Canale, M. (1983). From communicative competence to communicative language pedagogy. In Richards, J. & Schmidt, R. (Eds) *Language and Communication* (pp. 2–27). Longman: London.

Canale, M. & Swain, M. (1980). Theoretical bases of communicative approaches to second language teaching and testing. *Applied Linguistics*, 1(1): 1–48.

Carrell, P. L. (1982). Cohesion is not coherence. *TESOL Quarterly*, 16(4): 479–488.

Carter, R. (1998) Orders of reality: CANCODE, communication, and culture. *ELT Journal*, 52(1): 43–56.

Carter, R. & McCarthy, M. (2006). *Cambridge Grammar of English: A comprehensive guide. Spoken and written English grammar and usage*. Cambridge: Cambridge University Press.

Carter, R., Goddard, A., Reah, D., Sanger, K. & Bowring, M. (2001). *Working with Texts*. London: Routledge.

Casanave, C. (1992). Cultural diversity and socialisation: A case study of a Hispanic woman in a doctoral program in sociology. In Murray, D. E. (Ed.) *Diversity as Resource: Redefining cultural literacy* (pp. 148–182). Alexandra, VA: TESOL.

Celce-Murcia, M. (1995). The elaboration of sociolinguistic competence: Implications for teacher education. In Alatis, J. E., Straehle, C. A. & Ronkin, M. (Eds) *Linguistics and the Education of Language Teachers: Ethnolinguistic, psycholinguistic, and sociolinguistic aspects. Proceedings of the Georgetown University, Round Table on Languages and Linguistics*, 2005 (pp. 699–710). Washington, DC: Georgetown University Press.

Celce-Murcia, M. (2007). Rethinking the role of communicative competence in language teaching. In Alcón Soler, E. & Safont Jordà, M. P. (Eds) *Intercultural Language Use and Language Learning* (pp. 41–57). Berlin: Springer.

Celce-Murcia, M., Dörnyei Z. & Thurrell, S. (1995). A pedagogical framework for communicative competence: A pedagogically motivated model with content specifications. *Issues in Applied Linguistics*, 6(2): 5–35.

Chafe, W. & Danielewicz, J. (1987). Properties of spoken language. In Horowitz, R. & Samuels, S. J. (Eds) *Comprehending Oral and Written Language* (pp. 83–113). New York: Academic Press.

Chalker, S. (1996). *Linking Words*. London: Collins.

Chen, X. (2010). Discourse-Grammatical Features in L2 Speech: A corpus-based contrastive study of Chinese advanced learners and native speakers of English. Unpublished PhD thesis, City University of Hong Kong.

Cheng, W. (2003). *Intercultural Conversation*. Amsterdam: John Benjamins.

Chiapello, E. & Fairclough, N. (2002). Understanding the new management ideology: a transdisciplinary contribution from Critical Discourse Analysis and new sociology of capitalism. *Discourse and Society*, 13(2): 185–208.

Chomsky, N. (1965). *Aspects of the Theory of Syntax*. Cambridge, MA: MIT Press.

Chouliaraki, L. & Fairclough, N. (1999). *Discourse in Late Modernity: Rethinking Critical Discourse Analysis*. Edinburgh: Edinburgh University Press.

Christiansen, T. (2011). *Cohesion: A discourse perspective*. Berne: Peter Lang Publishing.

Christie, F. and Derewianka, B. (2008). *School Discourse: Learning to write across the years of schooling*. London: Continuum.

Clark, H. H. & Bangerter, A. (2004). Changing ideas about reference. In Noveck, I. A. & Sperber, D. (Eds) *Experimental Pragmatics* (pp. 25–49). Houndmills: Palgrave Macmillan.

Clark, R. & Ivanic, R. (1997). *The Politics of Writing*. London: Routledge.

Clark, R & Ivanic, R. (1999). Raising critical awareness of language: A curriculum aim for the new millennium. *Language Awareness*, 8(2): 63–70.

Clyne, M. (1994). *Inter-cultural Communication at Work: Discourse structures across cultures*. Cambridge: Cambridge University Press.

Coe, R. (2002). The new rhetoric of genre: Writing political briefs. In Johns, A. M. (Ed.) *Genre in the Classroom: Multiple perspectives* (pp. 197–210). New Jersey: Lawrence Erlbaum.

Coffin, C. (2006). An investigation into secondary school history. In Christie, F. & Martin, J. R. (Eds) *Genre and Social Institutions: Social processes in the workplace and school* (pp. 196–230). London: Cassell.

Cohen, A. D. & Ishihara, N. (2005). A web-based approach to strategic learning of speech acts. Minneapolis, MN: Center for Advanced Research on Language Acquisition (CRLA), University of Minessota. Retrieved from http://www.carla.umn.edu/speechacts/research.html

Cook, G. (1998). The uses of reality: a reply to Ronald Carter. *ELT Journal*, 52(1): 57–63.

Cots, J. M. (2006). Teaching 'with an attitude': Critical Discourse Analysis in EFL teaching. *ELT Journal*, 60(4): 336–345.

Coxhead, A. (2000). A new academic word list. *TESOL Quarterly*, 34(2): 213–238.

Crombie, W. (1985). *Discourse and Language Learning: A relational approach to syllabus design*. Oxford: Oxford University Press.

Crozet, C., Liddicoat, A. J. & Lo Bianco, J. (1999). Intercultural competence: From language policy to language education. In Lo Bianco, J., Liddicoat, A. & Crozet, C. (Eds) *Striving for the Third Place: Intercultural competence through language education* (pp. 1–20). Melbourne: Language Australia.

Culpeper, J. (2011). *Impoliteness: Using language to cause offence*. Cambridge: Cambridge University Press.

Cutting, J. (2008). *Pragmatics and Discourse*, 2nd edn. London: Routledge.

de Beaugrande, R. (undated). The case against Critical Discourse Analysis reopened: In Search of Widdowson's 'Pretexts'. Retrieved from http://www.beaugrande.com/WiddowsonPretexts.htm

de Beaugrande, R. & Dressler, W. U. (1981). *Introduction to Text Linguistics*. London: Longman.

de Cock, S. (2010). Spoken learner corpora and EFL teaching. In Campoy, M. L., Bellés-Fortuno, M. B. & Gea-Valor, M. L. (Eds) *Corpus-based Approaches to English Language Teaching* (pp. 123–137). London: Continuum.

Devitt, A. (1991). Intertextuality in tax accounting. In Bazerman, C. & Paradis, J. (Eds) *Textual Dynamics of the Professions* (pp. 336–357). Madison, WI: University of Wisconsin Press.

Devitt, A., Reiff, M. J. & Bawarshi A. (2004). *Scenes of Writing: Strategies for composing with genres*. New York: Longman.

Dudley-Evans, T. (1997). Genre models for the teaching of academic writing to second language speakers: advantages and disadvantages. In Miller, T. (Ed.) *Functional Approaches to Written Text: Classroom applications* (pp. 150–159). Washington, DC: United States Information Agency.

Edmondson, W. (1981). Illocutionary verbs, illocutionary acts, and conversational behaviour. In Eikmeyer, J. J. & Rieser, H. (Eds) *Words, Worlds and Contexts* (pp. 485–499). Berlin, Federal Republic of Germany: de Gruyter.

Eggins, S. & Slade, D. (2005). *Analysing Casual Conversation* (paperback re-issue). London: Equinox.

Ellis, R. (2008). *The Study of Second Language Acquisition*, 2nd edn. Oxford: OUP

Enkvist, A. E. (1978). Coherence, pseudo-coherence and non-coherence. In Ostman, J. O. (Ed.) *Cohesion and Semantics* (pp. 109–128). Turku: Abo Akademi.

Fairclough, N. (1989). *Language and Power*. New York: Longman.

Fairclough, N. (1992a). *Discourse and Social Change*. Cambridge: Polity.

Fairclough, N. (1992b). (Ed.) *Critical Language Awareness*. Harlow: Longman.

Fairclough, N. (1992c). Introduction. In Fairclough, N. (Ed.) *Critical Language Awareness* (pp. 1–29). London: Longman.

Fairclough, N. (1992d). The appropriacy of 'appropriateness'. In Fairclough, N. (Ed.) *Critical Language Awareness* (pp. 33–56). London: Longman.

Fairclough, N. (1996). A reply to Henry Widdowson's 'Discourse Analysis: A Critical View'. *Language and Literature*, 5(1): 49–56.

Fairclough, N. (2000). *New Labour, New Language?* London: Routledge.

Fairclough, N. (2001). Critical Discourse Analysis as a method in social scientific research. In Wodak, R. & Meyer, M. (Eds) *Methods of Critical Discourse Analysis* (pp. 121–138). London, UK: Sage Publications.

Fairclough, N. (2003a). *Analysing Discourse: Textual analysis for social research*. London: Routledge.

Fairclough, N. (2003b). A reply to Henry Widdowson's 'Discourse Analysis: A critical view.' In Seidlhofer, B. (Ed.) *Controversies in Applied Linguistics* (pp. 145–152). Oxford: Oxford University Press.

Fairclough, N. (2005). Critical Discourse Analysis. *Marges Linguistiques*, 9: 76–94.

Fairclough, N. (2008). The language of Critical Discourse Analysis: Reply to Michael Billing. *Discourse and Society*, 19(6): 811–819.

Fairclough N. & Wodak, R. (1997). Critical Discourse Analysis. In van Dijk, T. (Ed.) *Discourse as Social Interaction* (pp. 258–284). London: Sage.

Fairclough, N., Mulderrig, J. & Wodak, R. (2011). Critical Discourse Analysis. In Van Dijk, T. (ed.) *Discourse Studies: A multidisciplinary introduction*, 2nd edn (pp. 357–378). London: Sage.

Feez, S. (2002). Heritage and innovation in second language education. In Johns, A. M. (Ed.) *Genre in the Classroom: Multiple perspectives* (pp. 43–69). Mahwah, NJ: Lawrence Erlbaum.

Feez, S. & Joyce, H. (1998). *Text-based Syllabus Design*. Sydney: National.

Fillmore, C. J. (1985). Frames and the semantics of understanding. *Quaderni di Semantica: Rivista Internazionale di Semantica Teorica e Applicata*, 6, 222–254.

Firth, J. R. (1957). *Papers in Linguistics 1934–1951*. Oxford: Oxford University Press.

Flowerdew, J. (1990). Problems of speech act theory from an applied perspective. *Language Learning*, 40: 79–105.

Flowerdew, J. (1993a). Concordancing as a tool in course design. *System*, 21(2): 231–244.

Flowerdew, J. (1993b). A process, or educational, approach to the teaching of professional genres. *ELT Journal*, 47(4): 305–316.

Flowerdew, J. (1997). The discourse of colonial withdrawal: a case study in the creation of mythic discourse. *Discourse and Society* 8(4): 493–517.

Flowerdew, L. (1998). Integrating 'expert' and 'interlanguage' computer corpora findings on causality: discoveries for teachers and students. *English for Specific Purposes*, 17(4): 329–345.

Flowerdew, J. (1999/2007). Description and interpretation in Critical Discourse Analysis. *Journal of Pragmatics*, 31: 1089–1099. Reprinted in Teubert, W. & Krishnamurthy, R. (Eds) *Corpus Linguistics: Critical concepts in linguistics* (pp. 42–53). London: Routledge.

Flowerdew, J. (2002). Genre in the classroom: A linguistic approach. In Johns, A. M. (Ed.) *Genre in the Classroom: Multiple perspectives* (pp. 91–102). Mahwah, NJ: Lawrence Erlbaum Associates.

Flowerdew, J. (2003a). Signalling nouns in discourse. *English for Specific Purposes Journal*, 22(4): 329–346.

Flowerdew, J. (2003b). Register specificity of signalling nouns in discourse. In Meyer, C. & Leistyna, P. (Eds) *Corpus Analysis: Language structure and language use* (pp. 35–46). Amsterdam: Rodopi Publishers.

Flowerdew, J. (2003c). A pedagogic grammar of signalling nouns in discourse. *Revista Canaria de Estudios Ingleses*, 44: 141–155.

Flowerdew, L. (2005). An integration of corpus-based and genre-based approaches to text analysis in EAP/ESP: Countering criticisms against corpus-based methodologies. *English for Specific Purposes*, 24: 321–332.

Flowerdew, J. (2006). Use of signalling nouns in a learner corpus. *International Journal of Corpus Linguistics*, 11(3): 345–362.

Flowerdew, L. (2008a). Corpora and context in professional writing. In Bhatia, V. K., Flowerdew, J. & Jones, R. (Eds) *Advances in Discourse Studies* (pp. 115–127). London: Routledge.

Flowerdew, L. (2008b). *Corpus-based Analyses of the Problem-solution pattern: A phraseological analysis*. Amsterdam: John Benjamins.

Flowerdew, L. (2008c). Determining discourse-based moves in professional reports. In Ädel, A. & Reppen, R. (Eds) *Corpora and Discourse: The challenges of different settings* (pp. 117–131). Amsterdam: John Benjamins.

Flowerdew, J. (2009). Corpora in language teaching. In Long, M. H. & Doughty, C. J. (Eds) *The Handbook of Language Teaching* (pp. 327–350). Oxford, UK: Wiley-Blackwell.

Flowerdew, J. (2010). Use of signalling nouns across L1 and L2 writer corpora. *International Journal of Corpus Linguistics*. 15(1): 34–53.

Flowerdew, J. (2011). Reconciling approaches to genre analysis in ESP: The whole can equal more than the sum of the parts. In Belcher, D., Johns, A. M. & Paltridge, B. (Eds) *New Directions in ESP Research* (pp. 119–144). Ann Arbor, MI: University of Michigan Press.

Flowerdew, J. (2012a). *Critical Discourse Analysis in Historiography: The case of Hong Kong's evolving political identity*. Houndmills: Palgrave Macmillan.

Flowerdew, J. (2012b). Corpora in language teaching from the perspective of English as an international language. In Alsagoff, L., McKay, S. L., Hu, G. & Renandya, W. R. (Eds) *Principles and Practices for Teaching English as an International Language* (pp. 226–243). New York: Routledge.

Flowerdew, L. (2012). *Corpora and Language Education*. New York: Palgrave Macmillan.

Flowerdew, J. & Forest, R. (2009). Schematic structure and lexico-grammatical realisation in corpus-based genre analysis: the case of 'research' in the PhD literature review. In Charles, M., Pecorari D. & Hunston, S. (Eds) *Academic Writing: At the interface of corpus and discourse* (pp. 15–36). London: Continuum.

Flowerdew, J. & Mahlberg, M. (2006). (Eds) *Corpus Linguistics and Lexical Cohesion. Special Issue of the International Journal of Corpus Linguistics*. Amsterdam: John Benjamins.

Flowerdew, J. & Miller, L. (2005). *Second Language Listening: Theory and practice*. London: Longman.

Flowerdew, J. & Wan, A. (2006). Genre analysis of tax computation letters: How and why tax accountants write the way they do. *English for Specific Purposes*, 25(2): 133–153.

Flowerdew, J. & Wan, A. (2010). The linguistic and the contextual in applied genre analysis: The case of the company audit report. *English for Specific Purposes*, 29(1): 78–93.

Foucault, M. (1982). The subject and power. In Dreyfus, H. & Rabinow, P. (Eds) *Michel Foucault: Beyond structuralism and hermeneutics*. Chicago, IL: University of Chicago Press.

Fowler, R. (1991). Critical linguistics. In Halmkjaer, K. (Ed.) *The Linguistic Encyclopedia* (pp. 89–93). London: Routledge.

Fowler, R. (1996a). On critical linguistics. In Caldas-Coulthard, C. R. & Coulthard, M. (Eds) *Texts and Practices: Readings in Critical Discourse Analysis* (pp. 3–14). London: Routledge.

Fowler, R. (1996b). *Linguistic Criticism*. Oxford: Oxford University Press.

Fowler, H. W. & Fowler, G. (1973). *The King's English*, 3rd edn. Oxford: Oxford University Press.

Fowler, R., Kress, G., Hodge, R. & Trew, T. (1979). (Eds) *Language and Control*. London: Routledge.

Francis, G. (1986). *Anaphoric Nouns*. Birmingham: English Language Research, University of Birmingham.

Frankenberg-Garcia, A. (2012). Raising teachers' awareness of corpora. *Language Teaching*, 45(4): 490–514.

Freadman, A. (1994). Anyone for tennis? In Freedman, A. & Medway, P. (Ed.) *Genre and the New Rhetoric* (pp. 43–66). Bristol: Taylor & Francis.

Freedman, A. (1987). Learning to write again: Discipline-specific writing at university. *Carleton Papers in Applied Language Studies*, 4: 95–116.

Freedman, A. (2006). Interaction between theory and research: RGS and a study of students and professionals working 'in computers'. In Artemeva, N. & Freedman, A. (Eds) *Rhetorical Genre Studies and Beyond* (pp. 101–120). Winnipeg: Inkshed.

Freedman, A. & Medway, P. (1994a). *Genre and the New Rhetoric*. London: Taylor & Francis.

Freedman, A. & Medway, P. (1994b). *Learning and Teaching Genre*. Portsmouth, NH: Heinemann.

Freire, P. (1985). *The Politics of Education*. London: Macmillan.

Fries, P. H. (1981). On the status of theme in English: Arguments from discourse. *Forum Linguisticum*, 6: 1–38.

Fries, P. H. (1995). A personal view of theme. In Ghadessy, M. (Ed.) *Thematic Development in English Texts* (pp. 1–19). London: Pinter.

Fung, L. & Carter R. (1999). Discourse markers and spoken English: Native and learner use in pedagogic settings. *Applied Linguistics*, 28(3): 410–439.

Garcés-Conejos Blitvich, P. & Fortanet-Gómez, I. (2008). The presentation of self in résumés: An intercultural approach. *English for Specific Purposes across Cultures* 5: 69–90.

Gaskell, D. & Cobb, T. (2004). Can learners use concordance feedback for writing errors? *System*, 32(3): 301–319.

Gavioli, L. (2001). The learner as researcher: introducing corpus concordancing in the classroom. In Aston, G. (Ed.) *Learning with Corpora* (pp. 108–137). Bologna: CLUEB.

Gavioli, L. (2005). *Exploring Corpora for ESP Learning*. Amsterdam: John Benjamins.

Gavioli, L. & Aston. G. (2001). Enriching reality: Language corpora in language pedagogy. *ELT Journal*, 55: 238–246.

Gee, J. P. (2011a). *An Introduction to Discourse Analysis: Theory and method*, 3rd edn. London: Routledge.

Gee, J. P. (2011b). *How to do Discourse Analysis: A toolkit*. London: Routledge.

Georgakopoulou, A. & Goutsos, D. (2004). *Discourse Analysis: An introduction*, 2nd edn. Edinburgh: Edinburgh University Press.

Gilquin, G. & Granger, S. (2010). How can data-driven learning be used in language teaching? In O'Keeffe, A. & McCarthy, M. (Eds) *The Routledge Handbook of Corpus Linguistics* (pp. 359–370). London: Routledge.

Gledhill, C. (2000). The discourse function of collocation in research article introductions. *English for Specific Purposes*, 19: 115–135.

Goffman, E. (1971). *The Presentation of Self in Everyday Life*. Harmondsworth: Penguin.

Goodwin, C. (1981). *Conversational Organization: Interaction between speakers and hearers*. New York: Academic Press.

Gozzi, R. Jr. (1991). New speech act verbs in American English. *Research on Language and Social Interaction*, 24: 447–457.

Grabe, W. (2002). Narrative and expository macro-genres. In Johns, A. M. (Ed.) *Genre in the Classroom: Multiple perspectives* (pp. 249–267). Mahwah, NJ: Lawrence Erlbaum.

Gramsci, A. (1971). *Selection from Prison Notebooks* (transl. Hoare, Q. & Nowell-Smith, G.). London: Lawrence and Wishart.

Granger, S. (2002). A bird's-eye view of learner corpus research. In Granger, S., Hung, J. & Petch-Tyson, S. (Eds) *Computer Learner Corpora, Second Language Acquisition and Foreign Language Teaching* (pp. 3–33). Amsterdam: John Benjamins.

Granger, S. (2004). Practical applications of learner corpora. In Lewandowska-Tomaszczyk, B. (Ed.) *Practical Applications in Language and Computers (PALC 2003)* (pp. 291–301). Frankfurt: Peter Lang.

Granger, S. (2011). From phraseology to pedagogy: Challenges and prospects. In Herbst, T., Uhrig, P. & Schüller, S. (Eds) *Chunks in the Descriptions of Language: A tribute to John Sinclair* (pp. 123–146). Berlin: Mouton de Gruyter.

Gregory, M. & Carroll, S. (1978). *Language and Situation: Language varieties and their social contexts*. London: Routledge & Kegan Paul.

Green, B. & Lee, A. (1994). Writing geography lessons: literacy, identity and schooling. In Freedman, A. & Medway, P. (Eds) *Learning and Teaching Genre* (pp. 207–224). Portsmouth, NH: Boynton/Cook (Heinemann).

Grey, A. (1990). *The Bangkok Secret*. Pan Books.

Grice, H. P. (1989 [1967]). Logic and conversation. In Grice, H. P. (Ed.) *Studies in the Way of Words* (pp. 22–40). Cambridge, MA: Harvard University Press.

Grimes, J. (1975). *The Thread of Discourse*. The Hague: Mouton.

Grundy, P. (2012). Teaching and learning pragmatics. *English Language Teaching Journal* 66(1): 120–122.

Gu, Y. (1990). Politeness phenomena in modern Chinese. *Journal of Pragmatics*, 14: 237–257.

Halliday, M. A. K. (1975). *Learning How to Mean: Explorations in the development of language.* London: Edward Arnold.

Halliday, M. A. K. (1978). *Language as Social Semiotic.* London: Edward Arnold.

Halliday, M. A. K. (1987). *Spoken and Written Language* (2nd edn). Oxford: Oxford University Press.

Halliday, M. A. K. (1989). *Spoken and Written Language.* Oxford: Oxford University Press.

Halliday, M. A. K. (2004). Things and relations: Regrammaticizing experience as technical knowledge. In Webster, J. J. (Ed.) *The Language of Science* (Volume 5 in the *Collected Works of M. A. K. Halliday*) (pp. 49–101). London: Continuum.

Halliday, M. A. K. (2006). Talk given at City University of Hong Kong. March.

Halliday, M. A. K. & Hasan, R. (1976). *Cohesion in English.* London: Longman.

Halliday, M. A. K. & Hasan, R. (1985/1989). *Language, Context, and Text: Aspects of language in a social-semiotic perspective.* Oxford: Oxford University Press.

Halliday, M. A. K. & Matthiessen, C. M. I. M. (2004). *An Introduction to Functional Grammar.* London: Edward Arnold.

Halliday, M. A. K., McIntosh, M. & Strevens, P. (1964). *The Linguistic Sciences and Language Teaching.* London: Longman.

Hammersley, M. (1997). On the foundations of Critical Discourse Analysis. *Language and Communication*, 17: 237–248.

Handford, M. (2010). *The Language of Business Meetings.* Cambridge: Cambridge University Press.

Hardt-Mautner, G. (1995). Only Connect: Critical Discourse Analysis and Corpus Linguistics, University of Lancaster. Retrieved from http://ucrel.lancs.ac.uk/papers/techpaper/vol6.pdf

Hasan, R. (1977). Text in the systemic functional model. In Dressler, D. (Ed.) *Current Trends in Text Linguistics* (pp. 228–246). Berlin: De Gruyter.

Hasan, R. (1979). On the notion of text. In Petofi, J. S. (Ed.), *Text Versus Sentence: Basic questions of text linguistics* (pp. 369–390). Hamburg: Helmut Buske.

Hasan, R. (1984a). Coherence and cohesive harmony. In Flood, J. (Ed.) *Understanding Reading Comprehension* (pp. 181–219). Newark, DE: International Reading Association.

Hasan, R. (1984b). The nursery tale as a genre. *Nottingham Linguistic Circular*, 13: 35–70.

Hasan, R. (1985). The structure of a text. In Halliday, M. A. K. & Hasan, R. (Eds.) *Language, Context, and Text: Aspects of language in a social-semiotic perspective* (pp. 52–69). Oxford: Oxford University Press.

Hasan, R. (1995). The conception of context in text. In Fries, P. H. & Gregory, M. (Eds.) *Discourse in Society: Systemic functional perspectives. Meaning and choice in language: Studies for Michael Halliday* (pp. 183–283). Norwood, NJ: Ablex.

Hasselgård, H. (2010). *Adjunct Adverbials in English.* Cambridge: Cambridge University Press.

Hatch, E. (1983). *Psycholinguistics: A second language perspective.* Rowley, MA: Newbury House.

Hatim, B. & Mason, I. (1990). *Discourse and the Translator.* Harlow: Longman.

Hawkins, E. (1984). *Awareness of Language: An introduction.* Cambridge: Cambridge University Press.

Heritage, J. (1997). Conversation analysis and institutional talk. In Silverman, D. (Ed.) *Quantitative Research: theory, method and practice* (pp. 161–182). London: Sage.

Hewings, M. & Hewings, A. (2002). 'It is interesting to note that…': a comparative study of anticipatory 'it' in student and published writing. *English for Specific Purposes*, 21(4): 367–383.

Hewings, A. & North, S. P. (2006). Emergent disciplinarity: a comparative study of theme in undergraduate essays in geography and history of science. In Whittaker, R., McCabe, A. & O'Donnell, M. (Eds.) *Language and Literacy: functional approaches* (pp. 266–281). London, Continuum.

Hobbs, J. (1978). Resolving pronoun references. *Lingua*, 44: 311–338.

Hobbs, J. (1979). Coherence and coreference. *Cognitive Science*, 3: 67–90.

Hodge, B. & Kress, G. R. (1979/1989). *Language as Ideology*. London: Routledge.

Hoey, M. (1983). *On the Surface of Discourse*. London: Allen & Unwin.

Hoey, M. (1991a). Another perspective on coherence and cohesive harmony. In Ventola, E. (Ed.) *Functional and Systemic Linguistics: Approaches and uses* (pp. 385–414). Berlin: Mouton de Gruyter.

Hoey, M. (1991b). *Patterns of Lexis in Text*. Oxford: Oxford University Press.

Hoey, M. (2005). *Lexical Priming: A new theory of words and language*. London: Routledge.

Hoey, M. (undated) retrieved from: http://www.onestopenglish.com/support/methodology/grammar-vocabulary-and-skills/whats-in-a-word/155130.article

Holmes, J. (1995). *Women, Men and Politeness*. New York: Longman.

House, J. & Kasper, G. (1981). Politeness markers in English and German. In Coulmas, F. (Ed.) *Conversational Routine: Explorations in standardized communication situations and prepatterned speech* (pp. 157–185). The Hague, The Netherlands: Mouton de Gruyter.

Huckin, T. (2005). Some useful tools and concepts for Critical Discourse Analysis. Unpublished talk, given at City University of Hong Kong.

Hudson, R. A. (1980). *Sociolinguistics*. Cambridge: Cambridge University Press.

Hunston, S. (2002). *Corpora in Applied Linguistics*. Cambridge: Cambridge University Press.

Hunston, S. (2007). Semantic prosody revisited. *International Journal of Corpus Linguistics*, 12(2): 249–268.

Hutchby, I. & Wooffitt, R. (2008). *Conversation Analysis* (2nd edn). Cambridge: Polity Press.

Huth, T. & Taleghani-Nikazm, C. (2006). How can insights from conversation analysis be directly applied to teaching L2 pragmatics? *Language Teaching Research*, 10: 53–79.

Hyland, K. (2000). *Disciplinary Discourses: Social interactions in academic writing*. Harlow: Pearson Education.

Hyland, K. (2004). *Genre and Second Language Writing*. Ann Arbor, MI: University of Michigan Press.

Hymes, D. (1962). The ethnography of speaking. In Gladwin, T. & Sturtevant, W. (Eds) *Anthropology and Human Behaviour* (pp. 13–53). Washington, DC: Anthropological Society of Washington.

Hymes, D. (l972a). Models of the interaction of language and social life. In Gumperz, J. J. & Hymes, D. (Eds) *Directions in Sociolinguistics* (pp. 35–71). New York: Holt, Rinehart and Winston.

Hymes, D. (l972b). On communicative competence. In Pride, J. B. & Holmes, J. (Eds) *Sociolinguistics: Selected readings*. Harmondsworth: Penguin.

Hymes, D. (1974). *Foundations in Sociolinguistics: An ethnographic approach*. Philadelphia, PA: University of Pennsylvania Press.

Hyon, S. (1996). Genre in three traditions: Implication for ESL. *TESOL Quarterly*, 30(4): 693–722.

Hyon, S. (2002). Genre and ESL reading: A classroom study. In: Johns, A. (Ed.) *Genre in the Classroom. Multiple perspectives* (pp. 121–141). Mahwah, NJ: Lawrence Erlbaum.

Ide, S. (1989). Formal forms and discernment: Two neglected aspects of universals of linguistic politeness. *Multilingua*, 8(2/3): 223–248.

Ishihara, N. (2010). Instructional pragmatics: bridging teaching, research, and teacher education. *Language and Linguistics Compass*. Retrieved from http://onlinelibrary.wiley.com/doi/10.1111/j.1749-818X.2010.00242.x/full.

Ishihara, N. & Cohen, A. D. (2010). *Teaching and Learning Pragmatics*. London: Pearson Education.

Ivanic, R. (1991). Nouns in search of a context. *International Review of Applied Linguistics*, XXIX(2): 93–114.

Jäger, S. (2001). Discourse and knowledge: theoretical and methodological aspects of a critical discourse and dispositive analysis. In Wodak, R. & Meyer, M. (Eds) *Methods of Critical Discourse Analysis* (pp. 32–62). London: Sage.

Jakobson, R. (1960). Closing statement: Linguistics and poetics. In Sebeok, T. A. (Ed.) *Style in Language* (pp. 350–377). Cambridge, MA: MIT Press.

Janks, H. (1999). Critical language awareness, journals, and student identities. *Language Awareness*, 8(2): 111–122.

Janks, H. & Ivanic, R. (1992). Critical language awareness and emancipatory discourse. In Fairclough, N. (Ed.) *Critical Language Awareness* (pp. 305–331). London: Longman.

Jaworski, A. & Coupland, N. (1999). (eds) *The Discourse Reader*. London: Routledge.

Jefferson, G. (2004). Glossary of transcript symbols with an introduction. In Lerner, G. (Ed.) *Conversation Analysis: Studies from the first generation* (pp. 13–31). Amsterdam: John Benjamins.

Jenks, C. J. (2011). *Transcribing Talk and Interaction: Issues in the representation of communication data.* Amsterdam: John Benjamins.

Jiang, X. (2006). Suggestions: what should ESL students know? *System*, 34(1): 46–54.

Johns, A. M. (1997). *Text, Role and Context.* Cambridge: Cambridge University Press.

Johns, T. (1997). Contexts: the background, development and trialling of a concordance-based CALL program. In Wichmann, A., Fligelstone, S., McEnery, T. & Knowles, G. (Eds) *Teaching and Language Corpora* (pp. 100–115). London: Longman.

Johns, A. M. (2002a). (ed.) *Genre in the Classroom: Multiple perspectives.* Mahwah, NJ: Lawrence Erlbaum.

Johns, A. M. (2002b). (ed.) Introduction. In *Genre in the Classroom: Multiple perspectives* (pp. 3–12). Mahwah, NJ: Lawrence Erlbaum.

Johns, T. (2002). Data-driven learning: The perpetual challenge. In Kettermann, B. & Marko, G. (Eds) *Teaching and Learning by Doing Corpus Analysis: Proceedings of the fourth international conference on teaching and language corpora*, Graz 19–24 July, 2000 (pp. 107–117). Amsterdam: Rodopi.

Johns, A. M. (2003). Genre and ESL/EFL composition instruction. In Kroll, B. (Ed.) *Exploring the Dynamics of Second Language Writing* (pp. 195–217). Cambridge: Cambridge University Press.

Johns, A. M., Bawarshi, A., Coe, R. M., Hyland, K., Paltridge, B., Reiff, M. J. & Tardy, C. (2006). Crossing the boundaries of genre studies: Commentaries by experts. *Journal of Second Language Writing*, 15: 234–249.

Johnson, B. (2008). *Discourse Analysis* (2nd edn). Oxford: Blackwell.

Jones, J. (2004). Learning to write in the disciplines: the application of systemic functional linguistic theory to the teaching and research of student writing. In Ravelli, L. & Elli, R. (Eds) *Analysing Academic Writing: Contextualized frameworks* (pp. 254–273). London: Continuum.

Jones, R. (2012). *Discourse Analysis: A resource book for students.* Oxford: Blackwell.

Jucker, A. H. (2009) Speech act research between armchair, field and laboratory: The case of compliments. *Journal of Pragmatics*, 41: 1611–1635.

Kaplan, R. (1966). Cultural thought patterns in intercultural education. *Language Learning*, 16(1): 1–20.

Kasper, G. (2006). Beyond repair: Conversation analysis as an approach to SLA. *AILA Review*, 19: 83–99.

Kasper, G. & Blum-Kulka, S. (1993). (eds) *Interlanguage Pragmatics.* New York: Oxford University Press.

Koester, A. J. (2002). The performance of speech acts in workplace conversations and the teaching of communicative functions. *System*, 30(2): 167–184.

Kramsch, C. (2000). Second language acquisition, Applied Linguistics, and the teaching of foreign languages. *Modern Language Journal*, 84: 311–326.

Kress, G. (1989a). *Linguistic Processes in Sociocultural Practice.* Oxford: Oxford University Press.

Kress, G. (1989b). Against arbitrariness: the social production of the sign as a foundational issue in Critical Discourse Analysis. *Discourse and Society*, 4(2): 169–191.

Kress, G. (2003). *Literacy in the New Media Age.* London: Routledge.

Kress, G. & van Leeuwen, T. (1996). *Reading Images.* London: Routledge.

Kristeva, J. (1980). Word, dialogue and the novel. In Roudiez, L. (Ed.) (transl. Gora, T., Jardine A. & Roudiez, L.) *Desire in Language: A semiotic approach to literature and art* (pp. 64–91). New York: Columbia University Press.

Kuiper, K. (2009). *Formulaic Genres.* Basingstoke, UK: Palgrave Macmillan.

Labov, W. (1972). Rules for ritual insults. In Sudnow, D. (Ed.) *Studies in Social Interaction* (pp. 120–169). New York: Macmillan, Free Press.

Laclau, E. & Mouffe, C. (1985/2001). *Hegemony and Socialist Strategy: Towards a radical democratic politics.* New York: Verso Books.

Lakoff, R. (1973). The logic of politeness; or, minding your p's and q's. *Papers from the 9th Regional Meeting, Chicago Linguistics Society* (pp. 292–305). Chicago, IL: Chicago Linguistics Society.

Lantolf, J. & Pavlenko, A. (2001). (S)econd (L)anguage (A)ctivity theory: understanding second language learners as people. In Breen, M. P. (Ed.) *Learner Contributions to Language Learning: New directions in research* (pp. 141–158). London: Longman.

Lave, J. & Wenger, E. (1991). *Situated Learning: Legitimate peripheral participation.* Cambridge: Cambridge University Press.

Lazaraton, A. (2002). *A Qualitative Approach to the Validation of Oral Language Tests.* Cambridge: Cambridge University Press.

Lee, D. & Swales, J. (2006). A corpus-based EAP course for NNS doctoral students: Moving from available specialized corpora to self-compiled corpora. *English for Specific Purposes,* 25: 56–75.

Leech, G. (1981). *Semantics* (2nd edn). Harmondsworth, UK: Penguin Books.

Leech, G. N. (1983). *Principles of Pragmatics.* London: Longman.

Leech, G. (1997). Teaching and language corpora: A convergence. In Wichmann, A., Fligelstone, S., McEnery, T. & Knowles, G. (Eds) *Teaching and Language Corpora* (pp. 1–23). London: Longman.

Leech, G. (2007). Politeness: Is there an east–west divide? *Journal of Politeness Research* 3: 167–206.

Leung, C. (2005). Convivial communication: recontextualising communicative competence. *International Journal of Applied Linguistics,* 15(2): 119–144.

Levinson, S. C. (1983). *Pragmatics.* Cambridge: Cambridge University Press.

Lewis, M. (1993). *The Lexical Approach.* Hove, England: Language Teaching Publications.

Lewis, M. (1997). (ed.) *Implementing the Lexical Approach.* Hove, England: Language Teaching Publications.

Liddicoat, A. J. (2007). *An Introduction to Conversation Analysis.* London: Continuum.

Liddicoat, A. J. & Crozet, C. (2001). Acquiring French interactional norms through instruction. In Rose, K. & Kasper, G. (Eds) *Pragmatics in Language Teaching* (pp. 125–144). New York: Cambridge University Press.

Limerick Corpus of Irish English. Retrieved from http://www.metafilter.com/99869/Online-Corpora.

LoCastro, V. (2003). *An Introduction to Pragmatics: Social action for language teachers.* Ann Arbor, MI: University of Michigan Press.

Lock, G. (1996). *Functional English Grammar: An introduction for second language teachers.* Cambridge: Cambridge University Press.

Lock, G. & Lockhart, C. (1998). Genres in an academic writing class. *Hong Kong Journal of Applied Linguistics,* 3(2): 47–64.

Longacre, R. E. (1976). *An Anatomy of Speech Notions.* Lisse: The Peter de Ridder Press.

Louw, B. (1993). Irony in the text or insincerity in the writer? The diagnostic potential of semantic prosodies. In Baker, M., Francis, G. & Tognini-Bonelli, E. (Eds.) *Text and Technology* (pp. 157–176). Amsterdam: John Benjamins.

Luke, A. (1994). Editor's preface. In Freedman, A. & Medway, P. (Eds.) *Genre and the New Rhetoric* (pp. vii–xi). London: Taylor & Francis.

Luke, A. (1996). Genres of power? Literacy education and the production of capital. In Hasan, R. & Williams, G. (Eds.) *Literacy in Society* (pp. 308–338). New York: Longman.

Luke, A. (2002). Beyond science and ideology critique: developments in Critical Discourse Analysis. *Annual Review of Applied Linguistics*, 22: 96–110.

Machin, D. & van Leeuwen, T. (2003). *Global Media Discourse: A critical introduction.* London: Routledge.

Mann, W. C. & Thompson, S. A. (1988). Rhetorical structure theory: Toward a functional theory of text organization. *Text*, 8(3): 243–281.

Mao, LuMing R. (1994). Beyond politeness theory: 'Face' revisited and renewed'. *Journal of Pragmatics*, 21: 451–486.

Marcuse, H. (1971). *Negations: Essays in critical theory.* Boston, MA: Beacon Press.

Markee, N. (2000). *Conversation Analysis.* Mahwah, NJ: Lawrence Erlbaum.

Markee, N. (2008). Toward a learning behavior tracking methodology for CA-for-SLA. *Applied Linguistics*, 29: 404–427.

Martin, J. R. (1983). Conjunction: The logic of English text. In Petöfi, J. S. & Sözer, E. (Eds.) *Micro and Macro Connexity of Texts* (pp. 1–72). Hamburg: Helmut Buske Verlag.

Martin, J. R. (1984). Language, register and genre. In Christie, F. (Ed.) *Children Writing* (pp. 2l–29). Geelong, Australia: Deakin University Press.

Martin, J. R. (1992). *English Text: System and structure.* Amsterdam: John Benjamins.

Martin, J. R. (1993). A contextual theory of language. In Cope, W. & Kalantzis, M. (Eds.) *The Powers of Literacy: A genre approach to teaching writing* (pp. 116–136). Pittsburgh, PA: University of Pittsburgh Press.

Martin, J. R. (1999). Grace: The logogenesis of freedom. *Discourse Studies*, 1(1): 29–56.

Martin, J. R. (2000). Beyond exchange: Appraisal systems in English. In Hunston, S. & Thompson, G. (Eds) *Evaluation in Text: Authorial stance and the construction of discourse* (pp. 142–175). Oxford: Oxford University Press.

Martin, J. (2004). Positive discourse analysis: power, solidarity and change. *Canaria de Estudios Ingleses*, 49: 179–200.

Martin, J. R. & Rose, D. (2003). *Working with Discourse.* London: Continuum.

Martin, J. R. & Rose, D. (2007). *Working with Discourse: Meaning beyond the clause* (2nd edn). London: Continuum.

Martin, J. R. & Rose, D. (2008). *Genre Relations: Mapping culture.* London: Equinox.

Martin, J. R. & Rose, D. (2012). *Learning to Write, Reading to Learn: Genre, knowledge and pedagogy in the Sydney school.* London: Equinox.

Martin, J. R. & White, P. R. R. (2005). *The Language of Evaluation: Appraisal in English.* London: Palgrave Macmillan.

Martin, J. R. & Wodak, R. (2003). *Re/reading the Past: Critical and functional perspectives on time and value.* Amsterdam: John Benjamins.

Matsumoto, Y. (1988). Reexamination of the universality of face: Politeness phenomena in Japanese. *Journal of Pragmatics*, 12: 403–426.

Matsumoto, Y. (1989). Politeness and conversational universals: Observations from Japanese. *Multilingua*, 8(2/3): 207–221.

Mautner, G. (2009a). Corpora and Critical Discourse Analysis. In: Bake, P. (Ed.) *Contemporary Corpus Linguistics* (pp. 32–46). London: Continuum.

Mautner, G. (2009b). Checks and balances: How Corpus Linguistics can contribute to CDA. In Wodak, R. and Meyer, M. (Eds) (pp. 122–143). *Methods of Critical Discourse Analysis.* London: Sage.

Maynard, D. W. & Heritage, J. (2005). Conversation analysis, doctor–patient interaction and medical communication. *Medical Education*, 39(4): 428–435.

McCarthy, M. (1991). *Discourse Analysis for Language Teachers.* Cambridge: Cambridge University Press.

McCarthy, M. & Carter, R. (1994). *Language as Discourse: Perspectives for language teaching.* London: Longman.

McCarthy, M. J. & Slade, D. (2007). Extending our understanding of spoken discourse. In Cummins, J. & Davison, C. (Eds) *International Handbook of English Language Teaching* (pp. 859–873). New York: Springer.

McCarthy, M, O'Dell, F. & Shaw, E. (1997). *Basic Vocabulary in Use: Self-study reference and practice for students of North American English.* Cambridge: Cambridge University Press.

McCarthy, M., McCarten, J. & Sandiford, H. (2005). *Touchstone.* Cambridge: Cambridge University Press.

McEnery, T. & Hardie, A. (2012). *Corpus Linguistics: Method, theory and practice.* Cambridge: Cambridge University Press.

Meyer, C. F. (2002). *English Corpus Linguistics: An introduction.* Cambridge: Cambridge University Press.

Meyer, R., Okurowski, M. E. & Hand, T. (2000). Using authentic corpora and language tools for adult-centred learning. In Botley, S., McEnery, T. & Wilson, A. (Eds) *Multilingual Corpora in Teaching and Research* (pp. 86–91). Amsterdam: Rodopi.

Miller, C. R. (1984). Genre as social action. *Quarterly Journal of Speech*, 70: 151–167.

Mitchell, T. F. (1957). The language of buying and selling in Cyrenaica: A situational statement. *Hesperis*, 26: 31–71. Reprinted in Mitchell, T. F. (Ed.) *Principles of Firthian Linguistics* (pp. 167–299). London: Longman.

Morley, J. & Bayley, P. (2009). (Eds) *Wordings of War: Corpus-assisted discourse studies on the Iraq war.* London: Routledge.

Morrison, A. & Love, A. (1996). A discourse of disillusionment: Letters to the editor in two Zimbabwean magazines after independence. *Discourse and Society*, 7: 39–75.

Mugford, G. (2008). How to be rude! Teaching impoliteness in the second-language classroom. *ELT Journal*, 62(4): 375–384.

Mukherjee, J. (2002). *Korpuslinguistik und Englischunterricht: Eine Einführung.* Frankfurt am Main: Peter Lang.

Mur Dueñas, P. (2007). 'I/we focus on ...': A cross-cultural analysis of self-mentions in business management research articles. *Journal of English for Academic Purposes*, 6: 143–162.

Murray, N. (2010). Pragmatics, awareness raising, and the cooperative principle. *English Language Teaching Journal*, 64(3): 293–301.

Murray, N. (2012). English as a lingua franca and the development of pragmatic competence. *ELT Journal*, 66(3): 318–326.

Nattinger, J. & de Carrico, J. (1992). *Lexical Phrases and Language Teaching.* Oxford: Oxford University Press.

Obama, B. (1995). *Dreams from my Father: A story of race and inheritance.* New York: Three Rivers Press.

Ochs, E. (1979). Planned and unplanned discourse. In Givon, T. (Ed.) *Syntax and. Semantics 12: discourse and syntax* (pp. 51–80). New York: Academic Press.

Ohta, A. S. (2001). *Second Language Acquisition Processes in the Classroom: Learning Japanese.* Mahwah, NJ: Erlbaum.

O'Keeffe, A. & McCarthy. M. (2010). (eds) *The Routledge Handbook of Corpus Linguistics.* London: Routledge.

O'Keeffe, A., McCarthy, M. & Carter, R. (2007). *From Corpus to Classroom: Language Use and Language Teaching.* Cambridge: Cambridge University Press.

O'Keeffe, A., Clancy, B. & Adolphs, S. (2011). *Introducing Pragmatics in Use.* London: Routledge.

Olshtain, E. & Cohen, A. D. (1983). Apology: A speech act set. In Wolfson, N. & Judd, E. (Eds) *Socio-linguistics and Language Acquisition* (pp. 18–35). Rowley, MA.: Newbury House.

Olshtain, E. & Weinbach, L. (1993). Interlanguage features of the speech act of complaining. In Kasper, G. & Blum-Kulka, S. (Eds) *Interlanguage Pragmatics* (pp. 108–122). Oxford: Oxford University Press.

Paige, D. (1984). *Food Processors Properly Explained*. New York: Elliot Right Way Books.

Painter, C. (2009). Language development. In Halliday, M. A. K. & Webster, J. (Eds) *Continuum Companion to Systemic Functional Linguistics* (pp. 1–17). London: UK.

Paltridge, B. (2001). *Genre in the Classroom*. Ann Arbor, MI: University of Michigan Press.

Paltridge, B. (2002). Genre, text type and the EAP classroom. In Johns, A. (Ed.) *Genre in the Classroom: Multiple perspectives* (pp. 73–90). Malwah, NJ: Lawrence Erlbaum.

Paltridge, B. (2004). The exegesis as a genre: An ethnographic examination. In Ravelli, L. & Ellis, R. (Eds) *Analyzing Academic Writing: Contextualised frameworks* (pp. 84–103). London: Continuum.

Paltridge, B. (2006). *Discourse Analysis: An introduction*. London: Continuum.

Paltridge, B. (2008). Textographies and the researching and teaching of writing. *Iberica, Journal of the European Association of Languages for Specific Purposes*, 15: 9–23.

Partington, A. (1998). *Patterns and Meanings*. Amsterdam: John Benjamins.

Pomerantz, A. (1984). Agreeing and disagreeing with assessment: Some features of preferred/dispreferred turn shapes. In Atkinson, J. M. & Heritage, J. (Eds) *Structure of Social Action: Studies in conversation analysis* (pp. 57–101). Cambridge: Cambridge University Press.

Raisanen, C. (2002). The conference forum: A system of interrelated genres and discursive practices. In Ventola, E., Shalom, C. & Thompson, S. (Eds) *The Language of Conferencing* (pp. 69–93). Frankfurt: Peter Lang.

Ravelli, L. J. (2004). Signalling the organization of written texts; hyper-themes in management and history essays. In Ravelli, L. J. & Ellis, R. A. (Eds) *Analysing Academic Writing: Contextual framework* (pp. 104–130). London: Continuum.

Reddy, M. J. (1979). The conduit metaphor – a case of frame conflict in our language about language. In Ortony, A. (Ed.) *Metaphor and Thought* (pp. 284–297). Cambridge, MA: Cambridge University Press.

Reisigl, M. (2008). Analyzing political rhetoric. In Wodak, R. & Krzyzanowski, M. (Eds) *Qualitative Discourse Analysis in the Social Sciences* (pp. 96–120). London: Palgrave.

Renkema, J. (2004). *Introduction to Discourse Studies*. Amsterdam: John Benjamins.

Renkema, J. (2009). *The Texture of Discourse: Towards an outline of connectivity theory*. Amsterdam: John Benjamins.

Richards, J. C. & Rogers, T. (2001). *Approaches and Methods in Language Teaching*. Cambridge: Cambridge University Press.

Richards, J. C. & Schmidt, R. (1983). (eds) *Language and Communication*. London: Longman.

Richterich, R. & Chancerel, J. L. (1980). *Identifying the Needs of Adults Learning a Foreign Language*. Oxford: Pergamon Press.

Römer, U. (2010). Using general and specialized corpora in English language teaching: Past, present and future. In Campoy-Cubillo, M. C., Belles-Fortuño, B. & Gea-Valor, L. (Eds) *Corpus-based Approaches to English Language Teaching* (pp. 18–35). London: Continuum.

Rosaldo, M. Z. (1982). The things we do with words: Ilongot speech acts and speech act theory. *Language in Society*, 11: 203–235.

Rose, K. R. & Kasper, G. (2001). *Pragmatics in Language Teaching*. Cambridge: Cambridge University Press.

Sacks, H. (1987). On the preferences for agreement and contiguity in sequences in conversation. In Button, G. & Leed, J. R. E. (Eds) *Talk and Social Organization* (pp. 54–69). Clevedon: Multilingual Matters.

Sacks, H., Schegloff, E. A. & Jefferson, G. (1974/1978). A simplest systematics for the organization of turn-taking for conversation. *Language*, 50(4): 696–735. Also in Schenkein, J. (Ed.) (1978). *Studies in the Organization of Conversational Interaction*. New York: Academic Press.

Schauer, G. A. (2010). Study abroad and its effect on speech act performance. In Martinez Flor, A. and Uso Juan, E. (Eds) *Speech act Performance: Theoretical, empirical and methodolgical issues* (pp. 91–108). Amsterdam: John Benjamins.

Schauer, G. A. & Adolphs, S. (2006). Expressions of gratitude in corpus and DCT data: vocabulary, formulaic sequences, and pedagogy. *System*, 34(1): 119–134.

Schegloff, E. (1972). Sequencing in conversational openings. In Gumpertz, J. J. & Hymes, D. (Eds) *Directions in Sociolinguistics: The ethnography of communication* (pp. 346–380). New York: Holt, Rinehart, & Winston.

Schegloff, E. A. (1987). Recycled turn-beginnings. In Button, G. & Lee, J. R. E. (Eds) *Talk and Social Organization* (pp. 70–85). Clevedon: Multilingual Matters.

Schegloff, E. A. (2007). *Sequence Organization in Interaction: A primer in conversation analysis* (volume 1). Cambridge, UK: Cambridge University Press.

Schegloff, E. & Sacks, H. (1973). Opening up closing. *Semiotica*, 8(4): 289–327.

Schegloff, E. A., Jefferson, G. & Sacks, H. (1977). The preference for self-correction in the organization of repair in conversation. *Language*, 53: 361–382.

Schegloff, E. A., Koshik, I., Jacoby, S., & Olsher, D. (2002). Conversation analysis and applied linguistics. *American Review of Applied Linguistics*, 22: 3–31.

Schiffrin, D. (1987). *Discourse Markers*. Cambridge: Cambridge University Press.

Schmidt, R. & Richards, J. C. (1980). Speech acts and second language learning. *Applied Linguistics*, 1: 129–157.

Schryer, C. F. (1993). Records as genre. *Written Communication*, 10(2): 200–234.

Scollon, R. & Scollon, S. (1990). Athabaskan–English interethnic communication. In Carbaugh, D. (Ed.) *Cultural Communication and Intercultural Contact* (pp. 259–290). Hillsdale, NJ: Lawrence Erlbaum.

Scollon, R. & Scollon, S. (1995). *Intercultural Communication*. Oxford: Blackwell.

Scollon, R. & Scollon, J. (2012). *Intercultural Communication: A discourse approach*. Oxford: Blackwell.

Searle, J. R. (1969). *Speech Acts*. Cambridge: Cambridge University Press.

Searle, J. (1975). Indirect speech acts. In Cole, P. & Morgan, J. L. (Eds) *Syntax and Semantics Volume 3: Speech Acts* (pp. 59–82). New York: Academic Press.

Searle, J. (1976). The classification of illocutionary acts. *Language and Society*, 5: 1–24.

Searle, J. (1979). *Expression and Meaning: Studies in the theory of speech acts*. New York: Cambridge University Press.

Searle, J., Bierwish, M. & Kiefer, F. (1980). Introduction. In Searle, J. R. Kiefer, F. & Bierwisch, M. (Eds) *Speech Act Theory and Pragmatics* (pp. vii–xii). Dordrecht: Reidel.

Seedhouse, P. (2004). *The Interactional Architecture of the Language Classroom: A conversation analysis perspective*. Oxford: Blackwell.

Sidnell, J. (Ed.) (2009). *Conversation Analysis: Comparative perspectives*. Cambridge: Cambridge University Press.

Sidnell, J. (2010). *Conversation Analysis: An introduction*. Chichester, West Sussex: Blackwell.

Simpson-Vlach, R. & Ellis, N. C. (2010). An academic formulas list (AFL). *Applied Linguistics*, 31: 487–512.

Sinclair, J. M. (1990). (ed.) *Collins COBUILD English Grammar*. London: HarperCollins.

Sinclair, J. M. (1991). *Corpus, Concordance Collocation*. Oxford: Oxford University Press.

Sinclair, J. M. (2001). Preface. In Ghadessy, M., Henry A. & Roseberry, R. L. (Eds) *Small Corpus Studies and ELT: Theory and practice* (pp. vii–xv). Amsterdam: Benjamins.

Sinclair, J. M. & Coulthard, R. M. (1975). *Towards an Analysis of Discourse: The English Used by Teachers and Pupils*. Oxford: Oxford University Press.

Sinclair, J. M. & Renouf, A. (1988). A lexical syllabus for language learning. In Carter, R. & McCarthy, M. (Eds) *Vocabulary and Language Teaching* (pp. 140–158). London: Longman.

Smart, G. & Brown, N. (2006). Developing a 'discursive gaze': Participatory action research with student interns encountering new genres in the activity of the workplace. In Artemeva, N. & Freeedman, A. (Eds) *Rhetorical Genre Studies and Beyond* (pp. 241–282). Winnipeg, Manitoba, Canada: Inkshed Publications.

Sperber, D. & Wilson, D. (1995). *Relevance: Communication and Cognition* (2nd edn). Oxford: Blackwell Publishers.

Stenström, A. M., Andersen, G. H. & Ingrid, K. (2002). *Trends in Teenage Talk: Corpus, compilation, analysis and findings*. Amsterdam: John Benjamins.

Stewart, D. (2010). *Semantic Prosody: A critical evaluation*. London: Routledge.

Stubbe, M., Lane, C., Hilder, J., Vine, E., Vine, B., Marra, M., Holmes, J. & Weatherall, A. (2003). Multiple discourse analyses of a workplace interaction. *Discourse Studies*, 5: 351–388.

Stubbs, M. (1994). Grammar, text and ideology: Computer-assisted methods in the linguistics of representation. *Applied Linguistics*, 15(2): 201–223.

Stubbs, M. (1996). *Text and Corpus Analysis*. Oxford: Blackwell.

Stubbs, M. (1997). Whorf's children: Critical comments on Critical Discourse Analysis (CDA). In Wray, A. & Ryan, A. (eds) *Evolving Models of Language* (pp. 100–106). Clevedon: Multilingual Matters.

Stubbs, M. (2001). Inference theories and code theories: Corpus evidence for semantic schemas. *Text*, 21: 437–465.

Stubbs, M. (2004). Language corpora. In Davies, A. & Elder, C. (Eds) *The Handbook of Applied Linguistics* (pp. 106–132). Malden, MA: Blackwell.

Swales, J. M. (1990). *Genre Analysis: English in academic and research settings*. Cambridge: Cambridge University Press.

Swales, J. M. (2002). Integrated and fragmented worlds: EAP materials and Corpus Linguistics. In Flowerdew, J. (Ed.) *Academic Discourse* (pp. 150–164). London: Longman.

Swales, J. M. (2004). *Research Genres*. Cambridge: Cambridge University Press.

Swales, J. M. & Feak, C. B. (2012). *Academic Writing for Graduate Students* (3rd edn). Ann Arbor, MI: University of Michigan Press.

Swales, J. M. & Luebs, M. (1995). Toward textography. In Gunnarsson, B-L. & Ècklund, I. (Eds) *Writing in Academic Contexts* (pp. 12–29). Uppsala: FUMS.

Taboada, M. (2004). *Building Coherence and Cohesion: Task-oriented dialogue in English and Spanish*. Amsterdam: John Benjamins.

Taboada, M. & Mann, W. C. (2006a). Applications of rhetorical structure theory. *Discourse Studies*, 8(4): 567–588.

Taboada, M. & Mann, W. C. (2006b). Rhetorical structure theory: Looking back and moving ahead. *Discourse Studies*, 8(3): 423–459.

Tadros, A. (1985). *Prediction in Text: Discourse Analysis monograph*. Birmingham: English Language Research, Birmingham, University of Birmingham.

Taguchi, N. (2012). *Context, Individual Differences, and Pragmatic Development*. Bristol: Multilingual Matters.

Tannen, D. (1989). *Talking Voices: Repetition, dialogue, and imagery in conversational discourse*. Cambridge: Cambridge University Press.

Tanskanen, S.-K. (2006). *Collaborating Towards Coherence: Lexical cohesion in English Discourse*. Amsterdam: John Benjamins.

Tardy, C. M. (2009). *Building Genre Knowledge*. West Lafayette, IN: Parlor Press.

Terkourafi, M. (2005). Beyond the micro-level in politeness research. *Journal of Politeness Research*, 1: 237–262.

Thibault, P. J. (2004). *Agency and Consciousness in Discourse: Self–other dynamics as a complex system.* London: Continuum.

Thomas, J. (1983). Cross-cultural pragmatic failure. *Applied Linguistics,* 4(2): 91–112.

Thomas, J. (1995). *Meaning in Interaction: An introduction to pragmatics.* Harlow: Longman.

Thompson, G. (1993). *Reporting.* London: Collins.

Thompson, S. (1994). Aspects of cohesion in monologue, *Applied Linguistics* 15(1): 58–75.

Thompson, G. (2004). *Introducing Functional Grammar* (2nd edn). London: Arnold.

Thornbury, S. (2005a). *Beyond the Sentence: Introducing Discourse Analysis.* Oxford: Macmillan Education.

Thornbury, S. (2005b). *How to Teach Speaking.* Harlow: Longman.

Thornbury, S. (2010). What can a corpus tell us about discourse? In O'Keeffe, A. & McCarthy, M. (Eds) *The Routledge Handbook of Corpus Linguistics* (pp. 270–287). London: Routledge.

Thornbury, S., & Slade, D. (2006). *Conversation: From description to pedagogy.* Cambridge: Cambridge University Press.

Titscher, S., Wodak, R., Meyer, M. & Vetter, E. (2000). *Methods of Text and Discourse Analysis.* London: Sage.

Tognini-Bonelli, E. (2001). *Corpus Linguistics at Work.* Amsterdam: John Benjamins.

Tribble, C. (2002). Corpora and corpus analysis: New windows on academic writing. In Flowerdew, J. (Ed.) *Academic Discourse* (pp. 131–149). London: Longman, Pearson Education.

Trimbur, J. (2002). *The Call to Write* (2nd edn), New York: Longman.

Uhrig, K. (2011). Business and legal case genre networks: Two case studies. *English for Specific Purposes,* 13(2): 127–136.

Upton, T. & Connor, U. (2001). Using computerised corpus analysis to investigate the textlinguistic discourse moves of a genre. *English for Specific Purposes,* 20(4): 313–329.

Ure, J. (1971). Lexical density and register difference differentiation. In Perren, G. E. & Trim, J. L. M. (Eds) *Applications of Linguistics: Selected papers of the Second International Congress of Applied Linguistics, Cambridge, 1969* (pp. 443–452). Cambridge: Cambridge University Press.

van Dijk, T. A. (1977a). *Text and Context: Explorations in the semantics and pragmatics of discourse.* London: Longman.

van Dijk, T. A. (1977b). Semantic macro–structures and knowledge-frames in discourse comprehension. In Just, M. A. & Carpenter, P. A. (Eds) *Cognitive Processes in Comprehension* (pp. 3–32). Hillsdale, NJ: Erlbaum.

van Dijk, T. A. (1980). *Macrostructures.* Hillsdale, NJ: Lawrence Erlbaum.

Van Dijk, T. A. (1993). Principles of Critical Discourse Analysis. *Discourse and Society,* 4(2): 249–283.

van Dijk, T. A. (2001a). Critical Discourse Analysis. In Tannen, D., Schiffrin, D. & Hamilton, H. (Eds) *Handbook of Discourse Analysis* (pp. 352–371). Oxford: Blackwell.

van Dijk, T. A. (2001b). Critical discourse studies. In Wodak, R. & Meyer, M. (Eds) *Methods of Critical Discourse Analysis* (pp. 63–86). London: Sage.

van Dijk, T. A. (2001c). Multidisciplinary CDA: A plea for diversity. In Wodak, R. & Meyer, M. (Eds) *Methods of Critical Discourse Analysis* (pp. 95–120). London: Sage.

van Dijk, T. A. (2008). *Discourse and Context: A sociocognitive approach.* Cambridge: Cambridge University Press.

van Dijk, T. A. (2011). *Discourse Studies: A multidisciplinary introduction.* London: Sage.

van Ek, J. A. & Alexander, L. G. (1975). *Threshold Level English.* Oxford: Pergamon for the Council of Europe.

van Ek, J. A. & Alexander, L. G. (1989). *Threshold 1990.* Cambridge: Cambridge University Press and Council of Europe.

van Ek, J. A. & Trim, J. L. M. (1998). *Threshold 1990: Council of Europe/Conseil de l'Europe.* Cambridge: Cambridge University Press.

van Leeuwen, T. (1996). The representation of social actors. In Caldas-Coulthard, C. R. & Coulthard, M. (Eds) *Texts and Practices: Readings in Critical Discourse Analysis* (pp. 32–70). London: Routledge.

van Leeuwen, T. (2004). *Introducing Social Semiotics*. London: Routledge.

van Leeuwen, T. (2008). *Discourse and Practice: New tools for CDA*. Oxford: Oxford University Press.

Ventola, E. (1987). *The Structure of Social Interaction: A systemic approach to the semiotics of service encounters*. London: Pinter.

Vygotsky, L. S. (1986). *Thought and Language*. Cambridge, MA: Massachusetts Institute of Technology.

Wagner, J. (2004). The classroom and beyond. *Modern Language Journal*, 88: 612–616.

Wallace, C. (1992). Critical literacy awareness in the EFL classroom. In Faircough, N. (Ed.) *Critical Language Awareness* (pp. 53–92). London: Longman.

Wallace, C. (2009). Critical language awareness: Key principles for a course in critical reading. *Language Awareness*, 8(2): 98–210.

Walters, F. S. (2007). A conversation-analytic hermeneutic rating protocol to assess L2 oral pragmatic competence. *Language Testing*, 24: 155–183.

Waring, H. Z. (2009). Moving out of IRF (Initiation-Response-Feedback): A single case analysis. *Language Learning*, 59(4): 796–824.

Waring, H. Z., Creider, S., Tarpey, T. & Black, R. (in press). A search for specificity in understanding CA and context. *Discourse & Society*.

Watts, R. J. (2003). *Politeness*. Cambridge: Cambridge University Press.

Watts, R. J. (2005). Linguistic Politeness Research: Quo vadis? In Watts, R. J., Ide, S. & Ehlich, K. (Eds) *Politeness in Language. Studies in its history, theory and practice*, 2nd edn (pp. xi–xlvii). Berlin: Mouton de Gruyter.

Wen, X. Y. (2007). On pragmatic information in learners' dictionaries, with particular reference to LDOCE4. *International Journal of Lexicography*, 20(2): 147–173.

White, R. (2001). Adapting Grice's maxims in the teaching of writing. *ELT Journal*, 55(1): 62–69.

Widdowson, H. G. (1978). *Teaching Language as Communication*. Oxford: Oxford University Press.

Widdowson, H. G. (1995a). Discourse Analysis: A critical view. *Language and Literature*, 4(3): 157–172.

Widdowson, H. G. (1995b). Review: Norman Fairclough: Discourse and social change. *Applied Linguistics*, 16(4): 510–516.

Widdowson, H. G. (1996). Reply to Fairclough: Discourse and interpretation: Conjectures and refutations. *Language and Literature*, 5(1): 57–69.

Widdowson, H. G. (1998a). Context, community and authentic language. *TESOL Quarterly*, 32: 705–716.

Widdowson, H. G. (1998b). The theory and practice of Critical Discourse Analysis. *Applied Linguistics*, 19: 136–151.

Widdowson, H. G. (2004). *Text, Context, Pretext*. Oxford: Blackwell.

Wierzbicka, A. (1985). Semantic metalanguage for a cross-cultural comparison of speech acts and speech genres. *Language in Society*, 14(4): 491–513.

Wierzbicka, A. (1987). *English Speech Act Verbs: A semantic dictionary*. Sydney: Academic Press.

Wilkins, D. A. (1976). *Notional Syllabuses*. Oxford : Oxford University Press.

Wilkinson, S. & Kitzinger, C. (2008). Conversation analysis. In Willig, C. and Stainton-Rogers, W. (Eds) *The Sage Handbook of Qualitative Research in Psychology* (pp. 55–71). London: Sage.

Willis, D. (1990). *The Lexical Syllabus: A New approach to language teaching*. London: HarperCollin.

Willis, J. & Willis, D. (1988). *Collins COBUILD English Course*. London: Collins.

Willis, D. & Willis, J. (1996). Consciousness-raising activities in the language classroom. In Willis, J. & Willis, D. (Eds) *Challenge and Change in Language Teaching* (pp. 63–76). Oxford: Heinemann.

Wilson, D. & Sperber, D. (2004). Relevance theory. In Horn, L. R. & Ward, G. (Eds) *The Handbook of Pragmatics* (pp. 607–632). Oxford: Blackwell.

Winter, E. O. (1974). *Repetition as a Function of Repetition: A study of some of its principle features in the clause relations of contemporary English*. Unpublished PdD thesis. University of London.

Winter, E. O. (1977). A clause relational approach to English texts: A study of some predictive lexical items in written discourse. *Instructional Science*, 6: 1–92.

Winter, E. O. (1979). Replacement as a fundamental function of the sentence in context. *Forum Linguisticum*, 4: 95–133.

Winter, E. O. (1992). The notion of unspecific versus specific as one way of analysing the information of a fund-raising letter. In Mann, W. & Thompson, S. A. (Eds) *Discourse Description: Diverse linguistic analyses of a fund-raising text* (pp. 131–170). Amsterdam: John Benjamins.

Wodak, R. (1999). Critical Discourse Analysis at the end of the 20th century. *Research on Language and Social Interaction*, 32(1&2): 181–193.

Wodak, R. (2001a). What CDA is about: A summary of its history, important concepts and its developments. In Wodak, R. & Meyer, M. (Eds) *Methods of Critical Discourse Analysis* (pp. 1–13). London: Sage.

Wodak, R. (2001b). The discourse-historical approach. In Wodak, R. & Meyer, M. (Eds) *Methods of Critical Discourse Analysis* (pp. 64–94). London: Sage.

Wodak, R. & Meyer, M. (2001). (Eds) *Methods of Critical Discourse Analysis*. London: Sage.

Wodak, R., de Cillia, R., Reisigl, M. & Liebhart, K. (1999). *The Discursive Construction of National Identity*. Edinburgh: Edinburgh University Press.

Wong, J. (2002). 'Applying' conversation analysis in Applied Linguistics: Evaluating English as a second language textbook dialogue. *International Review of Applied Linguistics (IRAL)*, 40(1): 37–60.

Wong, J. (2007). Answering my call: A look at telephone closings. In Bowles, H. & Seedhouse, P. (Eds) *Conversation Analysis and Language for Specific Purposes* (pp. 271–304). Bern: Peter Lang.

Wong, J. & Waring, H. Z. (2010). *Conversation Analysis and Second Language Pedagogy: A guide for ESL/EFL teachers*. New York: Routledge.

Woolf, V. (1931, 2006). *The Waves*. New York: Mariner Books.

Wray, A. (2002). *Formulaic Language and the Lexicon*. Cambridge: Cambridge University Press.

Yates, J. (1989). *Control Through Communication: The rise of system in American management*. Baltimore, MD: Johns Hopkins University Press.

Yule, G. (1996). *Pragmatics*. Oxford: Oxford University Press.

Index